School of American Research
Advanced Seminar Series

DOUGLAS W. SCHWARTZ, GENERAL EDITOR

# SCHOOL OF AMERICAN RESEARCH ADVANCED SEMINAR SERIES

*Published by Cambridge University Press*

Dreaming: Anthropological and Psychological Interpretations
BARBARA TEDLOCK

The Anasazi in a Changing Environment
GEORGE G. GUMERMAN

The Chemistry of Prehistoric Human Bone
T. DOUGLAS PRICE

The Emergence of Modern Humans: Biocultural Adaptations in the Later Pleistocene
ERIK TRINKAUS

The Olmec and the Development of Formative Mesoamerican Civilization
ROBERT J. SHARER and DAVID C. GROVE

The Anthropology of War
JONATHAN HAAS

The Evolution of Political Systems
STEADMAN UPHAM

Turko-Persian in Historical Perspective
ROBERT L. CANFIELD

Classic Maya Political History: Hieroglyphic and Archaeological Evidence
T. PATRICK CULBERT

*Published by the University of New Mexico Press*

Reconstructing Prehistoric Pueblo Societies
WILLIAM A. LONGACRE

New Perspectives on the Pueblos
ALFONSO ORTIZ

Structure and Process in Latin America
ARNOLD STRICKON and SIDNEY M. GREENFIELD

The Classic Maya Collapse
T. PATRICK CULBERT

Methods and Theories of Anthropological Genetics
M. H. CRAWFORD and P. L. WORKMAN

Sixteenth-Century Mexico: The Work of Sahagun
MUNRO S. EDMONSON

Ancient Civilization and Trade
JEREMY A. SABLOFF and C. C. LAMBERG-KARLOVSKY

Photography in Archaeological Research
ELMER HARP, JR

Meaning in Anthropology
KEITH H. BASSO and HENRY A. SELBY

The Valley of Mexico: Studies in Pre-Hispanic Ecology and Society
ERIC R. WOLF

Demographic Anthropology: Quantitative Approaches
EZRA B. W. ZUBROW

The Origins of Maya Civilization
RICHARD E. W. ADAMS

Explanation of Prehistoric Change
JAMES N. HILL

Explorations in Ethnoarchaeology
RICHARD A. GOULD

Entrepreneurs in Cultural Context
SIDNEY M. GREENFIELD, ARNOLD STRICKON, and ROBERT T. AUBEY

The Dying Community
ART GALLAHER, JR and HARLAND PADFIELD

Southwestern Indian Ritual Drama
CHARLOTTE J. FRISBIE

Lowland Maya Settlement Patterns
WENDY ASHMORE

Simulations in Archaeology
JEREMY A. SABLOFF

Chan Chan: Andean Desert City
MICHAEL E. MOSELEY and KENT C. DAY

Shipwreck Anthropology
RICHARD A. GOULD

Elites: Ethnographic Issues
GEORGE E. MARCUS

The Archaeology of Lower Central America
FREDERICK W. LANGE and DORIS Z. STONE

Late Lowland Maya Civilization: Classic to Postclassic
JEREMY A. SABLOFF and E. WYLLYS ANDREWS V.

# Classic Maya Political History

# CLASSIC MAYA POLITICAL HISTORY: HIEROGLYPHIC AND ARCHAEOLOGICAL EVIDENCE

EDITED BY
T. PATRICK CULBERT

*A SCHOOL OF AMERICAN RESEARCH BOOK*

Published by the Press Syndicate of the University of Cambridge
The Pitt Building, Trumpington Street, Cambridge CB2 1RP
40 West 20th Street, New York, NY 10011-4211, USA
10 Stamford Road, Oakleigh, Melbourne 3166, Australia



First published 1991
Reprinted 1994
First paperback edition published 1996

Printed in Great Britain at the University Press, Cambridge

*British Library cataloguing in publication data*

Classic Maya political history; hieroglyphic and archaeological evidence –
(School of American Research advanced seminar series). –
(A School of American Research book).
1. Mexico. Maya. Politics. Archaeological sources
I. Culbert, T. Patrick II. Series III. Series 306.20972

*Library of Congress cataloguing in publication data*

Classic Maya political history: hieroglyphic and archaeological
evidence / edited by T. Patrick Culbert.
p. cm.
"A School of American research book."
Includes bibliographical references.
ISBN 0 521 39210 1
1. Mayas – Politics and government. 2. Mayas – History.
3. Mayas – Antiquities. 4. Mexico – Antiquities.
5. Guatemala – Antiquities.
I. Culbert, T. Patrick.
F1435.3.P7C53 1991
972.81'016 dc20 89-78201 CIP

ISBN 0 521 39210 1 hardback
ISBN 0 521 56445 X paperback

wv

# Contents

# Figures

# Tables

# Contributors

T. PATRICK CULBERT, editor
*Department of Anthropology*
*University of Arizona*

WILLIAM L. FASH
*Department of Anthropology*
*Northern Illinois University*

NORMAN HAMMOND
*Department of Archaeology*
*Boston University*

CHRISTOPHER JONES
*University Museum*
*University of Pennsylvania*

PETER MATHEWS
*Department of Archaeology*
*University of Calgary*

LINDA SCHELE
*Department of Art*
*University of Texas*

PETER SCHMIDT
*Instituto Nacional de Antropologia e Historia*

ROBERT J. SHARER
*University Museum*
*University of Pennsylvania*

DAVID S. STUART
*Department of Anthropology*
*Princeton University*

GORDON R. WILLEY
*Peabody Museum*
*Harvard University*

LINNEA H. WREN
*Department of Art*
*Gustavus Adolphus College*

NORMAN YOFFEE
*Department of Anthropology*
*University of Arizona*

# Preface

The idea for the School of American Research Advanced Seminar that gave rise to this volume originated with Douglas W. Schwartz, who suggested to me the possibility of a seminar that would deal with Maya hieroglyphic inscriptions. In discussing the best manner to approach the topic, we decided that it would be exciting to bring together a group of specialists in epigraphy, archaeology, and art history to combine their different data and viewpoints in a new approach to understanding Classic Maya civilization. The time seemed ideal for such an effort. Glyphic decipherments had accumulated so rapidly that epigraphers were inundated by a sea of new data to which researchers not actively engaged in decipherment had had almost no exposure. Nothing could be more logical as a continuation of the S.A.R.'s tradition of ground-breaking seminars on the Maya than to combine the new mass of epigraphic data with the more traditional material from archaeology and iconography.

The first step in implementing the idea was to form an organizing committee consisting of Richard E. W. Adams, Christopher Jones, Norman Hammond, and me. The committee refined the scope and objectives of the seminar, made a list of potential participants, and prepared a proposal entitled "Elite Interaction in Classic Maya

Civilization." The proposal was accepted and the seminar was held at the School of American Research, Santa Fe, on October 20–24, 1986. Participants at the seminar were Clemency C. Coggins, William L. Fash, Norman Hammond, Christopher Jones, Peter Mathews, Linda Schele, Robert S. Sharer, Gordon R. Willey, Linnea H. Wren, and Norman Yoffee; I participated and served as chair of the seminar sessions.

Because so many new ideas were generated during the seminar discussions, the preparation of the manuscript for this volume involved an unusual amount of revision, sometimes even complete rewriting, of the papers that had been prepared before the seminar. Clemency Coggins, whose seminar paper (1986) covered both elite burials and the associated ideology, decided that her major interest lay in ideological matters outside the scope of the volume and that her paper should be published separately in shortened form (Coggins 1988). Linda Schele, whose original paper (1986e) had examined in detail all historical inscriptions across the lowlands between 9.12.0.0.0 and 9.13.0.0.0, changed her focus to the western region when it became clear that this region needed to be included for the volume to present the full political history of the Classic period. My own seminar paper, which had espoused a Tikal regional state, was drastically altered to provide regional coverage for the northeast Peten to complement the very full data on Tikal provided by Jones. Norman Hammond's original material was divided into two separate sections when he accepted two additional assignments needed to make the volume complete. One was the preparation of the Introduction to the volume (chapter 1). The second (chapter 11) is an overview of the structure of Maya polities that integrates the data on elites derived from inscriptions with information on other segments of society derived from archaeological sources. Hammond's holistic perspective which ties together all levels of Maya society is juxtaposed with Yoffee's, which focuses primarily upon elite interaction from the comparative viewpoint that his specialization in Mesopotamia makes possible.

Readers unfamiliar with Maya studies may be mystified by the profusion of different kinds of names applied to Maya individuals. Some researchers prefer sober lists of letters or numbers: Rulers A, B, and C of Tikal or Rulers 1, 2, 3, and 4 of Dos Pilas, for example. A second method simply describes Maya name glyphs in English, giving such intriguing appelations as Bird-Jaguar and Smoking Frog. Sometimes when the Maya *name* (not necessarily the phonetic value) of a glyph is known (e.g., the names of days or months), the name will be used, often in combination with an English term for a second name glyph. Cauac Sky and Cauac Shield are examples of such combinations. Another system, introduced at Palenque, uses only Maya words. Sometimes these are the same descriptive glosses for pictures in the glyphs as comparable English terms. Sometimes, they are actual phonetic readings, although the correctness of such readings is often a matter of dispute among experts. Suffice to say, there has been no accepted attempt to systematize Maya naming and the free-flow result is that some rulers have been tagged with a number of different names. The penultimate ruler of Copan, for example, has variously been called "Sun-at-Horizon," "New Sun-at-Horizon," "Madrugada" (Spanish for dawn), Yax Sun-at-Horizon, and Yax Pac (a phonetic reading that is the matter of some dispute). Rather than engage in lengthy and tortuous debates about the "best" or "correct" name variants, we have generally accepted the name favored by the author in this volume who deals primarily with the site in question, but have allowed other authors to use variants with the "primary" name mentioned occasionally in parentheses.

Throughout the volume, we have followed Maya calendrical dates with their equivalents in the Christian (Gregorian) calendar. In deriving equivalents, we have followed the Goodman-Martínez-Thompson correlation of the two calendars (see Hammond, this volume, chapter 1), the correlation favoured by all the participants. Although there is residual debate about the correctness of this correlation, we are, in essence, dealing with Maya time so that an alternative correlation would have no effect upon our deliberations.

To facilitate our interactions, we agreed upon definitions for some of the key concepts we would use. We defined *polity* as an autonomous political unit. A multi-center or complex polity (called regional state by some) may have more than one major center of population, and may result from amalgamation of formerly autonomous polities. An *elite* is a small group within the upper echelon of a society that exerts ideological political, social, or economic power or any combination of these. Finally, the *dynastic monument complex*, often called the "stela cult," is the assemblage of monumental art and inscriptions recording dynastic history, propaganda, and associated rituals. It may include any or all of stelae, "altars," lintels, architectural embellishments, and complete buildings.

Our participation at the seminar proved to be both an exciting professional enterprise and a warm collegial experience. We were stimulated by the sharing of ideas, disagreed (when we did so) amicably, and were heartened by the surroundings and hospitality of the School of American Research. We are deeply indebted to Douglas W. Schwartz for his original idea for the seminar and for his contributions over the years in fostering Maya studies in the Advanced Seminar series. We are grateful to Jonathan Haas for professional arrangements and his wise advice on the conduct of seminar sessions. We thank Cecile Stein for her help with a variety of matters and Jane Barberousse for her skill in arranging meals and seminar facilities. Finally, we are grateful to Jane Kepp for her advice and encouragement in preparing the manuscript for publication.

T. PATRICK CULBERT

# 1
# Introduction

NORMAN HAMMOND

This book is concerned with the historical reality recorded on Classic Maya monuments of the first millennium AD, its interpretation in terms of social and political interaction within and between states, and the better understanding of Maya civilization that is emerging from a more accurate perception of the role of its ruling elites.

Since Berlin (1958, 1959) and Proskouriakoff (1960) showed that the Classic inscriptions dealt with real people in historical time, there has been a rapid expansion of knowledge of the nature of the Maya writing system and the specific content of the texts. As a result, outline biographies of named individuals can now be elucidated and dynastic histories constructed for a number of sites. Epigraphers have estimated that some 50 percent of the extant Classic period inscriptions have now been read, and close to nine-tenths of the content of most of them can be understood.

Over the same three decades there has been a similar influx of data on other aspects of Maya civilization: four previous School of American Research Advanced Seminars examined the Preclassic rise, Terminal Classic collapse, and Postclassic transition of complex society in the lowlands, together with the patterns of settlement and community structure that formed the spatial matrix of that society (Adams

1977a; Culbert 1973; Sabloff and Andrews V 1986; Ashmore 1981a).

Other symposia have analyzed the agricultural foundations underlying those patterns (Harrison and Turner 1978; Flannery 1982). The manifestations of elite activity present in architecture, sculpture, burials, craft products, iconography, and inscriptions have been the subject of numerous particularizing studies. Yet Classic civilization itself, the phenomenon of unity and interdependence over more than six centuries and nearly a quarter million square kilometers, has not; nor has elite culture been related to its economic and social infrastructure on a broad scale, although the studies of individual sites such as Tikal and Copan have treated their subjects holistically. A holistic approach to Maya civilization was advocated by Willey (1980) and has become apparent in some recent studies of Maya art (e.g., Schele and Miller 1986).

The purpose of the S.A.R. Advanced Seminar embodied in this book was to consider both the infrastructure and the superstructure of Maya civilization in the light of the textual decipherments which have brought some Classic elites to the edge of history. The discussion of these advances, so rapid that many are yet unpublished and unsynthesized, brought together a group of epigraphers, art historians, and archaeologists to share information and begin to bring together the multiple sources of evidence now available for an understanding of Classic Maya society: stratigraphy, epigraphy, and iconography were seen as coequal and perhaps congruent sources of information on elite behavior. It was nevertheless clear that the inscriptions would be the focus of consideration: they provided data new to many of the group, and a prime purpose of this book is to assemble for the first time in the charts of historical events information that spans the Maya lowlands.

Because Emblem Glyphs are so fundamental in reconstructing the political history of the Maya lowlands, an article by Peter Mathews that outlines the structure and function of Emblem Glyphs follows this Introduction. The succeeding articles interweave the inscriptional record with the more familiar archaeological data to provide syntheses of the political histories of sites and, in some cases, entire regions. A number of concepts were axiomatic: the cultural unity of Maya elite activities as the principal definition of Classic civilization spatially and temporally; the impact of epigraphy in bringing it within the ambit of history; the realization that this was "winners' history," with the risk of partiality; and the development of scholarly approaches from the substantive to the theoretical that has accompanied a century of investigation and formed a cumulative data base for present and future considerations of Maya elites.

These approaches were brought to bear on a variable data base: of the four regions considered principally here, the western has abundant and well-published texts, but apart from Palenque has seen a minimum of published archaeological research. Schele's paper for the first time collates inscriptions from all the sites and provides a summary of political history. The Pasion region is likewise rich in Late Classic inscriptions, and also benefits from major archaeological projects at Altar de Sacrificios and Seibal. Mathews and Willey have integrated the data into a regional history that demonstrates what will be possible for other regions when more research has been done.

The southeast region has a significant number of inscriptions only at Copan and Quirigua but provides a good research area because both sites have been the location of recent major projects that included both excavation and epigraphy. The Fash/Stuart and Sharer papers lay out the results and demonstrate the interactions and antagonisms between these two sites, while their contrasting developmental trajectories provide an unusually clear example of both variation and mutual impact within a region.

The northeast Peten region is an area, frequently considered to be the heartland of Classic Maya civilization, with densely packed large sites, major projects executed at Uaxactun, Tikal, and Rio Azul, and an abundance of inscriptions covering the entire historical span of the Classic period. Tikal is probably the most intensively studied of all Maya sites. Jones' paper presents the history of the Tikal dynasty, and shows the integration that is possible when epigraphic data can be matched with superb stratigraphic control of architectural development and burials. Culbert's chapter treats of interaction between sites within and beyond the northeast Peten and raises the question of the size of Maya polities.

Sites in the north of the Yucatan Peninsula have far fewer inscriptions than those in the southern lowlands but are also now beginning to reach historical status, as Wren and Schmidt demonstrate. The emergence of a new political ideology at Chichen Itza is their primary theme, and one which marks the recent limit in time of the cultural system that generated the inscriptions forming the focus of this book.

In addition to the presentation of historical data and the substantive reconstruction of Maya history, the seminar was concerned with the ways in which the Maya elite interacted, with the objective of determining the nature and rules of interaction from the new epigraphic understanding, complemented by the data from iconography and archaeology. The rules were, of course, never made explicit in the inscriptions, but we had to hand a set of concrete examples from which to elicit the underlying structure. Some of the structure was vertical, linking the ruling elite to the lower levels of the social pyramid, while other, lateral links provided the great network of interaction that tied together elite lineages across the lowlands.

Much of this is inherent in the reconstructions of site and regional histories: in one paper here, emerging from the seminar discussions, Schele and Mathews describe a pattern of intersite visitation previously unrecognized in the literature and summarize data on such patterns of interaction as warfare and marriage. Mechanisms of elite interaction discussed at the seminar but not explicitly covered in the papers are reviewed in Culbert's summary chapter.

We then turned to a consideration of what the new conjunction of data tells us about the overall structure of Classic Maya society. Here, the lacunae in the inscriptional record are clear: the texts provide a limited story that concerns only the formal acts of a few members of the uppermost stratum of Maya society. Their purpose was not to recount dispassionate history but to present the protagonists in the best possible light. The texts relate a ruler to the cosmos and to his own deified ancestors but do not link him to the rest of society or give information about administration, economy, or trade. They recount victories, captures, and sacrifices but leave us to guess why the battles took place.

This is why, in reconstructing Classic Maya society, we need both archaeological and epigraphic data: the former to tell us about the lower echelons of society and about areas such as economics and trade where the inscriptions are silent; the latter to provide more specific detail about the structure and functioning of the elite than can ever be gained from excavated evidence. My own paper attempts such a holistic reconstruction of Classic Maya society and brings in comparative evidence from mainly historical cultures elsewhere. Yoffee's paper, which focuses upon elite interaction, provides in particular a view of Maya civilization from the perspective of Mesopotamia, where the combination of textual, iconographic, and archaeological evidence has been a rich source of scholarly advancement for far longer than it has in the Maya lands.

## GEOGRAPHICAL AND CHRONOLOGICAL FRAMEWORKS

Previous S.A.R. Advanced Seminar volumes have divided the Maya lowlands into archaeological zones, the details of which have changed slightly as knowledge has increased (see Sabloff and Andrews V 1986:Fig. 2.1 for the most recent version). This volume uses a broader framework of regions: the western, Pasion, northeast Peten, and southeast regions (Fig. 1.1). That only these four regions are taken for detailed scrutiny is due to the restricted distribution of Emblem Glyphs. Since polity interaction can only be discussed when polities are recognized, and the Emblem Glyph is the only signifier that we have (cf. Mathews; Mathews and Willey; Schele and Mathews, this volume), the area of consideration is confined to the southern lowlands where more than 85 percent of the known Emblem Glyphs occur. (Most of the others are around Uxmal and at Chichen Itza.)

This factor apart, the traditional boundary between the southern and northern lowlands is now much less solid than it used to be. Not only has the existence of a "central lowlands" focused on the Rio Bec area been mooted, and much of Quintana Roo linked to the south by the characteristics of the Coba polity and the "Petenized" sites south of it, but the presence of Yucatecan speakers as far south as the Usumacinta in the Classic period and the widespread interpenetration with Chol has indicated more unity than was once apparent. The unity of elite culture, expressed in iconography and hieroglyphic writing, has been a commonplace since the time of Stephens in the 1840s; its regional variations, most strongly expressed in architectural style, are sufficiently within a common tradition for the cultural frontiers with the highlands, the Mixe-Zoque and Zapotec across the Isthmus of Tehuantepec, and the peoples of lower Central America to have been long implicitly accepted, whatever the degree of proposed linguistic or cultural diffusion across them.

Similarly, traditional chronological boundaries have recently been re-examined. The tripartite division into Preclassic (Formative), Classic, and Postclassic, with the Classic beginning in AD 300 and ending in 900, was predicated on the sudden appearance, from a Preclassic

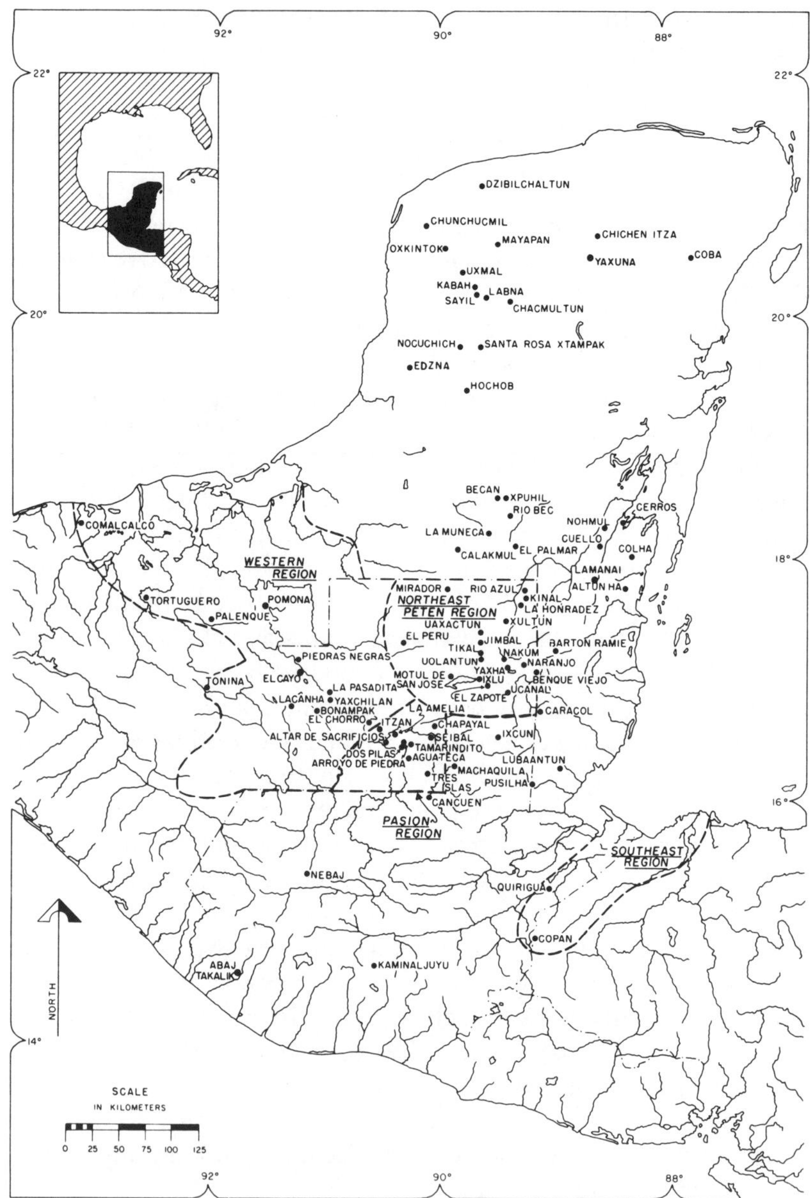


Fig. 1.1 The Maya lowlands: regions and sites.

base of farming villages, of ceremonial centers with vaulted stone architecture, polychrome pottery, and carved stone monuments with hieroglyphic inscriptions. These inscriptions bore Initial Series dates (so called because they always began the text) in the Long Count, a quasi-linear measuring of time from a base date in 3114 BC, divided into cycles of 400 "years," 20 "years," one "year" (actually 360 days), months and single days. Each day was also designated in two shorter cycles, of 365 days and 260 days, with the result that any one day had a unique definition within a period of over 5,000 years. The correlation between this native calendar and the Christian one, established by Joseph Goodman at the beginning of this century and refined by Martínez Hernández and Thompson (the G.M.T. correlation, used in this book), placed Maya civilization within real time, assigning it an antiquity comparable with the Byzantine Empire, or making the Late Classic apogee coeval with the T'ang Dynasty in China. It was this correlation and the temporal distribution of Initial Series dates that led to setting the boundaries of the Classic at AD 300 and 900.

A beginning for Classic civilization in AD 300 was called in question by the discovery of earlier monuments, such as Tikal Stela 29 at AD 292, the undated but stylistically Preclassic stelae of El Mirador, and the San Diego rock-carving. Monuments on the Pacific slope, such as Abaj Takalik Stelae 2 and 5, with their second-century AD or earlier dates and their clear resemblance to Polol Altar 1 in the lowlands, also demonstrated a longer and more complex development of the dynastic monument complex or "stela cult," as did the discovery of a plain stela of *c.* AD 100 at Cuello (Hammond 1982). Excavations, particularly at Tikal (Coe 1965a), demonstrated similar Preclassic origins for vaulted buildings, while the origins of Classic geometric and figured polychrome pottery in trichromes and polychromes of the Late Preclassic at Cuello, Holmul, and Nohmul (Pring 1977; Hammond 1982, 1984) showed that an autochthonous evolution of ceramic technology was more likely than the migrationist theories espoused by Gifford (1974) and Sheets (1971).

Subsequent widespread discovery of Preclassic cultural complexity at El Mirador (Matheny 1980), Edzna (Matheny *et al.* 1983), Cerros (Freidel 1979), Lamanai (Pendergast 1981), and Nohmul (Hammond *et al.* 1985) made it clear that "the Classic period is the second phase of Maya civilization" and "that to talk of 'Preclassic Maya civilization' is no longer a contradiction in terms: the outward and visible signs of

Classic civilization emerge from an already complex society" (Hammond 1986b:411; 1980:189).

In the same manner that elites and elite interaction began before the start of the Classic period, they obviously continued into the Postclassic. Sabloff (1985) emphasizes this continuity in a radical reformulation of Maya periodization that combines the entire interval from 300 BC to AD 1250 into a single Middle Phase.

Even with such continuity of elite culture, however, the inscriptions that were at the heart of our deliberations are still almost entirely confined to the Classic period. The wealth of detail and chronological precision that they provide – martial and marital interactions involving named individuals from known polities that can be pinned down to a specific day – continues to justify separating out the span of time when inscriptions occur.

The chronological framework we will use, therefore, delineates a Classic period beginning in AD 250 (in accordance with modern usage that attributes a slightly earlier start for the period) and ends at AD 900. An Early Classic from 250 to 600 is followed by a Late Classic from 600 to 800 and a Terminal Classic (a relatively recent invention that is now generally used) from 800 to 900 that encompasses the period of the collapse in the southern lowlands. Such additional elaborations as a Middle Classic (400 to 700), useful in the southeastern region (Fash and Stuart, this volume), and a Tecep that conflates the Terminal Classic and Early Postclassic in Belize are of regional utility but do not have relevance to our purposes.

## THE CONTEXTS OF MAYA INSCRIPTIONS

Classic Maya texts survive in contexts ranging from the monumental to the minuscule, from the most public assertions of regal power to the most private indications of ownership. All of them help to develop our understanding of the role of the elite in ancient Maya civilization, as would, had any survived, the codical books (which, at the time of the conquest of Yucatan, Diego de Landa described as containing "antiquities and their sciences") which were the precursors of the surviving codices and the Books of Chilam Balam.

Since no Classic books are known, although the rotted remains of several have been reported from tombs, the textual record is impoverished. It has been depleted still further over the past quarter century by looting, which has wrenched hundreds of monumental and portable inscriptions from their archaeological contexts, robbing them of their vital associations and the Maya of their history. The information that can be gained from a looted monument when its origin is established, as for instance with the *cahal* inscription of La Pasadita Lintel 2, is a poignant reminder of what has been lost.

The most spectacular vehicles for Classic inscriptions are the great stelae and their accompanying altars or zoomorphs, which stood in the plazas of Maya centers and proclaimed both dynastic history and the passage of time. Similarly public are the hieroglyphic stairways, half monument and half architecture. While the largest of these, on Copan Structure 10L–26, was a history of the kings of Copan, others, such as those at Dos Pilas, commemorated victories in battle and the capture of important lords. Elsewhere, as at Naranjo, such stairways could mark defeat by another polity which imposed a monumental commemoration on the vanquished.

Architecture was also the vehicle for roofcomb inscriptions, such as that on Temple VI (Temple of the Inscriptions) at Tikal, with its mythical dates, and those on façades, as with the zodiac on the Monjas Annex at Chichen Itza. The interiors of buildings held less publicly visible texts, including inscribed benches of the kind found in nobles' houses at Copan; wall panels with texts or images or both, for example at Palenque; those carved on lintels which would have been readable only by an observer lying on the floor or craning the neck; and those on murals, as at Uaxactun and Bonampak.

Murals with texts have also been found in tombs at Tikal and most recently at Rio Azul, where they commemorate both the lives of elite individuals and the cosmic framework within which those lives were passed. Similar to tombs in their chthonic location, but differing in function and in the nature of their texts, are caves such as Naj Tunich where the content of the murals runs from the solemn to the *risqué*.

All of these contexts are immobile: the inscriptions are in the location where the Maya intended them to be when they were carved or painted. The other major group of contexts consists of portable objects, mostly personal possessions, which although they often finished up in tombs were not always made for funerary purposes. The largest number of texts occurs on pottery vessels, many bearing the "Primary Standard Sequence," which Coe (1973) originally thought to be specifically funerary in content but which now seems to reflect the quotidian function and ownership of the pot and sometimes the name of the man who painted it (the signatures of stela sculptors have also been recognized) (Houston and Taube 1987; Stuart 1986a,b, 1988). Personal jewelry such as jade earflares could be "name-tagged," as Mathews and Pendergast (1979) showed for a pair from Altun Ha, while several of the carved bones from Tikal Burial 116, the tomb of "Ruler A/Ah Cacau" beneath Temple I, also bore the ruler's name glyph. The inscribed bone from a Late Preclassic burial at Kichpanha, several shells incised with texts from funerary and other contexts, jades such as the Pomona flare and the Kendal shell-effigy, and mundane objects like the Kendal axe are less consistently explicable but invaluable members of the corpus of early Maya texts.

## INTELLECTUAL FRAMEWORKS

A realization of the cultural unity of Maya civilization dates from at least as early as Stephens and Catherwood's visit to Palenque in 1840, when Stephens (1841, II:343) noted that "the hieroglyphs are the same as we found at Copan and Quirigua . . . there is room for the belief that the whole of this country was once occupied by the same race, speaking the same language, or at least having the same written characters." The inscriptions at Copan he believed to be historical in content, and the sites in general "the remains of a cultivated, polished and peculiar people, who had passed through all the stages incidental to the rise and fall of nations, reached their golden age and perished, entirely unknown" (Stephens 1841, II:356).

Stephens correctly surmised the nature of the Maya monuments and their inscriptions, but he could not read them. Constantine Rafinesque (1827) had identified the Palenque inscriptions, from Del Rio's publication of 1822, with the script in the Dresden Codex and with "a peculiar language, distinct from the Azteca, probably the Tzendall . . . spoken from Chiapa to Panama, and connected with the Maya of Yucatan," but had not guessed at their contents.

Reading of the glyphs did not begin for another generation, until Brasseur de Bourbourg (1864) published the Madrid transcript of Diego de Landa's *Relación de las cosas de Yucatán* with its "alphabet." De Rosny deciphered the directional glyphs in 1876, working from the Madrid and Paris Codices, and in 1882 Cyrus Thomas showed that inscriptions were read by pairs of columns from the upper left corner.

Ernst Förstemann (1880), curator of the Dresden Codex, used Landa's *Relación* and Stephens's publication of Pío Pérez's calendric treatise to demonstrate the Maya use of a vigesimal base and place notation, together with the signs for zero/completion. He then unraveled the Venus tables in the Dresden Codex and, using the "calculation of ages" based on the *katun* in Landa, demonstrated the existence and structure of the Long Count. Maudslay's work at Copan provided fresh data on which Förstemann could test his thesis, and in 1894 he read seven Initial Series dates on the Copan stelae. Finally Goodman, working from Förstemann's and Maudslay's data, anchored the Long Count to the Christian calendar, so that from 1905 onwards the Maya have been part of dated history.

While the dates on the monuments could now be precisely specified, what they commemorated still could not. Some dates, such as the katun period-endings, clearly marked the passage of regular blocks of time, while others, on the basis of the astrological emphasis of the codices, were identified with celestial events. Both Eric Thompson and Sylvanus G. Morley, the two most powerful epigraphers of the middle decades of this century, were convinced that the majestic march of time, depicted in such evocative images as the passing of the burden of the katun on Copan Stela D, would not have been sullied by the Maya with the quotidian concerns of human history. To Thompson (1950:155) the possibility that "Maya dates recorded on stelae may refer to historical events or even recount the deeds of individuals" was "well-nigh inconceivable. The dates surely narrate the stages of the journey of time with a reverence befitting such a solemn theme . . . To add details of war or peace, of marriage or giving in marriage, to the solemn roll call of the periods of time is as though a tourist were to carve his initials on Donatello's David."

This Arcadian view, which went along with a vision of Maya society as composed of happy peasants supporting a priesthood engaged in esoteric rites in "ceremonial centers" with few other inhabitants, was controverted by a series of discoveries, archaeological and epigraphic, in the late 1950s. The mapping of Tikal showed that the ceremonial centers were the cores of cities with populations in the tens of thousands, with a necessary complexity of social and political organization (Coe 1965b). Berlin's identification of the Emblem Glyph as a territorial or ethnic marker (1958), and of name glyphs for some Palenque rulers (1959), showed that at least some of the inscriptions included sublunary matters, while Proskouriakoff's (1960) elucidation of historical patterning in the inscriptions of Piedras Negras suggested that the texts dealt with human rulers who were the individuals portrayed on the monuments. Thompson (1960:v) quickly saw the implications of this, and by the time Kelley (1962a) had demonstrated a dynasty at Quirigua, and Proskouriakoff (1963, 1964) had outlined the biographies of Shield-Jaguar and Bird-Jaguar of Yaxchilan, he was convinced that his view "regarding the impersonality of the texts [was] completely mistaken" (Thompson 1971:v).

A parallel development in Maya epigraphy was the proposal (by no means the first) that the script was at least in part phonetic, made by Yurii Knorosov (1952; in English 1958). Some of his examples were poor, and Thompson (1953) disagreed with him as acidly as he had with Benjamin Whorf twenty years earlier. Some Mayanists, notably Michael Coe and David Kelley (see Kelley 1962b for a historical study of this topic), supported Knorosov, but general acceptance of the phonetic-structure thesis did not come until Floyd Lounsbury's (1973) demonstration that the T168 "ben-ich" prefix, a standard part of the Emblem Glyph, was to be read *ahpo/ahau*. Shortly thereafter, Lounsbury, Schele and Mathews (Lounsbury 1974; Mathews and Schele 1974) published their decipherment of the dynasty of Palenque, a dynastic sequence was proposed for Tikal (Coggins 1975; Jones 1977), and statements about parentage, capture, and sacrifice were added to those for birth and accession identified by Proskouriakoff in 1960 (see Schele 1982 for a recent summary). The ruling elites of some Maya polities had become historical individuals, their lives filled with known incidents and interactions.

Ideas about the social position of those elites developed in parallel with the decipherment of the script. Morley (1946:159), while noting the informative potential of Classic art, bemoaned the lack of direct contemporary evidence from the inscriptions. He felt that the Postclassic, as reflected in early colonial sources such as Landa's *Relación*, was an equally useful guide, and proposed an analogy with the city-states of Classical Greece, late medieval Italy, and north Germany. Such city-states were culturally homogeneous and politically independent, each headed by a hereditary ruler (in the Maya case the *halach uinic*) who succeeded by patrilineal descent. Brainerd, in his revision of *The Ancient Maya* (Morley and Brainerd 1956:143–5), dropped the European comparison but retained Morley's view of Maya rulership –

one that, as this volume shows, has proved remarkably durable. A more egalitarian model emerged from the Carnegie/Harvard group of scholars, based partly on Vogt's (1964) view of Zinacantan as preserving pre-Columbian traditions, partly on Thompson's (1954) priest-peasant model, and partly on early settlement pattern studies (Willey 1956). This model has been countered by the mass of data emerging from Tikal (Coe 1965b; Haviland 1966, 1967).

Studies of subsistence, a topic dormant since the Carnegie Institution's work at Chichen Itza, were revived when the mapping of Tikal suggested higher population size and density than extensive swidden farming could support. The recognition of additional and under-appreciated food sources, such as roots (Bronson n.d.), marine protein (Lange 1971), and tree crops (Puleston 1971), was followed by the identification of artificial econiches such as drained fields and hillside terracing (Siemens and Puleston 1972; Turner 1978) as facilities for intensive agricultural production. While very large areas of such constructions were proposed (Harrison 1978; Adams 1980; Adams, Brown, and Culbert 1981), with a concomitantly central role in the Maya economy, further research in the 1980s suggests that they were supplementary, scattered, and often both late and of short duration, the result perhaps of the Late Classic population peak rather than any sustained commitment to capital investment in agriculture.

Settlement pattern studies have also contributed to the view of both ancient Maya social structure and polity interaction. The initial stage of such studies, lasting more than a century, worked outwards from the individual polity and from the isolated "ceremonial center" which was seen as its core. The swings in interpretation – from the idea of Maya centers as pre-industrial cities, common from the time of Stephens in the 1840s to Thompson in the 1930s, to the notion of the "vacant center" with a rural hinterland, which was powerful for at least thirty years from the 1930s to the 1960s, and since then back to the urban model – need not concern us here: they have been much discussed (e.g. Becker 1979). What persisted through this initial stage, ending only with the impact of the regional approach in the Belize Valley project (Willey *et al.* 1965), was the fashion for treating the site and its monuments in isolation, with intersite comparisons then being made at the level of architectural or other stylistic commonalties, which were, of course, manifestations of elite culture.

The second stage was an examination of intersite contacts, beginning with a historicist approach (Sabloff and Willey 1967) and developing into an economic one with studies of Fine Paste pottery distribution and, especially, of obsidian trade. These economic approaches were stimulated by the ability of analytical methods to trace materials to their sources and thus to enable directional maps of exchange contacts to be built up. The individual polity centers were reduced to a series of points on the map: what was important were the lines linking those points with each other. Interaction between polities was certainly being observed, but the polities themselves were submerged in favor of the interaction, occasionally being lucky enough to win distinction as a "redistributive node."

This emphasis on the links rather than the linked continued with the proposition that ritual networking overlaid the economic networks: Freidel's (1981) theoretical construct of "pilgrimage fairs" as an integrative mechanism on the grand scale, and Freidel and Sabloff's (1984) notion of "ceremonial circuits" on Cozumel at the local level are examples of this trend. More recently there has been a return towards considering the polity as a focus of interest, while not discarding the interactive approach, exemplified by Price's (1977) "cluster-interaction" model.

Thus, since 1970 the view of Maya society as complex has converged with the results of epigraphic decipherment: this volume summarizes the evidence and the interpretations.

## METHODS OF APPROACH

There are three ways in which ancient Maya political structure has been studied, some noted above: they may be tagged "up, down, and sideways." The first, from the base upwards, begins with the ecological and economic foundation offered by the lowland zone and relates it to the differential distribution of Maya centers across the landscape and their relationship to topography, resources, and communications. This is an approach that can, if one is blinkered, utilize only the notion of *der isolierte Staat* (von Thünen 1875), taking a single polity and treating it as a "typical" specimen of development in which questions about social and economic stratification and control hierarchies are asked and answered entirely within the context of the polity itself. It can also be more fruitfully used if the polity is treated synecdochically and the insights gained from scrutiny of its workings applied to its less well-studied neighbors, but here is the accompanying danger that uniformity will be assumed and imposed, and a real diversity between polities masked. As an example, the internal analysis of the polity or "realm" of Lubaantun in southern Belize which I undertook in 1970 (Hammond 1972) is one which could easily be applied uncritically to the adjacent polity of Pusilha, given that it shares the same range of ecological zones and economic resources. Closer study of Pusilha, however, shows major differences in chronological sequence, florescence, participation in the use of the dynastic monument complex for political commemoration, and internal site organization. The differences are sufficiently great that even studying the interaction between these two polity centers a day's march (32 km) apart is a problem.

"Bottom-upwards" study can, of course, begin at a level above that of the individual polity or center, with a loss of detail and an increase in implicit assumptions of comparability. The same Lubaantun study examined the distribution of centers around the Maya Mountains and their relationship to major rivers and relief (Hammond 1972:Figs. 25, 26), a simple example in which all sorts of questions are innocently begged. Development of this approach into an examination of the spatial relationships of eighty-three centers across the whole southern lowland zone (Hammond 1974a) discarded even major environmental factors in an attempt to seek non-ecological bases for the distribution of Maya polities. With hindsight, the principal contribution was to show how limited a purely spatial approach could be, but the divergence between the patterns I discerned and those emerging with the decipherment of texts and increased understanding of the Classic political scene may prove a useful check to those working with only spatial patterning in prehistoric contexts. Renfrew and Level (1979) use both historically documented and prehistoric distributions to predict boundaries from polity center locations; the results are intriguing rather than accurate in the externally referenced tests, and show a heavy reliance on selection of the "right" slope parameter.

A second method of approach is from the top downwards, from the level of superstructure towards the relations of production and the productive forces that form the infrastructure of Maya civilization. Such approaches take the position that, far from being epiphenomenal, the evidence of iconography and text is basic in defining polity. The first "top-down" approach was that of Morley (1946:Plate

19), who used the number of monuments at a site and the extent of its visible architecture to create a four-level hierarchy. It was a very subjective assessment – Copan and Uxmal were ranked at the top level less on the amount of such superstructure present than on their beauty and preservation, while the gigantic but poorly explored site of Calakmul ranked no higher than the second class in spite of its 104 stelae, and Oxkintok, Izamal, and Seibal were all relegated to the third class.

The next approaches in this field were engendered by Berlin's (1958) recognition of Emblem Glyphs and the subsequent definition of dynastic sequences for Palenque, Piedras Negras, Tikal, Yaxchilan, and elsewhere. Here were political centers with named rulers, proclaiming their polity through the Emblem Glyph. That they were also proclaiming suzerainty over other realms was suggested by Barthel (1968b:121), who proposed that "on different time horizons there are groups of emblems that define the 'capitals' of the period," the "first concrete point of reference for the internal organization of the area of Classic Maya culture." On this "cosmosociological principle" Barthel suggested four regional "capitals" at each of three periods: for AD 650–700 he proposed Copan, Palenque, possibly Tikal, and an unknown site with an Emblem Glyph apparently based on T579; for AD 750–800, on the basis of the Emblem Glyphs present on Copan Stela A, he included Copan, Palenque, Tikal, and another unknown site he called *chan*; for AD 850, using Emblem Glyphs on Seibal Stela 10, he nominated Seibal, Tikal, chan, and yet another unknown site identified by an Emblem Glyph with an *ik* main sign.

Barthel's four-capitals model was adopted by Marcus (1973, 1976), who applied a formal central-place model to generate a network of hypothetical hexagonal territories, and also suggested that chan was Calakmul and ik Motul de San Jose. (While chan has since then found favor as El Peru, some scholars now prefer Calakmul or an unknown site.) Marcus developed from Barthel's model the proposition that where one center mentioned another's Emblem Glyph, but not vice versa, the latter was politically dominant over the former.

Several problems existed with both Barthel's model and Marcus's adaptation of it. There was a lack of corroborative evidence that these (or any other) centers were accepted by the Maya as having any supernal standing, and Motul de San Jose with its small size, few stelae, and short calendric span seemed a poor candidate in any case. The Seibal inscription seemed more likely to record local political interaction within the central Peten region (Hammond 1974b), a conclusion made even more likely given the patterns of warfare and marriage documented by Mathews and Willey and Schele and Mathews (this volume), and the mention of one polity by another seems to record relationships between autonomous equals rather than any hierarchy of political obligation.

The role of women in Classic Maya politics was pointed out by Proskouriakoff (1961b) and Marcus (1976), and has been subsequently shown to include at Palenque either rulership or regency, or both, and to be generally a vital factor in dynastic succession, vertically within the polity and laterally between polities (Mathews 1986; Fox and Justeson 1986). Inter-polity marriage was for alliance: its pattern of occurrence accords more closely with that of royal visits than with that of inter-polity warfare, the latter showing a non-congruent set of relationships carried out over shorter distances (Schele and Mathews, this volume, Figs. 10.6–10.8; Hammond, this volume, chapter 11). What is surprising, perhaps, is that some raids were carried out over such long distances: Machaquila to Motul de San Jose, Quirigua to Copan, and Tonina to Palenque are all substantial and arduous journeys, although many of the routes of attack included stretches of navigable river (e.g. Caracol–Naranjo, Dos Pilas–Seibal, Dos Pilas–Yaxchilan, Piedras Negras–Pomona, and Aguateca–Cancuen).

These are examples of the documented interactions between polities that we must use in trying to understand their internal structure (Hammond, this volume, chapter 11) as well as their elite relationships, and they show how valuable the "top-down" approach can be.

The third method of approach is "sideways," from outside the corpus of Classic Maya archaeological and epigraphic evidence. Some of these data are nevertheless Maya – the gnomic utterances of the *Books of Chilam Balam*, the clues given by early ethnographers such as Landa and Cogolludo, the evidence of colonial vocabularies and dictionaries, and the degree to which we can recognize prehispanic survivals in colonial Maya culture (Farriss 1984, 1986). Comparative material can also be sought in regions where formative and crystallized polities, Renfrew's (1975) "early state modules," existed in the past and where documentary records are more comprehensive and include categories of data, such as economic records, totally absent from surviving (and perhaps from all) Maya texts. The same dangers apply in historical as in ethnographic analogy, that visible homology will conceal vital diversity of deep structure, but with that caveat in mind a fruitful range of material can be employed, from the Mesopotamian polities (Yoffee, this volume) through the Bronze Age Aegean (Renfrew 1972) to the *señorios* of Chimu Peru (Netherly 1984) with their hierarchical bipartition, and the rise of the Capetian monarchy in France (Lewis 1982), where a clan-based system of descent that prevented the personal accumulation of power was replaced with the idea of the dynasty, with patrilineal primogeniture and undivided inheritance of the patrimony. A feudal approach to the Maya has already been canvassed by Adams and Smith (1981). In the work of Lewis (1982) we see how a dynasty emerges and consolidates its political and economic support, and in France we see the rise of a regional state such as Culbert (this volume) feels existed in the Maya lowlands, at least in the case of Tikal.

Some notion of Maya political organization might emerge from examination of what kinds of information texts contain and what they ignore, as Lamberg-Karlovsky (1986) has done in comparing the information content of Egyptian, Indus, and Mesopotamian inscriptions. The Maya are closer to Eygpt, with its recording of religious and cosmological elements and historical events such as conquest, than to the Mesopotamian concern with "monitoring production and distribution at several levels along a distributive chain" (Lamberg-Karlovsky 1986:151) or the Indus portable seals' apparent concern with individual and group identity.

This book, then, concerns the impact that the decipherment of Maya hieroglyphic writing has had upon our understanding of Classic Maya society. Substantively, it presents the first summarization of Maya political history based upon Classic-period inscriptions. It then moves to a consideration of what the inscriptions add to our understanding of elite interaction. Finally, it considers what the entire conjunction of epigraphic, iconographic, and archaeological data tells us about the structure of Maya polities and Maya society.

# 2
# Classic Maya Emblem Glyphs

PETER MATHEWS

One of the great breakthroughs in the decipherment of Maya hieroglyphic writing was the discovery by Heinrich Berlin in 1958 of a particular category of hieroglyph that he called "Emblem" Glyphs (Berlin 1958). Berlin had noticed that Emblem Glyphs had a fairly standard position and form in Maya texts: they occurred towards the end of passages, and they usually consisted of three signs – a prefix, a superfix, and a "main sign" (Fig. 2.1). The main sign of Emblem

Fig. 2.1 The standard form of the Emblem Glyph, using Tikal as an example. The prefix is commonly known as the "water group". The main sign is usually a single sign, but in some Emblem Glyphs is a consistent combination of two or more signs.

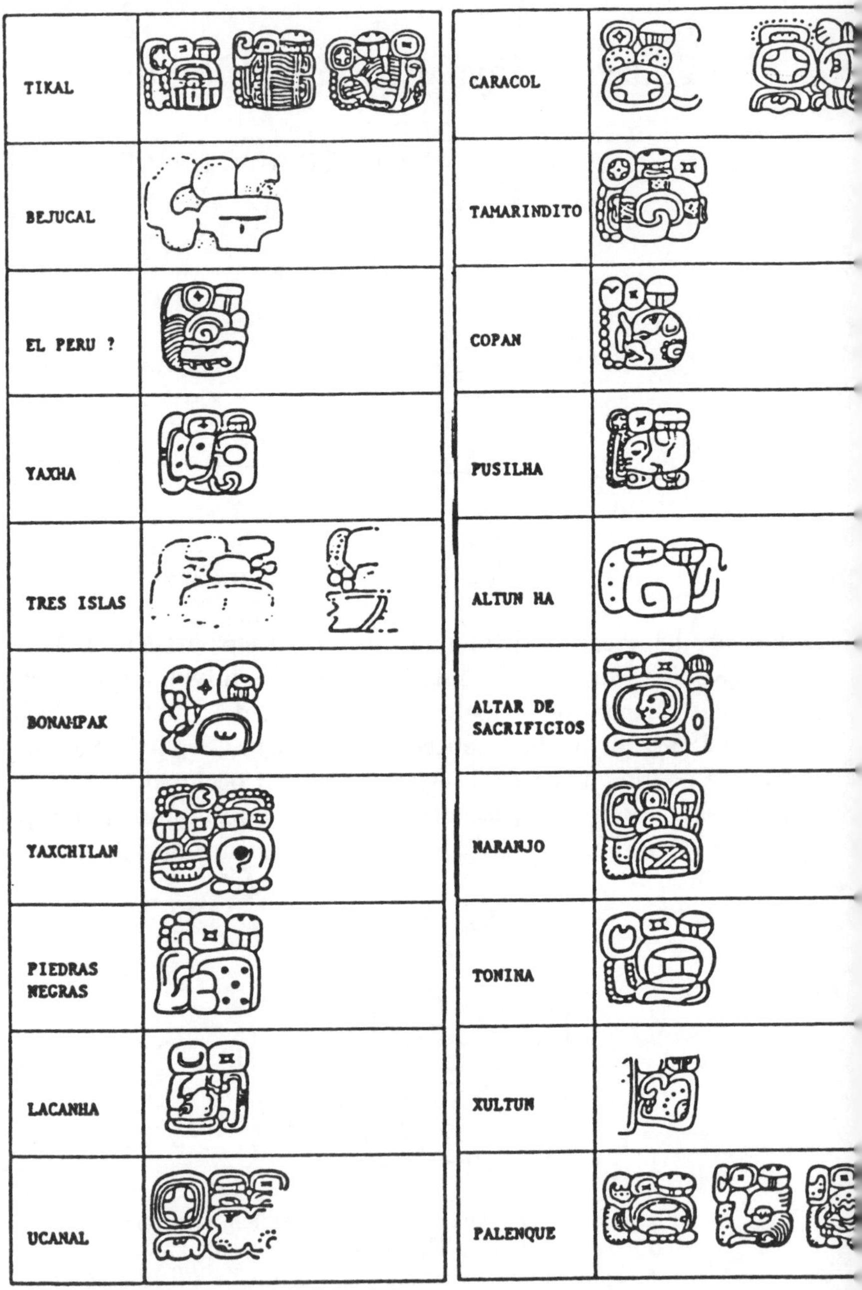

| | | | |
|---|---|---|---|
| TIKAL | | CARACOL | |
| BEJUCAL | | TAMARINDITO | |
| EL PERU ? | | COPAN | |
| YAXHA | | PUSILHA | |
| TRES ISLAS | | ALTUN HA | |
| BONAMPAK | | ALTAR DE SACRIFICIOS | |
| YAXCHILAN | | NARANJO | |
| PIEDRAS NEGRAS | | TONINA | |
| LACANHA | | XULTUN | |
| UCANAL | | PALENQUE | |

Fig. 2.2 Known Emblem Glyphs (in approximate order of appearanc

| | | | |
|---|---|---|---|
| S PILAS/ ATECA |  | SACUL |  |
| AN |  | IXTUTZ |  |
| UL DE JOSE |  | LOS HIGOS ? |  |
| ONA |  | UXMAL |  |
| LI PUNIT |  | CHICHEN ITZA |  |
| BAL |  | | |
| LUMKIN |  | | |
| HAQUILA |  | |  |
| RIGUA |  | |  |
| CUEN ? |  | |  |

Glyphs, Berlin noted, was different from site to site but fairly consistent within each site's inscriptions. Copan's Emblem Glyph, for example, occurs very commonly in the inscriptions of Copan, but only rarely in texts outside that site.

Berlin was not the first to notice the homogeneity of these glyphs: J. Eric S. Thompson had already isolated several Emblem Glyphs through the common use of their prefix (Thompson 1950:Fig. 43). Berlin, however, was the first to notice the geographical implications of this set of glyphs. He called them Emblem Glyphs because they seemed to be emblematic, in some ways, of the site in which they predominantly occurred. Berlin left open, however, the question of their precise significance, i.e., whether Emblem Glyphs represent the name of the city itself, or of the patron deity or ruling dynasty of the city.

In his article Berlin illustrated the Emblem Glyphs of eight Classic Maya sites and discussed possible Emblem Glyphs at six others. In the years following the publication of his article, many additional Emblem Glyphs have been noted, so that there are now some three dozen sites with securely identified Emblem Glyphs. In addition, Classic Maya inscriptions contain several Emblem Glyphs which are still not identified as to site (Fig. 2.2).

There is still considerable debate over the precise role of Emblem Glyphs. Proskouriakoff (1960:471) believed that they functioned as lineage or dynastic names; Barthel (1968a), who analyzed Emblem Glyphs in considerable detail, suggested that the prefix and superfix have a titular function, and that the main sign "seems to concern place-names as well as ethnic names" (Barthel 1968b:120, translation mine). Kelley (1976:215), on the other hand, argued cogently that the main signs of Emblem Glyphs are place-names.

Most, if not all, of today's generation of epigraphers follow Kelley in regarding Emblem Glyph main signs as toponyms. However, there is still some disagreement on two key questions concerning Emblem Glyphs. First, what is the specific function of the prefix and superfix of Emblem Glyphs, and hence what is the overall reading and function of Emblem Glyphs? Second, what are the implications of Emblem Glyphs for the sociopolitical and geopolitical organization of the Classic Maya? As we shall see shortly, the second of these questions is the more hotly debated at the present time, despite continuing uncertainty over the solution to the first.

## THE STRUCTURE AND FUNCTION OF EMBLEM GLYPHS

We have seen that Emblem Glyphs were isolated by Berlin largely because of their general consistency in form: usually they have a prefix, a superfix and a main sign. Ironically, it is the *in*consistencies of their form – the rarer variants of Emblem Glyphs – that give us the best clues as to their specific functions and reading (Fig. 2.3). Many Emblem Glyphs can, on occasion, have a subfix below their main sign. By far the most common subfix is T130 (T number from Thompson's [1962] catalog of glyphs), a sign whose value *wa* or *-w* is accepted by most epigraphers. Although it is possible that this sign acts as a grammatical suffix, it is more likely that it functions as a phonetic complement, indicating the final *-w* of some word. Since it is subfixed to the Emblem Glyph main sign, it might be reasonable to deduce that the T130 *-w* suffix is a phonetic complement to the main signs of Emblem Glyphs. However this would have the implication that all Emblem Glyph main signs – and there are some forty different ones known – are words that end in *-w*. This seems highly unlikely. Whenever the T130 subfix is present in an Emblem Glyph, T168 occurs as superfix, and so it is possible to hypothesize the subfix as a phonetic complement to the *superfix*, the two signs perhaps qualifying the main sign that they embrace.

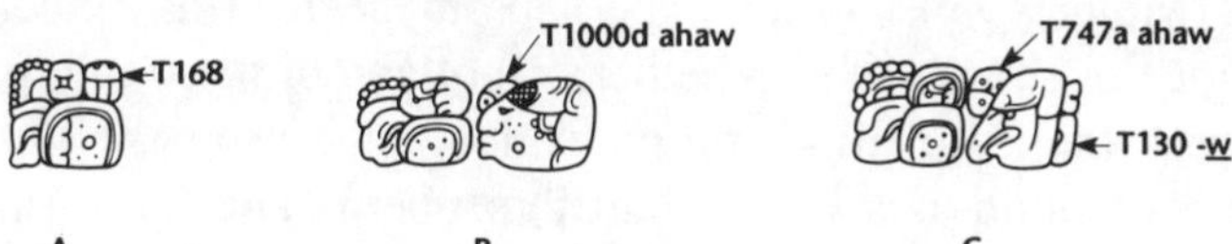


Fig. 2.3 Variant forms of Emblem Glyphs: *a* "standard" form of Piedras Negras Emblem Glyph; *b* early variant of the Piedras Negras Emblem Glyph with T1000d ahau replacing the T168 superfix; *c* early variant of the Piedras Negras Emblem Glyph with T747a ahau replacing the T168 superfix. Note the T130 *-w* postfix to T747a.

T168 is a sign whose derivation has been brilliantly worked out by Lounsbury (1973) as *ahpo* or *ahpop*, "ruler." Lounsbury argued that T168 later came to be read (especially in the Maya lowlands) *ahaw (ahau)*, "lord." This reading makes good sense in the context of Emblem Glyphs, in view of the T130 *-w* phonetic complement associated with them. It also makes good sense in view of the context of Emblem Glyphs, for they invariably occur towards the end of name phrases of Maya rulers and nobles, and thus presumably have a general function as royal or noble titles. I have argued elsewhere (Mathews 1985:32; Mathews and Justeson 1984:216–19) that occasionally there are aberrant Emblem Glyph compounds in which no T168 superfix occurs; in such cases, however, the glyph *following* the "Emblem Glyph" is a royal title. In most cases this title has the form T1000d or T747a, often with a T130 suffix (Fig. 2.3). These two signs are well recognized as head-variants of ahau (both occur, for example, as head variants of the day name Ahau). These variant Emblem Glyph forms show the substitution for T168 (as superfix to the main sign) of compounds that can be read ahau (and that follow the main sign). They therefore indicate that T168 is to be read ahau, and that the reading order of Emblem Glyphs was probably prefix+main sign+ahau.

The prefixes of Emblem Glyphs occur in several slightly variant forms, all belonging to what Thompson (1950:274–81) referred to as the "water group" of prefixes, owing to the presence of a row of dots or droplets in most examples. In addition to interpretations of water, the droplets have been interpreted as kernels of maize, beads of incense, and pebbles used in divination. Barthel (1968a:169–70) regarded Emblem Glyph prefixes as "patrilineal symbols." More recently, the droplets have been interpreted as drops of blood (Stuart 1984; Schele and Miller 1986:175–208), perhaps to be read as "precious, holy, divine" or some such. Whether or not any of these interpretations is correct, the Emblem Glyph prefix does appear to be less important to the compound as a whole than the superfix and main sign, for it is frequently absent from Emblem Glyphs, apparently without radically changing their meaning.

So far we have looked at the affixes of Emblem Glyphs, and have seen that they functioned as titles, even though the prefix is still not well understood. The main sign and its interpretation have yet to be discussed. We have seen that there are several possible interpretations: place-name, patron deity, dynasty, or lineage name, and ethnic group. Each of these has been argued for to some extent, but most epigraphers nowadays accept place-name as the most likely candidate. There are several reasons for this. First, several Emblem Glyph main signs occur in a verbal compound signifying "war" (Fig. 2.4), a compound first interpreted by Riese (1984a). In this compound they substitute with

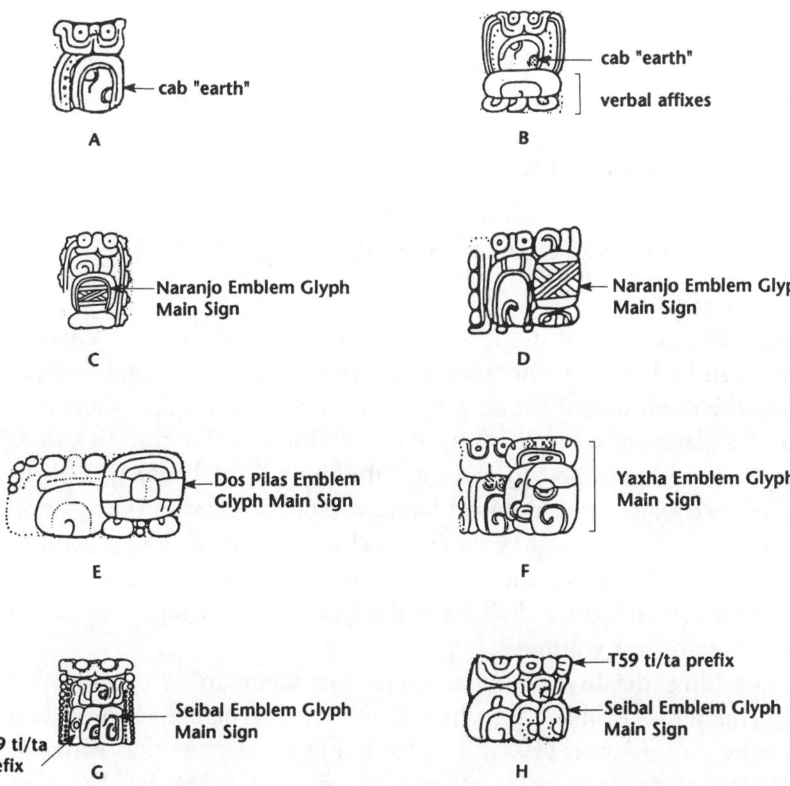


Fig. 2.4 War compounds with *cab* "earth" or Emblem Glyph main signs.

T526, *cab*, "earth" – a place-name *par excellence*. Second, in two examples from Seibal (Fig. 2.4g,h), the Emblem Glyph main sign is prefixed by T59, *ti/ta*. While there are several possible functions of *ti/ta*, the one that seems to fit here is that of spatial locative preposition "in, at (a place)." Finally, as Kelley (1976:215) has pointed out, most of the major categories of Maya glyphs have now been deciphered or at least are understood. If Emblem Glyphs do not include references to the individual sites or polities, then there seems to be no such reference in the Maya inscriptions. In view of the historical and political nature of the texts, this absence would be most odd.

We are left, then, with an interpretation of Emblem Glyphs that sees them functioning as royal titles (they invariably occur in royal name phrases) and read perhaps as "divine Tikal lord," etc. The "divine" interpretation of the prefix is still far from proven but is viewed favorably by many epigraphers. The main sign is viewed by most epigraphers as a place-name, referring either to the city itself or to the territory that it controlled or to both. And the "lord" is precisely the title that we would expect to find in a royal name phrase.

## SOCIOPOLITICAL IMPLICATIONS OF EMBLEM GLYPHS

Even if we are correct in the above interpretation of Emblem Glyphs, we are still left with the question of the main sign and its implications. Does the main sign of Emblem Glyphs – which most epigraphers now see as a place-name – refer to the city itself (or to part of the city), or to the territory controlled by the city, the polity? Do Emblem Glyphs occur as equals in the political landscape of the Classic Maya, or do they occur in some sort of hierarchical arrangement? The second of these questions is the most contentious issue currently concerning Emblem Glyphs, as we shall see in the following paragraphs, as well as elsewhere in this volume.

Regarding the first question, there now seems to be considerable agreement that Emblem Glyphs refer to a wider geographical area than just the city. Marcus (1973:913), for example, believes that Emblem Glyphs refer to "the site, as well as the territory subject to it." Whether or not this is the case (I believe that Marcus is correct), Emblem Glyphs can certainly be used in interpretations of Classic Maya political geography, for their very presence implies the functioning of local dynasties, and therefore of individual Maya sites. By looking at which Emblem Glyph sites were functioning at the same time, we can begin to attempt reconstructions of Classic Maya geography, and by considering other details, such as individual dynasties and their external contacts, we can begin to determine the relationships between the sites and attempt reconstructions of the Classic Maya political landscape.

As early as 1968 Barthel argued that Emblem Glyphs could be arranged in a hierarchical structure, and also that on occasion groups of four Emblem Glyph sites could be seen as directional capitals of the Maya world (Barthel 1968a). Barthel's arguments were embraced and greatly developed by Marcus (1973, 1976), who has done more than any other scholar to develop our knowledge and understanding of Emblem Glyphs. Marcus argued that sites with Emblem Glyphs were

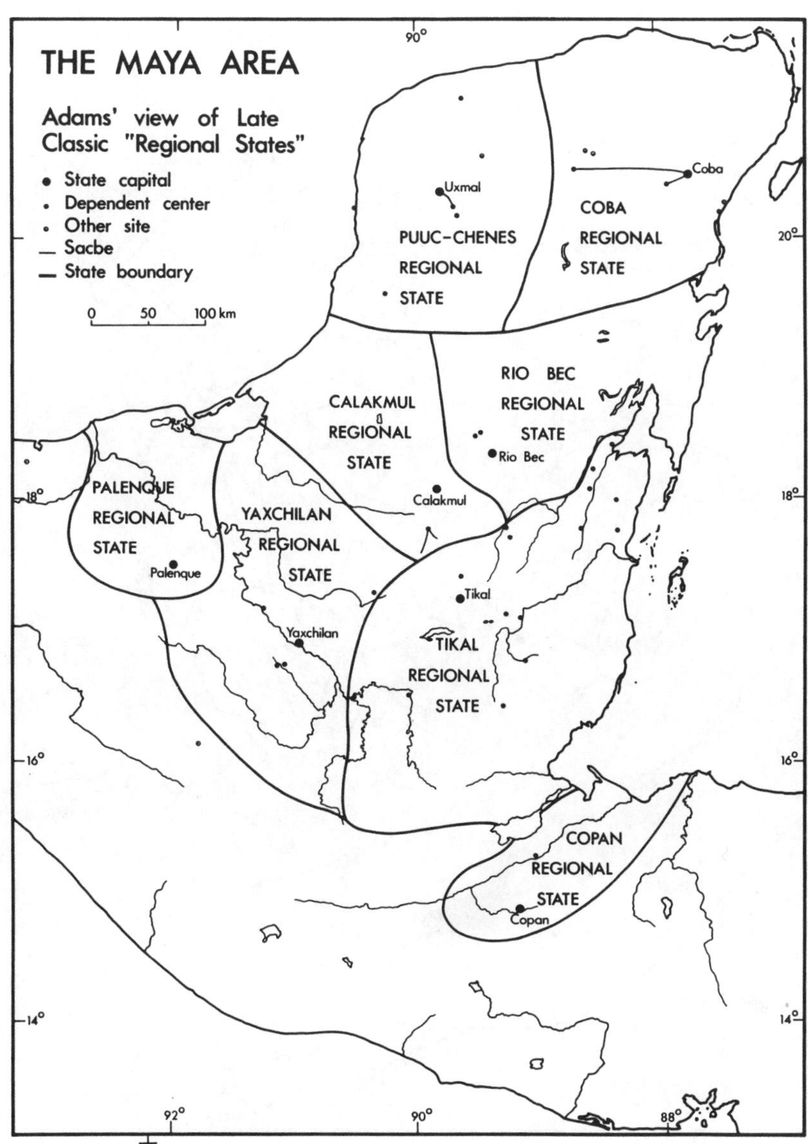


Fig. 2.5 Adams' (1986b) view of Late Classic political organization.

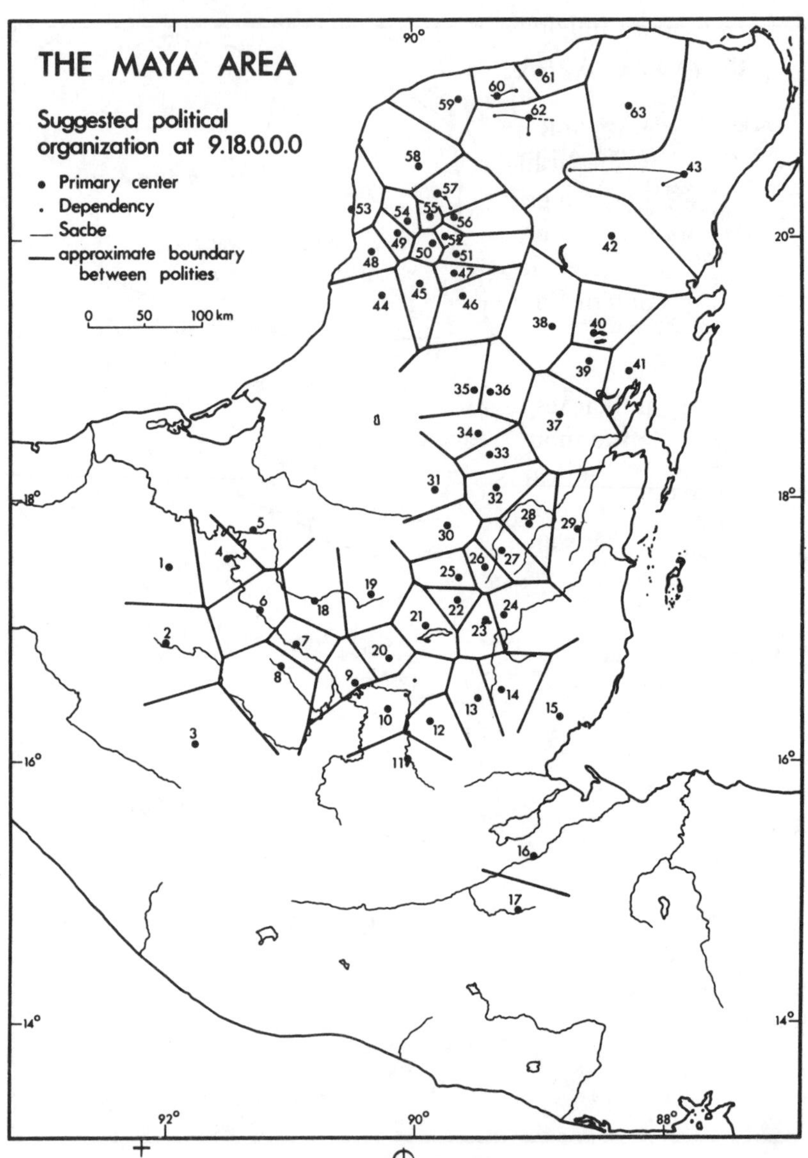


Fig. 2.6 Mathews' suggested Maya political organization and polity centers at 9.18.0.0.0 (AD 790).

politically more important than those with none. Furthermore, she argued that a hierarchy existed among sites with Emblem Glyphs: "If Site A was dependent to Site B, I expected Site A to mention Site B more often than Site B mentioned Site A" (Marcus 1976:10). Marcus arrived at a five-tiered hierarchy of Maya sites, in which centers with Emblem Glyphs comprise the first two ranks, sites in levels 3 and 4 have monuments but no Emblem Glyphs, and shifting hamlets comprise the lowest level. Into this hierarchy, Marcus incorporated Barthel's groups of four Emblem Glyph sites, recorded on Copan Stela A (9.15.0.0.0; AD 731) and Seibal Stela 10 (10.1.0.0.0; AD 849). Marcus considered these monuments to refer to the four capitals of the Maya world at their respective dates. The four sites (and they differed slightly on the two monuments) held sway politically over other sites, even those with Emblem Glyphs, in their respective regions. In other words, the lords of the four capitals were overlords of the Maya world, and other dynasties were inferior. This view leads to the argument for very large polities during the Classic Maya period: R. E. W. Adams (1986b:437) – largely following Marcus – has reconstructed eight "regional states" in the Late Classic Maya lowlands, with an average area of some 30,000 km$^2$ (Fig. 2.5).

My own view of Classic Maya political geography is somewhat different, for I do not see any hierarchical structure implied by Emblem Glyph patterns of occurrence. Rather, I see Emblem Glyphs, occurring in title phrases of Maya lords, as implying the *same* political rank – for the title involved is ahau, "lord". The Maya seem to have gone to some length when stating hierarchical political relationships (see Houston and Mathews 1985:Fig. 12); there is no implication of differential status in Emblem Glyph references.

If one considers all Emblem Glyphs to be references to sites and dynasties of equal political status, then there were at least as many polities functioning throughout the Classic Maya lowlands as there were Emblem Glyphs. I have argued for as many as two dozen independent polities in the southern Maya lowlands at 9.18.0.0.0 (AD 790; Fig. 2.6), and throughout the entire Maya lowlands at that date there might have been sixty or seventy autonomous "city-states," most with an area of about 2,500 km$^2$.

Which of these models is the more likely is the subject of some discussion in this volume, and no doubt will be a matter of debate for some time to come.

# 3

# Prehistoric polities of the Pasion region: hieroglyphic texts and their archaeological settings

PETER MATHEWS AND GORDON R. WILLEY

This essay is an attempt to define ancient lowland Maya political units from hieroglyphic inscriptions and their archaeological site contexts as these have been investigated in the Pasion Valley and its immediate environs in the southwestern sector of the Department of Peten, Guatemala. Hieroglyphic monuments are known from twenty-five sites in this region. Most of these monuments date from the Late Classic period although a few are Early Classic. Two of the larger sites have been excavated in some detail, and these excavations provide an archaeological sequence which begins as early as the Middle Preclassic period. Some glyphic recording has been done at almost all of the sites, and, in addition, minor excavations, surface survey, and mapping have been carried out at a number of the others.

## THE PASION REGION: NATURAL SETTING AND ARCHAEOLOGICAL BACKGROUND

The Pasion River rises in the hills of the Alta Verapaz and runs northward for about 100 km through the lowlands of the southern part of the Department of Peten, Guatamala. At a point near the major archaeological ruin of Seibal, the river turns sharply westward and flows some 50 km before joining with the Salinas-Chixoy system at the Mexican border. The Salinas-Chixoy-Pasion is then joined by the Rio Lacantun from the west, and with this last juncture the river system becomes the Usumacinta which, coursing northwestward, eventually reaches the Gulf of Mexico

The Pasion archaeological region (Fig. 3.1), as defined by us here, is essentially that of the Pasion drainage although we extend our region a bit northward beyond the Pasion-Chixoy confluence. In general, it is low-lying tropical rainforest country with some patches of savanna grasslands. Rainfall is high but broken by a January-to-April dry season. Vegetation, soils, and underlying geological structure have been described in some detail in two archaeological monographs on sites of the region (Willey and Smith, 1969:39–47; Willey *et al.* 1975:9–23), and we will not repeat this here; but, with reference to agricultural potential, we can summarize by saying that there are alluvial soils along the Pasion and its tributaries that are highly fertile and very suitable for intensive or short-fallow farming. There are also some large tracts of swampy riverine terrain that may have been tilled with artificial raised fields and drainage ditches (Adams 1983); however, definite evidence for such intensive agricultural fields is still lacking. Finally, further back from the streams are hill slopes with thinner soils which could have been cultivated under long-fallow swidden regimes.

The definition of a Pasion archaeological region within the larger Maya lowlands area is still somewhat tentative, but ceramics set it apart from other regions of the Peten, especially the Late Classic ceramics which include some regionally characteristic Tepeu tradition types and varieties as well as Terminal Classic Fine Oranges and Fine Grays. In architecture, hieroglyphic stairways are regionally characteristic. But one of the strongest internal bondings making for a Pasion cultural region or subarea of the lowlands is the hieroglyphic textual material. These texts offer indisputable evidence that the various sites within the region interacted politically with each other in an intensive way, especially during the Late Classic period. The outer geographical boundaries of the region must remain approximate. Hammond and Ashmore (1981:Fig. 2.1), in their definition of regions or "zones" in the Maya lowlands, draw a Pasion zone which extends from the Rio Lacantun eastward to the Caribbean and Lake Izabal. We think this is too large, given the present state of knowledge, and prefer to restrict

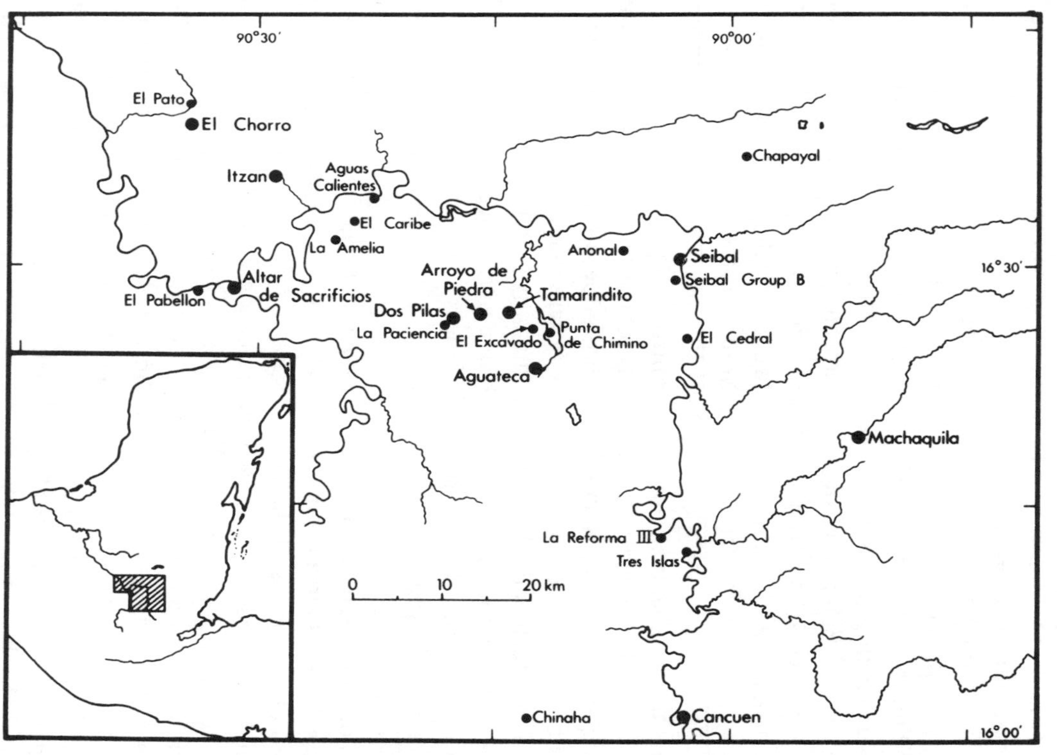


Fig. 3.1 Archaeological sites in the Pasion region.

ourselves as we have. Thus, we begin with the archaeological site of Cancuen in the southeast and go downriver to Altar de Sacrificios, extending only a short distance north of Altar de Sacrificios to take in such sites as El Chorro. It is possible that a Pasion region might also include the course of the Chixoy-Salinas, going some distance southward, or upstream, from Altar de Sacrificios, but such an extension should await more exploration.

From the number of these sites and their distribution, it seems safe to say that the Pasion region was densely settled in prehistoric times. For residential, as opposed to ceremonial center, settlement, we have only one extensive and detailed study, that for the peripheries of Seibal (Tourtellot 1988); however, there are many indications, gathered from "spot-checking" along the river banks (Willey 1973), that small mounds or "house-mounds" are virtually continuous throughout the region.

The spacing, hierarchical relationships, and dynastic historical relationships of the Pasion region centers are the central themes of our essay. Preliminarily, and very generally, we note these centers to be anywhere from 15 to 5 km apart although some of the smaller ones may be closer than 5 km to each other, and to larger centers.

Of the twenty-five sites included in this study, site plans exist for seventeen, which have been drawn by various people: Morley, Shook, Bullard, Ian Graham, von Euw, Tourtellot, and Houston and Dixon (See Table 3.1 for details). These plans enable a preliminary assessment for the ranking of the Pasion region sites, especially when considered in combination with other indications of site importance, such as the number of courtyards (Adams 1981; Adams and Jones 1981), the number of monuments, and the presence or absence of an Emblem Glyph.

All of these criteria are tabulated in Table 3.1. It can be seen that the Pasion region centers fall quite clearly into two groups: those sites with Emblem Glyphs are larger and have more monuments than sites without Emblem Glyphs. The areas of the sites with Emblem Glyphs range from 7.739 km$^2$ (Seibal) down to 0.51 km$^2$ (Anonal); the sites without Emblem Glyphs are smaller than 0.015 km$^2$. It should be pointed out here that site areas, which were calculated by Mathews, include only areas of concentrations of sizeable mounds. Also, of course, some maps are less complete and/or reliable than others. The Seibal and Altar de Sacrificios maps are undoubtedly the most reliable;

Table 3.1. A *comparison of Pasion region sites by site size and number of monuments*

| Site | Emblem Glyph | Site plan | Site area ($km^2$) | Number of courtyards | Number of monuments | |
|---|---|---|---|---|---|---|
| | | | | | Total | Carved |
| Seibal | + | 4,6 | 7.74 | 23 | 85 | 29 |
| Altar de Sacrificios | + | 3 | 0.57 | 8 | 58 | 36 |
| Dos Pilas | + | 4,7 | 0.51 | 16* | 52 | 35 |
| Cancuen | + | 6 | 0.32 | 8* | 24 | 6 |
| Aguateca | + | 4,7 | 0.23 | 7* | 24 | 11 |
| Tamarindito | + | 7 | 0.20 | 7* | 11 | 11 |
| Itzan | + | 4,7 | 0.10 | 7* | 32 | 24 |
| Arroyo de Piedra | + | 7 | 0.07 | 6* | 12 | 4 |
| Machaquila | + | 4 | 0.07 | 10 | 27 | 18 |
| El Chorro | + | 5 | 0.06 | 5* | 17 | 17 |
| Anonal | + | 6 | 0.05 | 5* | 2 | 2 |
| El Caribe | — | 2 | 0.01 | 3 | 3 | 3 |
| La Paciencia | — | 7 | 0.008 | 2* | 2 | 0 |
| La Amelia | — | 2 | 0.008 | 3 | 3 | 3 |
| El Excavado | — | 7 | 0.004 | 2* | 2 | 2 |
| El Pabellon | — | 1 | 0.003 | 1 | 1 | 1 |
| Aguas Calientes | ? | 1 | 0.001 | 1 | 1 | 1 |
| Tres Islas | + | — | — | — | 3 | 3 |
| La Reforma III | ? | | ? | ? | 2 | 2 |
| Punta de Chimino | ? | | ? | 1* | 2? | 2? |
| Seibal Group B | — | | ? | ? | 1 | 1 |
| Chapayal | — | | ? | ? | 1 | 1 |
| Chinaha | ? | | ? | ? | 1 | 1 |
| El Cedral | — | | ? | ? | 1 | 1 |
| El Pato | ? | | ? | ? | ? | ? |

The data tabulated here are based on site plans surveyed by several people (Column 3): (1) Sylvanus G. Morley; (2) Edwin M. Shook; (3) William R. Bullard; (4) Ian Graham; (5) Eric von Euw; (6) Gair Tourtellot III; (7) Stephen D. Houston and (in most cases) Boyd Dixon. Site areas have been calculated by Mathews, and courtyard counts by Adams (1981:Table 9.8) and Mathews (indicated by asterisks). Monument counts for Dos Pilas, Tamarindito, Arroyo de Piedra, La Paciencia, and Punta de Chimino have been augmented by information kindly supplied by Stephen Houston (personal communication, 1985–6).

those of Dos Pilas, Cancuen, Aguateca, Tamarindito, Arroyo de Piedra, and Anonal are also quite accurate and complete. The plans of Itzan and Machaquila are incomplete, and their site areas are almost certainly underestimated in Table 3.1. Similarly, the areas of El Caribe, La Amelia, El Pabellon, and Aguas Calientes are probably understated.

Courtyard counts for the Pasion region centers range from twenty-three down to five for the sites with Emblem Glyphs, and three or fewer for those without Emblem Glyphs. Finally, numbers of monuments range from eighty-six (total, with thirty-four carved) down to two in the sites with Emblem Glyphs, and from three down to one in sites without Emblem Glyphs.

Thus, the tabulations of Table 3.1 confirm a general correlation between site area, number of courtyards, and number of monuments, and the presence or absence of an Emblem Glyph. This, in part, sets up the potential for an evaluation of site hierarchies and geopolitical organization in the Pasion region. The remaining evidence for such an evaluation lies in the hieroglyphic texts at the various sites, and what they say about the local rulers and their relationships with neighboring lords.

The archaeological chronology of the Pasion region, as it is known especially from the excavations at Altar de Sacrificios (Willey 1973) and Seibal (Willey *et al.* 1975), begins with substantial Xe and Mamom Middle Preclassic occupations and continues through a vigorous Chicanel sphere Late Preclassic. The Protoclassic is then well represented at Altar de Sacrificios although not at Seibal. Similarly, the Early Classic is represented by both ceramics and stelae at Altar de Sacrificios but is exceptionally weak at Seibal. The Tepeu Late Classic ceramic sphere is present at both Altar de Sacrificios and Seibal, and there are Late Classic monuments at both sites. The Terminal Classic appears at Altar de Sacrificios as what might best be described as a "squatter" ceramic complex, characterized by Fine Paste wares. At Seibal a related ceramic complex is present, but here the site enjoyed a major building and monument phase. Both sites were apparently abandoned shortly after AD 900. The other sites of the Pasion region probably fall into this Middle Preclassic-through-Terminal Classic range although most await excavation. We know, however, that all twenty-five sites were active in the Late Classic.

## THE SITES: ARCHAEOLOGICAL AND EPIGRAPHIC SUMMARIES

The hieroglyphic record of the Pasion region is one of the best in the Maya lowlands, with over 200 carved monuments (Table 3.2) from our twenty-five sites under consideration. Dedicatory Dates span more than 400 years, from 9.1.0.0.0 to 10.3.0.0.0 (AD 455–889). In addition, there are at least twelve sites from among our twenty-five which

Table 3.2. *The Pasion region: monument totals by site*

| Site | Stelae t. | Stelae c. | Altars t. | Altars c. | Panels t. | Panels c. | HS. c. | O. c. | Totals t. | Totals c. | No. of glyphs | Dates t. | Dates e. | DD. e. |
|---|---|---|---|---|---|---|---|---|---|---|---|---|---|---|
| Aguas Calientes | 1 | 1 | — | — | — | — | — | — | 1 | 1 | 54 | 4 | 4 | 1 |
| Aguateca | 13 | 10 | 11 | 1 | — | — | — | — | 24 | 11 | 250 | 23 | 20 | 6 |
| Altar de Sacrificios | 20 | 17 | 29 | 10 | 7 | 7 | — | 2 | 58 | 36 | 752 | 41 | 33 | 20 |
| Anonal | — | — | — | — | 2 | 2 | — | — | 2 | 2 | 18 | 1 | 0 | 0 |
| Arroyo de Piedra | 7 | 4 | 5 | — | — | — | — | — | 12 | 4 | 93 | 6 | 4 | 3 |
| Cancuen | 12 | 3 | 11 | 2 | — | — | 1 | — | 24 | 6 | 152 | 5 | 3 | 3 |
| Chapayal | 1 | 1 | — | — | — | — | — | — | 1 | 1 | 38 | 1 | 0 | 0 |
| Chinaha | 1 | 1 | — | — | — | — | — | — | 1 | 1 | 9 | 1 | 1 | 1 |
| Dos Pilas | 20 | 20 | 16 | 2 | 9 | 6 | 4 | 3 | 52 | 35 | 853 | 66 | 42 | 14 |
| El Caribe | 2 | 2 | — | — | — | — | — | 1 | 3 | 3 | 23 | 3 | 0 | 0 |
| El Cedral | — | — | — | — | 1 | 1 | — | — | 1 | 1 | 4 | 0 | 0 | 0 |
| El Chorro | 5 | 5 | 7 | 7 | — | — | 2 | 3 | 17 | 17 | 310 | 10 | 5 | 5 |
| El Excavado | — | — | — | — | 2 | 2 | — | — | 2 | 2 | 33 | 1 | 0 | 0 |
| El Pabellon | 1 | 1 | — | — | — | — | — | — | 1 | 1 | 24 | 1 | 1 | 1 |
| El Pato | | | | | | | | | ? | ? | | | | |
| Itzan | 20 | 17 | 6 | 1 | 4 | 4 | 2 | — | 32 | 24 | 343 | 24 | 19 | 4 |
| La Amelia | 2 | 2 | — | — | — | — | 1 | — | 3 | 3 | 103 | 12 | 7 | 3 |
| La Paciencia | — | — | — | — | 2 | — | — | — | 2 | 0 | 0 | 0 | 0 | 0 |
| La Reforma III | 2 | 2 | — | — | — | — | — | — | 2 | 2 | ? | ? | ? | ? |
| Machaquila | 18 | 13 | 6 | 2 | 2 | 2 | — | 1 | 27 | 18 | 553 | 34 | 31 | 11 |
| Punta de Chimino | 1? | 1? | 1? | 1? | — | — | — | — | 2? | 2? | ? | ? | ? | ? |
| Seibal | 55 | 21 | 27 | 5 | 1 | 1 | 1 | 1 | 85 | 29 | 283 | 29 | 24 | 14 |
| Seibal Group B | 1 | 1 | — | — | — | — | — | — | 1 | 1 | 16 | 1 | 0 | 0 |
| Tamarindito | 7 | 7 | — | — | — | — | 3 | 1 | 11 | 11 | 215 | 17 | 15 | 3 |
| Tres Islas | 3 | 3 | — | — | — | — | — | — | 3 | 3 | 137 | 12 | 7 | 3 |
| Totals | 192 | 132 | 119 | 31 | 30 | 25 | 14 | 12 | 367 | 214 | 4,263 | 292 | 216 | 92 |

HS. Hieroglyphic Stairways
O. Other monuments (the two Altar de Sacrificios "others" are vases).
DD. Dedicatory Dates.
t. total.
c. carved.
e. [illegible]

have Emblem Glyphs. Fig. 3.2 illustrates time-lines of monumental activity for the various sites, with solid lines representing definite continuation of monumental (and dynastic) activity, and dashed lines representing probable activity (i.e., a short break in the record that more probably indicates a missing monument than a cessation of activity at the site). Fig. 3.3 shows datable monuments of the Pasion region, arranged by the *hotun* in which their Dedicatory Date occurred. Fig. 3.4 is similar but includes all dates, not just Dedicatory Dates. While it seems likely that other Pasion region sites with monuments will be discovered, our list probably includes all of the larger ones. Other sites of the region are most likely small residential mounds of the kind alluded to previously. One assumes that such domestic mound clusters or hamlets were affiliated to nearby monument sites or centers (see Willey 1973:64).

Our knowledge of the twenty-five Pasion region sites is very uneven; as noted, only two have been excavated in detail. We are dependent upon a few test excavations, surface collections and observations, and inspection of the exposed monuments for our knowledge of the others. We are especially grateful to Ian Graham, who has made available to us his wealth of data on Pasion region sites, in the form of preliminary drawings of monuments, and site plans and field notes. We are also very grateful to Stephen D. Houston for information in the form of site plans and notes on monuments and ceramics from several of the Pasion region sites. We have also made use of hitherto unpublished site plans of El Chorro and Anonal, made by Eric von Euw and Gair Tourtellot III, respectively. Let us review the twenty-five sites, taking them in alphabetical order.

*Aguas Calientes.* The site is on the south side of the mainstream of the lower Pasion, situated a little less than a kilometer from the river's bank. An L-shaped palace-type mound is the principal structure here, and it was associated with the only stela at the site. The text of this stela is not very clear, but it appears to refer to and portray a local ruler who was under the dominance of the Dos Pilas/Aguateca dynasty, *c.* 9.18.0.0.0 (AD 790).

*Aguateca/Dos Pilas.* Aguateca is on a high limestone escarpment on the west side of the Laguna Petexbatun; Dos Pilas is located some 11 km to the northwest. The two sites shared the same ruling dynasty,

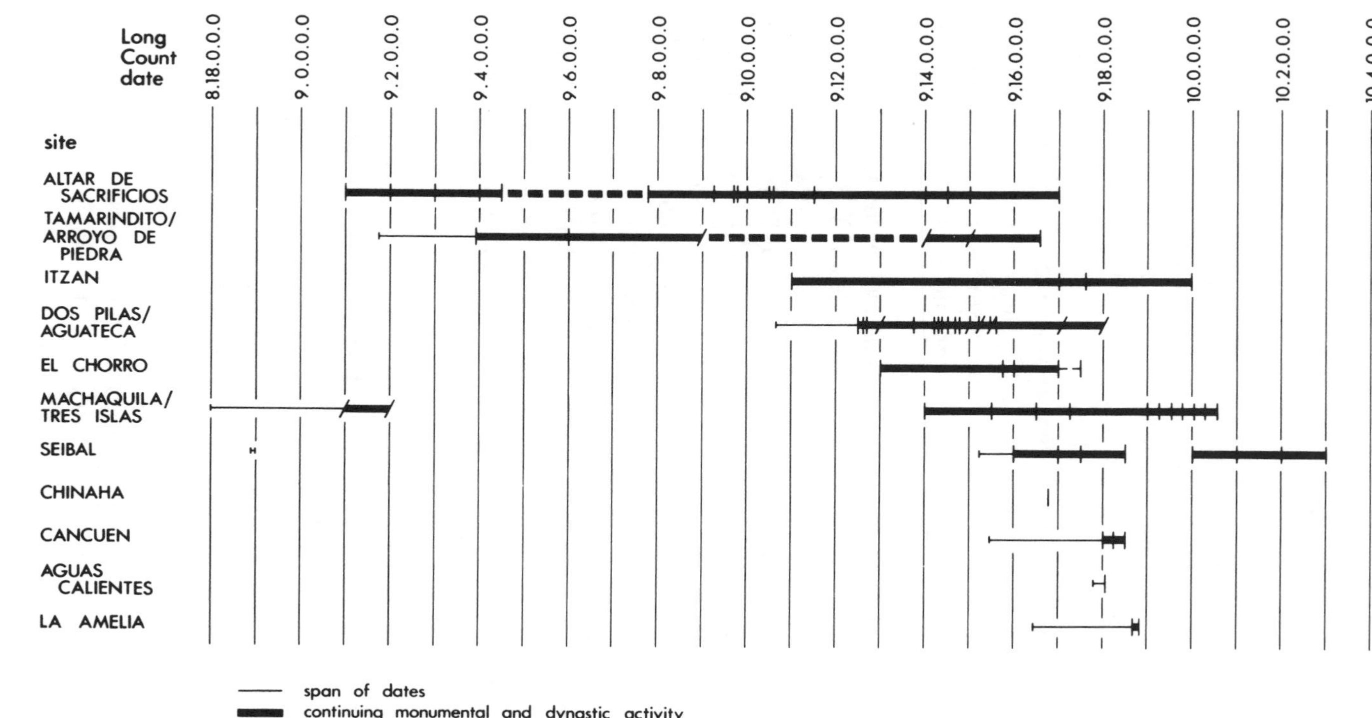


Fig. 3.2 Spans of monumental activity in the Pasion region.

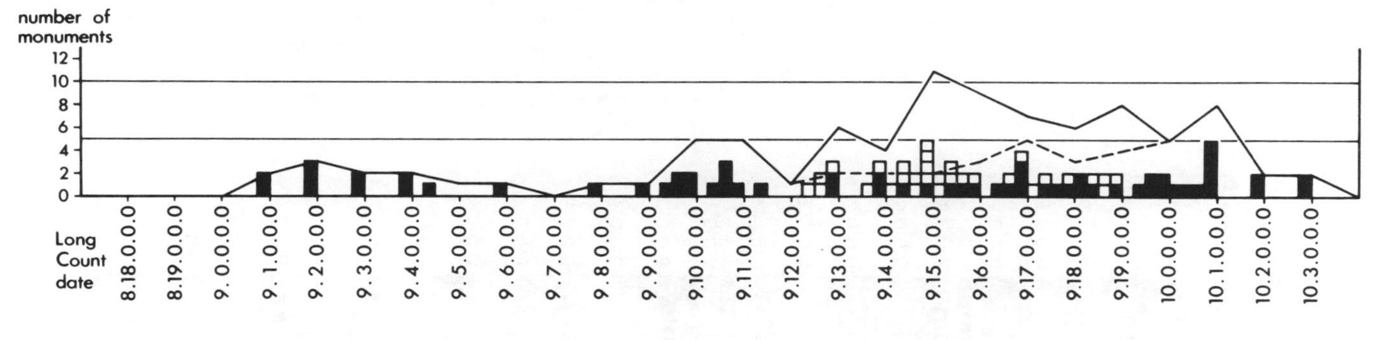


Fig. 3.3 Pasion region monuments, tabulated by Dedicatory Date.

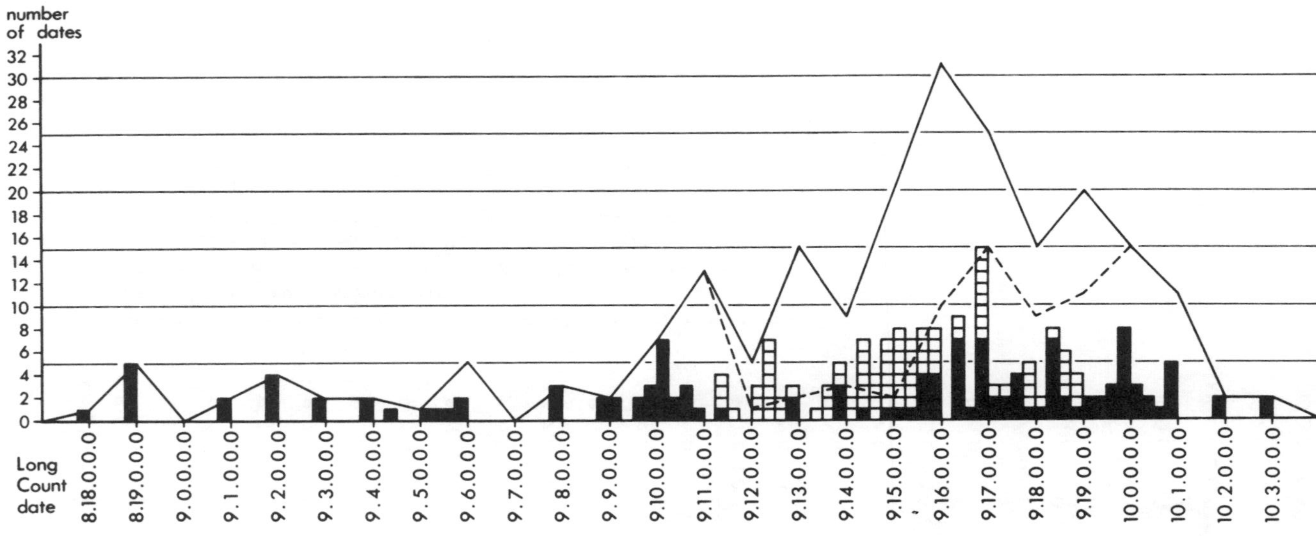


Fig. 3.4 Pasion region dates, tabulated by hotun.

which has been discussed in detail by Houston and Mathews (1985) and Johnston (1985). We know of at least five rulers in the dynasty, from 9.10.12.11.2 (AD 645) until *c.* 9.18.10.0.0 (AD 800). Sometime during Ruler 3's reign (*c.* 9.15.0.0.0; AD 731), the main focus of the dynasty moved from Dos Pilas to Aguateca. The expansionistic activities of the dynasty are well documented; shortly after 9.18.10.0.0 (AD 800), however, the dynasty went into rapid decline. Its power was eclipsed by 9.19.0.0.0 (AD 810).

*Altar de Sacrificios.* The site is on a small islet of high ground in the swampy, seasonally flooded, terrain of the south bank of the Rio Pasion, just above that river's confluence with the Chixoy. The principal large mounds are arranged in three plaza groups, covering an area about 400 by 400 m. This is at the higher, or eastern, end of the little islet; to the west, the islet, which is still reasonably well-drained ground, continues for another 700 m, and there are a number of small residential-type mounds on this part of the site. The principal mounds – including one quite tall pyramid and several large, palace-type platforms, as well as the ranges of a ball court – number about thirty (Willey and Smith 1969; Smith 1972). Large-scale excavations were carried out at Altar de Sacrificios from 1959 through 1963 (Willey 1973), with deep cuts into the larger mounds and extensive horizontal clearings in many places. Operations in Group B, the setting of the tall pyramidal structure, revealed an early occupation of the Middle Preclassic period (Xe and Mamom sphere phases), and toward the end of this period the first ceremonial platforms or pyramid bases were constructed. In the Late Preclassic and Protoclassic periods, Altar de Sacrificios became an impressive ceremonial center, with the final phase of the Structure B-1 pyramid being completed at the end of the Protoclassic or the beginning of the Early Classic period (Adams 1971; Smith 1972; Willey 1973). The earliest stela date at the site is found in association with this pyramid and commemorates a katun-ending of 9.1.0.0.0 (AD 455). It still remains something of a moot question as to whether Tzakol horizon pottery has its inception at Altar de Sacrificios at this time. The beginning dates for Tzakol ceramics in the northeast Peten, at Uaxactun and Tikal, are well over a century earlier than 9.1.0.0.0. This observation has a bearing on the timing of the spread of lowland Maya Early Classic culture (Willey, 1985a; Lincoln 1985).

Altar de Sacrificios seems to have suffered the Early Classic "hiatus" in the latter part of the sixth century AD, but the site recovered its status as an important center early in the Late Classic period. Virtually all of the large Group A palaces were built in the Late Classic, and some constructional activity continued into the Boca phase which is the chronological equivalent of Tepeu 3 – approximately AD 800–900, or the Terminal Classic period. Some Fine Paste wares began appearing at Altar de Sacrificios in Boca times, and following the Boca phase, the Jimba phase (AD 900–950) is completely dominated by Fine Paste pottery of the Tres Naciones Group (Rands, Bishop, and Sabloff 1982). After that, Altar de Sacrificios was abandoned.

Altar de Sacrificios has the longest monument sequence of any site in the Pasion region: from 9.1.0.0.0 (AD 455; Stela 10) until 9.17.0.0.0 (AD 771; Stela 15). In citing Stela 15 as the latest monument from Altar de Sacrificios, Mathews differs from J. A. Graham (1972:13–15, 103–5), who proposed that Stela 2 from that site dated to 10.1.0.0.0 (AD 849). Mathews prefers to date Stela 2 to 9.14.10.0.0 (AD 721) following Morley (1944:171). There are records of at least ten rulers in the Altar de Sacrificios monument span, and with three gaps in the sequence there were probably more rulers, of whom there is now no trace. Three rulers (A–C) date between 9.1.0.0.0 and 9.4.10.0.0 (AD 455 and 524). This was followed by a hiatus which lasted over sixty years, or until 9.7.15.12.9 (AD 589). This date was a very important one at Altar de Sacrificios: it was the accession date of a new (and apparently youthful) ruler (D), who remained in power until 9.10.0.0.0 (AD 633). Then followed, apparently, four rulers (E–H), in quick succession, until 9.11.10.0.0 (AD 662). Ironically, the later monuments at Altar de Sacrificios are among the worst preserved, but there seem to have been at least two more rulers (I, J) in the sequence – both reigns bracketed by hiatuses.

*Anonal.* This little center lies about 5 km west-northwest of the main center of Seibal (Tourtellot 1988). As such, we looked upon it in our surveys as being within the "sustaining area" of Seibal; however, Anonal was certainly a small ceremonial or administrative center. While there are other small temple pyramid complexes within the Greater Seibal zone, Anonal is clearly the largest of these, and Tourtellot has described it as being more varied architecturally than the others. It appears to have two pyramids and a possible vaulted building. Two carved panels were found. The earlier is badly weathered but dates stylistically to the Early Classic: *c.* 9.5.0.0.0 to 9.9.0.0.0 (AD 534–613). The other is much later, referring to Ruler E of Seibal (*c.* 10.0.0.0.0–10.1.0.0.0; AD 830–49), who is named as the overlord of the local Anonal individual who, however, is declared an *ahau* in his own right, with his own Emblem Glyph. Test diggings in the site revealed deep Escoba Mamom refuse covered by Late Classic constructional fill. The last deposition would be consistent with the late panel at the site, but no refuse or signs of the Early Classic period were encountered.

*Arroyo de Piedra/Tamarindito.* These two sites lie 8 km and 4 km, respectively, east of Dos Pilas. They share the same Emblem Glyph and, apparently, the same ruling dynasty. Of the two sites, Tamarindito is the larger, and also the one with the longer range of dates: from 9.1.17.10.8 to 9.16.11.7.13 (AD 472 to 962) – though there are many gaps in the sequence. The following dynastic summary considers both sites.

The first documented ruler of Tamarindito was born on 9.1.17.10.8 (AD 472) and was ruling by 9.3.19.0.0 (AD 513; Stela 5). There is then a short hiatus until Stela 4 (9.5.4.5.8–9.6.0.0.0; AD 538–554), which names another ruler (B) as in power on 9.6.0.0.0 (AD 554). A new ruler (C) was in power by 9.9.0.0.0 (AD 613); his accession date was possibly 9.8.19.11.16 (Arroyo de Piedra Stela 1; AD 613). It is quite likely that there were additional rulers between Rulers A, B, and C.

Following Ruler C there is a long hiatus, until after 9.12.0.0.0 (AD 672). Tamarindito Hieroglyphic Stairway 3 names a ruler (E) as a contemporary of Dos Pilas Ruler 2 (who was in power between 9.13.6.2.0 and 9.14.15.1.19; AD 698–726). Ruler E's parents are named, and his father probably preceded him as ruler D of Tamarindito. Dos Pilas Ruler 2 is also named on Arroyo de Piedra Stela 7, although the context is unclear. On Stela 3 of Arroyo de Piedra he is again named, although the reference is posthumous (9.15.0.0.0; AD 731); by now Dos Pilas has gained control over Arroyo de Piedra and Tamarindito. The local ruler (G) is named along with his parents (his father – Ruler F? – was a lord of Tamarindito; his mother was a lady of Dos Pilas); also named, as overlord, is Ruler 2 of Dos Pilas. Perhaps Dos Pilas gained control of the two cities through the marriage of their princess into the Tamarindito dynasty – or perhaps this was a marriage forced on Tamarindito and Arroyo de Piedra by their stronger neighbors. At any rate, it appears that by this time Dos Pilas and Aguateca had politically absorbed Tamarindito and Arroyo de Piedra, but allowed the local hereditary dynasty to continue as nominal rulers. This situation remained until the end of Tamarindito's recorded history.

On Tamarindito Hieroglyphic Stairway 2 another local ruler (H) is referred to. His accession date was on 9.16.9.8.11 (AD 760), but the focus of the Stairway text was a battle waged by Ruler 4 of Dos Pilas. The latest date on the Stairway is 9.16.11.7.13 (AD 762).

The latest known reference to the Tamarindito dynasty is on Aguateca Stela 7 (9.18.0.0.0; AD 790), to an individual we shall designate as Ruler I. It is not known, however, if he actually ruled over Tamarindito and Arroyo de Piedra, or how many rulers may have been between him and Ruler H, but the reference is evidence that Dos Pilas and Aguateca were still in control of Tamarindito and Arroyo de Piedra at this time.

*Cancuen*. This is the largest known site upriver from Seibal. Visited briefly by Maler (1908) and Morley (1937–8, II), it was mapped and test-excavated by a Peabody Museum party from Seibal in 1967 (Tourtellot, Sabloff, and Sharick 1978). It consists of two, or perhaps three, ceremonial groups within an area of about 600 by 550 m. There is a temple complex group and a palace-acropolis group, a hieroglyphic stairway being located within the latter. The pottery recovered from the recent tests is mostly Tepeu 2 in date although there are some sherds which fit more comfortably on a Tepeu 3, or Terminal Classic, time level. Resemblances to Seibal types are close. Smaller residential-type house mounds are located between the ceremonial groups and continue for at least 400 m north of the main center.

There are three stelae and assorted other monuments at Cancuen. The known dates fall between 9.18.0.0.0 and 9.18.10.0.0 (AD 790–800), and there were probably two rulers during this span. There are, however, earlier references to Cancuen, based on foreign occurrences of the Cancuen Emblem Glyph. Ruler 4 of Dos Pilas/Aguateca includes among his titles "Captor of the Cancuen lord." The capture apparently took place some time before 9.15.9.17.17 (AD 741), and Cancuen was then probably under the control of Dos

Pilas/Aguateca; by 9.18.0.0.0 (AD 790), however, Cancuen seems to have been independent again.

*Chapayal.* This site lies away from the Pasion course, some 15 km to the northeast of Seibal. It is known by a single broken stela whose text refers to Ruler D of Seibal (a ruler of the Dos Pilas/Aguateca dynasty), who we know was in power between 9.17.0.0.0 and 9.18.10.0.0 (AD 771–800).

*Chinaha.* Lying some distance to the west of Cancuen, this site is known from a single panel which has been dated by Dillon (1978) at 10.2.0.12.8 (AD 870), but in Mathews' opinion its date is much more likely to be 9.16.15.4.8 (AD 766).

*El Caribe.* This is a lower Pasion site, about 3 km inland from the river and southwest of Aguas Calientes (Morley 1937–8, II:294–300). With a total area of about 130 by 110 m, there is a single pyramid and several very long, palace-like structures. The same ruler is probably portrayed on the two known El Caribe stelae, and it seems likely he was in power some time between about 9.16.0.0.0 and 9.18.0.0.0 (AD 751–90).

*El Cedral.* This small site is some 10 km upriver from Seibal. A single panel fragment from here appears to be Late Classic in style and execution although it is unlike any sculpture from the Pasion region.

*El Chorro.* The location is about 20 km north-northwest of Altar de Sacrificios, on the little tributary of the Usumacinta. Seventeen carved monuments are known from here although only a few have well-preserved dynastic information. There are five monuments with decipherable dates, their time span being from 9.13.0.0.0 to 9.17.0.0.0 (AD 692–771). A looted stela, now in Poptun, has the El Chorro Emblem Glyph, and presumably came from the site. If so, it expands the dating range to 9.17.10.0.0 (AD 780). There were probably at least six rulers in this period of known dates. In addition, there are possible references at nearby Itzan to the capture of an El Chorro lord around 9.17.0.0.0 (AD 771), and somewhat earlier another El Chorro lord appears to have been captured by Ruler 4 of Dos Pilas. It appears, however, that these captures had no immediate effects on the viability of the El Chorro dynasty. There has been some confusion about the naming of El Chorro. When Eric von Euw visited the site he named it San Lucas. It has since been renamed El Chorro. Houston and Mathews (1985) mistakenly referred to the site as El Pato; the name El Chorro should be used in all future references to this site.

*El Excavado.* This is a small site located between Aguateca and Tamarindito. Two carved panels have been reported: they are badly weathered but probably date to about 9.11.0.0.0 (AD 652).

*El Pabellon.* Across the Salinas-Chixoy from Altar de Sacrificios is the little site of El Pabellon (Morley, 1937–8, II:325–7). Associated with the largest mound of a little mound group is a stela with the date of 9.10.0.0.0 (AD 633). The name of the protagonist does not seem to be that of the contemporary Ruler D of nearby Altar de Sacrificios; perhaps a lieutenant of Ruler D's was in charge at El Pabellon at this time.

*El Pato.* This site, a small one with only a few mounds, could well be part of El Chorro (Ian Graham, personal communication 1986).

*Itzan.* This site is on a little tributary of that name which flows into the lower Pasion from its north side, at a point about 13 km north-northeast of Altar de Sacrificios. The ruins are on a bluff top above the stream arroyo. Itzan was explored by a Peabody Museum field party during the period of their work at Seibal (Tourtellot, Hammond, and Rose 1978). Two plaza groups of mounds were mapped within a 300 by 300 m area. One large construction complex includes both palace structures and a pyramid. There is a causeway connected with the site. About eighty potsherds were recovered from minor digging and from the surface. These were identified as Preclassic and Late Classic, with one Terminal Classic Fine Orange fragment in the lot. The broken and weathered monuments of Itzan enable only a partial reconstruction of its dynastic history. The earlest textual references to Itzan, in fact, are at Dos Pilas, to a "Lady of Itzan," who married Ruler 1 of Dos Pilas and was the mother of Ruler 2 (*c.* 9.11.0.0.0; AD 652). The latest known Itzan date is 9.19.19.16.0 (AD 829), recorded on Stela 6. We can reconstruct at least five rulers of Itzan over its known 180-year history, although there were almost certainly more, for there are two long hiatuses in the known sequence: from *c.* 9.12.13.0.0 to *c.* 9.15.10.0.0 (AD 685–741), and from *c.* 9.17.12.0.0 to *c.* 9.18.17.0.0 (AD 782–807). Although Itzan history is very sketchy, it appears that the dynasty remained independent throughout its Late Classic history.

*La Amelia.* This is on a little tributary stream flowing into the south side of the lower Pasion, about 3 km southwest of El Caribe (Morley 1937–8, II:301–9). A compact little acropolis of seven mounds measures about 100 by 65 m. Two stelae and six panels from a stairway have inscriptions. The monuments mention the accession (on 9.18.11.13.4; AD 802) of a lord of the Dos Pilas/Aguateca dynasty. His name is the same as that of Seibal Ruler D – though the two might well have been different individuals. He is also recorded as subordinate to Ruler 5 of Dos Pilas/Aguateca.

*La Paciencia.* This small site lies 1 km southwest of Dos Pilas. It has two panels, both plain (Stephen Houston, personal communication 1985–6).

*La Reforma III.* This small site is located on the Pasion, a short distance downstream from its confluence with the Machaquila. The sad fate of two stelae from this site has been recounted by Maler (1908:37–8) and Morley (1937–8, II:247–8). The site itself appears to have consisted of only a few small earth mounds.

*Machaquila/Tres Islas.* Machaquila lies on the south bank of the Machaquila River, which flows into the Pasion not far from the site of Tres Islas. The two sites share the same Emblem Glyph, but have monuments of very different dates: Tres Islas from 9.1.0.0.0 to 9.2.0.0.0 (AD 455–75), and Machaquila from 9.14.0.0.0 to 10.0.10.17.5 (AD 711–841). Tres Islas is a baffling site: one of the three stelae there was associated with a sub-stela cache, but there is no known mound construction anywhere nearby. The ruler named in 9.2.0.0.0 (AD 475) has the Machaquila Emblem Glyph among his titles. There are several other personages named on the Tres Islas monuments, including one who has in his name a glyph very similar to the Cancuen Emblem Glyph.

During the 130-year span of Machaquila monuments, there were six rulers. For the first three (A–C) only isolated references survive, although they include parentage statements which state that Ruler A was the father of Ruler B, who in turn was the father of Ruler C. It is probable that Ruler C was in power for well over a *katun*; following his death three reigns are documented (Rulers D–F), for periods of about fifteen, ten and fifteen years, respectively. Machaquila appears to have remained independent, untouched by the political intrigues going on in the central part of the Pasion region. In fact, the only known foreign reference to Machaquila is at Cancuen: this is probably because the wife of Machaquila Ruler B was a lady from Cancuen.

*Punta de Chimino.* This is another small site in the Petexbatun zone. Reportedly, there were two monuments at the site, but these have been looted (Stephen Houston, personal communication 1986).

*Seibal.* Seibal has been explored recently by a Harvard University/Peabody Museum expedition working in the 1960s (Willey *et al.* 1975; Sabloff 1975; Willey 1978; Smith 1982; Tourtellot 1986). The ruins are on some high limestone hills on the west bank of the Pasion, near the point where the river makes its great bend to the west. The terrain here is generally higher than downstream at Altar de Sacrificios, and the hills on which the site is located, and which rise steeply to 100 m above the level of the river, are the highest terrain above its course through the Peten lowlands. This rather spectacular setting, together with the numerous great mounds of the ruin, make it the most impessive of the Maya centers of the Pasion region, and in sheer constructional volume it is certainly the largest. There are three main groups of structures, Groups A, C, and D. These are all found, each on its separate natural hilltop, within a square kilometer which abuts the river bank. The groups are connected by a causeway system. There are pyramids, large platforms, and numerous smaller structures within each group. Groups A and C both possess a ball court. There is also a Seibal Group B; however, this group, which was so designated by Morley (1937–8, II) many years ago, is better considered as one of the outlying minor centers rather than as a part of central Seibal (see below).

Extensive excavations were made in all three groups, and the stratigraphy from these excavations reveals a culture sequence beginning in Middle Preclassic Xe phase times and running through

Mamom Middle Preclassic, the Late Preclassic and Protoclassic Cantutse phase, the Early Classic Junco phase, the Late Classic Tepejilote Tepeu phase, and the Bayal Boca phase of the Terminal Classic (Smith 1982). The ceramic spheres and complexes are much the same as those found at Altar de Sacrificios (Adams 1971; Sabloff 1975). Deep cuts have revealed plaza floorings and small platform structures dating back as early as Middle Preclassic Mamom times. In the Late Preclassic Seibal was a major center. Many of the largest pyramids and palace-type platforms at the site were built in this period as the abundance of Chicanel sphere pottery attests. Both Groups A and D served as political and ritual foci. Surveys and excavations on the outlying peripheries of Seibal (within a 5 by 5 km rectangle drawn around the main center) have revealed house-mound evidence of a substantial population. Gair Tourtellot (1986), who conducted the Seibal peripheral studies, estimates a total population of 10,000 inhabitants for a Greater Seibal. In these peripheral surveys several minor temple constructions were found to date from the Late Preclassic.

In the Protoclassic Seibal suffered a decline, both as a ceremonial center and as a populous community. This reduction of its fortunes continued on into the Early Classic period; however, there is ceramic and some architectural evidence for a modest occupation of the site until, apparently, the sixth century AD when there may have been an abandonment, or near abandonment, during the Classic "hiatus."

In the Late Classic period, the equivalent of Tepeu 1 times, both the main center and the peripheries of Seibal were heavily reoccupied. This was not a slow population growth, such as that seen for the long Middle-to-Late Preclassic continuum; rather, the evidence suggests a sudden re-population of Seibal, with peoples coming from other localities. These may have been nearby places in the Pasion drainage, such as Altar de Sacrificios or the Petexbatun zone sites; or, perhaps, these settlers came from more distant places, as, for instance the Tikal-Uaxactun vicinity. Whatever their point of origin, they were very much in the Maya lowland cultural and ceramic traditions, bringing in typical Tepeu pottery. But the point to be made is that Seibal, after being pretty much deserted for a century or more, was now reoccupied.

Groups A and D both flourished during the Seibal Tepejilote Tepeu phase (Tepeu 1 and 2 times). Old Late Preclassic temples and platforms in these groups were built over in this Late Classic resurgence, and in the peripheries old Late Preclassic residential platforms were used as construction bases for numerous new Late Classic houses. The Tepejilote Tepeu phase came to an end at about AD 830 (10.0.0.0.0). The final Seibal phase, the Bayal Boca, was characterized by the appearance of Fine Orange and Fine Gray pottery of the Tres Naciones ceramic group. Some of the decorative motifs on the modeled-carved wares of the group are virtually identical to a new style of stelae carving introduced at 10.1.0.0.0 (AD 849). At this late time monumental dedications were made in the South Plaza of Group A, including five stelae with period-ending dates of 10.1.0.0.0, and others dated 10.2.0.0.0 (AD 869) and 10.3.0.0.0 (AD 889). At some time not long after 10.3.0.0.0 Seibal was abandoned.

For such a large site, and one with such a long and well-known archaeological sequence, Seibal's hieroglyphic record is exceptionally short and sporadic. There are, to be sure, very early records of Seibal at 8.18.19.8.7 and 8.19.0.0.0 (AD 415 and 416), with the first of these accompanied by a long explanatory text naming a Seibal lord (A). But as these texts, which occur on the Hieroglyphic Stairway of Structure A-14 in Group A, are early "historical" references which were carved some 335 years after the Cycle 8 dates referenced, their true historical accuracy might be questioned.

A cluster of three dates commemorated both at Dos Pilas and at Aguateca tell us something of Late Classic Seibal in their mention of a battle which resulted in the capture and sacrifice of a Seibal lord (B) by Dos Pilas Ruler 3. The date of the battle was 9.15.4.6.4 (AD 735) – a date falling into the Tepeu 2 ceramic time period – and it initiated a long interval during which Seibal was politically subordinate to the Dos Pilas dynasty; how long before 9.15.4.6.4 Ruler B was in power at Seibal is unknown, for no earlier record of him survives at Seibal. The previously mentioned Hieroglyphic Stairway at Seibal, dedicated on 9.16.0.0.0 (AD 751), is carved in the Dos Pilas style, and although it names a Seibal lord (C), he is subordinate to Ruler 4 of Dos Pilas/Aguateca who is commemorated on that stairway which was apparently built and carved by Dos Pilas rulers as part of their imposition of dominance over Seibal. This 9.16.0.0.0 dedication of the Seibal Hieroglyphic Stairway is the earliest, presumably contemporary, monumental hieroglyphic dedication at the site.

Stelae 5, 6, and 7 at Seibal, dating from 9.17.0.0.0 to 9.18.10.0.0

(AD 771–800), record another lord (Seibal Ruler D) of the Dos Pilas/Aguateca dynasty, one who is also named at Chapayal and, apparently, at La Amelia. He acceded to power at Seibal on 9.17.0.0.0 and appears to be a different person from the contemporary ruler (5) of Aguateca. It seems probable that the Dos Pilas/Aguateca control over neighboring sites was beginning to break up at this time (Houston and Mathews 1985:18–24). In fact, after 9.18.10.0.0 there is a thirty-year hiatus at Seibal, during which Dos Pilas' control over the site ended, and after which lords with the Seibal Emblem Glyph in their name phrases ruled again.

The most frequently recorded date at Seibal is 10.1.0.0.0 (AD 849) which, as mentioned, is on five stelae in the South Plaza of Group A. It names a Seibal lord (E) as ruler. He was also in power a katun earlier, on 10.0.0.0.0 (AD 830), and his title, "he of 1 day," may indicate that his accession was on 9.19.19.17.19 (recorded on Stela 11), and that his reign was one day old at the beginning of the new *baktun*, 10.0.0.0.0

There were at least two other rulers of Seibal, with known dates of 10.2.0.0.0 (AD 869; Ruler F) and 10.3.0.0.0 (AD 889; Ruler G). In addition, there are some other stelae which cannot clearly be dated, and which apparently name at least one more ruler (X). We follow John A. Graham (1973:213–17) in dating these monuments between 10.2.0.0.0 and 10.3.0.0.0. In other words, it is most likely that Ruler X was in power at Seibal between the reigns of Rulers F and G.

By 10.3.0.0.0, or shortly thereafter, no more monuments were carved at Seibal or indeed anywhere else in the Pasion region.

*Seibal, Group B.* This small satellite center, originally visited and designated by Morley (1937–8, II:252, 264–6; V:Plate 199b), is 2 km south of the Seibal main center. This site is neither as large nor as architecturally complex as Anonal. A stela, associated with a small pyramid, is all-glyphic and very late – dating to the reign of Seibal Ruler E (*c.* 10.0.0.0.0–10.1.0.0.0; AD 830–49).

## SPECULATIVE FORMATIONS OF PASION REGION POLITIES

Figure 3.5 illustrates site interactions in the Pasion region, where each arrow between two sites indicates a hieroglyphic reference by one site

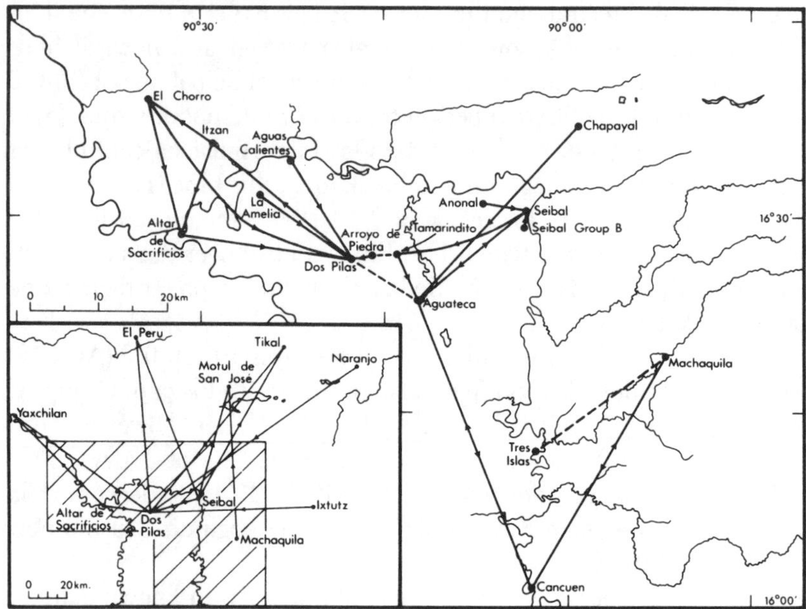


Fig. 3.5 Site interaction in the Pasion region.

to the other. But are these references to equals, or are they indications of site hierarchies?. Our arguments in answer to this question are based on Emblem Glyph usage, as well as on the specific interpretation of the intersite references.

Emblem Glyphs have long been used as indicators of Classic Maya political organization, especially in the pioneering studies of Joyce Marcus (1973, 1976). However, our interpretation of Emblem Glyphs and their political implications differs somewhat from that of Marcus. Emblem Glyphs occur within the name phrases of rulers: clearly their overall function is as royal titles. Indeed, the superfix of Emblem Glyphs – the so-called *ben-ich* superfix – is read ahau, "lord," the highest of Maya royal titles. The main signs of Emblem Glyphs substitute in one glyphic compound with *cab*, "land, earth," so there are grounds for arguing that Emblem Glyph main signs are place-names. Finally, the fact that two contemporary rulers of Palenque and Tortuguero have the same Emblem Glyph indicates to us that the Emblem Glyph main sign is a reference to a political area, rather than to the city or town, and that both rulers were of ahau rank in this political area. The alternative interpretation would be that the two close neighbors, Palenque and Tortuguero, had the same name, which we think less likely.

Thus, we believe that Emblem Glyphs, which function specifically as royal titles, "lord of *x* polity," are also indications of functioning Classic Maya polities; by compiling Emblem Glyph references at particular points in time – e.g., on katun-endings – we can begin to reconstruct maps of the geopolitical organization of the Pasion region during the Classic period. In these reconstructions we must also consider the nature of intersite references, which on occasion can indicate site hierarchies: even where two sites have Emblem Glyphs, one can be subservient to the other.

Local Emblem Glyphs occur in twelve of the twenty-five Pasion region sites considered in this paper. But not all occur contemporaneously. In the maps at the end of this chapter (Figs. 3.6–3.17), which represent reconstructions of the Pasion region geopolitical organization on each katun-ending from 9.10.0.0.0 (AD 633) through 10.1.0.0.0 (AD 849), the greatest number of contemporaneous polities is six.

## *The Preclassic period*

Before the appearance of hieroglyphic texts to aid us, what were the possible polities of the Pasion region in Preclassic times? For any such speculations we must depend upon site sizes and geographical locations of sites. For the Middle Preclassic period it is the general assumption, for the Pasion Valley as well as the Maya lowlands as a whole, that polities were, in effect, small autonomous villages. The Altar de Sacrificios and Seibal Xe and Mamom phase occupations would be examples. There seem to be no clearly defined site hierarchies that would suggest territorial polities. At both Altar de Sacrificios and Seibal, however, there were Mamom phase small temples or platforms that look like corporate constructions and that might signal the beginnings of site hierarchies.

By the Late Preclassic-Protoclassic there can be no doubt that complex society, with ruling elites, sustaining farming populations, and site hierarchies, had developed in the Pasion region as elsewhere in the Maya lowlands. At this time both Altar de Sacrificios and Seibal were clearly organizational centers. Political territorialism was underway. How large were the polities? Was there a dominant site for the entire

Pasion region? Seibal appears to have been the biggest in the number and bulk of its elite-type constructions. Was it a regional capital? The capital of what we are defining as the Pasion region? In the Protoclassic centuries (AD 1–300) Altar de Sacrificios may have become more important than Seibal. But were either of these sites, or any others of the Pasion, "capitals" of the "Pasion region"? The fact that there is no good evidence for such a large regional state in the ensuing Classic period throws doubt upon its presence earlier.

### *The Early Classic period*

There is no doubt that political territories were in existence in the Pasion region during the Early Classic. Allusions to late Cycle 8 rulers (AD 337–435) on later monuments at both Tres Islas and Seibal offer some support for this statement, and the early Cycle 9 dedicatory monuments (AD 435–534) at both Tres Islas and Altar de Sacrificios confirm it. To what extent these were developments out of Late Preclassic-Protoclassic polities or states must remain speculative.

At Altar de Sacrificios a Ruler A is commemorated on Stelae 10 and 11, dating to 9.1.0.0.0 and 9.2.0.0.0 (AD 455 and 475), respectively. At 9.3.0.0.0 (AD 495; Stela 13, Altar 3) another ruler (B) is in power; and by 9.4.10.0.0 (AD 524; Stela 12) Ruler C has taken over: and one of the two is portrayed on Stela 18F at 9.4.0.0.0 (AD 514).

Around this time dynastic activity is also recorded at Tamarindito in the Petexbatun, with Stela 5 commemorating the first known ruler (A) of the Arroyo de Piedra/Tamarindito sequence at 9.3.19.0.0 (AD 513). His successors were in power in the following katuns: Ruler B by 9.6.0.0.0 (AD 554; Tamarindito Stela 4) and Ruler C by 9.9.0.0.0 (AD 613; Arroyo de Piedra Stela 1).

Back at Altar de Sacrificios, after a hiatus during katuns 5 and 6 (AD 534—73; Willey 1974), there was the accession of a new ruler (D) at 9.7.15.12.9 (AD 589), who we think was responsible for the resurgence of the site during the subsequent Late Classic period.

Thus, the Early Classic record, with its stelae and Emblem Glyphs, supports the idea of political formations. Judging from the geographical closeness of Altar de Sacrificios and the Petexbatun sites, these Early Classic polities were relatively small territories, and, again, it seems unlikely that there was anything like a large "Pasion Valley regional state."

### *The Late Classic period: beginnings.*

Despite the "hiatus," the Late Classic period sees dynastic continuities at both Altar de Sacrificios and Arroyo de Piedra/Tamarindito. At the former, Ruler D continued to rule until 9.10.0.0.0 (AD 633; Fig. 3.6). Ruler E, apparently his son, succeeded him by 9.10.0.6.13 (AD 633; Sculptured Panel 1), dying either on 9.10.3.17.0 (AD 636; Stela 4 and Sculptured Panels 1 and 2) or on 9.10.4.1.3 (AD 637; Stela 4, Sculptured Panel 2, and a Pasion complex polychrome vessel; Adams 1971:Plate 53a). In any event, his successor (Ruler F) was in power by 9.10.10.0.0 (AD 642; Stelae 4 and 5), and Rulers G(?) and H continued until at least 9.11.0.0.0 (AD 652). As noted, Ruler C of Arroyo de Piedra was in power by 9.9.0.0.0 (AD 613), but the length of his reign is uncertain. At Itzan the Hieroglyphic Stairway, dated to 9.11.0.0.0 (AD 652; Fig. 3.7) falls in this early part of the Late Classic.

### *The Late Classic period: establishment of the Dos Pilas dynasty*

Some time around 9.10.10.0.0 (AD 642), one of the most significant events in the political history of the Pasion region took place: the arrival of the lords of Dos Pilas. There is a hieroglyphic reference to the apparent founder of the dynasty, Ruler 1, acceding to power on 9.10.12.11.2 (AD 645) and ruling for over forty years. He used the Tikal Emblem Glyph in his name, indicating that he was perhaps a member of the Tikal royal family (perhaps a younger son of a Tikal king) who had moved south to establish his own realm. Certainly one gets the impression that the Dos Pilas dynasty was intrusive into the lower Pasion. Perhaps in an attempt to consolidate its recently acquired position, Dos Pilas was very active in both marriage alliances and warfare. Dos Pilas Ruler 1 married a woman from Itzan – the earliest surviving reference to that site – and a woman from Dos Pilas (Ruler 1's sister?) married the king of El Chorro at about this time.

Ruler 1 of Dos Pilas also embarked on a series of battles, his most famous conquest being the capture of "Torch Macaw," on 9.11.11.9.17 (AD 664). The latest known date for Ruler 1 is 9.13.0.0.0 (AD 692). On 9.13.6.2.0 (AD 698) his son (Ruler 2) succeeded, ruling for almost thirty years. He and his successors were responsible for greatly increasing Dos Pilas' sphere of influence and political domain (Figs. 3.8–3.13).

### *The Late Classic period: expansion of Dos Pilas' dynastic power*

Probably in an attempt to consolidate their foothold in the Pasion region, the Dos Pilas dynasty intermarried with the rulers of Itzan and El Chorro. Their next step was political expansion and absorption, and their first victim was their closest neighbor, the dynasty of Tamarindito/Arroyo de Piedra. On Tamarindito Hieroglyphic Stairway 3 (which has no preserved date but which was probably carved *c.* 9.13.0.0.0–9.14.0.0.0; AD 692–711), Ruler 2 of Dos Pilas is named, apparently on the occasion of a royal visit to Tamarindito. There is no indication in the text that the local ruler (E) is subservient to him. Arroyo de Piedra Stela 7 also names Dos Pilas Ruler 2 probably at 9.14.0.0.0 (AD 711), but the nature of the reference is not clear. Stela 3 of Arroyo de Piedra, dated at 9.15.0.0.0 (AD 731), again mentions Ruler 2 of Dos Pilas (an anachronism, for his successor, Ruler 3, was in power by this time); however, by this time the Dos Pilas ruler is explicitly stated to be the overlord of the local ruler, Ruler G (Stephen D. Houston, personal communication 1984). It is noteworthy that Ruler G's father was a Tamarindito lord, his mother a lady from Dos Pilas: a third case of a marriage alliance between Dos Pilas and another dynasty.

Thus, it appears that by 9.15.0.0.0 (AD 731) if not by 9.14.0.0.0 (AD 711) Dos Pilas had control over Tamarindito and Arroyo de Piedra (Figs. 3.9–3.11), but the political process had begun somewhat earlier, with a Dos Pilas woman marrying into the Tamarindito/Arroyo de Piedra dynasty and her son becoming ruler of the site as a vassal of the Dos Pilas regime.

Ruler 3 of Dos Pilas/Aguateca, who acceded to power in 9.15.4.5.15 (AD 735), continued his predecessor's militaristic policies. On 9.15.4.6.4/5 (AD 735) he won a great victory over Seibal, capturing its king whom he sacrificed six days later. Seibal was to remain under Dos Pilas' control for about the next seventy years (Figs. 3.12–3.14). Ruler 3 stayed in power for almost fifteen years. His successor, Ruler 4, also engaged in warfare, capturing a lord of Cancuen, a lord of El Chorro, and, perhaps, one of Yaxchilan. It was he who ordered the carving of the Seibal Hieroglyphic Stairway, thus setting in stone Dos Pilas' hegemony over Seibal. It was during his reign that the territory held by Dos Pilas/Aguateca probably reached its maximum extent (Fig. 3.13).

### *The Late Classic period: the decline of Dos Pilas*

It would appear that Dos Pilas Rulers 3 and 4 were responsible for shifting the focus of the dynasty from Dos Pilas to Aguateca (Figs 3.13 and 3.14). The latest monument at Dos Pilas refers to Ruler 4 while the latest at Aguateca (Stela 7), which dates to 9.18.0.0.0 (AD 790) refers to Ruler 5 of the Dos Pilas/Aguateca dynasty. Ruler 5 is also named at La Amelia, as overlord of the local ruler. The local lord has the same name as that of a contemporary recorded on Seibal Stelae 5, 6, and 7 and Chapayal Stela 1. It is unlikely, however, that the two were the same person: there are different accession dates recorded at La Amelia and Seibal. It is possible that the name was some form of generic name or title for a lord of secondary status, under the direct control of the Dos Pilas/Aguateca ruler. But it is also possible that these "secondary" lords were by this time very largely autonomous, and that the hold of Dos Pilas/Aguateca over surrounding areas was breaking up. Indeed, after these references, all pre-9.19.0.0.0 (AD 810), no more is heard of Aguateca/Dos Pilas: its power was eclipsed.

The end of the Dos Pilas dynasty is surely related to the emergence or resurgence of other sites at this time. Machaquila and Itzan continue to thrive, and Cancuen appears to reassert its independence between 9.18.0.0.0 and 9.18.10.0.0 (AD 790 and 800; Fig. 3.14).

### *The Late Classic period: Cycle 10*

Late monuments in the Pasion region are located at three sites: Itzan, Machaquila, and Seibal (Figs. 3.15–3.17). At Itzan, the latest monument is Stela 6, which records a bloodletting by a ruler (E) on 9.19.19.16.0 (AD 829). His accession had taken place twenty-two years earlier, on 9.18.17.13.0 (AD 808) and he is the last known ruler at the site.

At Machaquila, Ruler D came to power on 9.18.9.15.10 (?; AD 800), and ruled until after 9.19.0.0.0 (AD 810). His successor, Ruler E, acceded on 9.19.4.15.1 (AD 815), and ruled until after 9.19.10.12.0 (AD 821). He was succeeded by Ruler F, probably a son, who reigned from before 9.19.15.0.0 (AD 825) to some time after 10.0.10.17.5 (AD 845), the latest known date at Machaquila. Thus Machaquila presents a dynastic sequence from 9.14.0.0.0 (AD 711) until after 10.0.0.0.0 (AD 830) with no breaks and apparently unaffected by the happenings in neighboring territories to the west.

The main focus for the very late epigraphic history of the Pasion is, of course, Seibal. After the Dos Pilas hegemony ended at 9.18.10.0.0 to 9.19.10.0.0 (AD 800–20), a new regime took over at Seibal. These new rulers included the Seibal Emblem Glyph in their name phrases. It is possible that they were descendants of old Ruler B of the site, but it is more likely that they were foreigners. The first of these new rulers (E) celebrated katun-endings at 10.0.0.0.0 and 10.1.0.0.0 (AD 830 and 849; Fig. 3.17). His personal name is a compound of six phonetic signs – an indication of a foreign name. He built Structure A–3 and dedicated Stelae 8, 9, 10, 11, 12, and 21. Definitely two, possibly three, or maybe more rulers of this dynasty followed after about 10.2.0.0.0 (AD 869). The somewhat non-Classic Maya Stelae 2, 3, 13, 14, and 19 pertain to this period. Only one of these stelae, 3, has a Calendar Round date, but its Long Count placement is uncertain. The securely dated Seibal Stelae 18 and 20, placed at 10.3.0.0.0 (AD 889), may well be the last recorded dates in the Pasion region; if not, then the end must have come soon afterwards.

## SOME CONCLUDING COMMENTARY

### A *résumé of Pasion drainage political history*

Simple political entities – autonomous villages – must have started with the earliest Preclassic settlers in the region. As populations and agricultural settlement expanded, some kind of boundary definitions, however vaguely defined, must have been set by village communities. By the end of the latter part of the Middle Preclassic period (*c.* 600–300 BC) the Pasion Maya were probably beginning to think of some of these villages as "central places," and with this we have the beginnings of site hierarchies.

By the close of the earlier half of the Late Preclassic period (*c.* 100–1 BC) some of these central places, such as Altar de Sacrificios and Seibal, with their large pyramid and platform constructions, obviously had become politicoreligious centers.

David Freidel (1986b), among others, has argued that the transition from Preclassic to Classic was a time of crisis for many lowland Maya polities. Some did not make a successful transition; others did; and we see examples of this in the Pasion Valley. Thus, Seibal which, on the basis of site size, appeared to be the leading center in the Late Preclassic, went into semi-eclipse in the Protoclassic and Early Classic periods. In contrast, Altar de Sacrificios, which had been a somewhat smaller place in the Late Preclassic, flourished in the Protoclassic and Early Classic. In Freidel's opinion, the transition to the Early Classic was marked by ideological and political shifts. It should be noted, however, that at Altar de Sacrificios Early Classic stelae commemorations of rulers, which began at 9.1.0.0.0 (AD 455), were celebrated in plaza and pyramid contexts of buildings that had been functioning, and had been added to constructionally throughout the Preclassic and Protoclassic periods. This would suggest that, whatever the nature of the Late Preclassic to Classic changeover, there was some kind or degree of ideological–political continuity.

In total, Early Classic stelae dedications are relatively few for the Pasion region. In addition to the Altar de Sacrificios monuments, there are early Cycle 9 stelae at Tamarindito and Tres Islas. There are also hieroglyphic "historical" references at both Tres Islas and Seibal to late Cycle 8 events at these sites although the historical validity of these "back-references" is open to question.

Moving into the Late Classic, we see that the Early Classic Arroyo de Piedra/Tamarindito dynasty apparently persisted through the Classic Maya "hiatus" – usually placed at 9.5.0.0.0 to 9.8.0.0.0 (AD 534–93) – for there are two stelae dedications pertaining to rulers of the dynasty which fall on the 9.6.0.0.0 (AD 554) and 9.9.0.0.0 (AD 613) katun-endings. Altar de Sacrificios also may have had some dynastic continuity through the "hiatus" as a new ruler is inaugurated there at 9.7.15.12.9 (AD 589). The Arroyo de Piedra/Tamarindito and Altar de Sacrificios dynasties appear to have dominated the Petexbatun part of the Pasion region during the early part of the Late Classic, or from about 9.8.0.0.0 to 9.11.0.0.0 (AD 593–652) although toward the end of this time Itzan also emerged as an independent polity. Then came the establishment of the new, perhaps Tikal-related, dynasty at Dos Pilas. This Dos Pilas/Aguateca dynasty expanded aggressively over the years between 9.12.0.0.0 (AD 672) and 9.17.0.0.0 (AD 771), eventually controlling Arroyo de Piedra/Tamarindito and the Petexbatun sector, as well as sites as far east and south as Seibal, Chapayal, and Cancuen. Nevertheless, in spite of this Dos Pilas/Aguateca aggressiveness, Altar de Sacrificios, Itzan, and El Chorro maintained their independence, as did Machaquila. At some time around 9.19.0.0.0 (AD 810), the power of the Dos Pilas/Aguateca dynasty was broken. Former vassals, such as Cancuen and Seibal, now re-asserted their independence.

Beginning at about 10.0.0.0.0 (AD 830) Seibal became the dominant site of the Pasion region; indeed, from 10.1.0.0.0 (AD 849) on it is the only site in the region to erect dedicatory monuments or to carry out large-scale public building. This late florescence of Seibal was almost certainly under a new, and perhaps foreign, dynasty, although they continued with the old Seibal Emblem Glyph. Yet after 10.3.0.0.0 (AD 889), Seibal, too, ceased all elite-type activity.

### *The Pasion region and the larger Maya lowlands*

The Pasion region is a part of the larger lowland Maya cultural sphere. This is seen in ceramics, artifact types, architecture, and, of course, the hieroglyphic inscriptions. The Pasion region's participation in a lowland Maya cultural sphere had begun as early as the Middle Preclassic, if not before; it had been steadily maintained, if not increased, during the Late Preclassic; and in the Early Classic period there were direct contacts of an elite nature with regions where the pattern of stela erection was well established – presumably the northeast Peten.

On the Late Classic period level, as we move into the information provided by the numerous monumental hieroglyphic texts and the occasional special finds such as the "Altar de Sacrificios Vase," we are able to become quite specific about Pasion region site contacts with centers outside the region. The most numerous of these Pasion extra-regional contacts involve the site of Dos Pilas and the Dos Pilas/Aguateca dynasty. Indeed, the very beginnings of the Dos Pilas dynasty appear to be linked to such a contact with the great site of Tikal which lies over 100 km to the northeast. The presence of the Dos Pilas dynasty is first recorded shortly after 9.10.10.0.0 (AD 642) and is identified with the Tikal Emblem Glyph. The Dos Pilas rulers also took the same "family name" ("God K") as the rulers of Late Classic Tikal. At Tikal itself there is some confirmation of the relationship with Dos Pilas in that the death and burial of Dos Pilas Ruler 2 are recorded there on a carved bone found among the grave goods of his Tikal contemporary, Ruler A (Burial 116). The "newness" or intrusiveness of the Dos Pilas dynasty into the Rio Pasion region is suggested by the location of the Dos Pilas site, which is very near the much older dynastic center of Arroyo de Piedra, as well as in the absence of any earlier dynastic records, or even back-references, to Dos Pilas on any of the monuments of the Pasion region sites. It is true that Preclassic ceramics have been found at Dos Pilas, and we need to know more about the site's earlier history and stratigraphy as we attempt to resolve questions of intrusions versus continuities, but in the light of all of the inscriptional evidence one can hardly deny that the Dos Pilas dynasty had some ties with Tikal.

All of this takes on added interest when we consider the Dos Pilas–Tikal relationship in the context of the internal history of Tikal. The period from 9.8.0.0.0 to 9.12.0.0.0 (AD 593–672), during the latter half of which the Dos Pilas dynasty was becoming established in the Pasion region, was a "dark age" at Tikal. There are no known monuments there which date from this time; indeed, the fact that several earlier stelae seem to have been broken up between 9.10.0.0.0 and 9.12.0.0.0 (AD 633 and 672) suggests that there might well have been a major power struggle going on within the city, resulting in the overthrow of the existing (Early Classic) Tikal lineage. Coggins (1975), Haviland (1977:63; 1981:112), and Jones and Satterthwaite (1982:129), among others, have all made this argument. Coggins (1975) further suggests that the defeated lineage moved to Dos Pilas, and then later re-established itself at Tikal with Ruler A in 9.12.9.17.16 (AD 682). Certainly there is much to recommend the first part of this assertion – the movement of members of the royal Tikal lineage to Dos Pilas to establish a new dynasty there. However, we are less convinced than Coggins of a later move back to Tikal. Coggins' identification of a record of Ruler A's father on Hieroglyphic Stairway 1 at Dos Pilas is not correct: he is not mentioned at Dos Pilas, only at Tikal. Far more likely, in our view, is Haviland's argument that members of the defeated lineage settled Tikal Group 7F-1 as a "dower house" until they were able to re-establish themselves as rulers of Tikal (Haviland 1981). The Dos Pilas dynasty might have been a branch of this family, and, perhaps disgruntled with having to "wait in the wings" for so long at Tikal, they decided to settle elsewhere (Dos Pilas).

When Tikal Ruler A (or perhaps his father) finally re-established the family as rulers of Tikal, it can only have enhanced locally the prestige of the Dos Pilas lineage, who by this time were starting to assert their authority in the Pasion region. Tikal Ruler A's record of Dos Pilas Ruler 2's death and burial might have represented recognition of this increased authority, or it might simply have been a family affair, a record of the death of his relative, the lord of Dos Pilas.

By this time Dos Pilas was also involved with some other sites outside of the Pasion region. On their own monuments they make references to a site which is very probably El Peru and to the accession of a ruler of that site on 9.12.13.17.7 (AD 686). Such references to the accession of a foreign ruler in a distant city are extremely rare and presumably indicated a very strong relationship between El Peru and Dos Pilas. There is also a second probable El Peru reference at Dos Pilas during Dos Pilas Ruler 2's reign although the exact nature of the event or occasion cannot be translated.

There are also clues to ties between Dos Pilas and Naranjo, another major city outside the Pasion region. Naranjo had been conquered by Caracol in 9.9.18.16.3 (AD 631), and, following a brief occupation by the conqueror, it was apparently abandoned. About 9.12.10.0.0 (AD 682), Naranjo's dynastic sequence began anew and involved the so-called "Woman of Tikal," whose parents are named on Naranjo Stela 24. As her father has exactly the same name as Dos Pilas Ruler 1, it is more probable in this case that the Tikal/Dos Pilas Emblem Glyph actually refers to a "Woman of Dos Pilas," probably Dos Pilas Ruler 2's sister. A further Dos Pilas–Naranjo link may be reflected in Dos Pilas' victorious battle against Seibal Ruler B, the one occurring at 9.15.4.6.4 (AD 735), which is the two Calendar Rounds+one day anniversary of Naranjo's defeat at the hands of Caracol. As such, the Dos Pilas victory could well be a sort of compensation for the Naranjo defeat, an act carried out by a friendly lineage or at least one known to have been related to them by blood in later times. (Very probably there were astronomical motivations for these battle dates as well.)

There are Dos Pilas connections, too, with Yaxchilan. A political reference is made to a capture of a Yaxchilan lord on Dos Pilas Hieroglyphic Stairway 3. This monument presumably dates to between 9.15.10.0.0 and 9.16.10.0.0 (AD 741 and 761), a possible "time of troubles" at Yaxchilan, corresponding to the 9.15.10.17.14 to

9.16.1.0.0 (AD 742–52) interregnum between the death of the Yaxchilan ruler, Shield-Jaguar I, and the accession of Bird-Jaguar IV.

Lastly, in this accounting of Dos Pilas' extra-regional references, we should mention Ixtutz Stela 4 (9.17.10.0.0; AD 780), which carries an Aguateca/Dos Pilas Emblem Glyph, although the nature of this reference is unclear.

There are also a few other Pasion region sites whose extra-regional connections are recorded in glyphic texts. For instance, the "Altar Vase" found in a Late Classic grave at Altar de Sacrificios (Adams 1971:Figs. 92–4) apparently makes glyphic mention of Yaxchilan. Incidentally, the Dos Pilas (or Tikal) Emblem Glyph is also on the vase, and we think it likely that the intended reference is to Dos Pilas rather than to Tikal. Finally, there is a glyphic record that Machaquila Ruler B apparently captured a lord of the Motul de San Jose polity some time before 9.15.0.0.0 (AD 731). The last known ruler of Machaquila (F) is also possibly named at Motul de San Jose (*c.* 10.0.0.0.0 ?; AD 830), evidence, perhaps, of a lasting relationship between the two polities, in which Machaquila appears to have been dominant.

## *Speculation on political process*

What were the relationships between Classic period polities of the Maya lowlands? Were they hierarchically structured, and how were they formed? Joyce Marcus (1973, 1976) has addressed these questions, but it will be apparent by now that we do not share all her views, especially when she argues that all Pasion region sites were under the power of Tikal during Cycle 9 and then, in Cycle 10, ruled by Seibal. We see a far greater degree of site autonomy in the Pasion region. This is not to say that political hierarchies did not occur in the region, but we feel that specific textual references (of conquests, alliances, etc.) are required as evidence for hierarchies, rather than depending upon general principles of Emblem Glyph usage and statistical counts of Emblem Glyph occurrences. Also, political control and site hierarchies must have changed through time, so that chronology has to be taken into account.

The maps shown in Figs. 3.6–3.17 present our view of the Late Classic political situation, katun by katun, in the Pasion region. The most significant hierarchical formation was headed by Dos Pilas/Aguateca. This lineage gained control over what had previously been independent, autonomous polities or "primary" centers: Arroyo de Piedra, Tamarindito, Seibal, and Cancuen. These became "secondary" centers within the Dos Pilas/Aguateca hierarchy, each governed by a Dos Pilas overlord. Aguas Calientes, La Amelia, and Chapayal were also satellite centers of Dos Pilas/Aguateca during this time (*c.* 9.18.0.0.0; AD 790).

Meanwhile, such centers as Itzan, Machaquila, and probably Altar de Sacrificios appear to have remained independent. There is some doubt as to the status of El Chorro, which at least twice in its history seems to have had its rulers captured, first by Dos Pilas, later by Itzan. It is uncertain whether these defeats led to El Chorro's subordination, but present evidence suggests the site remained an independent, primary center.

Other primary centers had their hierarchies as well: El Pabellon was presumably a secondary center within the orbit of Altar de Sacrificios (however, it must be admitted that no direct textual confirmation of this remains). Anonal and Seibal Group B were quite clearly in some sort of secondary status to Seibal during the first years of Cycle 10. The statuses of El Caribe, El Excavado, La Paciencia, and Punta de Chimino are uncertain although from their sizes and locations it is very likely that they were within the Dos Pilas/Aguateca orbit.

Towards the end of the Late Classic, *c.* 9.17.0.0.0–9.19.0.0.0 (AD 771–810), there seems to have been an increase in the number of sites erecting stelae, with places like Aguas Calientes, La Amelia, and probably El Caribe and Chapayal, putting up their first monuments. At the same time there are indications of a breakdown in the Dos Pilas/Aguateca overlordship. We have already seen that Seibal, Chapayal, and La Amelia were ruled over by a lord or (more likely) lords different from the contemporary ruler of Aguateca. Were different individuals of the Dos Pilas royal lineage in power over different parts of the realm? Were they under some central control, as seems to have been the case at La Amelia? Or were junior members of the lineage becoming dissatisfied with their roles in society and grabbing power for themselves in outlying centers?

Much has been written of demographic pressures in the Maya lowlands as the Late Classic period progressed. If a proliferation of the aristocracy accompanied this, a stressful situation of rivalries and disloyalties could have developed. The extent to which such factors caused or aided the Terminal Classic "collapse" is a matter of interesting speculation. In the Pasion region it is difficult not to see the expansionism of Dos Pilas as a destabilizing trend – both in the region and more widely in the southern lowlands.

In closing, we would like to emphasize that we consider the aggressive expansionism of the Dos Pilas dynasty to be quite exceptional in Classic Maya history. For the most part, major Maya centers appear to have lived at peace (in the political sense) with their neighbors, and the vast majority of "capture" events recorded in the inscriptions refer to local raids, evidently for sacrificial victims. There are only a dozen or so instances of battles where both combatants have Emblem Glyphs (Mathews 1986). Apparently, such major battles were able to have a wide range of possible outcomes, although the sacrifice of the captured ahau was no doubt inevitable. In some instances (e.g. the Tonina capture of Lord Kan-Xul of Palenque) it seems that nothing else happened – the two sites continued on their two courses, with no degree of control over the "loser" by the "winner." In other cases (e.g. Quirigua–Copan), perhaps a royal marriage was imposed upon the "loser," thus forming a blood-alliance and perhaps giving the "winner" some degree of influence over the "loser," at least for a time. A different case is that of Caracol, which, towards the end of the Early Classic period, captured the ruler of Naranjo and apparently took control of the site (for there is a monument hiatus at Naranjo for the next fifty years). Apart from Caracol, however, it was only Dos Pilas (so far as we know) which backed up its military conquests with political control over its victim sites. That it did so, and in the process expanded its territory at least four-fold, is evident, but it is equally clear that Dos Pilas was not able to hang on to its gains for more than two or three generations.

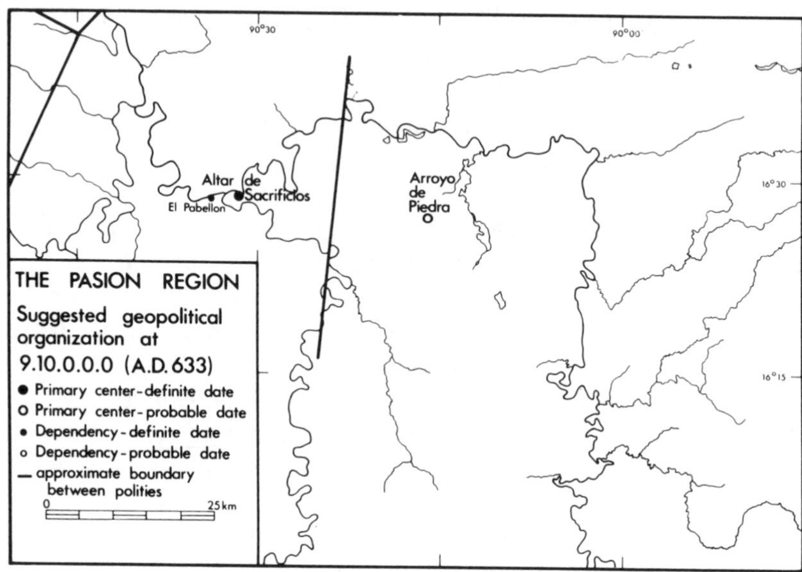


Fig. 3.6 The Pasion region: suggested geopolitical organization, at 9.10.0.0.0 (AD 633).

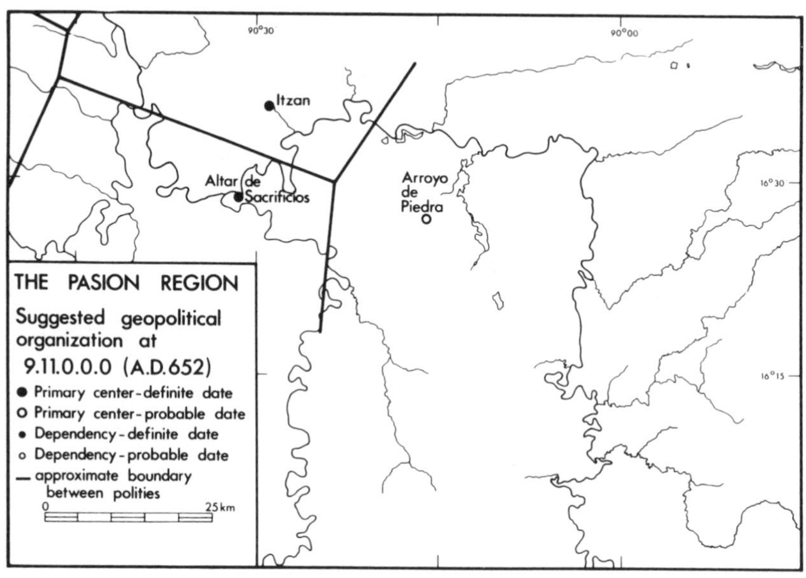


Fig. 3.7 The Pasion region: suggested geopolitical organization, at 9.11.0.0.0 (AD 652).

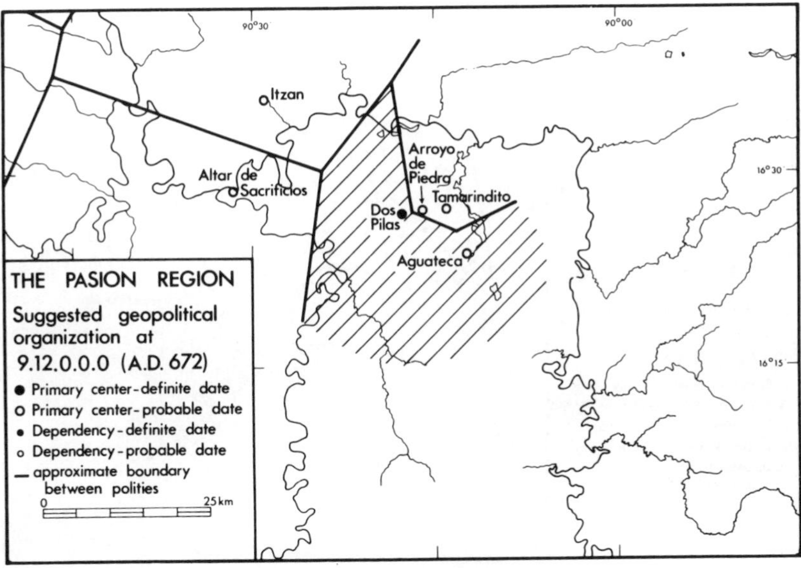


Fig. 3.8 The Pasion region: suggested geopolitical organization, at 9.12.0.0.0 (AD 672).

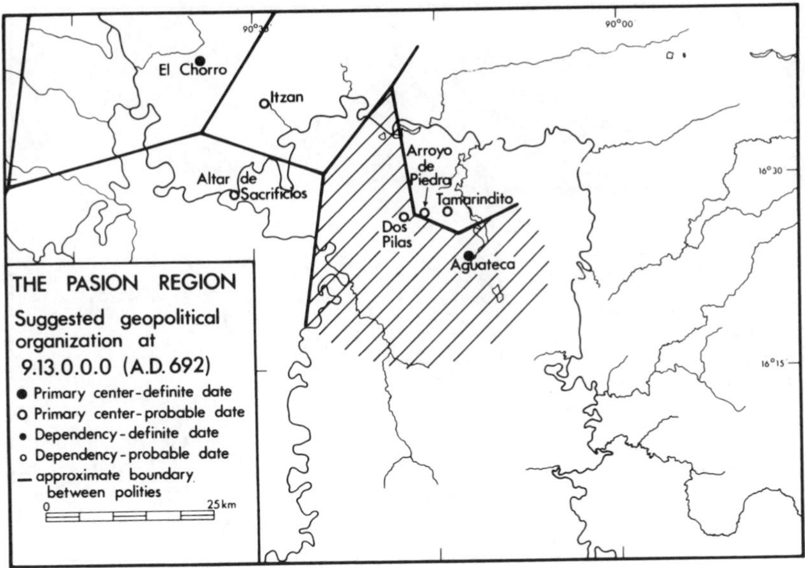


Fig. 3.9 The Pasion region: suggested geopolitical organization, at 9.13.0.0.0 (AD 692).

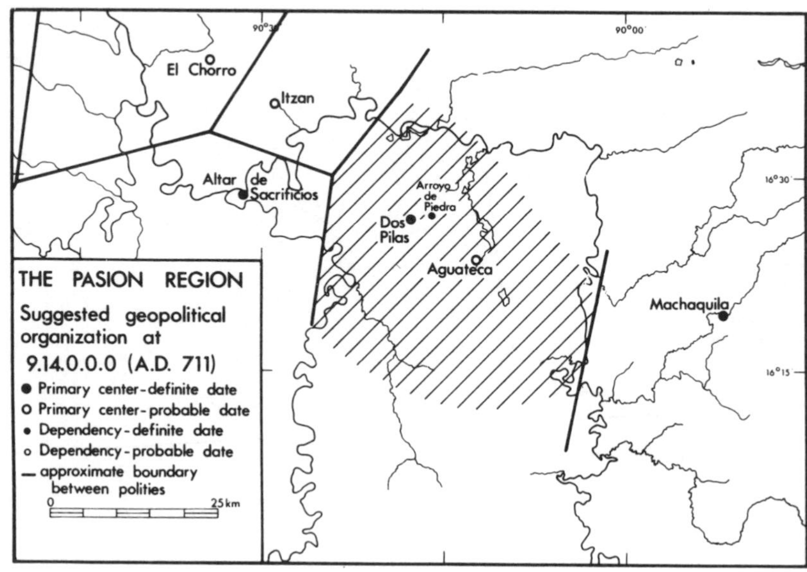


Fig. 3.10 The Pasion region: suggested geopolitical organization, at 9.14.0.0.0 (AD 711).

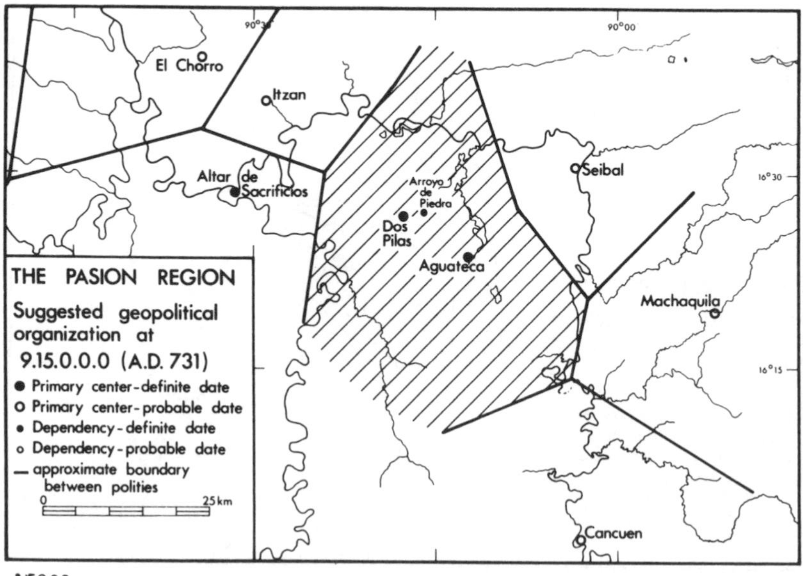


Fig. 3.11 The Pasion region: suggested geopolitical organization, at 9.15.0.0.0 (AD 731).

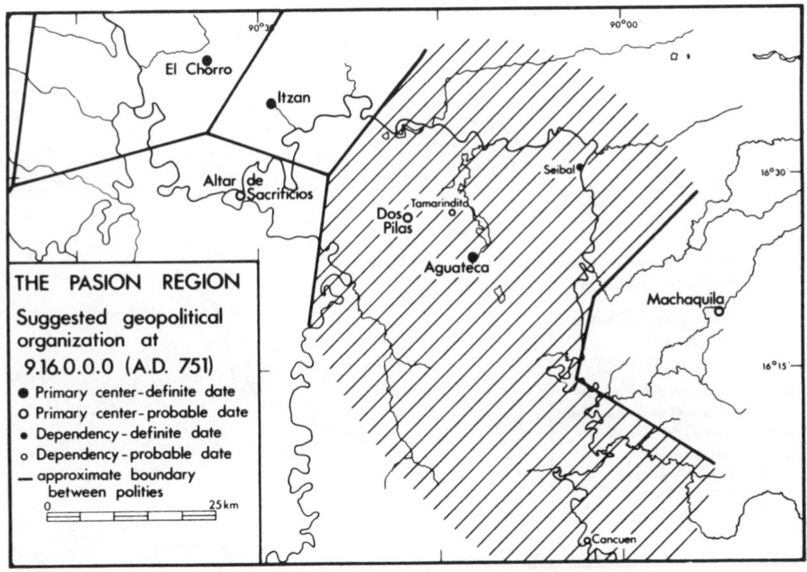

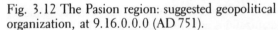

Fig. 3.12 The Pasion region: suggested geopolitical organization, at 9.16.0.0.0 (AD 751).

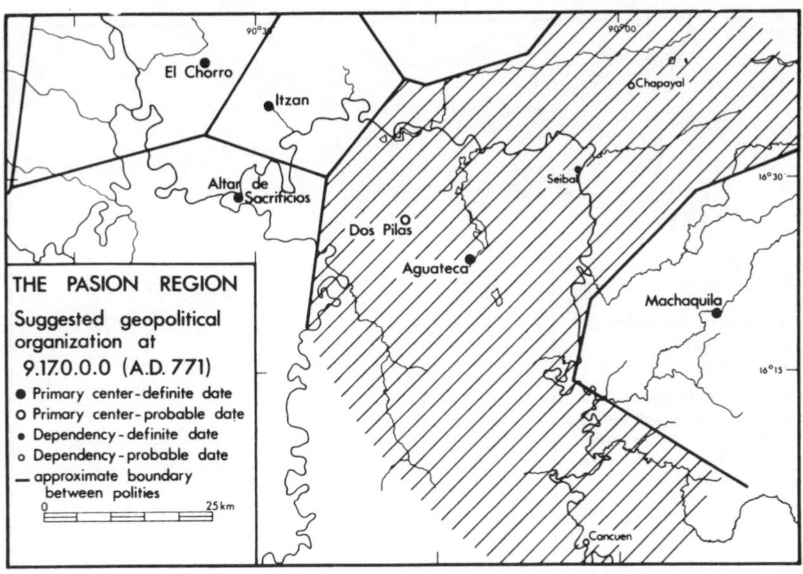


Fig. 3.13 The Pasion region: suggested geopolitical organization, at 9.17.0.0.0 (AD 771).

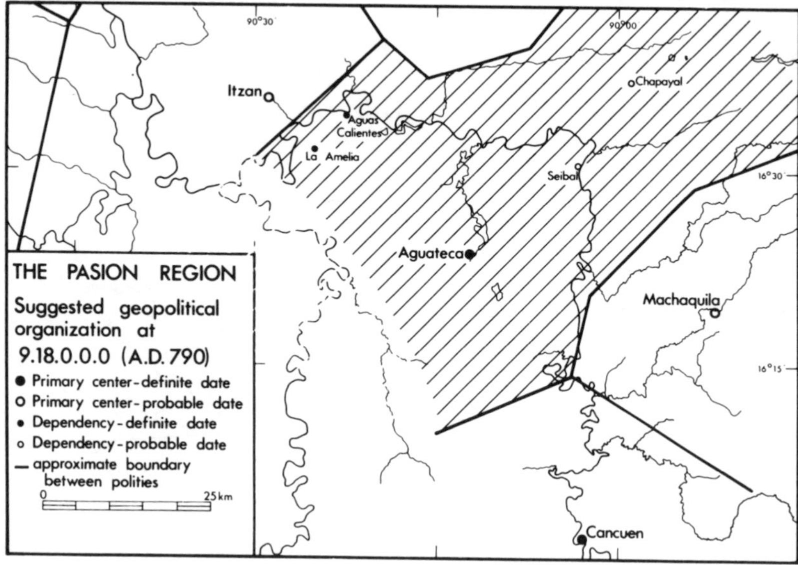


Fig. 3.14 The Pasion region: suggested geopolitical organization, at 9.18.0.0.0 (AD 790).

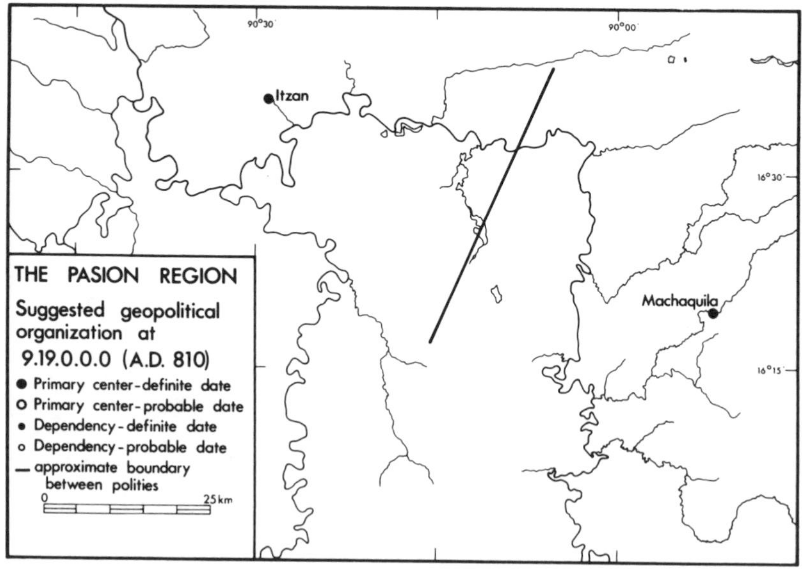


Fig. 3.15 The Pasion region: suggested geopolitical organization, at 9.19.0.0.0 (AD 810).

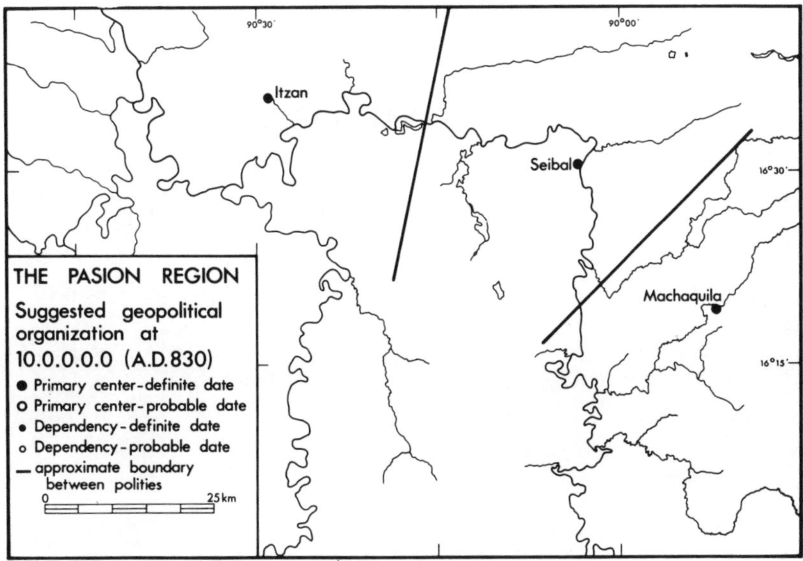


Fig. 3.16 The Pasion region: suggested geopolitical organization, at 10.0.0.0.0 (AD 830).

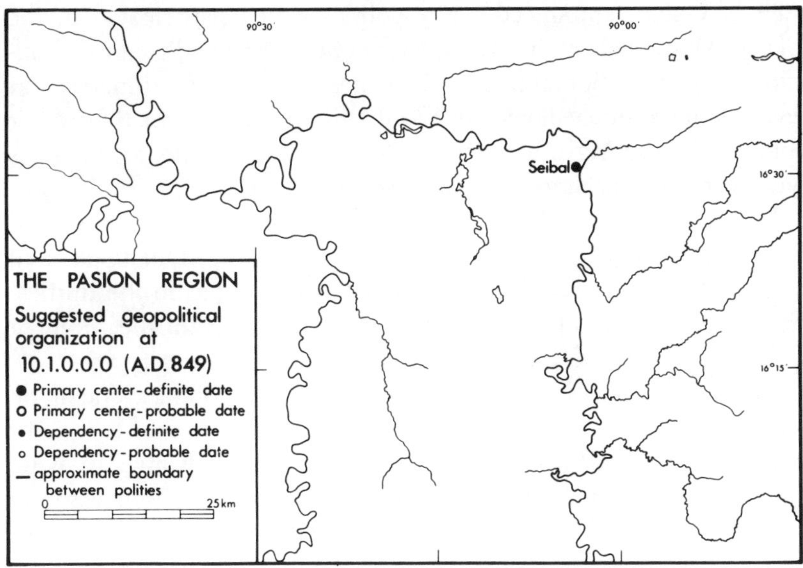


Fig. 3.17 The Pasion region: suggested geopolitical organization, at 10.1.0.0.0 (AD 849).

# 4
# An epigraphic history of the western Maya region

LINDA SCHELE

The region bordering the Usumacinta River and covering the modern state of Chiapas produced many polities which participated in the Classic Maya civilization. The largest of these include Palenque, Yaxchilan, Tonina, Bonampak, and Piedras Negras. Unfortunately, far less is known archaeologically about this western region than other zones of Classic Maya habitation. Only Palenque of the large polities has received sustained archaeological attention which is now published and available for study. Projects of shorter duration and limited goals have been conducted at Yaxchilan, Bonampak, and Tonina during the last decade, and at Piedras Negras in the thirties. Few of these studies have been published, giving us for the whole of Chiapas an archaeological history that is severely limited.

The epigraphic history of the western area is, in contrast, one of the most complete we have. Not only have these sites received long-term attention from epigraphers, but all are characterized by large surviving corpora of texts that are unusually long and detailed in comparison to other Maya sites. Piedras Negras and Yaxchilan were the focuses of Proskouriakoff's (1960, 1961a, 1963, 1964) seminal studies of the historical contents of Maya inscriptions. Palenque, Bonampak, and Tonina have been the sustained targets of epigraphic studies since

1973. The results of these studies have been detailed histories of each of these major cities and their subsidiary sites.

At Palenque, where comparison between archaeological and epigraphic data is possible and has been done, the two compare favorably.[1] However, for the western area as a whole, history must be reconstructed from epigraphic, iconographic, and stylistic analyses with archaeological data playing a minor role. Furthermore, because of the lack of deep excavations, archaeological information in general is limited to the Late Classic period – even at Palenque. This lack of penetration to deeper levels leads to further complications because the Early Classic history we have is usually, but not always, found in retrospective historical texts, as at Palenque, or in Early Classic monuments reused by Late Classic rulers, as at Yaxchilan.

The chart at the end of this chapter is an account of the history of the major polities – Yaxchilan, Bonampak, Palenque, Piedras Negras, and Tonina – as recorded in the inscriptions of each site. Sources for site histories are as follows:

1. Yaxchilan region: Proskouriakoff (1963, 1964), Tate (1986), Schele (1982), Mathews (1975, 1980, 1986, 1988), Coe and Benson (1966), M. Miller (1986), Schele and Freidel (n.d.), and personal communication with Peter Mathews and David Stuart.
2. Palenque region: Lounsbury (1974, 1980), Mathews and Schele (1974), Schele (1976, 1978–89, 1982, 1984a, 1986c), Coe (1974), Mathews (n.d.a), Kelker (1981), Riese (1978), personal communication with Floyd Lounsbury and Peter Mathews.
3. Piedras Negras region: Proskouriakoff (1960), Stuart (1985b), Johnston (n.d.), Houston (1983), personal communication with David Stuart and Peter Mathews.
4. Tonina: Mathews (n.d.b), Becquelin and Baudez (1982), personal communication with Peter Mathews.

Care must be taken in the use of the historical data from the inscriptions. First, we have only the records of the winners in a lifestyle characterized by internal competition between members of ruling lineages and tense, ever-changing relationships between different polities. Second, we must also recognize that the public inscriptions were primarily instruments of public propaganda and political policy. The Maya would be a rare people indeed if they had not shaded history to fit political purpose and adapted it to the world view with which they filtered experience. The written version of history must, therefore, be carefully compared to the archaeological record to determine how well the two data sets match, and when the archaeological data are not available, as in most of the western zone, we must be very careful about extrapolating too far beyond the raw data of the inscribed history. Finally, since the process of decipherment is ongoing, any analysis produced here has the disadvantages of representing my personal understanding of the inscriptions as well as a stage in the decipherment process. New discoveries made subsequent to this work surely will change our perception of the patterns of history recorded in the inscriptions and our attempts to explain those patterns will change in time.

## YAXCHILAN

Peter Mathews (1975) first noted the numerical ordering of the kings of Yaxchilan recorded on a set of Early Classic monuments, including Lintels 35, 37, and 47. Preceded by an ordinal number and a variant of the "successor"[2] glyph, the accession records of these Yaxchilan rulers allow us to reconstruct a detailed history. At the time of Mathews' original insight, only the lintels recording the fifth through the tenth rulers were known; however, the first lintel in the series was discovered in 1983 by Roberto Moll García (see *National Geographic Magazine*, October, 1985, p. 541). Together these four lintels give us the names in numerical order of the first ten kings of Yaxchilan's ruling dynasty.

The first ruler in this list, named with a set of male genitals resting on top of a jaguar head, was considered by his successors to have been the founder of the lineage (Schele 1986a). This status is confirmed on Lintel 22, where his name follows a "numbered successor" title (Riese 1984b) and the name phrase of the seventh king in the line. The purpose of the titular sequence is to identify the later king as the "seventh successor of Penis-Jaguar". Founders are also known for the Copan, Tikal, Naranjo, and Palenque lineages (Schele 1986a and Grube n.d.).

After making a field drawing of the newly discovered lintel, David Stuart (personal communication 1985) recognized that the rulers on the new lintel also appear with accession dates on Hieroglyphic Stairs 1. In that text, however, each ruler has a two-sentence text associated with his name: one detailing the date of his accession, and the other a later event attended by visitors from other sites (Schele and Mathews, this volume). David Stuart pointed out to me that the name of a visiting lord on the new lintel (C6–C7) also occurs on the Stairs (60–62). Furthermore, this visitor occurs in association with the third Yaxchilan king, whose name was Bird-Jaguar I (C4 and 52), in both texts. Without doubt the Hieroglyphic Stairs and the lintels record the same people and the same actions. The important information gained from this comparison is the dates of the events. The lintel series suppressed the dates of the kings' accessions and those of the actions of the visiting lords. Stuart demonstrated, however, that the Hieroglyphic Stairs 1 text assigns dates to both actions and lists the Distance Numbers between the recorded dates. Unfortunately, the stairs are in a very badly eroded condition and the reconstructions are, at best, problematic.

Nevertheless, combining Stuart's insights with those of Mathews allows the reconstruction of a chronology from early Yaxchilan and a clarification of the involved name phrases, especially of the kings. For example, the second ruler in the list, who is named with zoomorphic head and a jaguar on the lintel, appears on the stairs at 45 as "Shield-Jaguar". Unfortunately, only the earliest section of the stairs is preserved in a condition sufficient to allow even tentative decipherment. As a result, the reconstruction yields dates associated with the first three kings only, but this is enough tentatively to date the founding of the dynasty.

The first Calendar Round in the preserved text on Hieroglyphic Stairs 1 is 7 ____ 14 Zotz', giving the following possibilities:

| | | | |
|---|---|---|---|
| 8.13.9.14.1 | 7 Imix | 14 Zotz' | Aug. 6, 307 |
| 8.14.2.17.6 | 7 Cimi | 14 Zotz' | Aug. 2, 320 |
| 8.12.3.7.11 | 7 Chuen | 14 Zotz' | Aug. 11, 281 |
| 8.14.16.2.11 | 7 Chuen | 14 Zotz' | Jul. 30, 333 |
| 8.12.16.10.16 | 7 Cib | 14 Zotz' | Aug. 8, 294 |
| 8.15.9.5.16 | 7 Cib | 14 Zotz' | Jul. 27, 346 |

Mathews' original analysis of Yaxchilan's dynastic history gives us a bit of data that helps in the selection of one of these dates as a best guess. On Lintel 21, the date 9.0.19.2.4 (Oct. 16, 454) occurs with the seventh successor. Using twenty years per reign as an average[3] and six reigns preceding the seventh king, the reign of the founder ought to be about six katuns earlier or in the fourteenth katun. Ian Graham's

(1982:143) drawing and photograph of the stairs suggests Cimi as the most likely reading, giving the date 8.14.2.17.6 7 Cimi 14 Zotz' (Aug. 2, 320) as the tentative reconstruction of the accession date for Penis-Jaguar, with the reservation that the Chuen placement is also possible.

The record of the second successor, Shield-Jaguar, is entirely effaced, but the accession date of the third, Bird-Jaguar, is 2 ____ 14 Mol, giving these possibilities:

| | | | |
|---|---|---|---|
| 8.15.2.8.1 | 2 Imix | 14 Mol | Oct. 17, 339 |
| 8.17.15.3.1 | 2 Imix | 14 Mol | Oct. 4, 391 |
| 8.18.8.6.6 | 2 Cimi | 14 Mol | Sep. 30, 404 |
| 8.16.8.14.11 | 2 Chuen | 14 Mol | Oct. 10, 365 |
| 8.17.1.17.16 | 2 Cib | 14 Mol | Oct. 7, 378 |

The drawing and photograph favor a reading of Cib for the day sign, giving Bird-Jaguar a tentative accession date of 8.17.1.17.16 2 Cib 14 Mol (Oct. 7, 378).

Bird-Jaguar's accession is followed by a second date and event recording the action of a visiting lord who is also recorded on the newly found lintel. The Distance Number clearly has nine days and some number of uinals above ten but below fifteen. The day reached is 4 ____ 15+Uo or Zip. Chicchan, the ninth day after Cib, can occur with the 18th day of the month. These elements are enough to determine that the Distance Number is 12.9 and the date 8.17.2.12.5 4 Chicchan 18 Uo (Jun. 13, 379).

The fourth successor on the new lintel is named Yax-Antler-Skull. The date of his accession has three readable components 4 Lamat 11 ____, and the month sign is clearly one of the color months. The possibilities are as follows:

| | | | |
|---|---|---|---|
| 8.17.13.3.8 | 4 Lamat | 11 Ch'en | Oct. 21, 389 |
| 8.19.5.12.8 | 4 Lamat | 11 Yax | Nov. 2, 421 |
| 8.18.5.8.8 | 4 Lamat | 11 Zac | Nov. 27, 401 |
| 8.17.5.4.8 | 4 Lamat | 11 Ceh | Dec. 22, 381 |

Zac seems the least likely possibility on the photograph, and the 8.19 placement seems too late, if we are to allow time for the reigns of the fifth and sixth successors. Of the two remaining possibilities, I have chosen 8.17.13.3.8 4 Lamat 11 Ch'en (Oct. 21, 389) to leave more time for Bird-Jaguar's reign, but the earlier 4 Lamat 11 Ceh is just as likely.

The seventh successor has already been tied to the date 9.0.19.2.4 (Oct. 16, 454). No direct date survives with the ninth successor, Knot-eye Jaguar, but Lintel 37 records a date (9.3.13.12.19 1 Cauac 7 Yaxkin [Aug. 9, 508]) for the undeciphered "visitor" event that follows the accessions on Hieroglyphic Stairs 1. If the pattern for these two dates holds true, then the accession was several months earlier. Knot-eye Jaguar appears on Lintel 12 at Piedras Negras as the name of the first figure kneeling in front of the Piedras Negras king. The date of the pictured event is not secure, but it should correspond to one of the later dates on the lintel; I have chosen 9.4.3.0.17 (Oct. 19, 517), but one of the earlier Lintel 12 dates is also possible. Knot-eye Jaguar has dates on either side of 9.4.0.0.0 (Oct. 18, 514) making him the most likely king to be pictured on Yaxchilan Stela 27, a 9.4.0.0.0 monument.

The tenth successor, Tah-Skull II, acceded on 9.4.11.8.16 (Feb. 13, 526) with one of his accession-associated events on 9.5.2.10.6 (Jan. 16, 537) with lord "Cu-ix" from Site $Q^4$ (perhaps Calakmul, see Lintel 35). With this succession, the numbered order is no longer secure. We have a capture by a second king named Knot-eye Jaguar on 9.6.10.14.15 (Nov. 19, 564; Structure 44 steps) and a scattering monument (Stela 14) on 9.8.0.0.0 (Aug. 24, 593), but the name of the ruler did not survive. The accession of 6-Tun Bird-Jaguar, the father of the famous Shield-Jaguar, on 9.9.16.10.13 (Sep. 18, 629), brings us into the well-known period of Yaxchilan's history.

Mathews (1985:45) dates the founding of the Classic period dynasty at Tikal at around 8.10.0.0.0 (Oct. 25, 238), a chronology supported both by epigraphy and archaeology. If this is an accurate reconstruction, the Yaxchilan dynasty was established about eighty years later, or contemporary with the Leyden Plaque. This later placement does not require that Yaxchilan was settled at that time, but only that the later kings conceived that their dynasty was founded then. However, I suspect that this dating reflects real history, rather than propagandistic hoopla created by later kings. If so, then Yaxchilan and presumably Piedras Negras were slower by several katuns to adopt the political system of the Classic period than their precocious Peten neighbors.

Perhaps the most interesting implication of Yaxchilan's early history is that, from the earliest times, Yaxchilan kings interacted with other major polities, including Bonampak, Tikal, and Piedras Negras. Although the glyph recording the exact action done by the visitors is not deciphered, the context does not appear to indicate a hostile interaction.

Detailed history at Yaxchilan begins with Shield-Jaguar's reign, the subject of Proskouriakoff's (1963, 1964) early study and thus familiar to most Mayanists. Little has been changed in the intervening decades since her first analysis. Warfare, however, held a very important place in Yaxchilan's narrative record. From other studies (Mathews and Willey, this volume; and Schele and Freidel n.d.), we suspect this condition was not unusual during the Late Classic period. The Usumacinta region is unusual only in the prominence that was given to warfare in the public record.

The reign of Bird-Jaguar is particularly notable for the attention he gives to second-level nobles who were named with the title *cahal* (Mathews and Justeson 1984; Stuart n.d.). One of these cahals has been identified by Stuart (1989) as the brother of Bird-Jaguar's principal wife. Cahals or nobles of similar rank surely existed throughout the Classic period,[5] but during Bird-Jaguar's reign they attained an unprecedented prominence on monuments commissioned by the kings. I suspect that Bird-Jaguar was in fact a child of his father's old age and that he had older and more eligible rivals (Schele and Freidel n.d.) whom he had to outmaneuver during the ten-year interregnum that followed his father's death. Part of his strategy appears to have been establishing a network of alliances among the secondary lineages who would support his claim. His marriage to Lady Great-Skull-Zero and the alliance formed with her brother as patriarch of his lineage was a central part of that strategy.

During his reign, Bird-Jaguar also crossed the Usumacinta to visit La Pasadita in order to celebrate a period-ending with the cahal of that subsidiary site. His son Shield-Jaguar II shows up on monuments from Laxtunich, a subsidiary site as yet unidentified geographically.[6] The growing prominence of cahals and secondary *ahaus* in the Late Classic period suggests both a proliferation of the nobility through time and pressure on the central mechanisms of governance from that nobility (see also Fash and Stuart, this volume). One way to secure loyalty from them was to give them a piece of history in the form of their own monuments and in depictions of rituals by the high kings.

## BONAMPAK

The later history of Bonampak has been well published by Mathews (1980) and Mary Miller (1986); however, some of its earlier history is less well known. Bird-Jaguar of Bonampak is named with the sixth successor in the Yaxchilan series, placing his reign before the 9.0.19.2.4 (Oct. 16, 454) date associated with the seventh ruler. This association sets the beginning of Bonampak in Cycle 8. A Bonampak ruler nicknamed Fish-Fin appears in the Yaxchilan sequence associated with the ninth successor. Mathews (1975) has noted that this same ruler appears on two looted panels, probably from Bonampak proper, with contemporary dates. One of these, the Houston Panel, records rites on 9.3.0.14.13 (Nov. 19, 495) and 9.3.3.16.4 (Dec. 4, 498), while the Po Panel records the date 9.4.8.14.9 (Jun. 22, 523). Knot-eye Jaguar of Bonampak is named with the tenth successor of Yaxchilan, who succeeded on 9.4.11.8.16 (Feb. 13, 526).

I have seen snapshots of several new monuments that have been found at Bonampak since 1980, but these are not available for study. My recollection is that they record accessions and other events between 9.8.0.0.0 (Aug. 24, 593) and 9.15.0.0.0 (Aug. 22, 731), but until they are published we cannot complete Bonampak's dynastic sequence. Youths from Bonampak are shown on Piedras Negras Lintel 2 participating in ceremonies for the heir of Ruler 2 on 9.11.6.2.1 (Oct. 24, 658). Clearly Bonampak was an important site, equal to Yaxchilan in political and military importance from a time much earlier than previously suspected.

A looted column now in the St. Louis Museum (Liman and Durbin 1975) records a dedication rite on 9.14.3.8.4 (May 2, 715) performed by a Bonampak lord named Etz'nab-Jawbone. This Bonampak lord is called "the ahau of" Ruler 3 of Tonina, suggesting that in the period before the reign of Knot-eye Jaguar of Bonampak, Tonina had exerted influence, if not dominance, at the site. However, by 9.15.15.0.0 (Jun. 4, 746), the ruler of Lacanja records his own seating and the period-ending, carefully noting at the same time that he was the cahal of Knot-eye Jaguar. This Bonampak ruler should be the one immediately following Etz'nab-Jawbone. Clearly the patterns of subordinance and dominance were very complex, but perhaps they were also reasonably short-lived in the volatile context of the Late Classic period. Interestingly, a Bonampak ahau named Chuen was captured by

Shield-Jaguar of Yaxchilan on 9.14.17.15.11 (Jul. 14, 729). I suspect that alliances between polities of the Classic period were extremely volatile, or else the nobles of allied kingdoms arranged for battles even during times of alliance.

Perhaps the most interesting inter-polity relationship occurred during the reign of the last recorded ruler of Bonampak – Chan-Muan (acceded on 9.17.5.8.9 [Jun. 15, 776]). On Stela 2, the woman standing behind him is named as a lady of Yaxchilan (Mathews 1980:61). She was apparently the mother of the child whose heir-designation is shown in Room 1 of Temple 1. In the main text of Room 1, this heir is named in a relationship to Shield-Jaguar II of Yaxchilan (Schele 1982:172 and M. Miller 1986:35). The relationship glyph is badly eroded, but a comparison of all its versions in the various reproductions suggests it is T17d:668:174 *yichan*, a glyph that Stuart (1989) has recently identified as "mother's brother". This reading suggests that the king of Bonampak married the sister of the king of Yaxchilan, thus renewing (or confirming) an interrelationship that had existed between the two dynasties for hundreds of years.

In addition to giving a member of his family to Chan-Muan, Shield-Jaguar II also joined his Bonampak relative in war, taking a captive on 9.17.16.3.8 (Jan. 8, 787) (Mathews 1980:67). This capture is depicted over the central door of the temple of the murals, while the left door shows Chan-Muan talking to another captive four days later. This suggests that kings not only exchanged members of their families in marriage, but that they provided warriors and participated in each other's battles as allies. The lintel of the right-hand door of the same building records that an earlier king, Knot-eye Jaguar of Bonampak, took a captive in the land of the cahal who ruled Lacanja for him. This capture is put in the same narrative sequence as the captures of Shield-Jaguar II and Chan-Muan.

## PALENQUE

Palenque's epigraphic history is perhaps the most complete we now have from the Classic period, although the Early Classic history is not as well disseminated as the later history.[7] Almost all the dates from Palenque are firmly locked to a period-ending date, to a Long Count date, or to both, thus providing a well-documented and stable chronology for comparison with archaeological data. The one exception is the founder's dates as recorded on the Tablet of the Cross. The birth and accession of Bahlum-Kuk, the first king in the list, are recorded as 5 Cimi 14 Kayab and 1 Kan 2 Kayab, respectively, but the Distance Number between them, 1.2.5.14, does not fit. Since the dates of the person named immediately before Bahlum-Kuk are in Cycle 5 and those of the person after in Cycle 8, I deduce that the former was a legendary ruler from Olmec times and the latter was a historical ruler. The problem is to decide which category was meant for Bahlum-Kuk.

The clue seems to be in a later passage from the Group of the Cross in which a critical Late Classic date 9.12.18.5.17 3 Caban 15 Mol (Jul. 24, 690) is associated with the then reigning king, Chan-Bahlum. The verb starts with a God N glyph, followed by the title *Mah Kina* (written in two forms), a quetzal bird with a *na* sign attached, and *ta yotot*[8] "in his house". Chan-Bahlum is named as the actor. David Stuart found the clue to understanding this passage on an Early Classic stair under Temple 11 at Copan. There, a different dedicatory verb is followed by the Copan Emblem Glyph with a na "building" sign attached, ti yotot "in his house", and Mah Kina Yax-K'uk-Mo', who is well documented as the founder of Copan's lineage (Stuart and Schele 1986a; Schele 1986a). The Copan passage records the dedication of a temple house named "Copan lineage building, the house of Yax-K'uk-Mo' " by the successor who built it. At Palenque, Chan-Bahlum does the same thing by naming the Group of the Cross as "the Mah Kina Bahlum-Kuk building in the house of Chan-Bahlum". Clearly, Chan-Bahlum considered Bahlum-Kuk to be the founder of his dynasty, thus favoring an identification of Bahlum-Kuk as an historical person. In keeping with this interpretation, I have placed his birth at 8.18.0.13.6 (Mar. 31, 397) and his accession at 8.19.15.3.4 (Mar. 11, 431). This date for the beginning of Palenque's history fits well with the ceramic data published by Rands (1974) and in general the epigraphic data correspond to the archaeological history known from Palenque (Schele 1986b).

Little is known archaeologically from the Early Classic period, although a royal tomb from Temple 18a-sub dates ceramically to the reign of either Chaacal I or Kan-Xul I (Schele 1986b). David Stuart (personal communication 1984) has furthermore identified the name on an alabaster vase in the Dumbarton Oaks collection as that of the second successor, who has been affectionately nicknamed "Casper" (after the ghost). These data, skimpy though they are, suggest that Palenque's retrospective inscriptions record true history, not the inventions of later kings.

Pacal's reign is the most interesting in terms of inter-polity relationship. Stuart (personal communication 1984) identified the person on the Miraflores fragment as a cahal of Pacal. At the same time, Ahpo-Balam, the ruler of Tortuguero in the western zone, named himself an ahau of Palenque and child of ahaus of Palenque. At least during Pacal's reign, the kingdom extended toward the Usumacinta in the east and as far as Tortuguero in the west. Interestingly, the erection of inscribed monuments at Tortuguero ended with Ahpo-Balam's reign. Rands (personal communication 1975) report of a loss of affinities between Palenque and Tortuguero ceramics just at that time reinforces the implication – that Tortuguero withdrew from Palenque's sphere after Ahpo-Ba!am died. Other secondary texts and images inscribed on the substructure of House C seem to depict subordinates from the smaller centers within the polity who are shown giving public obedience to Pacal. In addition, a fragmentary text drawn by Maler (provided to the author by Karl Herbet Mayer) at the subsidiary site of Xupa relates to Pacal's reign.

Pacal also records war events involving a person from Site Q (either Calakmul or El Peru) and another person who may have been a sibling of Shield-Jaguar of Yaxchilan. Recorded on the Hieroglyphic Stairs, this war text clearly records the Yaxchilan Emblem Glyph in association with Shield-Jaguar's name and a capture verb. The person captured, however, was "a sibling", ( *yitan*[9]) of Shield-Jaguar, who was still twenty years from his accession at the time of the capture. Shield-Jaguar must, however, have already been the heir or I suspect that Pacal would have found it more advantageous to describe his captive as the "son of" the king rather than a "sibling of" the heir.

Other external involvement was rarely recorded by subsequent kings. Pacal's younger son, Kan-Xul was captured by Ruler 3 of Tonina. House AD, which he had commissioned as his accession monument, was finally dedicated by a non-royal noble named Xoc.[10] Kan-Xul's successor, Chaacal III, also was involved with an important cahal named Chac-Zutz'. This cahal not only erected his own panels, the Tablet of the Slaves, in his residential compound (Group IV), but he appears paired with Chaacal in the Tablet of the Scribe and Orator. As at Yaxchilan, the later rulers of Palenque broke earlier traditions by depicting these cahals in space that had been previously reserved for royal affairs. For example, the subordinates shown by Pacal on the substructure of House C have always been recognized for exactly what they are – people kneeling in subordination. In contrast, one would not be able to distinguish the relative ranks of Chac-Zutz' and Chaacal on the Tablets of the Scribe and Orator without information from the inscriptions.

## PIEDRAS NEGRAS

The earliest dated monument at Piedras Negras is Lintel 12 (IS date, 9.3.19.12.12 [Jul. 2, 514]), which depicts the earliest example of the composition that was later featured on Lintels 4 and 2. The protagonist on this early monument has been designated Ruler C by Johnston (n.d.). Its dates fall shortly before and after the end of Katun 4, a chronology confirmed by the identification of the first kneeling figure as Knot-eye Jaguar of Yaxchilan, who appears in the inscriptions of that site with contemporary dates and association (see Schele and Mathews, this volume). The other very early reference at Piedras Negras is found in a retrospective reference recorded on Lintel 2 to an event that took place only three years before the Lintel 12 IS date. Unfortunately, the damaged condition of Lintel 12 makes it impossible for me to compare the names to ascertain if the protagonists of the two events were the same or different persons. Lintel 2 may, therefore, refer to the ruler who preceded Johnston's Ruler C in office.

Yaxchilan's early texts suggest that the history of Piedras Negras began much earlier than Lintel 12's events. In the Early Classic Yaxchilan lintel set discussed earlier, a lord carrying the God N shell title and the Piedras Negras Emblem Glyph is associated with the seventh successor, who was reigning at Yaxchilan on 9.0.19.2.4 (Oct. 16, 454). An earlier lord may be associated with the first successor at Yaxchilan: a visitor to the first successor named "Ah Cauac" (a name used at Piedras Negras) and a turtleshell glyph, which may or may not refer to Piedras Negras.[11] The first reference in the Yaxchilan document established the existence of a Piedras Negras dynasty as early as the first katun of Cycle 9; the second may take it even further back in time. This possibility must be investigated with excavations which hopefully will yield buried monuments from the early history of the city.

The same relationship between Yaxchilan and Piedras Negras recurs on Piedras Negras Lintel 3 which records the participation of Bird-Jaguar of Yaxchilan in heir-designation ritual for the child who would become Ruler 4 (Proskouriakoff 1961b; Schele and Mathews, this volume). This scene figures prominently in our discussion of royal visits, but perhaps as interesting to the system of governance are the seven figures seated below the ruler's throne. One of them is an *Ah Nab*, a rank also found among the observers in the Bonampak murals (M. Miller 1986:40–2) and six of them are cahals. As at Bonampak and Yaxchilan, nobles of these ranks both participate in and witness the important dynastic events of the kings.

Internal relationships between the capital and subsidiary sites in the Piedras Negras polity are best studied in the inscriptions of El Cayo, which was ruled by cahals subordinate to the Piedras Negras royal family. The cahal whose history is recorded on the Dumbarton Oaks lintel featured his attendance at Ruler 3's three-tun anniversary of rule (Coe and Benson 1966:8). He emphasized his participation even though it occurred before he became ruler of El Cayo as if his own prestige had been enhanced by his participation. Panel 1 of El Cayo records another event, a dedication of some sort, that was enacted by a cahal named 4-Panak. At the time he was seven years old and still long from the throne of El Cayo. 4-Panak's father did not accede until forty-four days later and it was another nine years before 4-Panak himself would rule El Cayo. I cannot tell from the inscription what was dedicated, but it is associated with a place-name made of T5:528.116, a glyph that also shows up prominently as a location on Throne 1 of Piedras Negras. 4-Panak does this event *ichnal* "in the company of" Ruler 5 of Piedras Negras,[12] but I cannot tell if the event occurred at El Cayo or the capital.

In both these situations, the persons who participated in the ritual with the high king were children of cahals who were yet to become rulers of El Cayo. I suspect the true participants were the reigning cahals, but that their heirs and the children of their heirs went with them. The events were recorded by the children in retrospective histories that lent prestige to their own positions. If this is the case, then it provides insight into the importance secondary lords placed on participating in the rituals of the capital and the high king. The same sort of distributive prestige can be seen in an El Cayo lintel now in the Cleveland Museum of Art. The wife (or mother) of a later cahal (ruling shortly before 9.18.5.0.0 [Sep. 15, 795]) had her portrait carved on this lintel by the artist of Piedras Negras Throne 1.[13] Apparently, Ruler 7 lent the services of his best artist to an important cahal for commemorating an event in the life of his wife.

War iconography and events played a prominent part in the history of Piedras Negras throughout its lifetime. Lintel 12 shows foreign visitors, including Knot-eye Jaguar of Yaxchilan, attending the Piedras Negras ruler who stands before a captive. The same essential scene is repeated on Lintel 2 in which the visitors are youths from Bonampak and Yaxchilan, attending what I suspect was a coming of age rite for the Piedras Negras heir (Schele and Miller 1986:148–9). The protagonist is Ruler 2, but the heir apparently did not survive to take the throne. Interestingly, the text links this event with an earlier one that took place about three years before the Lintel 12 events so that the Piedras Negras rulers considered these events that involved foreign lords to have been particularly important to the prestige of their lineage.

Other war events are not recorded with the same detail although the Venus-Tlaloc war iconography and star-war events are particularly prevalent at Piedras Negras. The most telling of these is shown on Stela 12 which records (Schele and Miller 1986:219) the aftermath of a star-war with Pomona. The captives seated on the floor below a pyramidal platform are identified as cahals and I suspect they are from Pomona.

## TONINA

The earliest monument at Tonina, M106, is dated to 9.8.0.0.0 (Aug. 24, 593). We have no evidence for or against the existence of a Tonina polity earlier than this date. However, this date matches closely the beginning of the Late Classic florescence of Palenque and it is only forty years before the first dates at Tortuguero. Thus 9.8.0.0.0 may mark the time of a regional florescence of this central Chiapas zone. Curiously, Tonina seems to have retained Late Classic characteristics far longer than any other site in the lowland zone. Stela 106, dated at 10.4.0.0.0 (AD 909), is the latest known Classic Maya monument and, interestingly, it retains stylistic and iconographic integrity, a characteristic that cannot be claimed for the latest monuments at Seibal.

It should also be noted that the iconography of Tonina overwhelmingly refers to war and captive themes, although its royal portraits are consistent with the Maya tradition. The St. Louis column mentioned above suggests that Tonina exerted enough influence over Bonampak for a brief period during Katun 14 for an ahau of the Bonampak polity included the information that he was *yahau* ("the vassal of") Ruler 3. At least one Palenque king, Kan-Xul, was captured, and two other undated monuments record other Palenque captives with names not documented in that site's monuments. One of these monuments is associated with Ruler 8 whose dates fall between 9.17.18.13.9 (Jul. 17, 789) and 9.18.15.15.10 (May 30, 806). Although the date of the capture does not survive, it must have fallen near the end of Palenque's life as a coherent polity. Tonina must have been a bellicose neighbor whose depredations in Chiapas may have contributed to the collapse of the region, for Tonina certainly survived long after its rivals ceased to erect monuments.

## SUMMARY

Rands (1974, 1977) has reported several large Preclassic sites on the lower Usumacinta and large Preclassic settlements are known at Seibal and Altar de Sacrificios. The Classic peoples who inhabited Palenque, Piedras Negras, Yaxchilan, and Bonampak were presumably the inheritors of that Preclassic tradition although we do not have sufficient archaeology from any of the sites to determine what kind of Preclassic occupation each supported. If the epigraphic histories reflect the true happenings of the time, these polities of the west were not established until 80 to 160 years after the founding of the precocious dynasties of the central Peten. Those founding dates are recorded at least epigraphically in the Peten and in the west as belonging to the Early Classic period. Even at sites with deep and elaborate Preclassic occupations, the Classic Maya in general thought of their dynasty as being Early Classic, rather than Late Preclassic in origin. This oddity of dating may be the result of the little collapse that occurred at around 50 BC. Tonina appears to have been a polity of the Late Classic period only, since it has no date earlier than 9.8.0.0.0 (AD 593).

Each of the large western polities spawned a series of satellite population centers ruled by cahals or ahaus subordinate to the main kings. Yaxchilan had La Pasadita and Laxtunich, Piedras Negras had

El Cayo, and Palenque had Xupa, Miraflores, and Tortuguero. These cahals had the right from the beginning of the Classic period to commission and display monuments recording their own history, but these were always mounted only at their home sites or within their own residential compounds. By 9.16.0.0.0 (AD 751) at Yaxchilan and Piedras Negras, cahals are given billing with the high kings on public monuments commissioned by the kings. I suggest that this practice represents a change in political adaption responding to growing pressures on central authority from ecological, population, and social pressures.

The growing concentration on scenes of warfare and captive sacrifice in public space suggests that the western polities were engaged in constant warfare. Certainly the inscriptions record interactions of alliance and intermarriage between Bonampak and Yaxchilan and between Yaxchilan and Piedras Negras. In this fractured world, Tonina apparently coalesced as a polity in the low hills overlooking the Lacandon forest and the sustaining areas in the valleys south of Palenque. The military campaigns of the third king resulted in the capture and sacrifice of the contemporary king of Palenque, and it resulted in an ahau of Bonampak (perhaps even the king himself) recording in a public inscription that he was the vassal of the king of Tonina.

The intense warfare combined with other pressures from many different sources resulted in collapse in the three major polities and their satellites by 9.18.10.0.0 (AD 800) to 9.19.0.0.0 (AD 810). Seibal, Machaquila, and other sites in the Pasion had kings ruling during the first two katuns of Cycle 10 (AD 830–69), although at Seibal, they seem to have been invaders who moved into the vacuum left by the earlier defeat of Seibal by Dos Pilas. Yet while the great polities of the Usumacinta had dissipated by AD 800, Tonina, which had long been a predator on its lowland neighbors, survived in relative splendor to record the latest Long Count date known – 10.4.0.0.0 (AD 909).

*NOTES*

1. As fellows at Dumbarton Oaks in 1975, Robert Rands and I conducted a detailed study of archaeological, ceramic, and epigraphic data to reconstruct a history of Palenque. Although deep archaeology prior to AD 500 is not available for Palenque, we found consistent and detailed correspondences between

independently derived sets of ceramic, architectural, and epigraphic evidence.

2. Thompson (1950:161) read the normal "successor" glyph (T573) as *hel*, "change, successor". This suggested reading is used generally as the nickname of this glyph, but more recent evidence from its phonetic complements and its usages support a reading of *tz'ak*, the term used for "succession" in the Acalan document. The glyph Mathews first identified as "successor" at Yaxchilan is not T573. Rather it is T676, a glyph which can occur in Distance Numbers as "changeover" of days. No reading has been proposed for this glyph.
3. Following Mathews (1985), Jones (this volume) calculates the average reign between the 11th and 29th successor at 19.3 years. The Palenque data from the histories of fourteen rulers, most with a death or birth date combined with an accession date, gives the even higher average of 23.2. I have used a twenty-year average because this falls within known averages at these Maya sites and in many other pre-industrial civilizations around the world. If this average proves to be overly long, however, the reconstructed dates would fall one Calendar Round later.
4. This same lord appears on Naranjo Stela 25 (Stuart and Houston, personal communication 1989) associated with the earliest date of Naranjo Ruler 1. I suspect the Naranjo date (9.5.12.0.4) was the accession of Ruler 1. If so, then Naranjo St. 25 records that it happened, *u cab*, "in the land of", the Site Q ruler.
5. Indeed, Group 6G-XVI at Tikal (Laporte 1988) seems to have been the compound of just this sort of noble, but not royal, lineage. The protagonist of the text found on a Teotihuacan-style ball court maker calls himself the "ahau of" the high king of Tikal.
6. I have not included dates from the Laxtunich monuments because they are looted and I do not have reproductions available adequate to calculate the dates or actions. This is the famous and mysterious Lamb site (Lamb and Lamb 1951).
7. Palenque's history was reconstructed in a series of mini-conferences sponsored by Dumbarton Oaks between 1974 and 1979. Floyd Lounsbury, Peter Mathews, Merle Robertson, David Kelley, and Linda Schele were the original collaborators, but the study subsequently expanded to include David Stuart, Kathryn Josserand, and Nicholas Hopkins. Much of the argument is presented in the Palenque Round Table Series and in the series of workbooks from the Texas Workshop on Maya Hieroglyphic Writing.

8. The Tablet of the Cross text uses the *ta* spelling (T102) of this locative.
9. David Stuart in a letter to me dated in April 1988 suggested this reading for the T18:565:88 as "sibling". I have checked its occurrence throughout the corpus and found it to be an extemely productive reading that I now accept.
10. In earlier analyses of the Palace Tablet (Lounsbury, personal communication 1975; Schele 1979, 1982), we have proposed Xoc to be a ruler, but subsequent decipherments by Stuart (personal communication 1986) and Schele (1987) make it clear that Xoc never acceded to office. His role was to dedicate the house, probably after Kan-Xul's capture. There is nothing in his names or the events of his life to support his service in the role of ruler.
11. This turtleshell glyph does not have the ahau glyph required for an Emblem Glyph title so that it may simply be part of this lord's name.
12. Stephen Houston (1983) pointed out this occurrence of Ruler 5 at El Cayo in his discussion of Piedras Negras Ruler 5 and 6. David Stuart (personal communication in a letter dated March 1987) proposed this reading of T575.86:671. I have found that reading a productive one and accept it. Houston (1983) proposed that Ruler 5 and 6 were in fact the same person. He may be correct, but the name at the end of the text on Stela 16 recurs on the back of Throne 1 in what I think may be a parentage record. For the time being I am following Proskouriakoff's (1960) proposal of two rulers, while recognizing that the "Macaw-GI/Rabbit/Cauac Ahau" named on the two monuments is a person who was not a ruler.
13. David Stuart (1986a) has identified the *lu-bat* phrases on monuments as signatures of the sculptors.

| | Yaxchilan<br>Bonampak | Palenque<br>Tortuguero | Piedras Negras<br>El Cayo | Tonina |
|---|---|---|---|---|
| 8.14 (317) | | | | |
| | **8.14.2.17.6?? Penis-Jaguar, the lineage founder, accedes** | | | |
| | | | **Ah Cauac Turtleshell acts at Yaxchilan** | |
| 8.15 (327) | | | | |
| | **2nd successor (Shield-Jaguar I)** | | | |
| | | 8.15.16.0.5 unknown event at Tortuguero | | |
| 8.16 (357) | | | | |
| 8.17 (376) | | | | |
| | **8.17.1.17.16 Bird-Jaguar I, the 3rd successor, accedes** | | | |
| | 8.17.2.11.5 foreigner acts at Yaxchilan | | | |
| | **8.17.13.3.8?? Yax-Antler-Skull, the 4th successor, accedes** | | | |
| 8.18 (396) | | | | |
| | | 8.18.0.13.6 Kuk I born (lineage founder) | | |
| | 5th successor | | | |
| 8.19 (416) | | | | |
| | **6th successor (Tah-Skull I)** | | | |
| | Bird-Jaguar of Bonampak acts at Yaxchilan | | | |
| | | 8.19.6.8.8 Casper born | | |
| | | **8.19.15.3.4 Kuk I accedes** | | |
| | | **8.19.19.11.17 Casper accedes** | | |
| 9. 0 (435) | | | | |
| | **7th successor (Moon-Skull I)** | | | |
| | | | **Turtleshell acts at Yaxchilan** | |
| | 9.0.19.2.4 house event of Moon-Skull I (7th) | | | |
| 9. 1 (455) | | | | |
| | | 9.1.4.5.0 Manik born | | |
| | | 9.1.10.0.0 Chaacal I born | | |
| | **8th successor (Bird-Jaguar II)** | | | |

| | Yaxchilan<br>Bonampak | Palenque<br>Tortuguero | Piedras Negras<br>El Cayo | Tonina |
|---|---|---|---|---|
| | | | Zac-Imix, ahau of the king Turtleshell acts at Yaxchilan | |
| 9. 2 (475) | | | | |
| | | **9.2.12.6.18 Manik accedes** | | |
| | | 9.2.15.3.8 Kan-Xul I born | | |
| | **9th successor (Knot-eye Jaguar)** | | | |
| | Yax-Uc and Kan-Te, ahaus of the king Fish-Fin of Bonampak act at Yaxchilan | | | |
| 9. 3 (495) | | | | |
| | **9.3.0.14.13 dedication of monument by Fish-Fin of Bonampak** | | | |
| | 9.3.3.16.4 dedication of lineage house by Fish-Fin | | | |
| | | **9.3.6.7.17 Chaacal I accedes** | | |
| | 9.3.13.12.19 Ah Balam, ahau of the king Jaguar Paw-Skull of Tikal acts at Yaxchilan | | | |
| | | | **9.3.16.0.5 Ahau-in-hand rite for Ah Cauac Ah K'in** | |
| | | | **9.3.19.12.12 Ruler C does event** | |
| 9. 4 (514) | PE by Knot-eye Jaguar | PE by Chaacal I | | |
| | | | 9.4.3.0.17 Ruler C does event | |
| | 9.4.3.10.1 Knot-eye Jaguar acts at Piedras Negras | | 9.4.3.10.1 Ruler C does event | |
| | 9.4.8.14.9 event of Fish-Fin of Bonampak | | | |
| | | 9.4.9.0.4 Chaacal II born | | |
| | | 9.4.10.1.5 Chan-Bahlum I born | | |
| | | 9.4.10.4.17 Chaacal I dies | | |
| | **9.4.11.8.16 Tah-Skull II the 10th successor accedes** | | | |
| | Knot-eye Jaguar of Bonampak named in Yaxchilan text | | | |
| | | **9.4.14.0.4 Kan-Xul I accedes** | | |
| 9. 5 (534) | | PE by Kan-Xul | PE at Piedras Negras | |
| | 9.5.2.10.6 Yaxchilan event associated with an ahau of Site Q | | | |
| | | | **9.5.5.0.0 Ruler D PE** | |
| 9. 6 (554) | | PE by Kan-Xul | | |
| | | | 9.6.6.8.19? Ruler D does flint event | |
| | 9.6.10.14.15 Knot-eye Jaguar captures Etz'nab-Bat | | | |

| | Yaxchilan<br>Bonampak | Palenque<br>Tortuguero | Piedras Negras<br>El Cayo | Tonina |
|---|---|---|---|---|
| | | 9.6.11.0.16 Kan-Xul I dies | | |
| | | **9.6.11.5.1 Chaacal II accedes** | | |
| | | 9.6.16.10.7 Chaacal II dies | | |
| | | **9.6.18.5.12 Chan-Bahlum I accedes** | | |
| 9. 7 (573) | | 9.7.0.0.0 PE by Chan-Bahlum | | |
| | | 9.7.9.5.5 Chan-Bahlum I dies | | |
| | | **9.7.10.3.8 Lady Kanal-Ikal accedes** | | |
| 9. 8 (593) | PE at Yaxchilan & Lacanja | 9.8.0.0.0 PE by L. Kanal-Ikal | | 9.8.0.0.0 PE by Ruler 1 |
| | | 9.8.9.13.0 Pacal I born | | |
| | **9.8.9.15.11 star-shell war event by Muan-Chaan of Bonampak** | | | |
| 9.8.10 (603) | | | | |
| | | | 9.8.10.4.9 Ruler 1 does pre-accession rite | |
| | | | **9.8.10.6.16 Ruler 1 accedes** | |
| | | 9.8.11.6.12 Lady Kanal-Ikal dies | | |
| | | **9.8.11.9.0 Ac-Kan accedes** | | |
| | | | 9.8.13.10.0 Ruler 1 event | |
| | | | 9.8.15.0.0 Ruler's 1 PE | |
| | | 9.8.17.9.0 event | | |
| | | 9.8.17.15.14 event | | |
| | | 9.8.18.14.11 Pacal I dies | | |
| | | 9.8.19.4.6 Ac-Kan dies | | |
| | | 9.8.19.10.5 Ahpo-Balam born | | |
| | | **9.8.19.7.18 Lady Zac-Kuk accedes** | | |
| 9. 9 (613) | | 9.9.0.0.0 PE by L. Zac-Kuk | | |
| | | **9.9.2.4.8 Pacal II accedes** | | |
| | | | | **9.9.2.4.18 Ruler 1a erected M74** |
| | | 9.9.6.10.19 House C event | | |
| | | | 9.9.8.0.0 Ruler 1? event | |

| | Yaxchilan<br>Bonampak | Palenque<br>Tortuguero | Piedras Negras<br>El Cayo | Tonina |
|---|---|---|---|---|
| 9.9.10 (623) | | | | |
| | | | 9.9.11.12.3 Ruler 1? event | |
| | | 9.9.13.0.17 Lady Ahpo-Hel takes office | | |
| | | | 9.9.13.4.1 Ruler 2 born | |
| | | | 9.9.15.0.0 Ruler 1's PE | |
| | **9.9.16.10.13 6-Tun-BJ accedes** | | | |
| | | | 9.9.18.6.10 Ruler 1 event | |
| 9.10 (633) | | PE by Pacal | | Ruler 1a? erects stela (F34) |
| | | 9.10.2.6.6 Chan-Bahlum II born | | |
| | | | | 9.10.3.5.0 eroded (M75) |
| | | | 9.10.5.0.0 Ruler 1's PE | |
| | | | 9.10.6.2.1 Ruler 1 dies | |
| | | | **9.10.6.5.9 Ruler 2 accedes** | |
| | | | 9.10.6.6.4 Ruler 2 event | |
| | | 9.10.7.13.5 Lady Zac-Kuk dies | | |
| | | 9.10.8.9.3 Chan-Bahlum II is made heir | | |
| 9.10.10 (642) | | | | |
| | | 9.10.10.1.6 Pacal's father dies | | |
| | | | 9.10.10.8.14 Cahal Turtleshell-Death born | |
| | | **9.10.11.3.10 Ahpo-Balam accedes** | | |
| | | 9.10.11.9.6 Star-war of Ahpo-Balam | | |
| | | 9.10.11.15.4 Star-war of Ahpo-Balam | | |
| | | 9.10.11.17.0 Kan-Xul II is born | | |
| | | 9.10.12.3.10 Axe-war of Ahpo-Balam | | |
| | | | | 9.10.12.15.4 eroded (M75) |
| | | 9.10.13.0.0 PE at Tortuguero | | |
| | | 9.10.14.5.10 unknown event for Pacal | | |
| | 9.10.14.13.0 6-Tun-BJ captures a lord of an unidentified site | | | |
| | | 9.10.15.1.11 K'a event of Ahpo-Balam | | |

| | Yaxchilan | Bonampak | Palenque | Tortuguero | Piedras Negras | El Cayo | Tonina |
|---|---|---|---|---|---|---|---|
| | | | | | 9.10.15.2.15 Ruler 2 event | | |
| | | | | 9.10.16.13.6 Axe-war of Ahpo-Balam | | | |
| | | | | 9.10.17.1.2 capture and axe event | | | |
| | | | | 9.10.17.2.14 Star-war, capture, and ballgame of Ahpo-Balam | | | |
| | | | 9.10.17.6.0 Xoc born | | | | |
| | | | 9.10.18.17.19 Kan-Xul II's deerhoof event | | | | |
| | | | | | 9.10.19.5.9 13-tun anniversary of Ruler 2's accession | | |
| 9.11 (652) | | | 9.11.0.0.0 Pacal scatters | | | | |
| | | | | | 9.11.0.3.13 Ruler 3 born | | |
| | | | 9.11.1.12.8 13 haab anniversary of Chan-Bahlum's heir designation | | | | |
| | | | 9.11.1.16.3 war-axe event again Site Q? | | | | |
| | | | 9.11.2.1.11 dedication of House E | | | | |
| | | | | 9.11.3.3.10 12-tun anniversary of Ahpo-Balam's accession | | | |
| | | | 9.11.4.7.0 ancestor event for Pacal and Kan-Xul | | | | |
| | | | | | | | 9.11.5.0.0 scattering by (missing) |
| | | | | | 9.11.6.1.8 Ruler 2 kin-helmet event | | |
| | | | | | 9.11.6.2.1 Ruler 2 ahau-in-hand event | | |
| | | | 9.11.6.16.11 war event with Yaxchilan | | | | |
| | | | 9.11.6.16.17 bloodletting? of Pacal | | | | |
| | | | | | 9.11.9.8.12 Ruler 2 Venus war | | |
| 9.11.10 (662) | | | | | 9.11.10.0.0 Ruler 2 PE | | |
| | | | | | 9.11.12.7.2 Ruler 3 born | | |
| | | | | | | | 9.11.12.9.0 (missing) |
| | | | | | | | 9.11.12.17.0 event by Ruler 2 |
| | | | 9.11.13.0.0 ahau-in-hand Kan-Xul II | | | | |
| | | | | | 9.11.15.0.0 Ruler 2 PE | | |
| | | | | | 9.11.16.0.1 Ruler 2 accedes | | |
| | 9.11.16.2.8 6-Tun-Bird-Jaguar plays ball | | | | | | |
| | | | | 9.11.16.8.18 event at Tortuguero | | | |

| | Yaxchilan<br>Bonampak | Palenque<br>Tortuguero | Piedras Negras<br>El Cayo | Tonina |
|---|---|---|---|---|
| | | | 9.11.16.11.6 Ruler 2 Venus war | |
| | | 9.11.18.9.17 birth of Chac-Zutz' | | |
| | 9.11.18.15.1 Shield-Jaguar does a house event | | | |
| 9.12 (672) | | PE by Pacal | | Ruler 2 scatters and erects M113, M26 |
| | | 9.12.0.6.8 Lady Ahpo-Hel dies | | |
| | | | 9.12.2.0.16 Lady Katun-Ahau born | |
| | | 9.12.3.6.6 bloodletting by Pacal | | |
| | | | | 9.12.5.0.0 Ruler 2 PE |
| | | 9.12.6.5.18 Chaacal III born | | |
| | | | 9.12.6.5.9 Ruler 2 event | |
| | | 9.12.6.17.18 Ahpo-Balam dies | | |
| | | 9.12.7.0.0 Ahpo-Balam's burial?? | | |
| | | **9.12.7.1.19 accession of Muan-X** | | |
| | | **9.12.7.14.7 accession of Ah Ka'-Balam** | | |
| | | 9.12.8.10.0 Chaacal's father dies | | |
| | 9.12.8.14.1 Shield-Jaguar captures Ah Ahaual | | | |
| | | 9.12.9.7.12 house event of Ah Ka'-Balam | | |
| | 9.12.9.8.1 Shield-Jaguar accedes | | | |
| 9.12.10 (682) | | 9.12.10.0.0 Pacal PE | 9.12.10.0.0 Ruler 2 PE and presentation of captives | |
| | | 9.12.11.5.18 Pacal II dies | | |
| | **9.12.11.6.9 Ah Na-Chu-? accedes at Bonampak** | | | |
| | | **9.12.11.12.10 Chan-Bahlum accedes** | | |
| | | | 9.12.14.10.11 L. Katun-Ahau betrothed | |
| | | | 9.12.14.10.14 Ruler 2 dies | |
| | | | 9.12.14.10.17 + 1 L. Katun-Ahau lets blood | |
| | | | 9.12.14.11.1 Ruler 2 is buried | |
| | | | **9.12.14.13.1 Ruler 3 accedes** | |
| | | | 9.12.15.0.0 Ruler 3 PE | |
| | | | | **9.12.16.3.12 Ruler 3 accedes** |

| | Yaxchilan<br>Bonampak | Palenque<br>Tortuguero | Piedras Negras<br>El Cayo | Tonina |
|---|---|---|---|---|
| | 9.12.17.12.0 Shield-Jaguar captures Ah Zac-Chi-Pa-Ta | | | |
| | | | 9.12.17.13.1 Cahal Turtleshell-Death celebrates 3-tun anniversary of PN Ruler 3 | |
| | | 9.12.18.5.16 + Chan-Bahlum dedicates Grp. Cross | | |
| | | | 9.12.19.0.0 Ruler 3 PE | |
| | | 9.12.19.14.12 Chan-Bahlum bring god to their houses | | |
| 9.13 (692) | | | | Ruler 3 erects M21 |
| | | 9.13.0.4.12 Stone incensario cached in Grp. Cross | | |
| | | 9.13.0.7.0 Chaacal III's deerhoof event | | |
| | | | | 9.13.2.8.0 Ruler 3 does a kin-bowl event |
| | | 9.13.2.9.0 Chaacal III does event | | |
| | | | | 9.13.2.13.7 Ruler 3 plays the ballgame |
| | | | 9.13.3.15.13 Ruler 3 does event | |
| | | | 9.13.5.0.0 Ruler 3 PE | 9.13.5.0.0 Ruler 3 PE |
| | | | **9.13.5.2.9 Turtleshell-Death accedes as cahal** | |
| | | | | 9.13.7.6.5 Ruler 3 does event |
| | | | | 9.13.8.6.10 Ruler 3 does the mirror-in-hand event |
| | 9.13.9.14.14 Shield-Jaguar captures Ah Kan | | | |
| | | | 9.13.9.14.15 Ruler 4 born | |
| 9.13.10 (702) | | | 9.13.10.0.0 Ruler 3 PE | |
| | | 9.13.10.1.5 Chan-Bahlum dies | | |
| | | **9.13.10.6.8 Kan-Xul II accedes** | | |
| | 9.13.13.12.5 Lady Pacal dies | | | |
| | | 9.13.13.15.0 Chan-Bahlum leaves Xibalba | | |
| | | 9.13.14.8.0 Xoc takes mirror | | |
| | | | 9.13.14.11.1 Ruler 3 ahau-in-hand | |
| | | | 9.13.14.13.1 Ruler 3 1-katun anniversary | |
| | | | 9.13.15.0.0 Ruler 3 PE | 9.13.15.0.0 Ruler 3 PE |

| | Yaxchilan<br>Bonampak | Palenque<br>Tortuguero | Piedras Negras<br>El Cayo | Tonina |
|---|---|---|---|---|
| | | | 9.13.16.4.6 L. Ahpo-K'in born | |
| | 9.13.17.12.10 Bird-Jaguar born | | | |
| | | 9.13.17.15.12 Lady Xoc lets blood | | |
| | 9.13.17.15.13 Lady Ik-Skull in bundle rite | | | |
| | | | 9.13.19.13.1 L. Katun-Ahau ahau-in-hand rite | |
| | | | | 9.13.19.13.3 Ruler 3 captures Kan-Xul of Palenque |
| | | | 9.13.19.14.15 Ruler 4 born | |
| 9.14 (711) | | | | |
| | 9.14.1.17.14 Shield-Jaguar captures Ah Kan | | | |
| | | | 9.14.2.11.9 Ruler 3 event | |
| | 9.14.3.8.4 Etz'nab-Jawbone of Bonampak, the ahau of Ruler 3 of Tonina, dedicates an object | | | |
| | | | 9.14.5.0.0 Ruler 3 PE | **9.14.5.0.0 Ruler 4 PE** |
| | | 9.14.8.14.15 Xoc dedicates House AD of the Palace | | |
| | | | 9.14.9.7.2 Ruler 3's 57-tun birthday | |
| 9.14.10 (721) | | | 9.14.10.0.0 Ruler 3 PE | 9.14.10.0.0 Ruler 4 PE |
| | | **9.14.10.4.2 Chaacal III accedes** | | |
| | | 9.14.11.2.7 Kan-Xul leaves Xibalba | | |
| | | 9.14.11.12.14 Chac-Zutz' become governor | | |
| | 9.14.11.15.1 dedication of house sculpture by Lady Xoc | | | |
| | | 9.14.11.17.6 Chac-Zutz' captures Knot-Manik | | |
| | 9.14.12.6.12 sculpting of Lintel 26 finished | | | |
| | | | 9.14.12.7.2 Ruler 3's 3-katun birthday | |
| | | 9.14.13.11.2 axe-war by Chac-Zutz' | | |
| | 9.14.14.8.1 25-tun anniversary of reign for Shield-Jaguar | | | |
| | | | 9.14.14.9.18 Ruler 3 event | |
| | 9.14.14.13.17 dedication of Structure 23 by Lady Xoc | | | |
| | | | | **9.14.15.0.0 Ruler 5 PE** |
| | | | | 9.14.15.10.9 Ruler 5 erects M30 |

| | Yaxchilan<br>Bonampak | Palenque<br>Tortuguero | Piedras Negras<br>El Cayo | Tonina |
|---|---|---|---|---|
| | | | | 9.14.17.2.7 Ruler 5 does event |
| | 9.14.17.4.6? Birth of Knot-eye Jaguar | | | |
| | | | | 9.14.17.9.0 Ruler 5 scatters |
| | | 9.14.17.12.18 axe-war by Chac-Zutz' | | |
| | 9.14.17.15.11 Shield-Jaguar capture Ah Chuen | | | |
| | | 9.14.18.1.1 Chac-Zutz' does event | | |
| | | | **9.14.18.3.13 Ruler 4 accedes** | |
| | | | 9.14.18.5.7 Cahal Turtleshell-Death dies at El Cayo | |
| | | 9.14.18.9.8 Chac-Zutz' does event | | |
| | | 9.14.18.9.17 3-katun birthday of Chac-Zutz' | | |
| | 9.14.18.14.18 bloodletting by Shield-Jaguar | | | |
| | | | 9.14.18.15.1 unknown event at El Cayo | |
| 9.15 (731) | | | | |
| | 9.15.0.12.0 Shield-Jaguar captures Na-Cauac-Manik | | | |
| | | | **9.15.1.6.3 new cahal accedes at El Cayo** | |
| | | | | 9.15.3.7.5 Ruler 5 dies |
| | | | 9.15.3.8.0 unknown event at El Cayo | |
| | | | | 9.15.4.2.5 Ruler 5's apotheosis |
| | | | 9.15.5.0.0 Ruler 4 PE | 9.15.5.0.0 Ruler 6 PE |
| | | | 9.15.5.0.5 Ruler 4 event | |
| | | | 9.15.5.3.13 Ruler 4 7-tun anniversary | |
| | 9.15.6.13.1 Dedication of Structure 11 by Lady Rodent-Bone | | | |
| | 9.15.9.3.14 Knot-eye Jaguar of Bonampak takes a captive in the land of Lacanja | | | |
| | 9.15.9.17.16 Shield-Jaguar does staff event | | | |
| 9.15.10 (741) | | | 9.15.10.0.0 Ruler 4 PE | |
| | 9.15.10.0.1 major bloodletting event for Bird-Jaguar, his wife, mother, and brother-in-law | | | |
| | 9.15.10.17.14 Shield-Jaguar dies | | | |
| | 9.15.11.17.3 Lacanja cahal accedes | | | |
| | 9.15.13.6.9 Bird-Jaguar lets blood and plays the ballgame | | | |

| | Yaxchilan<br>Bonampak | Palenque<br>Tortuguero | Piedras Negras<br>El Cayo | Tonina |
|---|---|---|---|---|
| | | | 9.15.14.9.13 Ruler 4 event | |
| | 9.15.15.0.0 Lacanja cahal celebrates PE | | 9.15.15.0.0 Ruler 4 PE | |
| | 9.15.17.15.14 Lady Xoc dies | | | |
| | 9.15.18.3.13 Yaxchilan lord goes to PN | | 9.15.18.3.13 Ruler 4's 1-katun anniversary | |
| | | | 9.15.18.16.7 Ruler 7 born | |
| | 9.15.19.14.3 Bird-Jaguar's mother dies | | | |
| 9.16 (751) | | | | |
| | 9.16.0.13.17 Bird-Jaguar captures Chac-Cib-Tok' | | | |
| | 9.16.0.14.5 Bird-Jaguar's heir is born and is celebrated by bloodletting | | | |
| | **9.16.1.0.0 Bird-Jaguar accedes** | | | |
| | 9.16.1.0.9 Bird-Jaguar does the 4-Bat rite | | | |
| | 9.16.1.2.0 Bird-Jaguar does God K rite and tree-staff rite | | | |
| | 9.16.1.8.6 Bird-Jaguar does the basket rite with a cahal | | | |
| | 9.16.4.1.1 Bird-Jaguar captures Jewelled-Skull; his cahal captures Ahpo-Muluc | | | |
| 9.16.4.3.16 4- | | | Pa-na-ca is born at El Cayo | |
| | | | | 9.16.5.4.9 Ruler 8 born |
| | 9.16.6.13.1 Structure 24 is dedicated | | | |
| | 9.16.5.0.0 BJ lets blood at La Pasadita with his cahal | | 9.16.5.0.0 Ruler 4 PE | |
| | 9.16.6.0.0 Bird-Jaguar celebrates his 5th tun in office with his heir in the tree-staff rite | | | |
| | | | 9.16.6.9.16 Bat-Jaguar of Yax in bundle event | |
| | | | 9.16.6.10.19 Bat-Jaguar acts at PN | |
| | | | 9.16.6.11.17 Ruler 4 dies | |
| | | | 9.16.6.12.0 Ruler 4 is buried | |
| | | | **9.16.6.17.17 Ruler 5 accedes** | |
| 9.16.10 (761) | Bird-Jaguar scatters at Yaxchilan | | | |
| | | | | 9.16.10.16.13 event |
| | | | 9.16.12.2.6 dedication event at El Cayo | |
| | | | 9.16.12.4.10 Ah Chac-Zotz' accedes as cahal at El Cayo | |
| | | | **9.16.12.10.8 Ruler 6 accedes** | |
| | 9.16.13.0.0 Bird-Jaguar dedicates Structure 10 | | | |

| | Yaxchilan<br>Bonampak | Palenque<br>Tortuguero | Piedras Negras<br>El Cayo | Tonina |
|---|---|---|---|---|
| | | **9.16.13.0.7 Kuk II accedes** | | |
| | 9.16.15.0.0 Bird-Jaguar celebrates with the God K rite | | | |
| | 9.16.15.18.9 Bird-Jaguar sacrifices Ek'-Chan | | | |
| | 9.16.16.1.6 Bird-Jaguar does the staff rite | | | |
| | 9.16.17.2.4 Lady Ahpo-Ik' lets blood to dedicate Structure 21 | | | |
| | 9.16.17.6.12 Bird-Jaguar does the staff event | | | |
| 9.17 (771) | Shield-Jaguar II scatters? | | | |
| | | | 9.17.1.5.9 4-Pa-na-ca accedes as cahal at El Cayo | |
| | | | | 9.17.4.12.5 Ruler 7 dies |
| | **9.17.5.8.9 Muan-Chaan accedes** | | | |
| | | | | 9.17.5.17.5 apotheosis of Ruler 7 |
| | | | 9.17.9.5.1 Ruler 7 Venus war | |
| 9.17.10 (780) | Muan-Chaan scatters | | | |
| | | | 9.17.10.6.1 Ruler 7 event | |
| | | | **9.17.10.9.4 Ruler 7 accedes** | |
| | | 9.17.13.0.7 1-katun anniversary of Kuk's accession | | |
| | 9.17.16.3.8 Shield-Jaguar II of Yaxchilan captures Bat (recorded at Bonampak) | | | |
| | 9.17.16.3.12 Muan-Chaan captures "He of 5 Captives" | | | |
| | | | 9.17.16.14.19 Ruler 7 conquers Pomona | |
| | | | | 9.17.18.13.9 Ruler 8 does event |
| | 9 17.18.15.18 Muan-Chaan's mother lets blood | | | |
| 9.18 (790) | | | | 9.18.0.0.0 Ruler 8 PE |
| | 9.18.0.3.4 heir-designation of Muan Chaan's son at Bonampak | | | |
| | 9.18.1.2.0 dedication of Temple 1 | | | |
| | 9.18.1.15.5 Venus-war at Bonampak (Room 2) | | | |
| | | | | 9.18.2.13.3 Ruler 8 does event |
| | | | | 9.18.3.10.17 event |
| | | | 9.18.4.16.7 Ruler 7's 46th tun birthday | |
| | | | 9.18.5.0.0 Ruler 7 PE | |
| | 9.18.6.4.19 Shield-Jaguar II captures a lord | | | |

| | Yaxchilan<br>Bonampak | Palenque<br>Tortuguero | Piedras Negras<br>El Cayo | Tonina |
|---|---|---|---|---|
| | 9.18.6.5.11 Shield-Jaguar II captures a lord | | | |
| | 9.18.7.6.0 Shield-Jaguar II captures a lord | | | |
| | | | | 9.18.7.9.0 event |
| | | | | 9.18.7.13.0 event |
| | 9.18.7.16.9 Shield-Jaguar II does a deer event | | | |
| | 9.18.8.3.3 Shield-Jaguar II captures Ah-Zac-? | | | |
| | 9.18.8.10.12 Shield-Jaguar II does a "changeover" event | | | |
| | | 9.18.9.4.4 6-Cimi-Pacal accedes | | |
| | 9.18.9.6.6 Shield-Jaguar II captures God K-Cleft Sky | | | |
| | 9.18.9.9.14 Shield-Jaguar II captures a lord | | | |
| | 9.18.9.10.10 Shield-Jaguar II captures Ahpo-Pah | | | |
| 9.18.10 (800) | | | | |
| | | | | 9.18.15.15.0 Ruler 8 erects M95 |
| | 9.18.17.12.6 Tah-Skull III has Venus-war; captures Turtle-Bat | | | |
| | 9.18.17.13.10 Tah-Skull III does a balan-ahau event | | | |
| | 9.18.17.13.14 Tah-Skull III does a God K event | | | |
| 9.19 (810) | | | | |
| 10.0 (830) | | | | 10.0.7.9.0 Ruler 9 event |
| 10.1 (849) | | | | |
| 10.2 (869) | | | | |
| 10.3 (899) | | | | |
| 10.4 (909) | | | | 10.4.0.0.0 Ruler 10 PE |

# 5
# Cycles of growth at Tikal

CHRISTOPHER JONES

The decipherment of historical information from Maya monuments allows us to write a more detailed descriptive history of the Classic period. The hieroglyphic texts point to precise beginnings of reigns, conflicts between communities, visitations, genealogy, sovereign rulers and lesser lords. The carved portraits and scenes accompanying these texts enrich the written information with specific illustration of costume, hand-held objects, ritual actions and named captives, women, companions, and deceased ancestors. Taken together, the art and the inscriptions tell us much about individual rulers, the history of the sites, and even the social organization of the Classic Maya. As decipherment progresses, more and more of the unread statements will become accepted as real information.

The archaeological excavation of sites produces a set of data complementary to that of hieroglyphs and art. Although excavators have been able to date buildings by associated texts, the potential link between excavation and epigraphy has been slow in realization. For example, the earliest site to be excavated with a concentration on stratigraphy, Uaxactun, unfortunately had few surviving inscriptions linked to architecture and still has no named rulers.

Stratigraphic excavations allow an archaeologist to make statements of superimposition and, under certain circumstances, of contemporaneity as well. If a floor is seen to abut a wall in such a way that it covers an unplastered layer of fill under the wall, then a judgment can be made by the archaeologist that the floor completed the structure. The time-span between wall and floor, although a reality, can be judged negligible. In this way, passing from structure base to floor to structure base and so forth, observing junctures at every point, one can at times conclude that some structures and floors were to all intents and purposes contemporaries, parts of a single large construction project finished by widespread plaster floorings. Hammond (1975a:62) termed such programs *work projects*.

During the fourteen years of active Tikal Project excavation (1956–70), one of the principal research focuses was that of deep stratigraphy, especially as pursued by William R. Coe for the North Acropolis/Great Plaza, Group 5D-2 (Coe 1965a,b; Fig. 5.1). The strategy of the wide deep central trench and side tunnels in the Acropolis and the many long narrow trenches of the North Terrace and Great Plaza was to link platforms, structures, and stelae into a unified stratigraphic column wherein every construction, burial, cache, and monument could be chronologically related to every other. The results of the excavation are described by Coe in detail in Tikal Report 14 (Coe 1990).

Excavations directed by the author in the East Plaza (Group 5D-3) adjacent to the Great Plaza during the 1964 and 1965 field seasons revealed a series of platform floors similar to those in the Great Plaza. These results are described in Tikal Report 16 (Jones n.d.).

An excavation by Aubrey Trik in 1960 behind and under Structure 5D-1 (Temple I) allowed a linkage of the East Plaza floors with successive terraces and floors of the Great Plaza. These connections provided an opportunity to attach Long Count dates or their approximations to the structures in the East Plaza even though no hieroglyphic dates are associated directly with them. Through this line of inquiry, the East Plaza and adjacent areas could be added to the Great Plaza/North Acropolis stratigraphic column in order to broaden our perspective of Tikal's architectural growth beyond that of its immediate center.

Application of radiocarbon dating has in the past provided absolute dates to the central Tikal stratigraphic column, especially in the Preclassic levels (Coe 1965a,b). Some of the estimates based on these

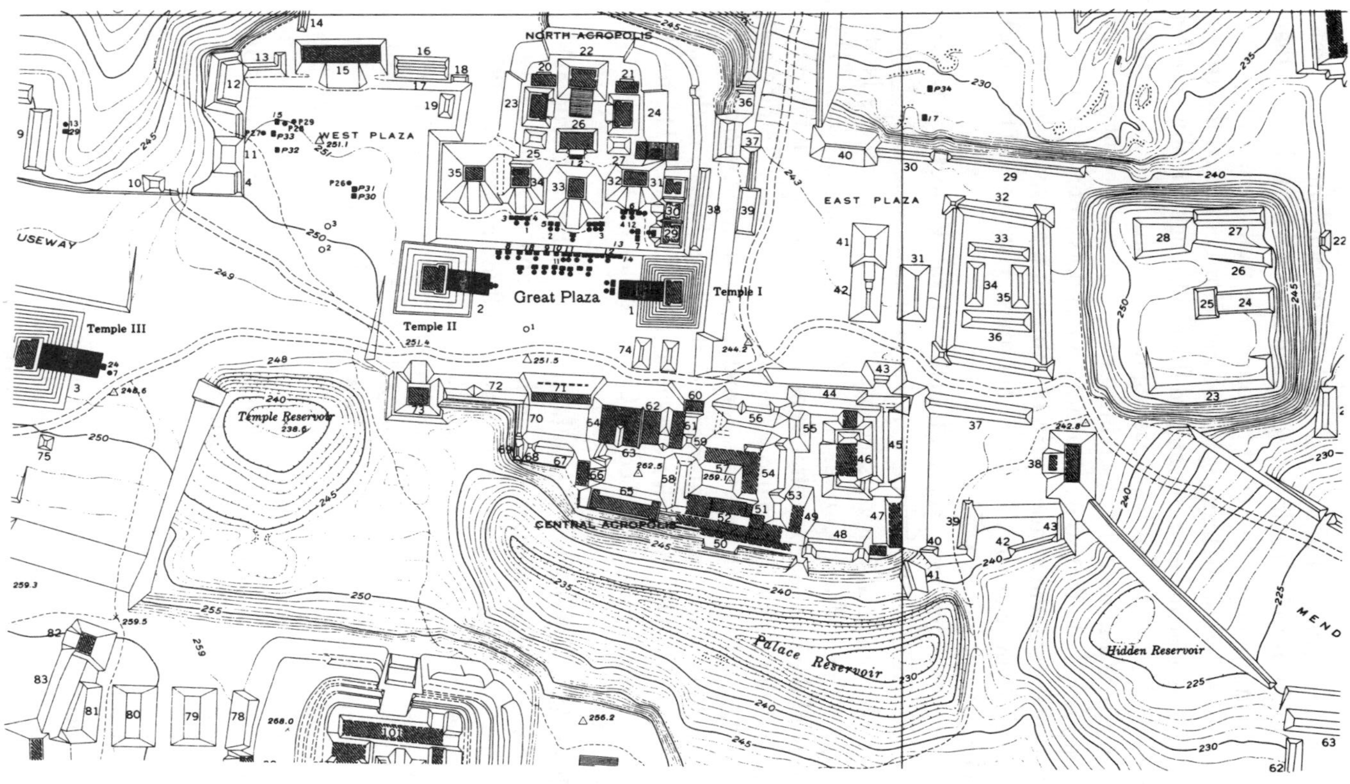


Fig. 5.1 Map of central Tikal, 1:2000 scale, from Tikal Report 11.

dates have been revised in the final report (Coe 1990). The only direct hieroglyphic dating for the group lay until recently in the 9.1.1.10.10 (AD 457) date painted on the wall of the Burial 48 chamber and the 9.13.3.0.0 (AD 695) date on Lintel 3 of Structure 5D-1 (Temple I).

Prior epigraphic studies (Coggins 1975; Jones 1977; Jones and Satterthwaite 1982) have identified historical dates and names in the Tikal inscriptions and have attempted to link burials with personages and reigns. Table 5.1 places the known Tikal rulers and their inaugural dates against a listing of successive katun (twenty-year) endings and Gregorian year equivalents. Dated inaugurals (i.e., transitions in rule) are in solid line; those for which we have no specific or approximate dates are in dashed line and are free to float a katun or more from where they are placed on the chart. Justifications for assignments of rulers to certain burials are summarized in Jones and Satterthwaite (1982:124–31).

In the attempt to connect the East Plaza constructions with those of the North Acropolis/Great Plaza area and to its burials, a cyclicity in Tikal construction seemed to emerge. At least seven times in the history of the site center (the horizontal lines on the right in Table 5.1) large-scale transformations or expansions of the site plan were effected as purposeful construction projects. Between those expansive episodes appear long periods in which efforts were concentrated on rebuilding within established themes. At times, there seemed to be correlations between the times of expansion and the presence of rulers who displayed outside connections in monument style or burial contents. This paper describes these perceived cycles of construction at Tikal, beginning with the earliest. Most of the description focuses on the East Plaza and Great Plaza/North Acropolis areas because stratigraphic interconnections are better known there. Some mention is made of the West Plaza, Central Acropolis, Twin Pyramid Groups and Great Temples when Long Count dates can be applied.

## 400 TO 200 BC

Early in this period, a building on a low south-facing platform, Structure 5D-Sub. 14-3rd, was constructed on the top of the bedrock hill (Coe 1965a:7–8). This is now dated to the mid-fourth century BC (Coe 1990). It can be considered the real beginning of the North Acropolis architecture, for subsequent versions of the complex follow its lead in focusing on a northern building which faces south. The structure was rebuilt twice prior to its demolition and replacement by Structure 5D-Sub. 1-2nd.

## 200 BC TO AD 1

Around 200 BC the Great Plaza remained unpaved. The Acropolis, however, was rebuilt many times larger than before, for the first time creating a large elevated paved platform in front of the principal structure. The new Structure 5D-Sub. 1-2nd continued to form the northern focus of the architectural complex, at first standing alone on the platform but later replaced by Structure 5D-Sub. 1 and joined by Structures 5D-Sub. 3, 4, 9, and 12-2nd through a lengthy span of architectural elaborations covering the next 200 years.

Thus these two early periods of Tikal's architectural history, not directly associated with inscriptions, seem to exhibit the 200-year cycle of expansion and consolidation exhibited in the later periods. It is interesting that the second two of the three Preclassic dates written in the façade text of Tikal Temple VI in AD 765 (1139, 457 and 156 BC) are each about fifty years away from the rough beginning dates of the two periods.

## AD 1 TO 200

The next major expansion of the site involved a refurbishing of the Acropolis (Floor 12) and the first paving of the Great Plaza (Floor 4B) as an introductory space in front of the Acropolis and Terrace. The West Plaza beside the Great Plaza also received its first pavement at this time. The East Plaza on the other side remained unplastered at first, but shortly afterward, as the Acropolis was repaved with Floor 11 and the Great Plaza with Floor 4A, the East Plaza received its initial plaster surface (Floor 5). Subsequent constructions for nearly 200 years afterward involved further reflooring of these surfaces and rebuildings of the old North Acropolis structures, 5D-22-6th replacing Sub. 1, etc.

Burials 166, 167, and 85 belong to the early years of the period following Floor 12. Coggins (1975:52–85) documents southern Maya connections in the Cauac ceramic complex pieces within these three burials and suggests that new leadership or at least new outside influences came into Tikal with them. Burial 85 is clearly the most important of the three, being both the richest and axial to the Acropolis (Coe and McGinn 1963). Present dating of Burial 85 is around seventy-five years later than the earlier estimates of 1 AD (Coe 1965a:14) but continues to be about fifty years after Floor 12 (Coe 1990).

Thus we seem to have an expansion of the site center beginning a few decades before an important burial. Responsibility for the initial paving of the Great Plaza and its adjacent West and East Plazas might have been either that of the person in Burial 85 or of an immediate predecessor. Whatever the case, new ceramic wares seem to correlate with a spurt of architectural expansion outward from the earlier limits.

By the time of Burial 85 the site center of Tikal had developed its basic pattern: a southward-facing Acropolis covering the burials of important people and crowned with a large pyramidal structure on the north, a multi-room building on the south, and one or more flanking pyramid structures. A wide terrace and stairway and a larger public gathering pavement fronted the hill to the south and in turn was flanked by east and west paved plazas of large size. There is no evidence of paved causeways leading into these side plazas this early, but the East Plaza at least is situated as a reasonable terminus for a trail leading up from the east or the southeast.

Following Burial 85 was an estimated 100-year time span (AD 75–170) in which renewal projects were again mostly confined to the North Acropolis: the laying of Floors 9, 8, and 7, two rebuildings of Structure 5D-22 (-6th and -5th) and a rebuilding of 5D-26 (-3rd). These projects pointedly maintained the forms begun earlier.

## AD 200

Another of the drastic changes in the Tikal site center occurred in the covering of Structure 5D-Sub. 3 with a broad high frontal Acropolis stairway (Coe 1965a:15–16). This provided for the first time a direct access to the top from the North Terrace and also affected a major shift in the Acropolis axis, the only one in the long history of the complex. The constructions received heavy burning just before Floor 6 continued, partially or completely, to bury the older pyramidal structures on top of the Acropolis. Floor 6 was then followed (after an estimated ten years) by Acropolis Floor 5, upon which were built new versions of the Acropolis buildings, Structures 5D-22-5th, 23-2nd.

Thus a rapid series of changes transformed the Acropolis within a time-span of thirty to forty years: the stairway, Floor 6, Floor 5 (around AD 200), and finally the new structures on the Acropolis top (Coe 1990). The changes involved continuity with the past in the retention of old Acropolis structure patterns, combined with an apparent wish to make dramatic and symbolic changes in the shift of axis, the direct-access stairway, the much larger Acropolis, and the larger structures.

Other changes occurred at Tikal at this time. Manik ceramics first made their appearance within the fills of the structures built upon Floor 5. Thus by the end of the Acropolis renovation sequence outlined above, Manik pottery had been in use long enough to have been included within the construction materials. Given the short span of time estimated between the initial reconstruction and structures, it is likely that the new ceramic type came with the beginning of the episode.

The first evidence for bas-relief carving at Tikal exists in some small fragments of carved stone found under Floor 5 and labeled Miscellaneous Stone 69 (Coe 1965a:Fig. 19; Jones and Satterthwaite 1982:Fig. 64 z-ff). The bas-relief carving suggests that the fragments derive from a stela front or an altar top. The small face on one fragment and the curl-nosed headdress on another might be from small subsidiary figures and do not in themselves imply that the monument was smaller than later Tikal stelae. In fact, the face and headdress together are similar to the human heads with curl-nose headdress which look down upon the main figures on Tikal Stela 29 (8.12.14.8.15; AD 292) and Stela 31 (9.0.10.0.0; AD 445). On Stela 36, which might be earlier than Stela 29, the main figure is himself wearing such a headdress.

Although the Miscellaneous Stone 69 carvings have been labeled Preclassic and compared to Miraflores carvings at Kaminaljuyu (Coe 1965a:17), they also fall within the range of the Early Classic Tikal style and might just as well represent the beginning of that tradition. Furthermore, the sealing of the fragments under Floor 5 does not make them earlier than Manik, since it is impossible to say that Manik ceramics were not being used at the time of the floor construction, only that they were not included within its fills.

Thus within a relatively short span of time around AD 200 marked changes took place in architecture, monument carving, and ceramic style. These changes further correlate with an interesting innovation within the historical record first pointed out by Peter Mathews (1985:31). Tikal rulers numbered themselves in a single sequence of successors, the earliest known of which is Jaguar Paw, listed as 9th ruler on an undated Manik ceramic complex cache vessel from the Central Acropolis (Coe 1965b:30). No precise inauguration date is known for Jaguar Paw. The 22nd, 27th, and 29th rulers are known by name glyph and inaugural date (on Stela 17, 21, and 22 respectively, and the 21st by name and burial (Burial 195, on MT. 216). The 11th, 13th, and 14th rulers are listed by name on a vessel of unknown provenance (Robicsek and Hales 1981:Fig. 76) in which Stormy Sky is named as 11th ruler (making his father Curl Nose a logical 10th ruler), Kan Boar's name follows with no number, a Skull name is listed as 13th, and Jaguar Paw Skull appears as 14th.

Taking the numbers at face value, there are a total of 348 tun years (360 days in length) from the inauguration date of Stormy Sky, the 11th ruler (*c.* 8.19.10.0.0; AD 426) to that of Ruler C, the 29th (9.16.17.16.4; AD 768). This makes an average reign for the eighteen rulers of 19.3 tuns each. Counting back from the 11th to a hypothetical 1st ruler, this average places the inauguration of the dynasty at 8.9.17.0.0 (AD 235). The average of 19.3 tuns is probably too short, however, considering that in the 50-tun span between the 14th and the 21st rulers, the average for seven rulers was known to drop to 7.2 tuns. By lengthening the average reign of the first ten rulers to 26 tuns, for example, one reaches a 1st ruler inauguration date of AD 170. Thus the establishment of a numbered succession at Tikal, certainly the earliest known stated establishment of a Maya dynasty in the Classic period texts, probably occurred some time around the above-mentioned changes in architecture, monument carving, and ceramics. Miscellaneous Stone 69 probably memorialized one of these first eight Tikal sovereigns.

The new leadership might have emerged out of the old leading families of Tikal, as suggested by the continuities in Tikal architecture from the Preclassic to the Classic (Coe 1965b:25–7). Lincoln (1985:55–7) has also argued that there is more continuity from Preclassic to Early Classic in Peten ceramics than has previously been recognized. Freidel and Schele (1983) have recently pointed out that Preclassic iconography and inscription are sufficiently known at this time to argue that the Early Classic Maya leadership was probably indigenous to the Peten area and that any non-Peten traits which come in are additions to a locally well-established matrix of religious concepts and symbols of political power.

As Coggins suggested a while ago (1975:59–62), the fall of the larger Preclassic site of Mirador to the north was probably caused by this new leadership centered at Tikal, Uaxactun, and perhaps other Peten sites. Thus the dramatic changes in the appearance of the Tikal Acropolis and surrounding site center seem to reflect important shifts of power throughout the Peten.

## AD 200 TO 400

The two centuries between a hypothetical 1st Ruler and Curl Nose are almost totally lacking in contemporary historical information. Stela 29, though it carries a date and a portrait, does not have a surviving name or event glyph. The Leyden Plaque tells of the inauguration of a Tikal ruler Moon Zero Bird at 8.14.3.1.12 (AD 320), a personage also mentioned in passing on the later Stela 31 (Mathews 1985:13–46). Mathews also points out that the two citings of a Jaguar Paw on Stela 31, first at 8.14.0.0.0 (AD 317) and then at 8.17.0.0.0, 60 tuns later, suggest the existence of two rulers with that name rather than just one. Because Burial 22 is stratigraphically about half-way through the 200 year period, it might not be the tomb of the later Jaguar Paw, 9th Ruler, but that of an earlier ruler, such as the man of Stela 29.

As Coe has remarked (1965b:24), early Manik tombs of the transitional Preclassic to Classic period were not found in the North Acropolis excavations. More recently, however, Juan Pedro LaPorte and Lillian Vega de Zea of the Proyecto Nacional Tikal (1986) have reported the discovery of several tombs, caches and a monument (Stela 39) from Structure 5D-86, east of the Mundo Perdido pyramid. The stela carries a 8.17.0.0.0 (AD 376) date and the name Jaguar Paw. On the basis of ceramics, they date the tombs to Manik I and II and suggest that the site of royal burials shifted temporarily from the North Acropolis to the Mundo Perdido complex. The reason for this shift is unknown, but suggests a temporary break with earlier Tikal leadership.

During the 200-year period, there is little evidence of construction in the Great Plaza or East Plaza. On the North Acropolis, however, there was a steady refurbishing of existing structures, first Structure 5D-23 and 26-1st, then 22-4th, then 22-3rd. Again, activity concentrated on rebuilding temples on the Acropolis rather than expanding or adding to the areas around it.

The Central Acropolis might have been the area of dramatic new construction activity toward the end of the period, however. The carved blackware vessel of a cache dedicatory to Structure 5D-46, the Early Classic Palace of the Central Acropolis carries the inscription: "his house, Jaguar Paw, Ruler of Tikal, 9th Ruler," indicating that the cache vessel was commemorative of the construction and that this important residence-type building was erected in that reign, which precedes the inauguration of Curl Nose at 8.17.2.16.17 (AD 379).

## AD 400

A new period of plaza repaving and architectural innovation seems to have occurred around AD 400 with the laying of a new Acropolis floor (Floor 4), a Great Plaza floor (Floor 2B) and the construction of two large structures on the east and west sides of the Great Plaza, later buried by Temples I and II (Structures 5D-1-2nd and 2-2nd). The first version of the Great Plaza ball court (Structure 5D-74-2nd) was also built with this floor. The East Plaza probably received a new flooring (Floor 3) around this time, although a strict stratigraphic contemporaneity with the other floors cannot be demonstrated because new terracing for the Great Plaza was not built at this time. The reflooring in all the areas is the first of the type called "smell floors" for the distinctive flinty odor that is given off when scratched with a trowel and that results from the use of chert fragments in the floor gravel. A Long Count fix for this extensive redesigning of the Tikal center may be provided by the fact that stratigraphically it precedes Burial 10 (Coe 1990).

Identification by Coggins (1975:144–8) of this burial as that of Curl Nose was based on the presence of ceramics judged seriationally earlier than those in the hieroglyphically dated Burial 48, a jade pendant in the shape of the curl-nosed animal of the Curl Nose name glyph, and the location of the Ruler's inaugural monument, Stela 4, in front of the tomb. The link is further confirmed by the position of the contemporary Stela 18 in the plaza in front of the tomb and by the presence of the inverted upper half of Altar 1 in front of Stela 4, indicating that the stela was not moved far to its inverted position where found (Jones and Satterthwaite 1982:14).

Although it is not clear if Structure 5D-34 was built immediately after the sealing of Burial 10 or after some intermediate constructions, the burial itself does appear to be later than the new floors. If the burial is that of Curl Nose, therefore, the floors should date from the decades just before the inauguration date of Stormy Sky at 8.19.10.0.0 (AD 436).

Curl Nose was apparently an important ruler in Tikal history. His successor and son Stormy Sky devoted a fourth of the Stela 31 inscription to him. A date on Stela 31 one year before his inauguration, 8.17.1.4.12 (AD 378), was repeated in Uaxactun and is interpreted by Mathews (1985:44) as the victory of Tikal over neighboring Uaxactun. The name of Curl Nose's father, Atl-Atl Cauac Shield, is Mexican in appearance. Whether or not Curl Nose was a foreigner from Teotihuacan or Kaminaljuyu, or a particularly outward-looking member of Tikal's own leading families, it is clear from the contents of his tomb that he was attracted to exotic ceramic styles and wares. The repaving of the three central plazas of the site, and the building of a ball court and large new east and west structures on the Great Plaza would be fitting actions for such an outward-sighted person.

It might be significant that the accession date of Copan's dynastic founder Yax-K'uk-Mo' falls around this time (Schele 1986a). The architectural expansion of Tikal's site core was perhaps mirrored in new "Classic Maya" sites, trade routes, and alliances expanding Tikal's sphere of influence. Peten Maya patterns of dynastic rule and monumentality were being established elsewhere, either in competition or in cooperation with Tikal.

## AD 400 TO 500

The century following the AD 400 building project again seems to involve the same kind of consolidation of the new architectural patterns as seen in the previous episodes. Burial 10 for the first time placed a royal burial out in front of the North Acropolis rather than within it, beginning a movement away from the Acropolis which continued throughout the Late Classic. Another pyramid-shaped temple building, Structure 5D-32-2nd was constructed to balance Structure 5D-34 on the other side of the Acropolis stairway, but a burial corresponding to it was not searched for beyond the later Burial 195.

Burial 48, apparently dated to 9.1.1.10.0 (AD 457) and linked to Stormy Sky by the presumed death date on the tomb wall, continued the Burial 10 pattern in its location at the base of the Acropolis. Structure 5D-33-3rd was built shortly afterwards over the site of the burial, forming a set of three fronting structures.

Stormy Sky was perhaps Tikal's most influential ruler. The earliest monuments in sites to the east such as Caracol and Quirigua are in many ways derivative of his Stelae 1, 2, and 28 (Jones and Sharer 1980:11–13). This whole period witnessed the establishment of the Classic Maya culture area. How much of the expansion to east and west out of the Peten core can be attributed to leadership from Tikal is not certain but seems to have been considerable, judging alone from the overwhelming uniformity in the writing system across this vast stretch of territory.

As Coggins (1975:183) pointed out in the carving of Stela 31, the best-known monument to Stormy Sky, a blending of Maya and Mexican traits is discernible, in that the costume and pose of the front figure hark back to the much older Stela 29 while the figures on the sides are in full Teotihuacan array. The ceramic pieces in Burial 48, though Mexican influenced, are also not as foreign as those of Burial 10. Stormy Sky seemed to be interested in re-establishing the Tikal modes that preceded his father, Curl Nose.

After Stormy Sky, a uniform series of "staff stelae" belonging to Kan Boar (Stelae 9 and 13), his son Jaguar Paw Skull (Stelae 3, 7, 15, 27) and Curl Head or an unknown ruler (Stelae 8 and 6) dominated the monument sequence from 9.2.0.0.0 to 9.4.0.0.0 (AD 475 to 514). These stelae are generally short in stature, and short in text as well, rarely stating much beyond the date, the ruler's name, and his immediate parentage. The staff held in the hand of all the portraits seems to be a walking and fighting implement. Along with the small bag held in the other hand, the staff appeared for the first time in these stelae but then continued to be depicted on the monuments of the Late Classic.

Construction between AD 400 and 500 follows established styles and locations, with, for example, Structure 5D-33-2nd replacing 33-3rd and 22-2nd replacing 22-3rd. In both of these cases, however, the large masonry and stucco decorations of the buildings are among the most impressive and beautiful known at Tikal (A. Miller 1986:Figs.

13–18), making it clear that the periods of conservatism in Tikal's architectural history are often the most productive.

## AD 500

Yet another widespread construction project transformed the Tikal center once again around the end of the staff stela sequence. Floor 3 of the North Acropolis, Floor 2A of the Great Plaza, and Floor 2 of the East Plaza provided new coverings for those surfaces. With them, a massive new acropolis-like platform (Platform 5E-1) was erected on the east side of the East Plaza and a set of twin four-stairway pyramids (Structures 5D-Sub. 16 and 5E-Sub. 1) were built in the approximate center of its large open space.

The dating of these floors and constructions is aided by the assessment (Coe 1990) that Stela 10, dating to 9.4.13.0.0 (AD 527) or slightly later, is in its original position and postdates this architectural renovation by only a few years. This suggests a date for the constructions in the first decades of the sixth century AD.

The East Plaza twin pyramids are apparent forerunners of the later Twin Pyramid Groups built every twenty tuns. As such, they probably housed the tun and katun ending ceremonies, although the stela enclosure and nine-doorway building typical of the later groups were not found in the East Plaza version. An extensive renovation to the stairways demonstrates that the structures were utilized for several katuns, unlike the later groups that were successively abandoned, probably at the ends of their katuns of use.

The East Acropolis was a massive platform. Large stucco masks flanked a western stairway leading from the East Plaza to a complex of later-dismantled buildings on its summit. The east terraces of the Great Plaza were also rebuilt with these floors, thus creating on both sides of the East Plaza an entirely fresh and imposing arena for the twin pyramids. On the Great Plaza was built the platform supporting Structures 5D-29, 30 and 31 (the three temples now north of Temple I). These structures might have continued the trend away from the North Acropolis for royal burials, although they have not been excavated for tombs.

In sum, the constructions associated with these new floors represent a significant transformation of architecture and function, apparently dedicating the once-open East Plaza to large public ceremonies. The

Plaza appears to have been the seat of the Tikal katun-ending ceremonies for at least a century, until the twin pyramids were replaced by the ball court and the twin pyramid functions shifted to new groups on the roadways leading out from the site core (Jones 1969).

Lasting from AD 514 to 534, Katun 4 was a turbulent period in terms of stela style. The katun began with Stela 6, the last of the staff stelae. Three years afterward the stela pair, 23 and 25, were carved, both dedicated to 9.4.3.0.0 (AD 517) and one featuring a woman on the front, the other a man. These are followed by Stela 12 and Stela 10 ten years later at 9.4.13.0.0 (AD 527).

These monuments break with the staff stela design, some going back to the earlier form of Stela 31 and others in having square cross sections, figures on the front and side surfaces, and text on the back. Stela 10 mentions Jaguar Paw Skull, who might have ruled well into this katun (Jones and Satterthwaite 1982:128). Mathews (1985:Fig. 17), on the other hand, has proposed the existence of rulers Bird Claw, Curl Head, and Jaguar Paw Skull II among the seven rulers intermediate between Jaguar Paw Skull the 14th and Double Bird the 21st, who was inaugurated at 9.5.3.9.15 (AD 537). Haviland (1985) has argued that some of the rulers of this period might have suffered exile from the site center and burial in the outlying Group 7F-1.

This large number of unknown (yet counted) Tikal rulers suggests that the katun saw changes and conflicts. Although we are not sure what these conflicts were, nor what names were associated with them, they correlate roughly in time with extensive floor renovations and architectural innovations of the central area. To be more precise, the huge construction projects were probably a few years later than AD 500, when the site was still within the conservative period of the staff stelae.

Little in the way of major change seems to have occurred in the century following. Structure 5D-22-1st was built, covering the architectural sculptures of 22-2nd with a structure of similar form and only slightly larger size.

## AD 600

The next dramatic construction event in the North Acropolis area comes with the building of Structure 5D-32-1st over Burial 195. This can be dated to some extent by the hieroglyphic inscription recovered from four wooden boards in the tomb (Coggins 1975:Fig. 89). The hieroglyphic date reads as 9.8.0.0.0 or 9.9.0.0.0 (AD 593 or 613). Two ceramic plates in the burial carry the ruler's name, Animal Skull, and the statement that he was the 22nd Ruler at Tikal. On one (Coggins 1975:Fig. 90a), the inscription was originally painted on the plate and then covered with stucco and a newly painted inscription stating a two-katun anniversary, presumably of the reign. If Double Bird, the 21st Ruler, was still ruling at 9.6.3.9.15 (AD 557), as stated on Stela 17, Animal Skull's reign should have continued at least two katuns farther to 9.8.3.9.15 (AD 596) and the burial should date to afterwards.

The stratigraphic connection between Burial 195 and other constructions is one of the best in the Tikal sequence. Structure 5D-32-1st covering the sealed burial is contemporary with a new North Acropolis surface (Floor 2), new versions of the southern corner temples on top of the Acropolis (Structures 5D-25 and 27) and the first versions of the northern corner temples (Structures 5D-20 and 21) that complete the eight-temple layout marking the world directions. The North Terrace was repaved and the front stairway rebuilt. The Great Plaza was paved once again and its eastern terraces entirely rebuilt along with Floor 1 of the East Plaza.

Floor abutments suggest that all of these constructions were finished at roughly the same time, including Floor 1 of the East Plaza. This in turn is contemporaneous with the East Plaza ball court (Structures 5D-42 and 5E-31) and its accompanying Mexican-style shrine building (Structure 5D-43). Also coeval with this floor are the massive two-tiered terraces separating the Central Acropolis from the East Plaza. Finally, the first version of the Maler Causeway leading north out of the East Plaza was built at this time.

The huge construction projects outlined above are thus tied by stratigraphy to Structure 5D-32-1st and the burial of Animal Skull, 22nd Ruler, probably sometime after AD 596. The reverential entombment and large burial temple make it clear that Animal Skull was a revered forebear, but the lack of monuments from this period prevents us from identifying the succeeding ruler who completed the project. He might have been Shield Skull, apparently named as son of Animal Skull on MT. 25 (Jones and Satterthwaite 1982:129).

Animal Skull himself is likely to have been an intruder or at least not a son of the preceding ruler, for the name glyph of *his* father is not Double Bird nor any other recognized Tikal royal name. Recently, Arlen Chase and Steven Houston (in Chase and Chase 1987:33; 60–1, 93) have reported a new altar inscription at Caracol, Belize, that cites a victory in war over a Tikal lord at 9.6.8.4.2 (AD 562). This could have been associated with the death of Double Bird, because the dates on his only monument, Stela 17, extend with certainty only up to 9.6.3.9.15 (AD 557), the one-katun anniversary of his inaugural.

Stela 17, as with many of the early monuments at Tikal, has been broken at its base, deliberately erased, and moved from its original setting. Although some Tikal stelae were broken up before this time and deposited in earlier fills, for example Stelae 33 and 35 and Miscellaneous Stone 34 (Jones and Satterthwaite 1982:117–18), many of them were placed within Structure 5D-33-1st around 9.12.9.17.16 (AD 682) or earlier (see below). The broken monuments suggest that a massive destructive campaign took place, the date of which should be between AD 557 and 682 for no later monuments received this treatment. The breaks in the stelae are clearly deliberate, showing the scars of a pecked line made to facilitate the fracture. Carving on others looks as though it had been deliberately rubbed smooth. Stela 31 tells the story best: broken off its base, the face of its ruler portrait battered, set upright in a temple room with some care and ceremony and buried by Structure 5D-33-1st.

The combination of purposeful destruction and later re-erection is best explained by a sequence of two separate motives rather than just one. The raid or conquest from Caracol would account for the massive destruction; a restoration or reintegration of the old Tikal line would explain the reverence later accorded the broken monuments.

The Ik period tombs of Tikal are characterized by eastern traits, as demonstrated in Coggins' descriptions of Burials 150, 72, and 200 (1975:321, 333, 365). Although Coggins does not specify it, I think Burial 195 also shares in the possession of these eastern traits, especially in the calligraphic style of the large stuccoed plates (MT 216 and 217) and in the cartouched portraits and inscriptions on the wooden boards (Coggins 1975:Fig. 89, 90). The introduction of Ik ceramic types in these Tikal burials would appear to be the result of the Caracol raid and its resulting change of leadership or alliance.

## AD 600 TO 700

Burial 23 and the accompanying Burial 24 continue the eastern connection in their ceramic contents (Coggins 1975:372–87). Coggins has suggested a dynastic discontinuity with the accession of Ruler A at 9.12.9.17.16 (AD 682), but this is contradicted by the parentage statement identifying Ruler A's father, Shield Skull, as a Tikal ruler, by the striking architectural similarity of the three sequent burial structures (Structures 5D-33, 1, and 73) and by the continuities in burial practices from Burials 23 to 116 (the red dot on the capstone, obsidian chips overlying the chamber, and the jaguar pelts – Coggins 1975:373). The first two of these traits are found in earlier tombs at Caracol and probably came into Tikal funerary practice from there (Chase and Chase 1987:61). Furthermore, Ruler A's first monuments, Stela 30 and Altar 14 at 9.13.0.0.0 (AD 692), have markedly eastern design connections in the giant *Ahau* glyph on the altar. Finally, the broken shale stela, Stela 34, which probably once stood at the top of the stairway of Structure 5D-2 (Temple II) and which style-dates to around 9.13.0.0.0, is small enough and so eastern in its material and style as to have probably been carried into Tikal from that region already carved (Jones and Satterthwaite 1982:75, Figs. 55c, 107a).

Thus the century or somewhat more between the purported Caracol war and the inauguration of Ruler A is one of continuity as a new Tikal rulership again became integrated into the older traditions. At its beginning, the first ruler, Animal Skull, reigned for at least a katun and was buried in front of the North Acropolis beside the tombs of distinguished Early Classic sovereigns. At the end of it, Ruler A declared himself the 260-tun reincarnation of the spirit of Stormy Sky (Coggins 1975:448; Jones and Satterthwaite 1982:73). The integrative process is similar to that effected by Stormy Sky himself many years before.

There are no inscribed objects within Burial 23 which identify the occupant as Shield Skull, the father of Ruler A. Therefore, the burial and its Structure 5D-33-1st cannot be identified with complete certainty as the burial place of Ruler A's immediate predecessor and dated to just before 9.12.9.17.16 (AD 682). On the other hand, the burial contents seriate to the final Ik ceramic period, so Shield Skull or his immediate predecessor are good choices for it.

The century seems one in which the dynamic construction changes connected with Burial 195 became fixed traditional modes. Structure 5D-33-1st continued the Acropolis-fronting pattern by refilling the axial position. After the East Plaza ball court obliterated the twin pyramid set, the (presumably) katun-ending ceremonies shifted to at least two groups newly built on the outskirts, Groups 4D-2 and 5B-1, possibly at AD 652 and 672 (Jones 1969:Fig. 2). Ruler A continued the Twin Pyramid Group sequence with the dated Groups 3D-1 and 5C-1 at 9.13.0.0.0 and 9.14.0.0.0 (AD 692 and 711). Two floors of the Tozzer Causeway directly behind the latter group are stratigraphically earlier and indicate that the important western entrance road was first built and then rebuilt before AD 711.

In the Central Acropolis, a façade sculpture on Structure 5D-57 dates the building to around 9.13.3.8.11 (AD 695) and fixes the important Structures 5D-52-2nd, 54-2nd, 61, and 58 to the years before that date (Harrison 1970:Chart 1). The first building of the East Plaza marketplace complex precedes Structure 5D-1 (Temple I) as does the first of the great temples, Structure 5D-2 (Temple II).

Thus there are several stratigraphic connections to Long Count dates which demonstrate that the Late Classic transformation of Tikal began early in the seventh century and continued steadily through it. Its tone is one of continuity, building upon the patterns begun at the time of Burial 195.

## AD 750

The next Long Count fix for the Great Plaza stratigraphy is the construction of Structure 5D-1 (Temple I), fixed by the firm identification of Burial 116 under the structure as that of Ruler A and therefore occurring just before the inaugural date of Ruler B at 9.15.3.6.8 (AD 734; Jones 1986). Little construction follows Temple I in the Great Plaza and North Acropolis, but in the East Plaza important events include the expansion northwards of the platform edge, the construction of Structure 5D-40 in the northwest corner, the final Maler Causeway, the completion of the marketplace quadrangle in the eastern half of the plaza, and the final Mendez Causeway to the southeast.

With Temple IV at 9.15.10.0.0 (AD 741), Temple VI at 9.16.15.0.0 (AD 766) and Twin Pyramid Group 3D-2 at 9.16.0.0.0 (AD 751), all at the ends of the three causeways leading out from the site center, these large and highly public constructions which follow Temple I make Ruler B (AD 734 to 768) rather than Ruler A the most prolific builder of his era.

Nevertheless, even though Ruler B can be called innovative in such items as the design of his stone monuments (Jones 1977:58), most of the forms which he used to create the impressive aspect of "metropolitan" late Tikal were already begun in previous reigns: the Twin Pyramid Groups, the Great Temples, the grand causeways, the stone-roofed market buildings, the grand Central Acropolis palaces. There is little that is truly innovative in these later construction projects, in spite of their massive scale and there is correspondingly no indication of dynastic intrusion in the hieroglyphic records after that of Animal Skull and Burial 195.

The turn of the century (AD 800) did not seem to bring with it another episode of change. In the Twin Pyramid Groups of Ruler C at 9.17.0.0.0 and 9.18.0.0.0 (AD 771 and 790) and in Temple III at 9.19.0.0.0 (AD 810), there is a strong conservatism in design.

## AD 900

By AD 800, Tikal should have been ready for another dynamic conceptual growth to follow upon the long period of building within established traditions. These traditions end with Temple III around 9.19.0.0.0 (AD 810) and Stela 11 and Altar 11 at 10.2.0.0.0 (AD 869). Instead of starting up again with a new construction program, as had happened every time before, Tikal stopped construction and monument carving and then apparently lost most of its population within a century.

A final episode in the East Plaza was the construction of a group of rectangular house-sized platforms in the northwestern quarter of the plaza. One of these was built directly on the ruins of the market quadrangle, Structure 5E-32. Although these platforms do not have Eznab (Tepeu III) ceramics within their fills, they are covered with them. The East Plaza ball court was repaired so that the game could continue. Eznab deposits were found within and outside the other East Plaza buildings and many Central Acropolis structures as well.

A date for this transformation is not certain, but Stela 11 and Altar 11, fixed at 10.2.0.0.0 (AD 869), are within the Tikal tradition in their shape, carving, costuming, text, and cache. It seems unlikely that a conservative Tikal leadership would have allowed a domestic compound to be built in one of its major public spaces. Thus a date after AD 870 is more likely, and the turn of the century (AD 900) is a reasonable approximation.

The details of the death of Tikal and the Classic Maya are still not clear. Seibal surely played a role, perhaps as a vassal of Chichen Itza. Eznab pottery designs are closely similar to those of Chichen Itza stone carving and became very popular with the families that set up houses in the East Plaza of Tikal.

Revived monumental activity in the old sites of Uaxactun and Yaxha and the establishment of new outlying sites such as Jimbal and Ixlu to the north and south of Tikal, with their stelae dating to the late ninth century and their concurrent use of the Tikal Emblem Glyph (Jones and Satterthwaite 1982:109–16), might have substituted in a way for the architectural growth missing at the Tikal center.

The old city-state seemed to be dividing up into smaller units. This might have been a more suitable means of organization in the new military and political environment in which the northern Yucatan Peninsula possessed most of the wealth and power. However, these new Peten sites soon ceased construction as well.

## CONCLUSIONS

The plentiful body of data from stratigraphic excavations at Tikal can be connected at times to the absolute dates which rise out of the inscriptions. There can be no doubt that this combination of rich excavation data and precise chronology makes Tikal a unique laboratory for the study of culture change over a long period of time.

The principle of stratigraphic contemporaneity has not been widely used in writing construction history. Its underlying basis, the judgment that certain floors were laid down to finish off buildings, has furthermore not been generally accepted as an indicator of widespread construction projects. This paper and, more importantly, the excavation reports of the Tikal Project, will hopefully promote the more general pursuance of the concept in future excavation strategies.

Beginning around 400 BC, the center of Tikal appeared to undergo dramatic shifts every 200 years, first around 400 BC with the first south-facing structure beginning the basic northern focus of the North Acropolis complex, then around 200 BC with the beginning of the

North Acropolis as an elevated platform crowned with structures, around AD 1 with the paving of the Great Plaza and adjacent West and East Plazas, around AD 200 with the much higher Acropolis, direct access and shift of axis, around AD 400 with the construction of the ball court and the predecessors of Temples I and II in the Great Plaza, and around AD 600 with the extensive repaving and construction programs accompanying Burial 195.

Three of these episodes (at AD 1, 400, and 600) are associated with burials (85, 10, and 195) with considerable outside influences apparent in their contents. Twice they can be linked to possible breaks in the dynastic sequence (in the rules of Curl Nose and Animal Skull). In both cases, later rulers (Stormy Sky and Ruler A) took pains to re-establish their connections with the broken dynastic line while also honoring the intruder.

In all three of the above cases, as well as in the 200 BC and AD 200 changes, the episodes appear to correspond with changes in the Tikal ceramic complex, commencing the Cauac, Cimi, Manik I/II, Manik III, and Ik complexes in sequence. Imix ceramics, first seen in Burial 116 around AD 732, do not have any such association with a dynastic change. In the case of the Ik complex, with Animal Skull, the disruption of the Tikal dynasty seems clear and the introduction of new ceramic modes in the royal burial collections is apparent.

Twice in the sequence there are intermediate spurts of construction growth within the roughly 200-year pulse, once with the new plaza floors, the East Acropolis and East Plaza Twin Pyramids around AD 500 and later with the Great Temple, causeway, and marketplace constructions around AD 750.

It is interesting that the approximate dates of these two episodes, 9.4.0.0.0 (AD 514) and 9.16.15.0.0 (AD 761) are roughly 260 tun-years apart and were inscribed together on the Temple VI façade inscription. The first is connected in time to a sudden change in monument-carving style and to a possible period of dynastic turmoil during Katun 4. The second displays no such dynastic difficulties. It is possible that these intermediate construction projects point to a speeding up of the "pulse" of Tikal construction history.

Norman Hammond (personal communication 1987) has pointed out that the 200-year period might relate to half-baktun cycles 197 years in length. These work out to the following:

*Cycles of Growth at Tikal*

| | |
|---|---|
| 7.8.0.0.0 (205 BC) | Structure 5D-Sub. 1-2nd |
| 7.18.0.0.0 (2 BC) | Burial 85 Ruler |
| 8.8.0.0.0 (199 AD) | Fall of Mirador |
| 8.18.0.0.0 (396 AD) | Curl Nose, Fall of Uaxactun |
| 9.8.0.0.0 (593 AD) | Animal Skull, invasion |
| 9.18.0.0.0 (790 AD) | Ruler C, large construction |

Although imprecise, this ten-katun cycle fits the times of change better than does the 256-year cycle of thirteen Ahau-katun names. The fifty-two year cycle of the Calendar Round would also create a 208-year cycle which again matches roughly the observed Tikal cycle.

It seems likely, however, that Tikal history was not heavily swayed by such conscious belief in rhythmic destiny. Rather, the cycle might simply be a natural reaction to times of sudden change. Consolidation of established power is necessary in these cases and can last a long time. Eventually, however, it must lead to stagnation and the need for new directions and leadership, which can be met in various ways, by invasion from outside, by expansion of the state, or by the resolution of a dynastic struggle.

The collapse of Tikal and the other Classic Maya cities in the ninth century AD might have been caused not by an internal failure of moral or political order at Tikal but rather by a shift of power to the northern Maya. If Wren and Schmidt (this volume) are correct in saying that the ball court and other principal "Toltec" buildings of Chichen Itza date from around 10.2.0.0.0 (AD 869) rather than a century later, then that city became the dominant power in the Maya area earlier than we had guessed. The architecture of "Toltec" Chichen Itza is clearly one of domination and conquest similar to that well understood at later Tenochtitlan.

As the author has argued in an earlier paper (Jones 1979), Tikal would not have prospered as it did for a thousand years were it not for its location on one of the best portage routes across the spine of the Yucatan Peninsula. One of the means devised during that time for the maintenance of the route was the political cooperation between the independent Maya city-states along those routes, from Copan to Palenque.

The system worked for a long time, but as with most civilizations based on transportation and trade, Tikal and the others eventually found themselves bypassed as canoe technology developed beyond the rivers and along the coasts. Chichen Itza's new military might and political hegemony would not have been possible without this technologically inevitable shift to coastal travel. In this shift, the north of the peninsula would logically become the best location from which to control the flow of Central American jade, gold, cacao, cotton, and other tropical products headed towards Central Mexico. The area around Tikal might simply have been from the beginning an impossible place in which to sustain a large community without wealth flowing through it from long distance trade.

Table 5.1. A *tentative correlation of Tikal constructions and rulers*

| Long Count date | Gregorian year equivalent | Inaugural date | Ruler's name and number | Assigned burial | Acropolis/ Great Plaza structures | Acropolis/ Great Plaza floors | East Plaza structures/ floors | Approx-imate date |
|---|---|---|---|---|---|---|---|---|
| 10.4.0.0.0 | 909 | | | | | | | |
| 10.3.0.0.0 | 889 | | | | | | | |
| 10.2.0.0.0 | 869 | | Stela 11 Ruler | | | | | |
| 10.1.0.0.0 | 849 | | | | | | | |
| 10.0.0.0.0 | 830 | | | | | | | |
| 9.19.0.0.0 | 810 | | | | | | | |
| 9.18.0.0.0 | 790 | | | | | | | |
| 9.17.0.0.0 | 771 | | Ruler C (29) | | | | | |
| | | 9.16.17.16.4 | —— | | | | | |
| | | | – – (28) – – | Bu. 196 | 73 | | Causeways, Market, etc. | (AD 750) |
| 9.16.0.0.0 | 751 | | Ruler B (27) | | | | | |
| | | 9.15.3.6.8 | —— | Bu. 116 | 1 | | | |
| | | | | | 2 | | | |
| 9.15.0.0.0 | 731 | | | | | | | |
| 9.14.0.0.0 | 711 | | | | | | | |
| 9.13.0.0. 0 | 692 | | Ruler A | | | | | |
| | | 9.12.9.17.16 | —— | Bu. 23 | 33 | | | |
| 9.12.0.0.0 | 672 | | Shield Skull | | | | | |
| 9.11.0.0.0 | 652 | | | | | | | |
| 9.10.0.0.0 | 633 | | | | | | Fl.1/ | |
| 9 .9.0.0.0 | 613 | | – – – – – – | Bu. 195 | 32, 20, 25, 27, 74 | Fl.2/1 | Ball Court | (AD 600) |
| 9.8.0.0.0 | 593 | | Animal Skull (22) | | | | | |
| 9.7.0.0.0 | 573 | | – – – – – – | | | | | |
| | | | Double Bird | | | | | |
| 9.6.0.0.0 | 554 | | (21) | | | | | |
| | | 9.5.3.9.15 | —— | | | | | |

Table 5.1. *Continued*

| Long Count date | Gregorian year equivalent | Inaugural date | Ruler's name and number | Assigned burial | Acropolis/ Great Plaza structures | Acropolis/ Great Plaza floors | East Plaza structures/ floors | Approx- imate date |
|---|---|---|---|---|---|---|---|---|
| 9.5.0.0.0 | 534 | | | | 22 | | | |
| | | | Jaguar Paw Skull (14) | | 29–31 | Fl. 3/2A | Fl. 2/ Twin Pyramids | (AD 500) |
| 9.3.0.0.0 | 495 | | | | | | | |
| | | 9.2.13.0.0 | | | | | | |
| 9.2.0.0.0 | 475 | | Kan Boar | | 33–2nd, 22–2nd | | | |
| 9.1.0.0.0 | 455 | 9.1.1.10.0 | | Bu. 48 | 33–3rd | | | |
| | | | Stormy Sky (11) | | | | | |
| 9.0.0.0.0 | 436 | | | | | | | |
| | | 8.19.10.0.0 | | Bu. 10 | 34, 32–2nd | | | |
| 8.19.0.0.0 | 416 | | | | | | | |
| 8.18.0.0.0 | 396 | | Curl Nose | | 1, 2, 74 (–2nd) | Fl. 4/2B | Fl. 3 | (AD 400) |
| | | 8.17.2.16.17 | | | | | | |
| 8.17.0.0.0 | 376 | | Jaguar Paw (9) | | | | | |
| 8.16.0.0.0 | 357 | | – – – – – | | | | | |
| 8.15.0.0.0 | 337 | | Moon Zero Bird | | 22–3rd | | | |
| | | 8.14.3.1.12 | | | | | | |
| 8.14.0.0.0 | 317 | | | | | | | |
| 8.13.0.0.0 | 297 | | – – – – – | Bu. 22 | 22–4th | | | |
| 8.12.0.0.0 | 278 | | Stela 29 Ruler | | | | | |
| 8.11.0.0.0 | 258 | | | | 23, 26 | | | |
| 8.10.0.0.0 | 238 | | | | | | | |
| | 218 | | | | 22–5th, 23–2nd, 26–2nd | Fl. 5 | | (AD 200) |
| | 199 | | | | | Fl. 6/3A | | |

| | | | | | | |
|---|---|---|---|---|---|---|
| | 179 | | 26–3rd | | | |
| | 159 | | | | | |
| | 139 | | | Fl.7 | | |
| | 120 | | 22–5th | Fl.8 | | |
| | 100 | | | Fl.9 | | |
| | 80 | | 22–6th | | | |
| | 61 | Bu. 85 | | Fl.10/3B | Fl.4 | |
| | 41 | Bu. 167 | | Fl.11/4A | Fl.5 | |
| | 21 | Bu. 166 | Sub.11, 12 | Fl.12/4B | (West Plaza) | (AD 0) |
| AD | 1 | | | | | |
| BC | 17 | | Sub.3 | | | |
| | 37 | | | | | |
| | 57 | Bu. 164 | | | | |
| | 76 | | Sub.1, 9 | | | |
| | 96 | | Sub.4, | | | |
| | 116 | | | | | |
| | 136 | | | | | |
| | 155 | | | | | |
| | 175 | | | | | |
| | 195 | | Sub.1–2nd | | | |
| | 215 | | | | | |
| | 234 | Bu. 122, 123, 126 | | | | |
| | 254 | | | | | |
| | 274 | | | | | |
| | 294 | | | | | |
| | 313 | | | | | |
| | 333 | | | | | |
| | 353 | | Sub.14 | | | |

# 6
# Polities in the northeast Peten, Guatemala

T. PATRICK CULBERT

This paper summarizes information relevant to the regional history of the northeast Peten to complement the very rich data on Tikal provided by Jones (Jones and Satterthwaite 1982; Jones 1986; this volume), Coggins (1975, 1979), Schele (1986e; Schele and Freidel n.d.), and Molloy (n.d.). The viewpoint taken is an expansive one that sees the region as an interactive whole in which the histories of individual sites must be understood within a framework that stresses interaction between sites both within and outside of the region. The amount of long-distance political interaction proposed here does not seem to me very compatible with the vision of small, independent polities favored by most participants at the seminar, a question that is addressed in the final section of the paper.

The northeast Peten is a critical area for understanding Maya Classic period development and organization. The area contained very large and abundant sites (Hammond 1974a) and was probably the most densely populated part of the Maya lowlands in the Classic period (Culbert and Rice n.d.). It was in the northeast Peten that the dynastic monument complex ("stela cult") first took root in the lowlands and from which it spread outward to other lowland areas. For the Early Classic, only the northeast Peten provides a conjunction of archaeological, epigraphic, and iconographic information that bears upon the question of political organization and interaction. For the Late Classic, when data from throughout the lowlands are much more abundant, the northeast Peten continued to have large sites, important rulers, and far-flung connections with other regions.

Sites in the northeast Peten have been the object of a large amount of archaeological research. The Carnegie Institution's investigations at Uaxactun (Ricketson and Ricketson 1937; A. L. Smith 1937, 1950; R. E. Smith 1937) put Maya Classic sites on the archaeological map, so to speak. They were followed by more than twenty years of field research by the Tikal Project (Coe 1965a,b, 1990; Coggins 1975, 1979; Jones and Satterthwaite 1982; Jones n.d., this volume, are particularly relevant to this paper) and the Proyecto Nacional Tikal (Laporte and Fialko n.d.) that have deeply influenced (some would say biased) our interpretations of the Maya. More recently, R. E. W. Adams' work at Rio Azul (Adams 1984, 1986a,b, 1987) has added another multi-year project at a major site and the Caracol Project of A. F. and D. Z. Chase (Chase and Chase 1987; Houston 1987), just outside the Peten but directly relevant, is beginning to provide important new data.

Inscriptions are abundant in the northeast Peten, although at some sites they are poorly preserved, badly looted and/or not yet studied. Next to Tikal, Uaxactun has the fullest record although it has not been completely analyzed. Naranjo (Closs 1985; Schele 1986e) provides inscriptions that are very important to understanding Late Classic interaction. El Peru, which was perhaps the site of the looted Site Q antiquities (Houston and Mathews 1985:14–15), has a long and important history as do the still little-reported Yaxha and Xultun. When the records of all these sites have been more fully investigated, they will undoubtedly clarify our understanding of political structure and interaction.

## THE LATE PRECLASSIC (300 BC–AD 250) AND EARLY CLASSIC (AD 250–534)

There is a monumental architecture of Late Preclassic date at a number of northeast Peten sites, but because there is no epigraphic record we must infer social complexity from the archaeological record. The Preclassic architecture at Tikal has been documented (Coe 1965a, 1990; Jones, this volume; Laporte and Fialko n.d.) and the number and size of structures is impressive. There were very large structures and a substantial population at Rio Azul (Adams 1987), and numerous, although not very large, public structures at Uaxactun (Ricketson and Ricketson 1937). All of these sites, however, are dwarfed by the size of Mirador in the northwest Peten (Dahlin 1984; Matheny 1986). Mirador is so large that our entire concept of Preclassic Maya civilization seems destined for revision once the site has been more fully investigated. It has already been suggested that the fall of Mirador may have been connected with the Early Classic florescence elsewhere in the lowlands (Coggins 1979).

Now that the Preclassic is better known, the Early Classic no longer appears to represent a leap in level of complexity nor a sudden infusion of a set of new traits. It does, however, mark the beginning of the epigraphic record and the full dynastic monument complex. Although dynastic monuments occurred in the Guatemalan highlands and Pacific slope before they are attested in the lowlands, the northeast Peten, especially the Tikal/Uaxactun zone, is where they first provide a continuous record in the lowlands. Tikal Stela 29 (8.12.14.8.15; AD 292) is the earliest known stela in the region, although Mathews (1985:31) suggests that the Tikal dynasty may have begun about 8.10.0.0.0 (AD 238) and Jones (this volume) suggests an even earlier starting date around AD 170.

Mathews (1985) has reviewed the data on Cycle 8 inscriptions (all those before AD 435). Although the addition since his article of Rio Azul Stela 1 (8.17.16.8.0; AD 393) expands the area in which such inscriptions occur, all are still within 100 km of Tikal. Sites with Emblem Glyphs during Cycle 8 include Tikal, El Peru, Rio Azul, Yaxha, Xultun, and Bejucal (accepting Cycle 8 style dates for Yaxha and Xultun). With the exception of Bejucal, all these sites are at least 40 km distant from each other and have long histories that continue into the Late Classic. Bejucal is an anomaly. It is only 20 km west of Tikal, and has inscriptions for only forty years at the end of Cycle 8. Justeson (personal communication) suggests that the cessation of monuments at Bejucal at about 8.18.0.0.0 (AD 396) might be seen as an indication of Tikal expansion. It is possible to outline a domain for Tikal during Cycle 8 and early Cycle 9 (AD 376–495). The Tikal Emblem Glyph was used at Uolantun (5 km southeast) and El Zapote (25 km south) and Mathews (1985) believes both to have been dependencies of Tikal. Around 8.17.1.4.12 (AD 378), Uaxactun

(20 km north) was added to the Tikal realm. Thus a circle of at least 20–25 km radius seems to have been dominated by Tikal in the early fifth century.

Uaxactun–Tikal interrelationships provide the clearest case of Early Classic political interaction attested in the inscriptions (Mathews 1985:33–46). The event at 8.17.1.4.12 (AD 378) that was commemorated at both sites has been amply considered elsewhere (Coggins 1975, 1979; Mathews 1985; Laporte and Fialko n.d.; Schele and Freidel n.d.; Molloy n.d.). The consensus at the seminar is that it involved a takeover, probably by conquest, in which Smoking Frog of Tikal gained the throne of Uaxactun. Because Uaxactun does not display its own Emblem Glyph during the Early Classic, Mathews (1985) believes that it remained under Tikal control. Schele and Freidel (n.d.) have concluded that although Curl Nose was a separate ruler of Tikal, he ruled under the aegis of Smoking Frog because his inscriptions refer to him as a *y'ahau* ("his ahau") of Smoking Frog and he enacts an important ritual (perhaps his inauguration) "in the land of Smoking Frog." Laporte and Fialko (n.d.), on the other hand, believe that after Smoking Frog (whom they believe to have been a Tikal ruler) held the throne at both Tikal and Uaxactun, the two sites were ruled by separate, but closely related ruling lines. Whatever the political relationship between the two sites, it is important that Uaxactun continued to exercise the elite prerogatives of monument carving, temple erection and rich burials through most of the Early Classic. These prerogatives were to be lost when Uaxactun was under Tikal aegis in the Late Classic.

Adams (1987) takes a very expansive view of Tikal political power. He believes that Tikal conquered Rio Azul during Cycle 8 or early Cycle 9 (AD 376–495), creating a domain that extended 100 km to the north. He bases his interpretation on altars at Rio Azul that show kneeling prisoners similar to those in murals recently discovered at Tikal (Laporte and Fialko n.d.) and on his conclusion (Adams 1986b) that the insignia of Ruler X at Rio Azul indicate that he was a relative of Stormy Sky of Tikal. Although Laporte and Fialko (n.d.) seem to find such an expansion of Tikal's domain possible, the participants at the Santa Fe seminar could not accept a realm of such size.

There can be no doubt that Tikal experienced Teotihuacan influence during the latter part of Cycle 8 and that such influence was in some way involved with the 8.17.1.4.12 interaction with Uaxactun and the inauguration of Curl Nose at Tikal shortly thereafter (Coggins 1975, 1979). Tikal Burials 10 and 48, probably those of Curl Nose and his successor, Stormy Sky, include many imported vessels, some probably of actual Teotihuacan manufacture. Stuccoed decoration on some of the vessels includes obvious Mexican iconography, although perhaps mediated through the Mexican-related center at Kaminaljuyu in the Guatamalan highlands. Tikal Stela 31, in which Stormy Sky is flanked by two individuals (believed by Schele and Freidel [n.d.] to be two portraits of Curl Nose) in Mexican regalia including Tlaloc shields and spear-throwers strengthens the inference of Mexican contact. Evidence uncovered by the Proyecto Nacional Tikal (Laporte and Fialko n.d.) in the Lost World Pyramid Group and Group 6C-XVI makes Teotihuacan contact seem even more direct. Talud-and-tablero architecture begins in the Lost World complex by the start of the Early Classic and Mexican iconography is added around 8.17.0.0.0 (AD 376). A "ball court marker" with Teotihuacan form and iconography bears a hieroglyphic inscription that commemorates the 8.17.1.4.12 (AD 378) date and names Smoking Frog three times.

Teotihuacan influence was by no means confined to Tikal. My observation of the ceramics at Rio Azul suggests that the site has more cylindrical tripods of Mexican shape and with decorative elements such as "coffee-bean eyes" than are found at Tikal, and there is a small talud-and-tablero altar at Rio Azul like one discovered in Grp. 6C-XVI at Tikal (Laporte and Fialko n.d.). None of the excavated Rio Azul burials, however, displays as much Teotihuacan iconography as Tikal Burials 10 and 48. Mexican influence at Uaxactun seems less strong than at Tikal and Rio Azul. Cylindrical tripods occur in burials, but none has Teotihuacan iconography (Smith 1955). Nor is there known talud-and-tablero architecture at Uaxactun. Yaxha, which although little investigated is already known to have talud-and-tablero architecture and a Tlaloc stela, will certainly show more evidence of Mexican contact when further research has been done at the site.

Researchers vary in their evaluations of the strength and nature of Teotihuacan influence in the Maya lowlands and the related question of the origin of Curl Nose. Mathews (1985) and Schele and Miller (1986) take little notice of the Teotihuacan presence. Several scholars envision local Maya as using Teotihuacanos, perhaps resident in the lowlands as merchant colonies, to gain support in local political maneuvering. Laporte and Fialko (n.d.) see the accession of Curl Nose as marking the triumph of the local *Ma'Cuch* lineage over two rival lineages and imply that connections with Teotihuacanos may have been useful in the process. Schele and Freidel (n.d.) identify Curl Nose as the son of the preceding ruler, Great Jaguar Paw, based upon the conclusion that the glyphs that identify Curl Nose's father are simply a title of Jaguar Paw. They consequently envision no break in the continuity of the Tikal dynastic line, but consider that the adoption of a new, Teotihuacan-inspired form of warfare aimed at conquest was critical in establishing Tikal's dominance in the Early Classic Peten. Jones (this volume), although taking no position on the origin of Curl Nose, speaks of "new trade routes and alliances expanding Tikal's 'sphere of influence.'"

Other researchers see Curl Nose as an outsider interposed in the Tikal dynasty as a result of Teotihuacan pressure. Coggins (1975, 1979) believes that Curl Nose was from outside the northeast Peten and was a Mexicanized Maya from either Kaminaljuyu (1975) or Mirador (1979). Molloy (n.d.) believes that there was outright conquest of parts of the Maya lowlands by Teotihuacan and that Tikal was ruled by a cadre of Mexican rulers all bearing the Curl Nose glyph. I do not find the arguments for a local origin of Curl Nose (and Smoking Frog) robust and am still attracted by the possibility that they may have originated in Kaminaljuyu.

There is no information about interaction between sites in the northeast Peten during the first quarter of Cycle 9 (AD 435–543). This was a time during which inscriptions at Tikal were brief and uninformative (Jones, this volume) and those at other sites have received little attention. This was, however, the time of an explosive spread of the dynastic monument complex into all regions of the southern lowlands and into the north as far as Oxkintok. One must ask what role the northeast Peten had in this spread. Given Mirador and the size of Preclassic sites in several regions of the lowlands, the extension of the dynastic monument complex can hardly be seen as the start of civilization, nor does anyone advocate political unification of the lowlands. Sharer (this volume) does suggest that a branch of the northeast Peten elite may have been established at Quirigua to start the dynasty there, but his suggestion is based upon stylistic rather than epigraphic evidence. Yaxchilan was visited by an emissary from Tikal in 9.3.13.12.1 (AD 508) and one from El Peru in 9.5.2.10.6 (AD 537) (Schele and Mathews, this volume), but there is no indication that such visits involved political influence. We must await further research before anything much can be said about interaction within or outside of the northeast Peten in early Cycle 9.

In summary, I would argue that the northeast Peten was the most highly developed region of the lowlands through most of the Early Classic period. There can be no doubt about the area's epigraphic priority, and although it can be argued that there has been too little archaeological research in other regions to uncover much Early Classic evidence, there seems little reason to project that such research would reveal remains of the scale known to exist at northeast Peten sites.

Epigraphic evidence about regional interaction in the northeast Peten is minimal for the Early Classic and almost entirely derived from Tikal. Tikal seems to have been a multicenter polity by the late 8th Cycle, and the mechanisms of interaction – war, conquest and royal visits – that are much better attested in Late Classic times were already present in the Early Classic. Given the disagreements that still exist about political structure in the more thoroughly known Late Classic, it will be some time before the Early Classic picture is established.

## THE HIATUS (AD 534–93) AND LATE CLASSIC (AD 593–830)

The political history of the northeast Peten begins to become clearer during the time of the "hiatus" at the end of the early Classic (9.5.0.0.0–9.8.0.0.0; AD 534–93) (Willey 1974) and adds increasing data during the Late Classic (9.8.0.0.0–10.0.0.0.0; AD 593–830). With the larger amount of epigraphic data available, events at individual sites can be brought into perspective only through a regional and even interregional framework. In the earliest segment of time to be considered in this section (9.5.0.0.0–9.13.0.0.0; AD 534–692), Caracol, just outside the Peten in Belize, was the dominant political center and the northeast Peten was in relative decline. Beginning slightly before 9.13.0.0.0 (AD 692), there was a resurgence at Tikal and Naranjo that led to a brilliant century in the history of the northeast Peten. By about 9.17.0.0.0 (AD 771) there are signs of political fragmentation that led eventually to the Classic Maya collapse.

The story of the hiatus (9.5.0.0.0–9.8.0.0.0; AD 534–93) and Tepeu 1 (9.8.0.0.0–9.13.0.0.0; AD 593–692) must begin at Caracol.

Caracol thrived during the hiatus (Chase and Chase 1987) with a full set of monuments, a list of rulers, and major construction activity. The recently discovered Altar 21 (Houston 1987; Chase and Chase 1987:60–1; Schele and Freidel n.d.) reports that Caracol waged two successful wars against Tikal on 9.6.2.1.11 (AD 556) and 9.6.8.4.2 (AD 562). The latter defeat may help explain features in Tikal's history that have been enigmatic. Jones (this volume) believes that it may have occasioned a rash of monument destruction that took place some time after the erection of Stela 17, the last secure date on which is 9.6.3.8.15 (AD 557). Stela 17 is the only monument dedicated to the ruler Double Bird whom Jones suggests may have been deposed or killed as a result of the battle with Caracol. After Stela 17, there were no monuments for more than a century, a break that both Jones (this volume) and Schele and Freidel (n.d.) attribute to Caracol domination of Tikal. Several important burials supply information about intervening rulers however. Inscriptions on ceramics indicate Burial 195 to have been that of Animal Skull, whose *hel* number indicates him to have been the immediate successor of Double Bird. Animal Skull's father, however, was not Double Bird, but a man who does not bear the Tikal Emblem Glyph (Jones, this volume). Jones suggests the possibility that Animal Skull may have been either a foreigner or a local from outside the line of succession who was imposed as a result of the defeat by Caracol. Coggins (1975) has noted the southeastern connections of ceramics in Burials 23 and 24 which followed Burial 195, connections that might now be posited to directly relate to Caracol. Burial 23 may have been that of Shield Skull, possible son of Animal Skull and father of ruler A (Ah Cacau). On Altar 14, paired with Stela 30 as Ruler A's first monuments at 9.13.0.0.0 (AD 692), there is a giant Ahau, a device common at Caracol. After these monuments, however, Ruler A abandoned Caracol-related customs as Tikal regained power under his direction.

There are varying interpretations of events of this period in Tikal's history. In the version just given Jones (this volume) suggests that Animal Skull was an intruder in the Tikal dynasty. Coggins (1975) and Chase and Chase (1987) suggest instead that Shield Skull may have been an interloper. All the interpretations, however, stress the possibility of a break in dynastic succession and evidence for connections with Caracol or the region southeast of Tikal.

The case of Caracol and Naranjo (Schele 1986e) provides even more solid evidence of an expansive military policy of Caracol that included forays into the Peten. Caracol defeated Naranjo twice, in 9.9.18.6.3 (AD 631) and 9.10.3.2.12 (AD 636). After commemorating the second defeat in 9.10.10.0.0 (AD 636), Naranjo carved no more monuments for forty years. Whether Caracol forces occupied or controlled Naranjo during this interval cannot be determined but they were at least present at the site long enough to build the substantial structures that contain the record of Naranjo's defeat. In the case of Naranjo, Caracol was capable of defeating and probably controlling a site at a distance of 50 km. If Tikal was also controlled through an imposed dynasty, Caracol's realm stretched nearly 100 km to the north and west. Caracol may have found an ally in that direction for Schele and Freidel (n.d.) identify a lord with the Site Q Emblem Glyph as involved in the humiliation of Naranjo prisoners.

In addition, the data suggest that neither Uaxactun nor Rio Azul was important in Tepeu 1. No major architecture at Uaxactun is securely dated to Tepeu 1 (A. L. Smith 1950) and R. E. Smith (1955:19) reports that even sherds from the phase were relatively scarce. The same situation prevailed at Rio Azul (Adams 1987:22), where Tepeu 1 ceramics are sparse and architectural activity was much less than in either Tzakol or Tepeu 2. Although there are sites about which little is known – Xultun, for example, has several stelae dated to Tepeu 1 – there seems to have been a period of relative stagnation in the central zone. I do not believe this period of inactivity can be understood except within a broader framework that takes into account the size and military success of Caracol.

Tepeu 2 saw the resurgence of both Tikal and Naranjo and was a time of great accomplishments in the northeast Peten that included huge architectural developments, important dynasts and a surging population. Caracol (Chase and Chase 1987:61) went into eclipse with no monuments between 9.12.0.0.0 (AD 672) and 9.18.10.0.0 (AD 800) except for an unusual slate stela at 9.13.10.0.0 (AD 702). Once again, I believe that events in the central zone must be considered in relation to regional and interregional interaction.

In the approach favored in Santa Fe that defines political territories on the basis of Emblem Glyphs, Tikal, Naranjo, El Peru, and Xultun would have been independent states in Tepeu 2. Even in this minimalist view, a site like Tikal would have included an impressive array of secondary sites and an enormous population within its realm.

A Thiessen polygon of Tikal with borders determined by locations of neighboring sites with Emblem Glyphs extends 50 km east–west and 60 km north–south, a total of 3,000 $km^2$. This area has been thoroughly sampled by settlement surveys (Culbert and Rice n.d.) and a conservative estimate of Late Classic population exceeds half a million inhabitants. The twenty-courtyard sites (Adams 1981) of Uaxactun and Nakum fall within the minimal Tikal realm. Neither site has Late Classic monuments until a stela was erected at Uaxactun in 9.16.0.0.0 (AD 751; Mathews 1985:46) and Stela U was erected at Nakum in 9.17.0.0.0 (AD 771). There was major construction, however, in both sites during Tepeu 2. At Uaxactun, Groups A and B were completely remodeled (Smith 1950). Almost all the new structures were of range rather than temple-pyramid type. Although there were numerous Tepeu 2 burials in Uaxactun, none of them was in a major tomb or richly furnished. Uaxactun seems to have lacked the elite prerogatives of tombs, temples, and monuments and it is easy to imagine the site serving as an administrative center under the aegis of Tikal. It would be pleasing to report that Nakum had a comparable focus upon structures of possible administrative function, but such was not the case. Most Late Classic structures there (Tozzer 1913) were temples rather than range structures. In summary, even if Emblem Glyphs are accepted as absolute indicators of political autonomy, the polities so defined had very large populations and included an array of major subsidiary sites.

Inscriptions from the northeast Peten are not so informative about political organization as those from other areas. Inscriptions from several important sites are still undeciphered or too badly eroded to provide much data. In addition, the conservative style of central-zone monuments leaves much unsaid. Small sites in the zone did not erect monuments in which *cahals* noted their overloads. The multi-figure compositions that tell of royal visits (Schele and Mathews, this volume) were not a part of the northeast Peten repertoire. Although many captives were depicted, they were rarely identified by Emblem Glyphs, and even where warfare between named sites is mentioned critical information about the fate of defeated sites may be lacking.

We do know from the inscriptions, however, a complex set of interrelations that connected Dos Pilas, Tikal, Naranjo, and El Peru in the time before and during the return of the northeast Peten to prosperity. I believe that these interactions are indicative of coordinated political and military activity at distances that are difficult to reconcile with a model that pictures small polities with a radius of effective influence on the order of 25 km.

The set of interactions began with the arrival of Ruler 1, the founder of the Dos Pilas dynasty, who was inaugurated in 9.10.12.11.2 (AD 645) (Houston and Mathews 1985) or a katun later (AD 665) (Closs 1985). Ruler 1 of Dos Pilas used the same sky glyph symbol in his name that was used by Tikal rulers and may very well have come from Tikal (Mathews and Willey, this volume). Closs (1985:77) and Molloy (n.d.) posit, although without specific glyphic basis, that he may have been a brother of Ruler A of Tikal. Throughout its history, Dos Pilas used the same Emblem Glyphs used by Tikal, a fact that cries for interpretation if we are to understand Late Classic history. In other cases where sites used identical Emblem Glyphs, they are presumed to have been part of a single polity even when, as in the case of Palenque and Tortugero, the sites name different rulers. Although Dos Pilas and Tikal are much farther apart than other sites that shared Emblem Glyphs, one must at least raise the question whether they may not also have been some sort of single or joint polity (see Molloy n.d.).

In addition to whatever role Tikal played in starting the Dos Pilas dynasty, it may also have been involved at Seibal where it has been suggested (Sabloff 1975; Mathews and Willey, this volume) on the basis of ceramic similarities that the site was recolonized from the Tikal/Uaxactun area in late Tepeu 1 after near abandonment toward the end of the Early Classic.

Mathews and Willey (this volume) outline the creation by Dos Pilas of a multicenter polity in the Pasion region. In addition, Dos Pilas was politically active in the central and northeast Peten. The accession of Jaguar Paw-Jaguar of Site Q (believed by Schele and Freidel [n.d.] to be Calakmul and by others to be El Peru) on 9.12.13.17.7 (AD 686) was commemorated at Dos Pilas, a rare instance of an inauguration being mentioned at a foreign site. Schele and Freidel (n.d.) believe that Dos Pilas installed Jaguar Paw-Jaguar as their vassal, a status he occupies in kneeling before a Dos Pilas (or Tikal) lord on a looted pot reported by Houston and Mathews (1985:Fig. 10). Dos Pilas also fostered the rejuvenation of the Naranjo dynasty by sending Lady Six Sky, daughter of Ruler 1 of Dos Pilas, to Naranjo (see below). The relationships between Dos Pilas and Tikal are clouded by uncertainty about Site Q (see below), but they continued until the death of Ruler 2 of Dos Pilas which was commemorated on the carved bones in the tomb of Ruler A at Tikal (Jones 1986).

Ruler A took the throne of Tikal on 9.12.9.17.16 (AD 682). He was the son of the preceding ruler Shield Skull and therefore a scion of the dynasty that Caracol may have imposed at the site. Nevertheless, as he began to move Tikal into a period of renewed power he wrapped himself in the mantle of an earlier Tikal line by invoking the memory of the Early Classic ruler Stormy Sky. The rejuvenation of Naranjo began with the arrival of Lady Six Sky from Dos Pilas on 9.12.10.5.12 (AD 682), only 116 days after the inauguration of Ruler A. Coba, far to the north, may have been tied into the scheme of interaction because a stela there also records the date of Lady Six Sky's arrival. The birth of Smoking Squirrel (a probable but not specifically attested son of Lady Six Sky) five years later and his inauguration at the age of five were key events in Naranjo's rise. Smoking Squirrel further reinforced ties to Dos Pilas or Tikal by later mentions of two separate women (one of whom may have been his wife) with the Tikal/Dos Pilas Emblem Glyph. Closs (1985) believes that Lady Six Sky outlived Smoking Squirrel and eventually became ruler of Naranjo in her own right. If so, she continued to use the Dos Pilas/Tikal Emblem Glyph and after her reign Naranjo entered a period of nearly three katuns without further inscriptions.

Naranjo and Tikal undertook nearly simultaneous military campaigns in the process of re-establishing their prestige. Naranjo (Schele and Freidel n.d.) engaged in four war events between 9.13.1.3.19 (AD 693) and 9.13.2.16.10 (AD 695). The last event featured the capture of a lord of Ucanal, indicating a sphere of operation to the south and into what must have been the old Caracol territory. The phrase "he of Dos Pilas/Tikal" occurs in the record of this capture (Schele 1986e), suggesting some sort of cooperation between Naranjo and one of these sites. On 9.13.3.7.18 (AD 695), less than a year after the last of Naranjo's war events, Ruler A undertook his first recorded war. It seems to have involved the capture of Jaguar Paw-Jaguar of Site Q, suggesting that Tikal's thrust was toward the west or northwest. It seems unlikely that the inauguration of Ruler A and arrival of Lady Six Sky within a few months and the rapid succession of Naranjo's and Tikal's military campaigns in opposite directions were coincidental. An alliance between the two sites involving coordinated activities to restore the grandeur of the central Peten must be considered a possibility.

If Dos Pilas and Tikal were allies, and Jaguar Paw-Jaguar was a vassal of Dos Pilas, the capture of Jaguar Paw-Jaguar by Ruler A of Tikal is puzzling. It is possible to imagine scenarios to explain the event. Jaguar Paw-Jaguar might have rebelled against his vassalage and his punishment been assigned to Ruler A who was in need of an important prisoner to use in the dedication ceremonies for Temple 1, the lintels of which record the capture of Jaguar Paw-Jaguar. It is also possible, however, that Dos Pilas and Tikal were rivals rather than allies, a solution favored by Schele and Freidel (n.d.) and Molloy (n.d.). All of these possibilities must remain in the realm of speculation, however, until more details are forthcoming from the inscriptions. It is particularly important to investigate additional inscriptions from El Peru to see whether there were interactions with Tikal or Dos Pilas.

Whatever the ties that interlinked sites in Tepeu 2, they do not seem to have endured for more than a century. As indicated in my summary articles (Culbert 1988b; this volume), following Fash (1985; Fash and Stuart, this volume), I believe that an increase in the number of sites with their own monuments and Emblem Glyphs that began in 9.17.0.0.0 (AD 771) was a sign of dilution of royal authority and, eventually, of political fragmentation that led to the collapse of Classic Maya society.

## THE SIZE OF MAYA POLITICAL UNITS

The foregoing summary of northeast Peten history assigns a more dominant role to long-distance political interaction than many other Mayanists might prefer. This reflects my disagreement with the consensus opinion of seminar participants about the size and degree of isolation of Maya political units. The consensus strongly favored a structure of small-scale political units, attributing political independence to each site that possessed an Emblem Glyph. In my summary articles (1988b, this volume), I have expressed reservations about this consensus without (given my role as summarizer) spelling out my objections. In this section, I will consider the evidence that bears upon the question and my reasons for believing that the issue remains unresolved.

I have recently (Culbert 1988b) reviewed the development of ideas about the size of Maya polities. In brief, modern reconstructions of Maya society began with a city-state model closely connected with the Morley (1946) and Thompson (1954) vision of vacant ceremonial centers, low population, and swidden agriculture. With the rejection of the Morley–Thompson model in the 1970s, there was increasing discussion of regional states based upon hierarchies in the size of sites (Adams and Jones 1981) and Marcus' (1976) hierarchical interpretation of the distribution of Emblem Glyphs. The pendulum has now swung back again with a renewal of a model of small-scale polities that is based almost entirely upon epigraphic data.

The primary basis for arguing that Maya political units were of small scale is the conclusion that each site that had its own Emblem Glyph was politically autonomous. If such was the case, there were, indeed, a large number of polities and the number tended to increase through time (see the charts in Mathews 1985). I would argue, however, that the equation of Emblem Glyphs with autonomy has been treated more as an article of faith than as a matter to be demonstrated by the careful evaluation of evidence. The reason for accepting the equation lies in the uses of Emblem Glyphs rather than in the nature of the glyph itself. Although there is residual disagreement, most epigraphers now believe that Emblem Glyphs were the names of polities. Because two or more separate locations can use the same Emblem Glyph, the glyph must represent the total polity rather than just its principal center. Because it would be easy to amass a tiresome worldwide list of historical examples in which what had once been independent polities kept their names, and often their rulers, after being incorporated into other polities, there has been no attempt to claim a general principle that having a name makes a polity independent.

There are, however, examples of kinds of Emblem Glyph usage that support the conclusion that politically dependent sites do not have their own Emblem Glyphs. (1) There are cases in the Usumacinta zone where the political structure is clearly expressed in inscriptions. Governors of cahal rank serving at smaller sites express their fealty to *ahaus* who ruled at larger sites. In these cases, the smaller sites do not use Emblem Glyphs. There are, however, only a few cases in which political relationships are so clearly expressed and they are confined to the western region – the only region where the rank of cahal appears with any frequency. (2) More widespread are cases in which two or more sites simultaneously use the same Emblem Glyph. In most such cases, the sites sharing an Emblem Glyph are close to each other and one is considerably larger. Such smaller sites probably were subsidiary parts of a larger polity, although there is usually nothing explicit in the inscriptions to rule out the possibility that some cases may represent competing sites claiming leadership of the same polity. Also, the case of the shared Emblem Glyphs of Tikal and Dos Pilas – two large sites separated by a considerable distance – has not been considered to represent a single polity. (3) There are instances in which small sites with inscriptions have no known Emblem Glyph. They may well have been dependencies of larger sites, but the small sites usually have few inscriptions and it may well be that Emblem Glyphs simply fail to occur in the preserved sections of their inscriptions. (4) Finally, there are cases of sites that have been defeated by others ceasing to erect monuments implying that they have lost the prerogative of inscriptions (and Emblem Glyphs).

There are also cases, however, that contradict an assumption that Emblem Glyphs invariably indicate autonomy. (1) There are several cases in which rulers who explicitly acknowledge overlords at other sites continue to use their own Emblem Glyphs. The Tamarindito polity was taken over by Dos Pilas about 9.15.0.0.0 (AD 731), but continued to have its own rulers who use the local Emblem Glyph (Houston and Mathews 1985; Mathews and Willey, this volume). Similarly, the ruler of Anonal expresses subservience to the lord of Seibal, but uses the Anonal Emblem Glyph (Mathews and Willey, this volume) and a lord of Bonampak uses the Bonampak Emblem Glyph while under the aegis of a Tonina ruler (Schele, this volume). Jaguar Paw-Jaguar of Calakmul or El Peru, even if he was a vassal of Dos Pilas as Schele and Freidel (n.d.) believe, still used his own Emblem Glyph. These cases demonstrate that secondary status within a larger polity did not automatically result in the loss of a polity's Emblem Glyph. (2) There are no known cases in which a polity that was incorporated within a larger polity changed its Emblem Glyph to that of its new master. (3) There are cases in which a lord uses two Emblem Glyphs simultaneously (Justeson, personal communication). In several instances a ruler of Bonampak uses both the Bonampak and Lacanha Emblem Glyphs; Yaxchilan rulers habitually name themselves with the Emblem Glyph of Yaxchilan followed by that of a second, perhaps different, site; Cauac Sky of Quirigua uses the

Emblem Glyphs of both Quirigua and Copan after capturing 18 Jog of Copan. These examples demonstrate that the Maya themselves considered it possible to name a site with its Emblem Glyph even when it was clearly not a separate and independent political unit.

From the foregoing evidence, it seems far from conclusively established the possession of an Emblem Glyph is an absolute and reliable indicator of political autonomy. Cases that support the conclusion are not overwhelmingly abundant and there are many contradictory examples. It is particularly dangerous to reconstruct political histories for sites such as Xultun, where inscriptions are very poorly preserved and so far offer no evidence aside from a few dates of stelae and the fact that a Xultun Emblem Glyph occurs. In reconstructing Maya political practices, we must allow for considerable variability in the manner in which relationships between sites were arranged. A small site incorporated into the political sphere of an expanding large neighbor might be treated very differently in terms of leadership and elite privileges (including Emblem Glyphs) than a major site subjugated in war.

If the general argument for small-scale polities based upon Emblem Glyph distribution is tenuous, that for larger political units is equally so. Now that Marcus' (1976) hypothesis about hierarchical ordering based upon non-reciprocal mentions of sites in the inscriptions of other sites has been superceded by actual translations, the general argument for large political units rests almost entirely upon archaeological evidence of the size of sites. Even granted the inadequacy of many site maps and the fact that none of them makes allowance for different dates of mapped structures, there can be little doubt that Late Classic sites with inscriptions differed drastically in size and that the differences suggest a structure in some regions (Adams and Jones 1981). What can be challenged is whether differences in site size correlate very well with political structure, something that has been assumed to be the case in regional state models.

Proponents of small- and larger-scale polities also differ in their evaluations of the primary function of Maya warfare. Nobody would deny that the capture and sacrifice of prisoners was important in ritual, nor can there be any doubt that warfare sometimes resulted in the conquest of territory. Nevertheless, the relative importance of these aspects is a matter of disagreement. The argument that war was indicative of expansive military policy has always been central to the hypothesis that the Maya created regional states (e.g., Molloy n.d.). More recently, there has been increasing emphasis, particularly among epigraphers, upon the view that the ceremonial and ideological functions of Maya warfare were more important than political ones. Epigraphers stress the fact that many prisoners lack names or, if named, lack Emblem Glyphs, and that there are cases in which known rulers were captured without apparent serious disruption of the size or fortunes of their sites. This view is expressed in Schele and Mathews' assertion (this volume) that "It now appears that most Maya warfare probably consisted of relatively small-scale raiding, the main aim of which was to obtain live victims for sacrifice." In seminar discussions, the Aztecs' "Flowery War" for the purpose of obtaining sacrificial victims was proposed as a possible model to characterize Maya warfare.

If such was the case, the Maya must be considered unique among societies of their scale and complexity. The Classic Maya had a very high population density accompanied by agricultural intensification. For such a society not to make territorial and resource aggrandizement a major priority of military activities would be almost without anthropological and historical precedent. The Aztec war of flowers cannot be claimed as a parallel case. Although the capture and sacrifice of prisoners was an important part of Aztec ritual and political legitimization, it was not the primary function of militarism, but an adjunct to armies of expansion that built a tribute empire by conquest. In fact, Hassig (1988) has recently argued that the war of flowers was no more than an early stage of military activity the eventual objective of which was conquest.

## SUMMARY AND CONCLUSIONS

The crucial point in the foregoing section is that the "typical" size of Maya polities is an unresolved issue. Arguments in favor of both small- and larger-scale polities are based upon data that remain tenuous and contradictory. The two regions for which we have the best epigraphic evidence offer contrasting cases. The Usumacinta zone (Schele, this volume) seems to have been one in which the major political centers retain their independence through the Late Classic and devoted their belligerence to such smaller targets as Lacanha and Pomona. In the Pasion region (Mathews and Willey, this volume), Dos Pilas put together a sizeable multi-center polity by a variety of mechanisms that included outright conquest.

To say, as Mathews and Willey (this volume) do, that Dos Pilas was an anomaly and that western sites were typical seems to me to reach an unwarranted conclusion. Operating with the assumption that sites were small and autonomous with borders that can be easily determined by noting which sites did or did not have Emblem Glyphs risks the danger of neglecting important evidence of interaction. I do not believe that the political history of the Maya lowlands can be reconstructed without adopting a regional, and even interregional, perspective. In considering the history of the northeast Peten, it seems very important to me that the fortunes of individual sites are correlated, either positively or negatively, with those of other sites. Tepeu 1 was a period of diminished activity (and even diminished population) at several northeast Peten sites; that this occurred at a time when Caracol pursued an active military policy that included intervention in the northeast Peten was probably not coincidental. The resurgence of the northeast Peten in Tepeu 2 corresponded with the decline of Caracol and involved a set of interactions that linked the elite of Dos Pilas, Tikal, Naranjo, and El Peru. Important dynasts came to the thrones of these sites within a relatively short interval and, at least in the case of Dos Pilas and Naranjo, involved individuals foreign to the sites. It is possible, as Closs (1985) suggests, that Dos Pilas, Tikal, and Naranjo were all ruled by members of a single great dynastic family or, as Molloy (n.d.) suggests, that Dos Pilas and Tikal comprised a single polity. Military campaigns that re-established the power of Tikal and Naranjo occurred at nearly the same time and were probably coordinated rather than coincidental. In the light of this evidence, interactions between sites seem critical to understanding the history of the northeast Peten. I will not at this point posit a specific political structure or comparative model for the Late Classic Maya. Alliance, confederacy, perhaps even a loosely structured joint polity ruled by members of a single family, are all possibilities. The important issue is to debate alternatives, test them with data already available and, in the long run, gather the additional epigraphic and archaeological data that will be necessary for more definitive conclusions.

*ACKNOWLEDGMENTS*

This paper has been through several drastic revisions as my knowledge of the Maya expanded thanks to the generosity of a number of colleagues. I was deeply influenced by both the papers and discussions of my colleagues at the Santa Fe seminar, even in cases where I may disagree. I have profited over the years from discussions of the Maya with John P. Molloy, who was the first to convince me of glyphic evidence for the territorial expansion of Maya states. I have also profited from my years of association with Richard E. W. Adams whose ideas about Maya regional states have influenced me in ways that are obvious. Additional suggestions about this paper for which I am grateful were provided by John S. Justeson, Michael B. Schiffer, and John W. Olsen.

# 7
# Dynastic history and cultural evolution at Copan, Honduras

WILLIAM L. FASH AND DAVID S. STUART

Over the course of the past fifteen years, a series of archaeological projects has been carried out in the Copan Valley. While differing in goals, theory, and methodology, all of these projects have yielded data bearing on the evolution of the Copan polity. They have also been committed to articulating the archaeological record with that of the inscribed stone monuments found at numerous sites in the valley. While some of these studies have also held different opinions regarding the respective reliability of (emic) epigraphic and (etic) archaeological data, all would agree that both sets of information are useful and necessary for a better understanding of the Maya past.

The feedback between the analysis of the excavated materials and the study of the hieroglyphic records also serves as a means by which we may evaluate the potential and the relevance of both sets of data. Events and processes in which the two do not agree are of particular interest because they allow us to analyze which may be more reliable or informative in a given situation. Unquestionably, the inscriptions give us more explicit information on dynastic history, legitimation strategies, and the timing and protagonists of Classic Maya warfare than we could ever hope to recover in a non-literate context. However, the public political claims made by members of rival polities can often best be tested using archaeological data, rather than relying on propagandistic statements and symbolism employed by historical actors with vested interests. Here we will concentrate on those aspects of the archaeological and epigraphic records which bear most directly on the evolution of the Copan polity through time and space.[1] The archaeological remains of the Copan Valley provide important insights into the social and demographic context of cultural and political changes among the several polities which recorded Classic Maya inscriptions in the southeastern Maya zone.

Much has been written about the degree to which Copan owes its peculiarities of art style and evolution to its geographic position. Scholars such as Morley, Spinden, and Proskouriakoff discussed the similarities and differences between the monuments of Copan and the northeast Peten, always with the idea that Copan's elites were strongly influenced by, if not directly derived from, the Maya who controlled such centers as Tikal. Morley's ideas were the basis of John Longyear's ceramically based interpretations of Peten-zone "penetration" at Copan in the Early Classic. This traditional view posits that the Copan Valley was colonized by Maya-speakers who brought the Initial Series and other trappings of the Classic Maya cultural tradition from the central Peten shortly after 9.0.0.0.0 (AD 435), and then commenced erecting inscribed monuments in the Classic period tradition. In Longyear's words, "a band of Classic Maya, devotees of the hierarchic cult which was flourishing in the Guatemala Peten, arrived in the valley and proceeded to bind the Archaic peoples to their doctrine" (Longyear 1952:68). Important new archaeological, epigraphic, and linguistic evidence has accrued since that time, and this new evidence and recent interpretations of it will be considered here.

Morley also held the belief that Quirigua was a colony of Copan, noting the similarities in layout and their shared citation of the date 9.15.6.14.6.6 Cimi 4 Tzec (AD 738; Morley 1920:273, 428). Again Morley's ideas were seconded, this time by an epigrapher who believed he had adduced evidence for a genealogical link between Quirigua's most prolific monument-builder and one of the outstanding Copan kings (Kelley 1962a:238). Proskouriakoff (1973:168) viewed the key passages analyzed by Kelley differently, and remarked that the prominence of the date at Quirigua "suggests that the ruler of Quirigua had the upper hand in this encounter, especially since we hear no more of 18 Jog at Copan after this date, and soon afterward Quirigua becomes a major center of stelae erection." Marcus (1976:135) and Sharer (1978:16) go farther and interpret the relevant clauses as statements of the capture of Copan's 18 Jog by the Quirigua ruler Two-Legged (=Cauac) Sky, with Quirigua becoming a fully independent center thereafter. This interpretation holds today, but there are a number of interesting new twists to the history which we will pursue here.

The relationship of Copan to the minor centers in its immediate hinterland, particularly Los Higos and Rio Amarillo, also provides data on the nature of all three sites. Morley (1920) again viewed these "minor ceremonial centers" as colonies, and, following him Marcus (1976:148) described them as "offshoots." Gary Pahl (1977) preferred to see them as largely independent minor centers, demonstrating local autonomy by erecting their own monuments. There is validity to both these interpretations, or at least it would seem so from the analysis of their inscribed monuments, and newly found ones within the Copan Valley which date to AD 756–822. These monuments and their implications for the evolution and nature of the Copan polity specifically, and Classic Maya political structure in general, will be a major focus of discussion here. The roles of warfare, regional politics, and royal patronage in the Late Classic Copan polity have been the subject of much research in recent years, and new data and interpretations will be presented.

In pursuing these questions, we shall proceed chronologically from earliest to latest. This is done both for ease of presentation and so that larger questions regarding the nature of Classic Maya polities, and the social context and uses of monumental state art and records, can be seen from an evolutionary perspective.

## PRECLASSIC AND EARLY CLASSIC ORIGINS IN THE COPAN VALLEY

The origin of Copan as a Maya center is still a debated issue. There is now a wealth of new data which bear upon this problem. New excavations conducted in the Copan Valley have unearthed a number of important Early Classic, and Preclassic, occupation levels and other ceramic-laden archaeological contexts (Baudez 1983a; Fash 1983a). The earliest Copan ceramics contain forms and decorative modes that clearly associate them with contemporary Preclassic, and Early and Middle Classic sites in the southern Maya area, i.e., the Pacific coast and adjacent uplands of Chiapas and Guatemala, as well as Chalchuapa in El Salvador. The presence of complex ("Olmec") iconography on burial ceramics from Copan ties in with the evidence for participation in the Olmec symbol system which is strongly visible at Pacific coast and piedmont centers such as Abaj Takalik. Fragments of three pot-belly statues have been found in Copan, which also argues for strong highland/Pacific coast input in Preclassic Copan society.

Lyle Campbell's extensive study (1977) of the linguistic identities of the Preclassic inhabitants of this area argues persuasively that the southern Maya area was originally Xincan and Mayan, and that the Mayan speakers were not "highland Mayan" (Mamean or Quichean), whom he argues to have been intrusive to the area in the Postclassic, but extremely ancient ancestors of Cholan. There is still considerable debate among epigraphers and linguists regarding whether the residents of Kaminaljuyu were ancient ancestors of Xincan or Cholan speakers. Justeson, Norman, Campbell, and Kaufman (1985) provide evidence that Kaminaljuyu was ancestral to lowland Maya, based on linguistic and archaeological evidence for interaction among the lowland Maya and between the lowland Maya and highland Maya and non-Maya ethnic groups. This monograph shows further that the ancestral lowland Mayan language involved must date back to at least the Middle Preclassic. While the linguistic evidence is not site specific, it shows that there was an ancestral lowland Mayan linguistic presence in the vicinity of Copan, whose descendant – Cholan – is precisely the subgroup of Mayan inscribed on the Late Classic monuments of Copan.[2]

Thus, rather than viewing the Copan Valley as being "colonized" by Mayan speakers who displaced or placed themselves above an indigenous non-Maya population in the Early Classic, we believe that the initial inhabitants of the zone were either Mayan, or Xincan intimately familiar with ancestral Cholan Mayan peoples, customs, and language. The question then becomes, what was the nature of interaction which encouraged or caused the adoption of hieroglyphic writing, stela dedication, and other hallmarks of "Classic" Maya culture by what had previously been a small and rather undifferentiated group of Mayan (or Xincan) speakers, far removed from the "core" area of lowland Classic Maya civilization?

Unfortunately, archaeological data on this problem are not as abundant as one would hope, owing to both the depth of the Early

Classic deposits and a (relative) paucity of research directed at addressing this issue. The textual record is also incomplete, since the vast majority of the Early Classic stelae were deliberately buried and/or mutilated by subsequent rulers. Although there is archaeological evidence for an increase in population in the Early Classic over the preceding Late Preclassic, there is at present no evidence for monumental constructions or ritual buildings of any consequence. Even in the site core (hereafter referred to as the "Main Group"), Cheek (1983) has evidence for modest constructions, but no associated sculpture nor evidence for monumental architecture until about AD 400. Of considerable interest here is the fact that a cache found in association with the earliest structure in the Main Group contained a polished blackware effigy-head vessel virtually identical to some found in Kaminaljuyu at the same point in time. One should also note that the earliest polychrome ceramics in Copan are more similar to those of the Guatemalan highlands than they are to anything from the Peten area. Thus, Copan's affiliations with the southern (highland and Pacific coastal) Maya, rather than the lowland Maya, continued through the Early Classic.

The earliest clearly contemporary date in the Copan inscriptions is recorded on the recently discovered Stela 63 (Fig. 7.1). The Initial Series date of this inscription reads 9.0.0.0.0 8 Ahau 14 Ceh, a date falling in AD 435. This monument was placed inside a structure now buried within the pyramidal base of the final version of Structure 10L-26. The fill used to bury this early edifice was placed there 200 years after the construction of the building. This indicates that this stela and the structure built to house it were accessible and in use – perhaps sacrosanct – for a very long time, before finally being absorbed in a much later construction. This conclusion is supported by the fact that four subsequent rulers at the site made reference to the date, event, and protagonist recorded on Stela 63; the "display of the Manikin Scepter" by the ruler Yax-K'uk-Mo' (founder of the Copan dynasty) on this important period-ending was a signal event in the history of this Classic Maya polity.

Another early sculpture – Stela 35 – does not carry an inscription in the part that has been preserved, but stylistically appears to be contemporaneous with Stela 63. Our colleague Linda Schele believes that it may be a portrait of Yax-K'uk-Mo'. In his analysis of this monument, Claude Baudez (1983b:187) dates it to about 9.0.0.0.0 and also

Fig. 7.1 The Initial Series of the upper fragment of Copan Stela 63.

states that its style may be attributable as much to highland as to lowland influence. This plus the ceramic evidence would tend to support an indigenous, highlands/Pacific coast interaction sphere for the origins of complex society and monument dedication practice in Copan in the Early Classic, with room for interaction with, though probably not hegemony by, emerging elites in the southern lowlands. It should be emphasized, however, that we have not yet got to the bottom of the cultural deposits under Structure 10L-26, and there may very well be more to the early written history of the Copan polity than we can presently report. Robert Sharer's ongoing investigations of the early architecture buried under the final phase East Court of the Acropolis may very well also yield important new information on this subject.

There is some intriguing evidence that although Yax-K'uk-Mo' is cited by later rulers as the founder of the Copan dynasty, he was apparently not the first ruler at the site. Fifty years after the commemoration of Stela 63, there is a back reference to an earlier individual named on Stela 24, who is cited as the "first to be seated as *ahau*" (i.e., accede to office; Fig. 7.2). This individual's glyphic name is not that of Yax-K'uk-Mo'. This raises the question of whether Yax-K'uk-Mo' was from a different lineage (or faction) than this earlier, "first seated" ruler. Present evidence suggests that there were several

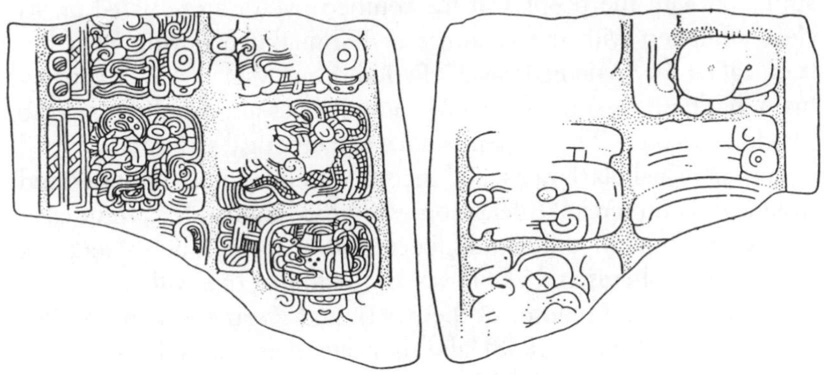

Fig. 7.2 Stela 24, Copan, with the Initial Series date 9.2.10.0.0 (AD 485) on the front side, and on the back the statement "first to be seated as ahau," followed by the name of an individual not from the Yax-K'uk-Mo' dynasty. Drawing by David Stuart.

segmentary lineages in the Copan Valley competing for power at this time, as the large land-holding families in the valley accrued power and prestige. It is plausible that the descendants of Yax-K'uk-Mo' were either genealogically or politically tied to him, and not to the ruler(s) who preceded him. Much remains to be done before we will be able to resolve this question satisfactorily.

## MIDDLE CLASSIC COPAN: POLITICAL CONSOLIDATION AND TERRITORIAL EXPANSION

Beginning in the early fifth century AD, Yax-K'uk-Mo' consolidated a corporate political entity from which subsequent rulers claimed orderly succession. Placed directly in front of Stela 63 was a hieroglyphic step, inscribed with a long text including the name of the fourth ruler in the Yax-K'uk-Mo' dynasty, Cu-Ix, and dated to *c.* AD 470. The Initial Series Date of Stela 24 was long ago deciphered as falling on 9.2.10.0.0 (AD 485; Morley 1920:78). Like the other monuments inscribed at about this time, Stela 24 was found in a battered, broken state, buried beneath the base of Stela 7 in the locality presently covered by the modern village of Copan Ruinas.

The ceramics in use in the Copan Valley during the reign of Yax-K'uk-Mo' and his first eleven successors show evidence for continued affiliation with the peoples in the southern Maya area. Based on its clear affiliation with the ceramics of Kaminaljuyu during what has been called the "Middle Classic" Period, René Viel (1983) designated his Acbi-phase ceramics (dated AD 400–700) as also pertaining to the "Middle Classic." The preponderance of cylindrical slab-footed tripod vessels, polished blackwares, and incised vessels bespeaks intensive and sustained commercial interaction with the highlands, presumably through Kaminaljuyu or an affiliated port of trade. The presence of Thin Orange sherds and whole vessels (including one with an incised Tlaloc face on the interior of the bowl), and green obsidian (Willey, Leventhal, and Fash 1978) also indicate that goods having their ultimate origins in central Mexico were items prized by the Middle Classic Copan elites. Some researchers have also made a case for the iconography of Stela 6 showing evidence of contacts with Teotihuacan (Hellmuth 1976). Although there are alternative explanations for the iconography of Stela 6, nonetheless we would be remiss not to recognize the overwhelming archaeological evidence for interaction with the highlands during the Middle Classic.

There is virtually no evidence for trade of polychrome ceramics or other elite items from the southern lowlands to Copan during the Middle Classic period. This fits in well with previous patterns since, as we have seen, Copan's strongest ties during the Preclassic and Early Classic are with the areas to the west and south, and not to the lowlands. However, the large centers in the northeast Peten do seem to have served as a model for the Copan elite to emulate. This is seen in the presence of plaster masks adorning the substructure of a large pyramidal structure buried underneath Structure 10L-26 (Stromsvik 1952:198) in the tradition of the plaster masks adorning Late Preclassic structures in numerous sites in the Peten and adjacent Belize. Such masks are also found on a substructure buried underneath the final phase architecture of the East Court of the Copan Acropolis, uncovered in 1989 by Sharer, David Sedat, and Alfonso Morales (provisionally designated "Ante Platform"), which even has Peten-style apron mouldings. Emulation of lowland elite political symbolism is also evident in the portraits of the rulers themselves on such monuments as Stelae E, P, and 7.

There are contemporary monuments which contain references to the 1st, 4th, 7th, and 10th through 16th rulers. The 11th ruler, Butz Chan, is of considerable interest here in that one of his monuments (Stela P) cites what Linda Schele (personal communication 1989) interprets to be the Emblem Glyph of Los Higos (Fig. 7.3a). This same glyph is also cited by the 13th ruler, 18 Jog, on Stela A (Fig. 7.3b), and these references may mean that these rulers claimed some sort of hegemony over the La Venta Valley or at least the site of Los Higos (Fig. 7.3c). The junior author, however, notes that this glyph may also simply be read *ba ahau*, and be a lordly title, rather than a reference to the polity of Los Higos. New archaeological evidence needs to be acquired in order to test Schele's hypothesis, and help us to understand if there was sustained and serious domination of Los Higos by Copan, or an attenuated and fleeting influence, or little or no control of this area by the Copan elites. We will return to this question in our consideration of late eighth-century regional politics, below.

In the final century of the Middle Classic (AD 400–700), a ruler of considerable virtuosity reigned in Copan. Named "Smoke Jaguar" by Riese (1983) and referred to by the authors as "Smoke-Imix-God K,"

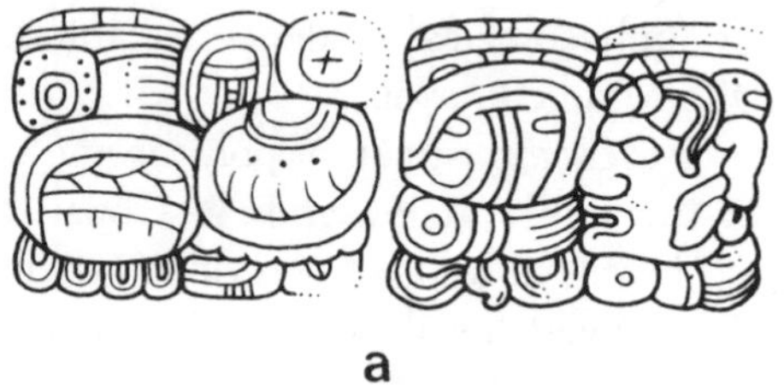

a

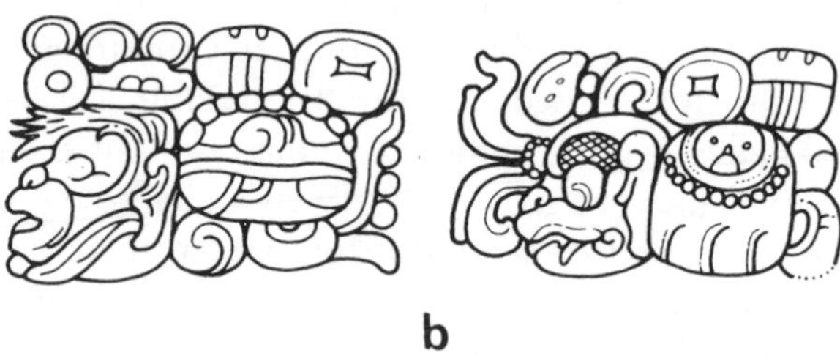

b

c

Fig. 7.3 Examples of the Los Higos Emblem Glyph (or *Ba Ahau* title): *a* Stela P, east side; *b* Stela A, west side; *c* Los Higos, Stela 1. Drawings by Barbara Fash.

this individual was responsible for the dedication of Stelae I, 1, 2, 3, 5, 6, 10, 12, 13, 19, and 23, Altars K, H', and I', the Hieroglyphic Steps of the original version of Structure 10L-2 in the Main Group, and quite probably a number of constructions now buried beneath the later buildings of the Copan Acropolis. The archaeological record indicates considerable population growth during his reign, and an increase in societal complexity. Fash (1983b) has argued that the Copan polity was rapidly evolving the size and complexity concomitant with a state level of socio-political integration by the end of Smoke-Imix-God K's reign. However, discovery and excavation of more seventh-century Copan settlements is necessary before one can demonstrate a population of 10,000 people in the Copan-sustaining area during the reign of Smoke-Imix-God K.

One of the more remarkable legacies of this prolific ruler's reign is the series of monuments (Stelae 10, 12, 13, 19, and 23) which were erected on the edges of the Copan pocket of the Copan Valley system. A number of different interpretations have been offered to account for these stelae, from Morley's giant sundial theory (1920:133) to Proskouriakoff's association of ancestors with sacred mountains (1973:171), to Spinden (1913) and Marcus' (1976:129; see also Leventhal 1979) demarcation of the limits of the polity's domain. The inscriptions themselves will no doubt help to resolve this question, once they have been satisfactorily read. At least one ancestor, the founder Yax-K'uk-Mo', is cited prominently on Stelae 10 and 12, and the idea of demarcating the ruler's territory certainly seems plausible. One should also note that the distribution of the monuments – at least in the eastern entrance to the Copan pocket – conforms to a series of sight-lines such as might be used in a rapid communications system. Of course, such systems are a common feature throughout the world, and we should not be surprised that the Maya would have employed them, especially in an area of rugged terrain such as Copan. The potential implications of this observation, however, are more interesting. The senior author has suggested (1983b:225) that this network of monuments may in fact have served defensive purposes, implying preparedness on the part of the Copan elites for attack from outside the Copan pocket.

In this context one takes special interest in the iconography of Stela 6, one of the last monuments commemorated by Smoke-Imix-God K. On it one finds abundant "year sign" and Tlaloc iconography. Proskouriakoff (1973:171) was the first to demonstrate an association between year signs and warriors, citing the example of Piedras Negras Lintel 1. The combined Tlaloc/year sign iconography is also prominent on the two monuments (Aguateca Stela 2 and Dos Pilas Stela 2) which proclaim the capture of the Seibal ruler Jaguar Paw (see Mathews and Willey, this volume). In Copan the only other time it is used prominently is on the seated figures of the Hieroglyphic Stairway, where the presence of shields and spears with the same figures, and abundant war and sacrifice iconography in the temple façade show that these symbols served to identify the ruler as a warrior. Linda Schele

(1986d) has pursued this question further with comparative evidence from other sites, and has come to the same conclusion.

Thus, late in his reign, it seems that Smoke-Imix-God K not only took steps to insure the defensibility of his kingdom, but sought to portray himself as an able warrior, complete with potent supernatural support and symbolism. Does this mean that Copan was being threatened, or was beginning to be worried, by intra-regional rivals? In comparing the Copan and Quirigua inscriptions, Stuart made an epigraphic reading that may help answer this question. On Altar L of Quirigua (Fig. 7.4), there is a portrait of a figure seated cross-legged within a quatrefoil, in typical Copan style. The figure is identified by a series of glyphs which read "Smoke-Imix-God K," the standard name

Fig. 7.4 Altar L of Quirigua. Drawing by Barbara Fash, after Maudslay (1889–1902, II:Plate 49).

phrase of the Copan ruler. This poses the possibility that Smoke-Imix-God K may have conquered or otherwise secured the fealty of the elites of Quirigua.[3] If this were true, it would place the subsequent capture of Copan's next ruler, 18 Jog, by his Quirigua rival Cauac Sky, in sharper focus. Cauac Sky apparently obtained his political independence from Copan in this way, and his "independence day" is recorded on five different Quirigua monuments, and to this day much remarked upon. It would also explain the explosive growth of Quirigua following the capture: Cauac Sky would have been the Maya equivalent of David defeating Goliath, reaping a political windfall from his dramatic victory.

## LATE CLASSIC COPAN: WARFARE, POLITICS AND PATRONAGE IN THE EVOLUTION OF DYNASTIC POWER

The onset of production of Copador pottery in southeastern Mesoamerica corresponds with a series of changes in interaction and economy in the area. Whereas during the Middle Classic, Copan's strongest ties were to the Upper Motagua and the highlands of Guatemala to the west, and the adjacent La Venta Valley to the east, at the end of that period their exchange to the west was severed (perhaps owing to the devolution of the Kaminaljuyu polity at this time) and Copan's interaction shifted to sites found to its south and east. The precise dating of the initial production and redistribution of Copador is still a matter of debate, but most authorities on the subject place it somewhere between AD 650 and 731, with AD 650–700 being the placement preferred by the Copan Project ceramicist (Viel 1983). This would correspond approximately with the end of the reign of Smoke-Imix-God K, which as noted may have been a time of political expansion within the Copan region itself. Copan's response to this set of events, and arguably as much attributable to internal growth and differentiation, was to become a regional center for the production and redistribution of polychrome ceramics. Ronald Bishop's neutron activation work suggests that the clay sources used in the production of Copador polychrome were to be found somewhere in the Copan Valley, leading to the conclusion that Copan was the production center for this widely traded ware. Following this interpretation, the Copan polity engaged in sustained and intense exchange systems with numerous localities in the southeast periphery where Copador has been found. Demarest (1988) has pursued this further, suggesting that through the acquisition and redistribution of Copador pottery, and pilgrimages to Copan, other nascent or established elites in western El Salvador (and western and central Honduras) were able to reinforce their own status through contacts with and emulation of the royal court of Copan.

This idea has much archaeological support in Copan. There are vast quantities of central Honduran Ulua (or "Ulua-Yojoa") polychrome pottery found in excavations in the Copan pocket. The most remarkable aspect of their distribution is that they are not restricted to elite contexts, or even to burial contexts, but show up in the middens of even the most humble house-mounds on the outskirts of the Copan pocket (Fash 1983a:406). Thus, exchange with areas to the south and east resulted in the importation of great quantities of polychrome pottery, and possibly other commodities as well (Leventhal, Demarest, and Willey 1982). One of the more interesting aspects of the excavations conceived and directed by William Sanders in the Second Phase of the Copan Project was the discovery and exposure of a courtyard or plaza group which housed what may have been immigrants to the Copan Valley from central Honduras (Gerstle 1987). It would appear that Sanders has managed to acquire some very compelling evidence for a patron–client system for the Copan Maya with Gerstle's investigation of Patio D of Group 9N-8. Higher concentrations of Ulua polychrome ceramics were found here than anywhere else in the Copan Valley, and a distinctive (lower Central American) tripod metate as well as unusual or unprecedented architectural forms and burial patterns point to non-Copan sources for the occupants of Patio D. The family or other corporate group in question was apparently attached to the larger, indigenous corporate group which owned the resided in Group 9N-8, but kept at something of a social distance. There was no direct access from Patio D to the central part of the site where the most important members of the indigenous lineage lived. Furthermore, infant and child mortality were much higher in Patio D than in the other patios at the site, suggesting that malnutrition and/or disease were more of a problem here than among the households of the indigenous lineage members and clients. The quality of the architecture and graves, however, prevents us from claiming these people were slaves; they lived in well-constructed masonry buildings and had some of the best-built and -stocked tombs on the site. They appear to be clients who were dependent upon and lived with a long-established elite land-holding lineage in the valley.

Although polychromes from other production areas in the southeastern periphery enjoy a wide distribution in the Copan Valley, polychromes imported from other Maya centers are exceedingly rare. Those which have been found derive either from the Main Group or from elite class residential groups in the urban core of Copan. Demarest's model of status reinforcement may also apply equally well to the Copan elites, who through acquisition of lowland Classic Maya objects sought to reify their own exalted positions. And in this context, we are led to consider the famous citation of other lowland centers on Stela A.

Thomas Barthel (1968b) and Joyce Marcus (1976) both considered the text of Copan Stela A, with its citation of four emblems. Cited are Copan, Tikal, Calakmul (or, according to recent fieldwork, possibly El Peru), and Palenque. Their apparent association with "four skies" and the four cardinal directions was adduced as evidence that these four centers were the most important ones in the Maya lowlands at that point in time. Some suggest that 18 Jog may actually be claiming some sort of dominion over the other three centers. As this point it cannot be said that a consensus exists among epigraphers regarding the meaning of this inscription. Whether 18 Jog was claiming dominion over the other centers, or some sort of military-political alliance, or something else altogether, none of his claims did him much good. A scant six years after the dedication of Stela A, he was captured by the Quirigua ruler Cauac Sky.

The date 9.15.6.14.6 6 Cimi 4 Tzec (3 May, AD 738) is recorded five times in the inscriptions of Quirigua, and only once (on Step 41 of the Hieroglyphic Stairway) at Copan. The reading of "capture" was first proposed by Joyce Marcus, though as noted Proskouriakoff (1973:168) was the first to propose that Quirigua had the upper hand in whatever encounter was being recorded. There are two different versions of the verb, one of which is similar to the "capture" glyph identified by Proskouriakoff (1964) at Piedras Negras. The other version of the verb contains an axe, and some epigraphers refer to this glyph as the "axe event." Linda Schele, George Stuart, and David Stuart were the first to identify this "axe event" glyph as being associated with scenes of decapitation in Maya funerary ceramics (personal communications 1984). It would therefore appear that the event which took place in AD 738 was not merely the capture of 18 Jog, but rather his decapitation, at the hands of Cauac Sky.

In the case of Quirigua, an unprecedented expansion takes place on the heels of this event (Sharer 1978). Not only do more monuments go up at Quirigua than ever before, they are erected in a manner very reminiscent of that at Copan. Morley (1920:428) long ago recognized the similarities in layout between the two sites, a pattern which led him to conclude that Quirigua was in fact a colony of Copan. However, given our new knowledge of the historical connections between the two, let us consider some new interpretations of the old material. Rather than being coerced into imitating Copan, it would appear that Cauac Sky's efforts were in fact a deliberate ploy to "one-up" his former masters.

Copan's Stela J, the famous mat stela, commemorated the accession of 18 Jog at 9.13.3.6.8 7 Lamat 1 Mol (AD 695). This places the accession monument of 18 Jog squarely at the entrance to the Main Group at its eastern entry, exactly at the terminus (or beginning) of the *sacbe* (causeway) leading to the "Las Sepulturas" residential ward (Fash and Long 1983:Map 12 "Grupo Principal"). Morley (1920:204) noted that Stela J was probably the first monument erected after the Great Plaza was laid out. Such a prominent placement seems perfectly in line with a stela of this importance. In Quirigua, the only stela with a mat pattern, Stela H, is placed at the entrance to the site in an equivalent position to Copan's Stela J, in front of the canoe port reconstructed by Sharer and his colleagues. Furthermore, like Copan's Stela J, it was the first stela erected after the Great Plaza area was laid out; the slightly earlier Stela S was placed at a site at some distance from the Main Group. And although there is no mention of accession in the inscription itself, the mat iconography (symbolic of royal power) on this monument is in keeping with the theme of the assumption of power. Clearly, this is a direct emulation of the Copan pattern. Cauac Sky not only recorded his victory over Copan, he sought to build his own version of the rival city on a grander scale, with a larger Great Plaza, with taller and more imposing stelae, with more elaborate full-figure glyphs, larger and more complex zoomorphic altars, marble temples, etc. Although Cauac Sky made a valiant effort to follow through with his vision, his successors had a much tougher go of it.

Quirigua, with a much smaller resident population than Copan, was not able to follow through with this grand plan, and ends up making a parody of itself.

Copan, on the other hand, was down but not out. It became apparent some time ago that the supporting population of Copan did not decline in size or productivity as a result of losing its ruler (Fash 1983b; 1986a). Much has been made of the fact that no stelae were erected in Copan for nineteen years following the capture (decapitation) of 18 Jog. Given the prolific record of the Copan kings (particularly 18 Jog and Smoke-Imix-God K), this pause was considered most noteworthy and significant. Berthold Riese (1986) was the first to point out, however, that this cessation in erection of stelae was at least partially explainable by the fact that the Copanecs were busy with the construction and embellishment of the final version of Structure 10L-26, with its elaborate Hieroglyphic Stairway. The stairway itself, Riese observed, was the equivalent of some twenty Copan stelae in scope and sophistication. There was a stela at its base, Stela M, which Morley (1920:279) and others think was the crowning statement of the monument as a whole. But what was the message of this magnificent structure, bearing as it did the longest single hieroglyphic inscription of the New World?

In January 1986, a large-scale, multi-disciplinary research project was initiated by the senior author, dedicated to the excavation, proper recording, reconstruction, interpretation, and analysis of the architectural sculpture which adorned the temple and Hieroglyphic Stairway of Structure 10L-26. Based on the interpretations of the project epigraphers (Stuart and Schele), we began the project with two hypotheses regarding the stairway inscription. The first was that the Copan example, like the hieroglyphic stairways at several other Maya centers, represented a conquest monument imposed upon a subjugated center by its conquerors from another site, in this case Quirigua. The second hypothesis was that the Hieroglyphic Stairway was an indigenous reaffirmation of power, citing the glorious history of the previous Copanec kings in an effort to downplay the loss of 18 Jog and exalt both his predecessors and successors in the local dynastic sequence. The latter hypothesis held that the purport of the monument was to restore faith in the sacred and secular basis of the original Copan dynasty, and enable the population to rally anew behind their divine king. We set out to resolve which of the two hypotheses was best supported by the data by conducting new excavations of the building, and by a renewed effort at recording the stairway inscription.

These new investigations of Structure 10L-26 have succeeded in clarifying a number of issues. The drawings of the stairway inscription done by the chief artist Barbara Fash have been checked and analyzed by the project epigraphers, with a number of important results. The stairway inscription has been shown to detail the exploits of at least ten Copan kings over the period AD 565–756. The primary theme of the stairway text is the citation of the birth, accession dates, important rites, and death dates for the Copan rulers. Our new excavations also recovered fragments from the temple inscriptions which, like those unearthed by the Peabody and Carnegie expeditions, cite the rulers' names and at least one accession date. The parts of the temple inscriptions found and re-articulated to date show that it was at least in part a list of kings: the names of the 15th, 14th, 12th, and possibly the 11th rulers are recorded.

The seated figures on the Hieroglyphic Stairway in all likelihood represent the earlier Copanec kings as revered ancestors, and our excavation and re-articulation of the temple fragments has shown that there were six royal portraits adorning the temple façade. The eccentric flint lances found by Stuart in the cache beneath the altar forming the base of the Hieroglyphic Stairway (Fig. 7.5) represent other accoutrements of distinguished warriors. Of considerable interest is the fact that many of the temple inscription blocks make extensive use of Tlaloc heads and year signs as decorative (non-diagnostic) signs in glyphs (the diagnostic parts of the same glyphs being easily identifiable). The association of Tlaloc iconography with warriors gives one the feeling that even the inscription here was being labeled as a warrior text.

One of the more intriguing finds to come out of our work on Structure 26 was the finding and fitting of a number of fragments of tenoned mosaic sculpture masks which were originally inset into Temple 26's façade. The re-articulation of these mask fragments (largely the handiwork of Barbara Fash) resulted in the reconstruction of a very distinctive deity, whose circular eyes give him a "goggle-eye" or Tlaloc aspect. The lines above the eyes, and the mouth are also reminiscent of Tlaloc visages within and outside the Maya area. It is apparent from our plotting of the sculptures and the actual motif

Fig. 7.5 The Hieroglyphic Stairway cache objects. Inside the lidded ceramic censer were placed the two jades, the flint lance, the spiny oyster shell, and the sting-ray spines. The lanceolate eccentric flints were placed next to each other in a vertical position, adjacent to the censer vessel. Photograph by Reyna Flores.

counts that there were six such masks adorning the temple: one on each corner, one at the center of the east side, and one over the central doorway on the west side. They must have been a very predominant aspect of the iconography of Temple 26 on all four sides of the building (Fash 1988).

Accompanying the Tlaloc masks were a number of other related symbols and themes. The portrait figures from the temple carried a shield in the left hand and probably a lance in the right, like the bottommost (*in situ*) seated figure on the stairway. Other symbols include rectangular shields not carried by the rulers (shown in warrior scenes at other Maya centers), scalloped shells and large conch shells (Underworld markers). Temple 26 is blatantly dedicated to themes of war and sacrifice, as was the annex building (Structure 10L-230) attached to its south side, which was decorated with sculptures of fleshless human long bones and skulls, reminiscent of the skull rack at Chichen Itza.

Although the decapitation date is indeed mentioned on the Stairway text, it does not appear that the text is out to glorify Quirigua or its rulers. To date no blocks have been found which cite the names of any Quirigua kings, not even Cauac Sky. The names and dates are purely Copanec, and the inscription seems to pay special homage to the illustrious predecessor of 18 Jog, Smoke-Imix-God K. Given the new reading of Quirigua Altar L, one begins to wonder if the citation of the Quirigua Emblem (Maudslay 1889–1902, V:32) may not be in conjunction with his subjugation of the Quirigua lineage prior to the demise of 18 Jog. Indeed, Stuart and Schele (1986b:14) note that what may be the actual dedicatory date of the stairway is followed not by the name of the king who commemorated it, but rather by the name of Smoke-Imix-God K. The bottom section of the stairway, presumably the first to be read, deals primarily with historical data relating to the reign of Smoke-Imix-God K. The citation of earlier ancestors in the other parts of the inscription re-affirmed the legitimacy of Smoke-Imix-God K, as well as that of the rulers who followed him, but it appears that his was the memory most recalled and revered in this critical site history.

All present evidence leads to the conclusion that Structure 10L-26 and its Hieroglyphic Stairway represent an indigenous re-affirmation of Copan power, rather than a conquest monument imposed upon it by the Quirigua lineage. This has several implications for our understanding of Maya warfare in the Late Classic period. First, Classic period bellicose encounters did not necessarily result in the absorption of one polity into the economic or political orbit of another. This is demonstrated by the historical record at the two sites. Although Cauac Sky (on Quirigua Stela A) claims dominion over Copan by listing its Emblem in his epithets, the first Copan monument (Structure 10L-26) following the demise of 18 Jog lets us know otherwise. The archaeological evidence also shows no great influx of Copan goods, or citizens, into Quirigua following AD 738, nor as we noted does Copan's supporting population go into a reduction of numbers or necessarily of productivity. Nonetheless, there was apparently a material incentive behind this act of war: Cauac Sky obtained his independence from his former masters. Second, even if warfare did not always involve massive transfers of arable land, people, goods, and services,[4] it was unquestionably a very potent source of ideological and secular power. This is demonstrated clearly by the radical transformation of Quirigua on the one hand, and the extreme elaboration and impressiveness of Copan Structure 10L-26 on the other. For the victor, the event was a watershed; for the loser, it was a time to retrench and revive the glorious times of old. Indeed, Structure 26 provides good evidence for the validity of Kautz and Jones' (1981) thinking on revivalist movements and their formulation in times of stress. In terms of the ruling elite of Maya society, warfare was indeed an important mechanism of culture change.

A final turn to our story of legitimation in the wake of the sacrifice of 18 Jog concerns not the kings who immediately follow him, but rather what may have been his grandson or other two-generation-removed relative. The 16th king of Copan is referred to by a variety of names in the literature: "Yax Sun-at-Horizon," "Yax Pac," "New Sun-at-Horizon," "New Horizon," "Madrugada" (Dawn), and "Rising Sun." On Stela 8 of Copan, we find glyphs which state that this ruler was the son of a woman from Palenque. As a means of status reinforcement, the 15th ruler of Copan married a Palenque woman, in order to bring added prestige to his offspring. One of those offspring became the last and in many ways most celebrated dynast in the history of Copan.

WILLIAM L. FASH and DAVID S. STUART

# THE REIGN OF YAX SUN-AT-HORIZON: ROYAL PATRONAGE AND THE DISSOLUTION OF DYNASTIC POWER IN THE COPAN POLITY

The archaeological record indicates quite clearly that Copan continued to grow in size and complexity through the reign of its last ruler, Yax Sun-at-Horizon, attaining the size, hierarchical structure, and organizational requirements of most definitions of the pre-industrial state (Fash 1983b; Sanders and Webster 1988). Indeed, the polity grew to such a size that the limits to growth, within the 24 $km^2$ or so of the Copan pocket proper, were reached, and the population began to suffer from its own excesses. This can be seen in the evidence amassed by William Sanders and David Webster in their continuing research into Copan Valley settlement patterns, and the study of the human skeletal remains by Rebecca Storey. The most fertile sectors of the pocket, the alluvial bottomlands, were mainly taken up by settlements, and the next best terrains (the high river terraces and gently rolling piedmont) were rapidly undergoing the same transformation. This left only the upper slopes with their thin layers of topsoil for cultivation, with detrimental long-term ecological consequences. The human skeletal remains show that, at the close of the eighth century, the majority of the population (whether urban or rural) shows signs of malnutrition and/or disease (Storey 1983). Copan eventually became the victim of its own success for, with the last recorded monument in Copan on Altar L in AD 822, the centralized ruling apparatus collapses, leaving the resident population in the valley to tend their property and continue living in much the same way as before. Interestingly enough, Sanders', Webster's, and Ann Freter's work indicates that they did so for quite some time after the end of centralized rule (Sanders and Webster 1988; Webster and Freter n.d.).

What bears discussion here is the evidence for interaction between the important lineage heads in the valley, and the next-to-last ruler of Copan, which shows royal patronage in a clear fashion, and has also been interpreted to mean that there was a visible weakening of centralized rule just before its demise. This interaction has left a remarkably clear legacy in the archaeological record. The first clear record of interaction between an elite family and the royal line was the hieroglyphic bench discovered by Richard Leventhal at Structure 9M-

158 in 1977 as part of Gordon Willey's Copan Valley Project (Willey, Leventhal, and Fash 1978). Peter Mathews deciphered the dedicatory date, verb, and protagonist of the bench inscription to be 9.17.10.0.0 12 Ahau 8 Pax (AD 782), "scattering," (by) Yax Sun-at-Horizon (personal communication 1977). The inscription was commemorated at this elite residential compound (a "Type 3" site, by the Willey and Leventhal [1979] typology) by the reigning dynast, who sought to show his concern for the welfare of these prominent citizens by performing a period-ending ("scattering") ceremony within the confines of their most impressive masonry structure.

Another, even more elaborate hieroglyphic bench was uncovered by David Webster and Elliot Abrams (1983) as part of William Sanders' large-scale excavations in the same residential zone. The bench was found within the central room of a large vaulted masonry structure (designated 9N-82) which was the most sumptuous building of the site of Group 9N-8, a Type 4 site (the largest and highest-status type-site in the Willey and Leventhal [1979] typology). As noted above, the head of this particular lineage had sufficient land holdings and/or other sources of wealth to be able to attract clients to his residential group from outside his immediate family, and even from outside the Copan pocket. Of the people within his inner circle, at least two were of sufficient status to merit having sculpture adornment on their own buildings. The largest structures of Patios B and C were both embellished with sculpture, including a hieroglyphic text on the exterior façade of Structure 9N-69. But Structure 9N-82 was clearly the palace of the lineage head, and its sculpture gives a unique window into inter-elite interactions during Copan's apogee. A series of publications are in press or in preparation on the subject of this sculpture (Fash 1986c, 1989; Webster 1989; Sanders 1989), and the interested reader is referred to them for details used to support the summary presented below, as well as alternative viewpoints (Baudez 1989).

The hieroglyphic inscription of the central room of Structure 9N-82 contains sixteen glyphs, and is sustained by six pillars carved with the images of atlantean figures. The text begins with a Calendar Round date falling within the reign of the ruler Yax Sun-at-Horizon, followed by the verb and the name of the protagonist. The verb contains the compound *yotot*, long recognized in the codices as having the meaning "in the house (or temple)." The event, then, takes place within the structure, and is assumed to have to do with the dedication of the building itself. The name of the protagonist is one which does not appear in any of the texts from the Main Group. Its only other known occurrence is on the inscription from Altar W', which is believed originally to have been placed in front of this structure (Webster, Fash, and Abrams 1986). The glyph following the name of the protagonist of the temple event is a "child of mother" expression, with the mother being identified as "Lady Ahau Kin." This name is believed to signify that the mother was conversant with calendrics and writing, following the meaning given by Landa to the term "Ahau Kin." This makes extremely good sense, given the iconography of the exterior façade of the building, and the sculpture associated with the preceding version of this structure (see below). Following the name of the mother are a series of poorly understood glyphs, with a secondary clause at the end of the text interpreted by Schele to mean that a ceramic offering was brought to the dedication ceremony by the ruler of Copan, Yax Sun-at-Horizon. It is obvious that although the protagonist is powerful enough to be commemorated on his own bench throne and palace structure, he derives some of that power from his association (whatever its nature) with the reigning king.

The façade iconography has been reconstructed, based on the position of the fallen elements and comparative evidence (Fash 1986b,c, n.d.). On either side of the central doorway leading into the bench were niches, framed by a split serpent head. Emerging from the jaws of the serpent were anthropomorphic deities, whose conch-shell inkpots and pectoral element enable us to identify them as variants of Michael Coe's (1977) "Monkey-Man" God of Writing. This same deity was found in a full-round presentation in association with the preceding version of this same structure (designated Structure 9N-82 C 2nd), indicating a continuity of worship of this god, possibly as the lineage patron (Fash 1986c). Furthermore, a burial found in association with the earlier building contained a jadeite bar pectoral identical to the one worn by the seated human figure placed front and center over the doorway leading into the bench of the final phase structure, which Fash believes to be a portrait of the protagonist of the bench inscription and the head of the localized lineage (Fash 1986b). Furthermore, one of the atlantean supports of the bench contains a portrait of an ancestor in the position of a *Pauahtun* (the guise in which the Monkey Man was portrayed at this building), indicating that the predecessor of the protagonist has become apotheosized at death as the lineage patron himself. All of this serves to indicate that the elite lines in Copan were not only involved in ancestor and lineage-patron worship (Fash 1986c), they were able to commission and dedicate finely carved sculpture monuments in their own honor.

An even more striking case of the importance of the elite lineages residing outside the Main Group of Copan comes from the site now occupied by the modern village, termed "Group 9" by Morley (1920). Altars T and U were both found in this area, and it has long been known that Yax Sun-at-Horizon's one katun anniversary (9.17.12.5.17; AD 783) is recorded on Altar T. But it has been only recently that Stuart and Schele have shown that an entirely different person is the focus of both these altars. Named with a crossed-bands sign, sky, and a skull glyph, this character is named in association with the hotun ending 9.18.5.0.0 (AD 795), and a seating event that took place within five years of that date. The office into which he accedes does not appear to be that of the high king, and his parentage statement says that he is the son of Yax Sun-at-Horizon's mother, but sired by a different father (presumably after the death of the 15th Copan ruler, Smoke Shell; Schele and Grube 1987). The inscriptions suggest that he is an ahau who is eligible to carry the Copan Emblem Glyph, but who holds office under the authority of Yax Sun-at-Horizon.

In 1988, excavations conducted on Structure 22A by Sheree Lane as part of the Copan Acropolis Project uncovered a small hieroglyphic altar with a thirty-glyph text inscribed on its top. The text cites the Period Ending 9.17.10.0.0 (AD 780) and Yax Sun-at-Horizon as the protagonist of the "scattering" event, but it also cites his half-brother and the date of his "seating." The building itself was decorated with *na* (house) and *pop* (mat) sculptures, and as such is labeled as the na pop (or popol na), the Mat House or Community House, if we may use analogy from the Popol Vuh and definitions in several Maya dictionaries for analogy. In the Popol Vuh, as Barbara Fash pointed out to us early on, the Mat (Community) House was where the lords convened, where all important community matters were discussed, and where disputes were adjudicated. Thus, the citation of the half-brother on this altar is a reflection of his importance in the political scheme of things. Besides this mention of him, and those on Altars T and U in Group 9, he is also cited on Altars G1 and G2 in the Great Plaza, further evidence of his status and power during the reign of Yax Sun-at-Horizon.

Apparently by 9.17.10.0.0 (AD 780), Yax Sun-at-Horizon was deeply interested in confirming his authority valley-wide by allowing his subordinates to erect inscribed monuments which emphasize their association with him. Furthermore, the emphasis on the cosmos seen in benches and temple façades with Pauahtuns and bicephalic monsters bespeaks an effort to lock each of the noble lines into the larger cosmological, as well as the local secular, order.

Outside the Copan pocket, the sites of Los Higos and Rio Amarillo also erect sculptured monuments at this time. Again, Morley's view of these sites was that they constituted outposts or satellites of Copan, and were dependent upon it (Morley 1920:381–6). More recently, Gary Pahl (1977) concluded that the recording of some possible non-Copan Emblem Glyphs on the monuments of the hinterland sites of Rio Amarillo and Los Higos indicate attempts on the part of these nascent elites to establish polities independent of Copan. Certainly both of the sites in question were placed in favorable ecological settings, and provided they could have attracted a large labor force, could well have begun to nucleate and prosper on their own. Still, one is struck by the similarity in sculpture style of the Los Higos stela, and the tenoned mosaic façade sculptures found at Rio Amarillo, with their counterparts (i.e., their models) at Copan. Also, the Pennsylvania State surveys have shown that there was never a large resident population in the Rio Amarillo Valley, and Stuart is skeptical that the glyph which Pahl identifies as a Rio Amarillo Emblem was really that; it may simply represent a title. Tenoned mosaic façade sculptures have been found at several sites in the area of La Entrada by Seiichi Nakamura and his colleagues (Nakamura 1985), and in examining some of them we were struck by their similarities with the Copan material. At one of the La Florida Valley sites with sculptured façades, El Abra, a tomb was found which contained an alabaster vase with glyphs carved in the tradition of the fine carved ceramics of Copan (i.e., Ardilla Incised). The inscription cites a Calendar Round date, the name of a local personage (presumably the occupant of the tomb), and, again, a relationship with the Copan king Yax Sun-at-Horizon. Also included in the tomb was a Copador cylinder (an obvious Copan import), and an Ulua polychrome cylinder (showing the strength of ties to central Honduras). All of these data indicate emulation of and in some cases direct contact with the court of Yax Sun-at-Horizon on the parts of the elites to the east of Copan. Certainly the prominent display of the Los

Higos Emblem and the portrait of the local ruler on Los Higos Stela 1 indicate a movement on the part of that site, at least, to political independence from Copan.

In 9.18.10.17.18 (AD 801), Yax Sun-at-Horizon erected Temple 18, a small structure which is conspicuously separated from the great ritual plaza of the East Court. The sculpture is carved in shallow relief and not meant to be read from any great distance. The dates celebrated are not period-endings and the iconography is that of war and captive sacrifice, presented in a very blatant way. The diminutive size of the structure in comparison to previous Acropolis temples implies a lack of support for any grandiose building plans, even for what has been interpreted (Baudez 1983a) as his funeral temple. The explicit if not gruesome treatment of the ruler as a bearer of trophy heads would seem to indicate that Yax Sun-at-Horizon was attempting to reinforce his prowess as a warrior on his final structure. We have noted that the emphasis on warrior iconography on Structure 26 was borne not of strength, but of weakness, following on the heels of a devastating military defeat. These characteristics of Yax Sun-at-Horizon's last temple suggest that his power was in fact waning, in the later years of his reign.

The picture from the valley is one of increasing demographic pressure, elevated infant mortality ratios, widespread malnutrition and/or disease in the context of a maladaptive settlement system which prompted a shift to areas ever farther from the Main Group for agricultural production. The regional picture is one of demographic and political expansion of rival (including possibly non-Maya) groups to the south and east, which may have been usurping clients and interaction nodes previously dominated by Copan. In short, grim tidings indeed, even for an energetic ruler such as Yax Sun-at-Horizon. On 9.19.0.0.0 (AD 810), the ruler of Quirigua (Jade Sky) records in the inscription of Structure 1B-1 of that site's Acropolis that Yax Sun-at-Horizon performed the "scattering" ceremony there. From all appearances, it seems that the rulers of Copan and Quirigua were able to set aside their previous differences, and band together at this late date. The fact that no other inscribed monuments go up at Quirigua after the erection of Structure 1B-1 suggests that it, too, suffered a political crisis at this time.

On Copan Altar L (Fig. 7.6), one finds the last attempt at hieratic art and state history on the part of the Copan elites. Carved on the south side is a scene showing Yax Sun-at-Horizon seated on his name

Fig. 7.6 Copan Altar L. Drawing by Barbara Fash.

glyph on the right, and another personage on the left, seated on a name read as U Ci Tok' ("Caretaker of Flint"). Between them is the Calendar Round date 3 Chicchan 3 Uo (placed at 9.19.11.14.5, or AD 822, by Grube and Schele 1987), and the verb for "seating." Apparently, on that date Caretaker of Flint dedicated this monument, set up in much the same way that Yax Sun-at-Horizon arranged the ancestor portraits on his Altar Q. According to the preserved south-side inscription, this was the date when Caretaker of Flint was, or was to be, seated as king. As Barbara Fash has pointed out to us, however, the remaining three sides of the altar were never finished; in fact only the north side was even started. This monument represents a very nice metaphor for the political collapse of Copan, because it shows that the support base for the ruler fell out from underneath him, before he could even finish the carving of his accession monument.

But who might have been the challengers to Yax Sun-at-Horizon, Caretaker of Flint, and Jade Sky in the latter years of Cycle 9? Given the internal evidence detailed above, it is tempting to assign at least some of the culpability for this set of events to the non-royal (and possibly rival royal) elite lineages in the Copan case. Rather than Eric Thompson's old model of a peasant revolt, this would represent a species of "nobles' revolt." This recalls Eric Wolf's work on the role, in the development of revolutions, of large populations of elite men whose hereditary position fits them to rise to positions of power in societies in which there are very few such positions compared with the number of individuals aspiring to them (Wolf 1969). On the other hand, we should leave open the possibility that rival polities in the southeastern periphery were involved. It seems quite evident that Copan functioned as a sort of "Gateway City" (Hirth 1978) during the Late Classic period (and possibly earlier), serving to link the more advanced polities of the southern periphery to the Maya area. It is quite conceivable that some of the non-Maya polities which were developing in central Honduras and western El Salvador were attaining state levels of population size and political unity at this time. Certainly the entire area was experiencing a demographic build-up, and any one of a number of polities, resentful of Copan's premier and exalted position, could have mounted a sizeable threat to the Copan rulership (see note 4). Again, we can only hope that such a set of events will eventually be revealed to us through the combined efforts of archaeologists and epigraphers.

## CONCLUDING THOUGHTS

The position of Copan on the outskirts of the Maya area gives us a chance to gauge the effectiveness of Classic Maya political and symbolic structures for a polity that was geographically marginal to the lowland "core" area of Classic Maya civilization. The inscriptions and art of Copan were among the most sophisticated ever produced by the ancient Maya, yet the archaeological evidence does not point to sustained exchange of goods or people from the Peten to Copan or vice versa. To understand the evolution of the Copan polity, one must concentrate on its internal dynamics, and on the polity's economic and political relations with the members of its regional interaction spheres, specifically the highlands and Pacific coast of Guatemala and adjacent Chiapas during the Preclassic through the Middle Classic periods, and the western and central sectors of Honduras and El Salvador during the Late Classic.

Nevertheless, we believe that Copan's participation in the lowland Maya cultural tradition was a key factor in its success through four centuries of dynastic rule. This is reflected in the tremendous quantity, as well as quality, of Maya-style sculpture and architectural monuments produced. There was obviously a strong desire to present the polity and its rulers as among the most distinguished Maya of their time. This places the citation of Copan with the other polities on Stela A in perspective, and explains why they resorted to an inter-dynastic marriage with another distinguished Cholan polity to re-invigorate and legitimate the Copan royal line in the face of a humiliating defeat at the hands of an intra-regional rival. In the same way, the elites within the Copan polity reinforced their exalted position through the acquisition of Peten polychromes and locally produced fine mosaic sculptures. Thus we suggest that although the actual materials exchanged may have been minimal (in contrast to the vast quantities of goods exchanged between Copan and its trading partners in the southeast), the prestige of the contacts, and the importance of royal interaction, were important variables in the formulation and maintenance of centralized authority structures in Copan.

In terms of political structure and cultural evolution, a number of insights into Classic Maya polities are provided by the Copan material. The monumental record indicates that successful maintenance of dynastic continuity was apparently a primary concern, and a key factor in the perpetuation of centralized rule. The importance of the ruler Yax-K'uk-Mo', of his 9.0.0.0.0 (AD 435) period-ending monument (left accessible for 200 years after its commemoration), and his citation as the founder of the Copan dynasty in the title strings of virtually every one of his successors, indicates a virtual obsession with providing tangible evidence of continuity, and the importance of the divine right to rule. The fact that this continuity is so explicitly and deliberately spelled out on the revivalist temple (Structure 10L-26) constructed to restore confidence in the ruling order on the heels of a humiliating military defeat shows just how critical this continuity was for maintaining royal authority in Classic Maya polities. Likewise, Altar Q is an eloquent ode to the importance of dynastic continuity, showing portraits of all the members of the Yax-K'uk-Mo' dynasty. The 16th ruler is shown on the date of his accession to power, symbolically receiving the blessing of all of his distinguished predecessors, and actually being presented with the baton of office by the founder himself.

The successful nucleation and expansion of the local resident population in Copan during the Middle Classic period enabled and may have encouraged the late fifth- and early sixth-century Copan rulers to attempt to expand their areas of political control and/or tribute collection to areas outside the Copan Valley. The possible claims of the 11th and 13th rulers to Los Higos, and of the 12th ruler to Quirigua, constitute phenomena which need to be tested with archaeological data. Of considerable interest from an evolutionary standpoint is that these possible forays beyond the Copan hinterlands occurred prior to the establishment of a state level of sociopolitical integration.

It seems likely that the ability of the ruler to acquire such distant prizes – particularly when achieved by force – was a key aspect of his prestige, and likely to increase his power among his local supporting population. Indeed, the expansion of Quirigua after Cauac Sky beheaded Copan's king 18 Jog is explicit evidence in favor of this interpretation. By the same token, the warrior iconography of the ruler portraits on Copan Structure 10L-26 show that the reaction to this potentially devastating military defeat was to emphasize the prowess of the earlier Copan kings as successful warriors!

Finally, the long-term success of an expanding, state-level Classic Maya polity bred a series of problems within the socio-economic system which the structure of the conservative political order apparently had difficulty coping with. The perpetuation of royal perquisites for the successive rulers, for their non-kingly descendants and cadet lineages, and the emulation of their life-style and status distinctions by other noble lines resulted in a system that was top-heavy. As noted, the structural problems posed by populations of elite men whose hereditary position fits them to rise to positions of power in societies where there are very few such positions available has been demonstrated by Wolf (1969) to have had a role in the development of revolutions. The strong dependence on the charisma and actions of the Classic Maya ruler, and the relatively underdeveloped nature of hierarchical institutions divorced from kinship lines, meant that it was difficult to accommodate the perceived needs and rival claims of the competing non-kingly factions in state-level Maya polities of the Classic period. The innovative approaches to this problem devised and implemented by the 16th Copan ruler indicate a willingness (arguably borne of need) to engage in power-sharing arrangements with important members of Late Classic Copan society. Unfortunately his efforts, apparently largely based upon his own prestige and performance of rituals at the hearths of his subordinates, were not sufficiently institutionalized to fend off the forces which culminated in the demise of dynastic power at Copan.

## *NOTES*

1. Most of the new epigraphic and archaeological data and interpretations presented here were obtained through the investigations of the Copan Mosaics Project, the Hieroglyphic Stairway Project, and the Copan Acropolis Project, all directed by the senior author and sponsored by the National Science Foundation, the National Endowment for the Humanities, the National Geographic Society, the Center for Field Research (Earthwatch), the Wenner-Gren Foundation for Anthropological Research, the H. John Heinz III Charitable Trust, the U.S. Agency for International Development, the Government of Honduras, and Northern Illinois University. We would like to thank the Honduran Institute of Anthropology and History for the privilege of carrying out this research, and the opportunity to help document and conserve the Copan sculptural corpus. We would also like to thank John Justeson, William Sanders, Barbara Fash, and the anonymous

archaeologist reviewer for reading the paper and providing important suggestions and constructive criticism.

2. Leroy Joesink-Mandeville (1987) believes that the Preclassic ("Archaic") Copanecs were Lencan. Given the current belief that most central and western Honduran Classic and Postclassic peoples were Lencan, this interpretation also merits serious consideration.
3. A plausible alternative explanation would see Quirigua Altar L as merely the record of a royal visit to Quirigua by the reigning monarch of Copan. We believe this interpretation to have less in its favor, because at other sites where such royal visits are recorded in the monuments, the visitor is always cited within the context of the actions of the host ruler (Schele and Mathews, this volume). There is no evidence that this is the case on Quirigua Altar L, which not only portrays Smoke-Imix-God K, but cites his most important period-ending (9.11.0.0.0; AD 652) as well.
4. William Sanders (personal communication) has suggested to Fash, that the capture and decapitation of 18 Jog might very well have been the result of a short-lived alliance between Cauac Sky and the heads of the non-Maya polities of the lower Motagua Valley, designed to prevent further expansion of Copan power and kingly pretensions in their area.

# 8
# Diversity and continuity in Maya civilization: Quirigua as a case study

ROBERT J. SHARER

Scholars today see Classic Maya civilization as extremely complex and diverse (Willey 1982; Morley, Brainerd, and Sharer 1983; Marcus 1983), both horizontally (marked by linguistic and ethnic distinctions) and vertically (marked by divisions between elite and non-elite and by wealth and status differences). At the same time, the traditional chronological periods into which archaeologists still divide Maya civilization often submerge real cultural continuity through time. Thus, while the Classic period is usually defined from about AD 250 to AD 900, most characteristics of Maya civilization crystallized at least five hundred years earlier during the Late Preclassic and continued for more than five hundred years later through the Postclassic.

Recognition of the diversity underlying our concept of Maya civilization has emerged from an unprecedented expansion in archaeological, art historical, epigraphic, and ecological research. Of course the most dramatic advances have been in the decipherment of Maya writing and its consequences – the emergence of Maya studies from a prehistoric to historical enterprise (Sharer 1978, 1985c). Although decipherment is obviously significant in its own right, epigraphic readings must also be tested against archaeological and other relevant data. Similarly, archaeological findings can be tested against the results of epigraphic or other research. It is with interdisciplinary research strategies that we are beginning to realize the full revolutionary consequences of decipherment – the emergence of a more comprehensive understanding of the ancient Maya based on the conjunctive research of archaeologists, epigraphers, and art historians.

In this paper I will explore some of the diversity that underlies our concept of Maya civilization, as revealed by recent research (see Webster 1988 for a consideration of the same theme, as seen from Copan). I will begin with an overview of Classic Maya civilization – its origins and the unifying characteristics of its elite subculture – followed by a closer examination of a regional case study in the southeast lowlands. The case study also illustrates the advantages of conjunctive research for increasing our knowledge of the Classic Maya.

## ORIGINS

The genesis of Maya civilization has been the subject of several traditional theories that, for the most part, have been based on rather simple unilineal models. The best known of these include the autochthonous Maya lowland theory, the Maya highland transplant, and, of course, the *cultura madre* theory, the latter looking farther into Mesoamerica to propose that Olmec civilization was the direct ancestor of Maya civilization. Suffice it to say that none of these theories accounts adequately for the complexity of the evolutionary process that led to civilization, either in the Maya area or elsewhere in Mesoamerica (Sharer and Grove n.d.).

It is now clear that Maya civilization was the product of a complex, multilinear process within a broad temporal and spatial framework. The relevant time frame probably includes the entire Preclassic era, *c.* 2,000 BC–AD 250, but the latter half of this period (Middle and Late Preclassic) was undoubtedly the most crucial. The relevant spatial distribution is a broad array of environmental zones and cultural regions, including both the lowland heartland of Classic Maya civilization (Hammond 1986a) and a far more vast "periphery" (Urban and Schortman 1986). In fact, one of the most important developments of the past few decades of Maya research has been the recognition that this so-called periphery – covering both the lowlands of Yucatan to the north and, to the south, a broad highland and coastal zone from Chiapas to El Savador and Honduras – played a crucial role in the evolution of Maya civilization (Sharer and Sedat 1987; Demarest n.d.).

The earliest evidence of complex sociopolitical evolution in the Maya area appears in the archaeological record of the southern periphery, including the Guatemalan highlands (Sanders and Murdy 1982; Sharer and Sedat 1987), the Pacific coast and piedmont (Graham 1976), Western El Salvador (Sharer 1978; Demarest 1986), and western Honduras (Fash 1982). These developments began during the Middle Preclassic with archaeological manifestations of social ranking or stratification, either with Olmec-style markers as at Abaj Takalik (Graham 1976) and Copan (Fash 1982), or without such links, as in the Salama Valley (Sharer and Sedat 1987). By the Late Preclassic a series of monuments is known from this same area carved with hieroglyphic texts that include ruling title and accession glyphs (such as the "seating" references on El Porton Monument 1 dated at *c.* 400 BC; see Sharer and Sedat 1987), along with depictions of rites associated with rulership (as with the hand-scattering scene on Kaminaljuyu Stela 10). It is now apparent that interaction among a series of complex regional societies in the southern periphery in the Middle and Late Preclassic was instrumental in the evolution of Classic Maya civilization (Sharer and Sedat 1987; Demarest n.d.).

To balance this perspective, a like amount of recent evidence bearing on the issue of the origins of Maya civilization comes from the lowland heartland itself. Excavations during the past decade have revealed clear indications of relatively swift Late Preclassic development at sites such as Cerros (Freidel 1979), Cuello (Hammond 1977), and Lamanai (Pendergast 1981), all located in the eastern lowlands of Belize (see Hammond 1986a). The most dramatic findings, however, come from the core of the lowlands, at the immense site of El Mirador (Matheny 1986). The El Mirador evidence, together with more recent data from the nearby and apparently contemporaneous site of Nakbe (Hansen 1987), indicates that the levels of Late Preclassic populations and organizational complexity in the lowlands were far greater than previously suspected, especially when combined with data from Preclassic sites in Belize and adjacent areas.

It is safe to assume that there was an evolutionary relationship between the Preclassic elite and the far better documented ruling class of the Classic era, although the details of this connection remain little known. But intervening factors undoubtedly complicated the link between Preclassic and Classic elites. These include the still poorly understood collapse of many Preclassic centers at the onset of the Classic period, including the apparently rather rapid decline of El Mirador. While it remains likely that the changes seen in the archaeological record reflect a critical transformation of the lowland elite-controlled political system at the onset of the Classic period (Freidel and Schele 1983), the degree to which this change was due to internal versus external factors – specifically influences from the southern Maya area (Freidel 1979, 1981; Sharer and Sedat 1987) – remains to be explicated. With the availability of more complete art historical and historical evidence in the Classic period, the role of external intervention in the political affairs of lowland centers such as Tikal can be discerned (Coggins 1975, 1976). It is probable that similar events had significant impacts on Preclassic political evolution, but lacking adequate iconographic and historical evidence these may remain invisible in the archaeological record.

## THE UNITY OF ELITE SUBCULTURE

A remarkable homogeneity in the inventory of material culture across time and space in the lowlands has long been recognized (Schortman 1986). For many years descriptions of Classic Maya civilization emphasized a dominant or even monolithic unity, epitomized, perhaps, by the outmoded "Old Empire" concept (Morley 1946). The homogeneity of Classic Maya civilization is most apparent in those aspects of material culture that reflect high sociopolitical status or ideological concerns – the manifestations of elite subculture within ancient Maya society. Our definition of Classic Maya civilization rests on traits that reflect the activities of the dominant but numerically minor stratum within society, including consistent preferences for exotic materials (jade, certain marine products, quetzal feathers, etc), art styles (painting and sculpture), writing and calendrical systems, clothing, symbols of office, architecture, and site planning. In fact, as we will see, there are considerable indications of diversity among the non-elite, representing the bulk of lowland Maya populations.

Thus our definition of Classic Maya civilization reflects the social stratum within each Maya polity that managed and directed the course of the polity. And to the degree that these polities formed an interdependent system of states, or peer polities, the economic, social, and ideological ties that created this network were maintained by the elite. Seen in a dynamic perspective, these elite-directed activities, both within and between the independent Maya polities fueled the evolutionary course of Maya society. Elites sponsored innovations that stimulated the cycles of growth and decline we are beginning to perceive throughout the course of Maya civilization. These range from the intensification of agriculture (Harrison and Turner 1978) to innovative political institutions.

As a significant example of the latter, it has been hypothesized that the major Classic period lowland polities were organized around a powerful political position, that of a ruler with an unprecedented concentration of authority – a kind of "god king" – who was legitimized by a synthesis of pre-existing and innovative forms, including the dynastic monument complex for display of genealogies and events used to reinforce political authority (historical texts and sculpted scenes), the hereditary transmission of power within the ruling lineage, and the monumental funerary temple dedicated to veneration of the divinity of the ruler (see Freidel and Schele 1983). While most of the diagnostics of this new political order were in place in the southern periphery and El Mirador by the Late Preclassic (see above), the complete integration of this assemblage may have first taken root in the lowlands at centers such as Tikal (A. Miller 1986). Thereafter this system appears to have been adopted with varying degrees of success at other major centers. Smaller or less-successful centers may never have adopted this form of centralized political authority, or come under the domination of their larger and more powerful neighbors, thus in some ways perpetuating older elite institutions and thereby contributing to the organizational diversity of the Maya lowlands.

## DIVERSITY

The temporal diversity of Classic Maya civilization has already been briefly characterized, given its origins from a mosaic of independent Preclassic centers both in the lowland core and in the surrounding periphery. Interaction within such a broad and diverse area – economic, social, and ideological networks – was essential for the maintenance of the system, and stimulated the evolutionary course of Maya civilization.

The spatial diversity of Classic Maya civilization originated in, and was maintained by, environmental and sociopolitical circumscription. Of course, these are familiar and justifiable attributes ascribed to the Maya highlands, but, although less dramatic, they were important (and until recently, often ignored) factors in the Maya lowlands as well. Social circumscription in the lowlands stemmed from multiple groups expanding and settling the landscape and, in the process, creating social and political territorial units that impeded fissioning from within and intrusions from without.

One important consequence of environmental and social circumscription may be found in the political structure of the Classic Maya. It seems clear that the Maya were never politically unified; from beginning to end their society was fragmented into a series of independent polities (Mathews 1986; Sabloff 1986; Mathews and Willey, this volume). The basis of this organizational diversity has been sought from several perspectives, but most derive from rather explicit analogies drawn from non-Maya ethnographic or historical sources. Recent attempts to model Classic sociopolitical organization include a "chiefdom-like" ranked society integrated by vertical patron–client obligations, based on ethnographic analogies with East African kingdoms (Sanders 1981). A feudal system, describing a more stratified organization integrated by both vertical obligations and horizontal marriage alliances, derived from analogies with a variety of societies (Western Europe, Japan, and East Africa), has been proposed by Adams and Smith (1977, 1981). And more recently, Sabloff (1986) has viewed the Classic Maya from the peer-polity perspective. In contrast to these models, which tend to see political power derived from control over production, Freidel (1981) has proposed a more dispersed and subtle system of political authority maintained by control over distribution, based on analogies of pilgrimages and market fairs. While these models offer useful insights, I remain convinced that our understanding of Classic Maya sociopolitical organization will benefit far more from inferences or direct analogies drawn from *Maya* archaeological, historical, and ethnographic data, in contrast to the application of models derived from outside (primarily Old World) sources (see Marcus 1983:469–70).

Another problem with models of this sort is that they explicitly or implicity portray Classic Maya sociopolitical organization as uniform across the lowlands. I would maintain that the available archaeological and ethnohistorical data clearly indicate that each polity varied to some degree in its organizational structure (Freidel 1983; see below), and that these variations contributed to the shifting patterns in the mosaic of independent Maya states that evolved through time.

The success of any given polity (measured by duration and size of architecture and settlement) can be assumed to have derived from a variety of factors, including location, environmental potential, economic conditions, organizational efficiency, prestige, military success, and the individual careers of rulers – especially their leadership capabilities and length of reign. We can glimpse the reflections of the operation of these factors in the obvious distinctions between centers (size, architectural complexity, etc.) and differences in their evolutionary careers (the timing of the rise and fall of individual centers, duration of and size of occupation, etc.). Although the issue of size of Classic Maya polities appears settled on the side of small-scale local states (Mathews 1986), we are just beginning to address questions as to the organizational diversity among these polities, and the delineation of their individual development trajectories.

While small-scale politically independent polities appear to have been the norm, important integrative factors also operated. Some of these involved political aggrandizement – brought about either by marriage alliances (Marcus 1976; Schele and Mathews, this volume), or conquest and military alliances (Webster 1977) – although such expansions appear to have been relatively fragile and short-lived. Other important integrative mechanisms were economic (Rathje 1971; Jones 1979) or ideological (Marcus 1976; Ashmore 1983). Overall, these and related integrative factors produced a degree of mutual interdependence among the lowland polities, characterized by at least one author as "a system of states" (Lowe 1985), that helps explain the less-than-random pattern visible in several episodes of growth and decline. In the central Maya lowlands we can see two or three cycles of this synchronized process at many sites – an expansion in the Late Preclassic and contraction by the Early Classic, a mid-Classic downturn, renewed expansion in the Late Classic and a most far-reaching decline in the Terminal Classic (Fig. 8.1).

The element of sociocultural diversity within Maya civilization is seldom emphasized, owing mostly to the difficulty in detecting this kind of variability in the archaeological record. In the Maya highlands, studies of contemporary language distributions and structure allow reasonable reconstructions of the time depth for these linguistic subdivisions (Kaufman 1976). Further north, Cholan languages are often assumed for much of the Classic period occupation, although given the extent of Postclassic depopulation over much of the central and southern Maya lowlands, information on reconstructed linguistic distributions in this area have been more elusive. But recent successes in decipherment of Classic Maya texts has allowed hypothetical identification of specific languages spoken at several Maya centers – findings that raise the possibility that Yucatec Maya was spoken more extensively than previously believed (Fox and Justeson n.d.). Regardless of such specific questions, it is becoming increasingly clear that Classic Maya civilization was sustained by a population that spoke more than one language (Justeson *et al.* 1985).

## DIVERSITY WITHIN CLASSIC MAYA CIVILIZATION: A CASE STUDY

The possibilities of more profound ethnic or cultural distinctions underlying Maya civilization has been investigated from several perspectives. It has been proposed that the Preclassic inhabitants of much of the southern Maya area were non-Maya (including Mixe-Zoquean and Xincan populations) – at a time when many of the elements of later Maya writing and sculptural style were apparently crystallizing in this very area (Lowe 1977; Campbell 1976). There has been some debate as to the ebb and flow of Maya and non-Maya populations within the southeastern periphery of the Maya area (Thompson 1970; Sheets 1983; Andrews 1977). Recently Schortman (1986) has postulated a plausible reconstruction of the dynamic interaction between Maya and non-Maya inhabitants of the Motagua Valley during the Classic period.

The conjunction of archaeological and historical evidence from the Classic era of the southeastern lowland periphery, dominated by Copan and Quirigua, allows a fairly confident reconstruction of both the origins and the evolution of Maya political elites in this region. These data offer a case in point to illustrate the diversity within Classic Maya civilization – specifically the contrast between an apparent indigenous emergence of a Maya elite dynastic center at Copan, and elite Maya colonization to establish dynastic rule at Quirigua, seemingly to extend control over the strategic lower Motagua region. At the same time, this evidence offers an example of the role of specific events and personalities in the development of Maya political centers and their hinterlands.

The wealth of new data and interpretations available from recent research at Copan are summarized by Fash and Stuart (this volume). Briefly, the well-documented Preclassic sequence at Copan (Fash 1982) indicates that its indigenous population was within the general cultural tradition often labeled "southern Maya" (Fash and Stuart, this volume). The Early Classic at Copan saw the emergence of a system of dynastic rule associated with carved monuments, consistent with the Classic lowland Maya elite tradition, but apparently without direct elite colonization from the Peten. The founder of Copan's Classic-period elite dynasty has been indentified as one Yax-K'uk-Mo' (Stuart and Schele 1986a). This elite tradition and the iconographic and epigraphic traits with Peten links, long noted in Copan's sculptural and inscriptional inventory, are seen as reflections of means used by the Copan dynasts to perpetuate their authority (Fash and Stuart, this volume). At the same time, there is solid evidence for more localized elite connections within the southeastern area, with Kaminaljuyu (Fash and Stuart, this volume), and to the non-Maya areas further into Central America (Miller 1983).

Quirigua has long been recognized as a Classic lowland Maya site, based mainly on its splendid Late Classic monuments (see Sharer 1988). The recent investigations of the Quirigua Project have, for the first time, placed the site in a broader temporal and spatial context (Ashmore 1980a; Ashmore and Sharer 1978; Sharer 1988), including its relationship with the surrounding lower Motagua region (Schortman 1980). The archaeological data, together with prior (Kelley 1962a) and conjunctive epigraphic studies (Jones 1983a, b; Jones and Sharer 1980; Sharer 1978; Ashmore 1984), allow a far more complete reconstruction of events, including those of newly discovered Early Classic Quirigua (Ashmore 1980b). Unfortunately, however, the crucial antecedents of the Preclassic period remain little known owing to the depth of alluvial deposition in the Motagua Valley.

The earliest known era of occupation at Quirigua spans the Terminal Preclassic and initial Early Classic period (*c.* AD 1–400). The sparse artifacts from this era reflect links with the generalized southern Maya Preclassic. But there is nothing at Quirigua that even approaches the time depth or scale of Preclassic occupation revealed at Copan, with its direct ties to Middle and Late Preclassic cultural developments in the southeastern Maya highlands and beyond (Fash 1982). The only evidence that might reflect an indigenous emergence of sociopolitical complexity at Quirigua are the fragments of two crude schist monuments, apparently related to the highland Preclassic pedestal sculptures, lifted from the alluvium north of the site core by Bandegua (the banana people). Conspicuous by their apparent absence are any architectural remains from this period. One mound group, located across the Motagua from Quirigua, has been hypothesized as Preclassic from its site plan (Ashmore 1980b), but this has yet to be verified by excavation.

The evidence becomes more plentiful in the middle period, the later Early Classic and first part of the Late Classic (*c.* AD 400–700). A small platform constructed on a prominent hilltop on the north side of the Motagua Valley, 4 km west of Quirigua's site core (known as Locus 002 or Morley's Group A), dates to this era (Ashmore 1980b, 1984). Monument 21 (Stela U) was found on a terrace beneath this structure; with a probable 9.2.3.8.0 (AD 478) Long Count inscription, it provides the earliest known historical date at Quirigua (Jones and Sharer 1980).

The earliest known remains of occupation and construction on the adjacent flood plain, apparently concentrated north and west of the later site core, were found deep beneath the modern surface. The focus of this occupation seems to have been a low platform (3C-1) that supported a small masonry substructure (Structure 3C-14). The latter is the probable original setting for Monument 26 (Ashmore 1980b), with its presumed portrait of an early ruler and text that includes two *hel* notations following a 9.2.18.0.? (*c.* AD 493) Long Count date (Jones and Sharer 1980; Jones 1983a). The arrangement and contents of the dedicatory cache beneath Structure 3C-14 are linked to contemporary elite-associated remains from Kaminaljuyu, Copan, and several central lowland sites (Ashmore 1980b). The contents of this cache are also closely tied to a disturbed deposit from Locus 002, apparently the remains of the original sub-stela cache of Monument 21.

The most plausible reconstruction, sees colonization by and establishment of a minor local ruling elite lineage or dynasty at Quirigua during the fifth century AD. A retrospective citation of this event, including, perhaps, a record of the founding ruler at Quirigua, may be found on Monument 3 (Stela 3), dated to AD 775, first pointed out by

Peter Mathews (personal communication; see Jones and Sharer 1980). The text on the west side records a 9.1.0.0.0 (AD 455) Long Count date, followed by a *Mah Kina* title and Quirigua Emblem Glyph. Regardless, the lack both of preceding sizeable occupation at Quirigua and of evidence for local evolution of sociopolitical complexity contrasts directly with the situation at Copan, and makes any thesis of *in situ* development of social stratification in the lower Motagua valley highly tenuous. Archaeological research within the Motagua valley region indicates that the elite of Quirigua were culturally distinct from the population that occupied the valley during the Classic period (Schortman 1986).

The source of the elite colonization of Quirigua is, in my opinion, most likely to have been the Peten, specifically the Tikal region. This conclusion is based on epigraphic and stylistic comparisons between Quirigua Monuments 21 and 26 and Early Classic monuments at Tikal (Stelae 2, 6, and 29) and Uaxactun (Stela 20), as discussed in a previous paper (Jones and Sharer 1980). Copan cannot be ruled out as a potential donor, but if it were the source of elite colonization at Quirigua, Copan's relative proximity would lead me to expect a far greater correspondence in elite-associated material culture than actually obtains between these two centers. As it stands, the material inventory of Early Classic Quirigua, including Monuments 21 and 26 and local polychrome pottery with Tzakol modes, has closer affinities with the Peten than with Copan. A hypothetical explanation for these events would posit an expansion from the Peten, perhaps sponsored by the rulers of Tikal, by an elite group that founded an outpost at Quirigua in order to control the Motagua trade route – a principal conduit for both jade and obsidian into the eastern lowlands, possibly stimulated by the development of an independent rival power at Copan.

Quirigua remained a very minor center for the remainder of the middle period. The most conspicuous event in the archaeological sequence is an apparent hiatus, probably dating to the early seventh century, marked by severe flooding and apparent course changes of the Motagua river. Following this disruption, Structure 3C-14 and Monument 26 were no longer the focus of Quirigua's floodplain center (Ashmore 1980b, 1984). A new residential and administrative complex was built farther south, probably to facilitate access to a changed river course, and established the foundation for the later growth of the Late

Classic site core (ibid; Jones and Sharer 1980). The new focus was a quadrangle, partially revealed beneath the later Acropolis construction, representing a typical Peten residential configuration (Plaza Plan 2; cf. Becker 1971). A crypt burial recovered from beneath its eastern shrine is consistent with the Peten tradition, and may be the interment of the ruler who founded the post-flood center.

During the latter portion of this middle period, Copan marked its authority over Quirigua, probably reflecting the larger site's control over the lucrative Motagua trade routes. Two carved monuments belong to this interval. One of these, Monument 12 (Altar L), which Satterthwaite (1979) dates at 9.12.0.0.0? (AD 672), is from the newly constructed site center and provides direct evidence of Copan's hegemony. David Stuart has identified both the name and portrait of the Copan ruler Smoke-Imix-God K on this Quirigua stone (Fash and Stuart, this volume). According to Satterthwaite (1979:40) Monument 12 records two historical dates, 9.11.0.11.11? (AD 653) and 9.12.0.17.0? (AD 673). It is likely that these dates refer to events involving Copan's control over Quirigua. The badly eroded Monument 20 (Stela T) from Locus 002, with a probable date of 9.13.0.0.0 (AD 692), also pertains to this era.

The late period at Quirigua, spanning the latter portion of the Late Classic (*c.* AD 700–900), is by far the best archaeologically and historically documented era (Sharer 1978; Ashmore and Sharer 1978; Jones and Sharer 1980; Ashmore 1984). Copan's hegemony over Quirigua continued into the eighth century, for as Stuart (1987) has shown, the 9.14.13.14.17 (AD 725) inauguration of the latter site's greatest ruler, Cauac Sky, is recorded on Monument 5 (Stela E) as occurring "in the territory of 18 Jog," ruler of Copan (aka 18 Rabbit). But this relationship ended some thirteen years into Cauac Sky's reign. A series of Cauac Sky's monuments record the capture and sacrifice of his former overlord, 18 Jog, in 9.15.6.14.6 (AD 738). This event clearly marks a turning point in the development of Quirigua. Thereafter Cauac Sky uses the title of 14 hel, probably signifying that he was the 14th ruler in a local Quirigua dynasty (a lineage of little-known historical origins, except for references to its apparent 3rd and 4th rulers recorded on Monument 26), although Riese (1986) has proposed this as a reference to his claim to be the 14th ruler at Copan (the unfortunate 18 Jog being the 13th ruler at that site).

Copan clearly suffered a setback in its fortunes after the humiliating loss of its powerful ruler. It now seems that 18 Jog was succeded by a little-known ruler, Smoke Monkey, who apparently erected no monuments during a reign of less than ten years (Stuart 1987), and may have been Cauac Sky's vassal. Regardless, Copan's prestige and power was not fully restored until the reign of its 15th ruler, Smoke Shell, who sponsored the complete rebuilding of Structure 10L–26 with its magnificent stairway that proclaims Copan's dynastic history in both text and sculpture (Fash and Stuart, this volume).

In the wake of Cauac Sky's triumph, Quirigua was substantially expanded in size, especially in a rebuilding of its central residential and administrative complex (the Acropolis) and in the creation of an adjacent public plaza of unprecedented size. The latter was crowned on its northern edge by a large platform used to support a series of monuments, including the largest Maya stelae known – dedicated, of course, to the glorious achievements of Cauac Sky. These building projects initiated an era of unprecedented growth in the size and complexity of Quirigua, although even at its peak, its total population probably never exceeded one tenth that at Tikal.

Evidence from beyond the site proper demonstrates that Quirigua's prosperity was paralleled by explosive development in much of the Motagua valley, especially in the rapid growth of residential and administrative centers at the head of a series of routes that led to the southeast, into Central America. It would seem that this prosperity derived from the usurpation by Quirigua and its valley allies of Copan's former control over trade along the Motagua route and between the Maya lowlands and lower Central America. These lower Motagua sites appear to have been ruled by a newly emerged local elite – their architectural and artifactual inventories depart from Classic lowland Maya traditions – that were none the less tied to Quirigua's destiny (Schortman 1980). Copan at about this time appears to refocus its external interaction to the southeast (see Fash and Stuart, this volume), in a direction away from Quirigua and the Motagua valley. One of the best reflections of this lies in Copan's control over the manufacture and distribution of Copador polychrome pottery (Beaudry 1987). At the same time, there is an almost complete absence of Copador or other polychrome vessels associated with elite activity at Quirigua and the lower Motagua sites – a possible reflection of the schism between the ruling houses of these two centers.

Cauac Sky survived to a ripe old age, ruling for nearly sixty years, a circumstance that probably accounts for a great deal of his success and impact on the developmental course of Quirigua. Although he appears overzealous in proclaiming his own importance (a Maya equivalent of Rameses II), there is little doubt that he profoundly changed the destiny of not only Quirigua, but much of the southeastern lowlands. One of the most instructive consequences of our new-found historical perspective on events of the Classic period has been the recognition of the impact on events made by individual (often long-lived) rulers, such as Cauac Sky, or Ah Cacau (Ruler A) at Tikal, and Pacal at Palenque.

The prosperity of Quirigua and the lower Motagua region continued after Cauac Sky, who died in AD 784. His successor (and son?) Sky Xul is best known for his commemorative monuments, the magnificently sculpted Monuments 15, 16, 23, and 24. Construction on Quirigua's Acropolis reached its culmination during the reign of the last historically known ruler, Jade Sky. The largest palace at Quirigua, Structure 1B-5, built about AD 810, was probably his residence. This construction, together with Structure 1B-1, situated across the plaza from this palace, indicate that Jade Sky maintained the prosperity of the Quirigua polity in the early ninth century.

At the same time, the authority of Jade Sky's contemporary, Yax Pac (Yax Sun–at–Horizon), was apparently being weakened in a changing political network characterized by newly emerging political elites both within and surrounding the Copan polity (Fash and Stuart, this volume). Copan's fortunes seem to have waned rapidly during Yax Pac's reign, culminating in the disintegration of the traditional dynastic political order shortly after AD 800 (Fash and Stuart, this volume), although a successor to Yax Pac, named U Cit Tok', has recently been proposed (Schele 1988). In a most interesting turn of events, based on references in the Structure 1B-1 texts (providing the last known Quirigua date at 9.19.0.0.0 or AD 810), it appears that Yax Pac may have taken refuge at Quirigua after being forced to abandon Copan (Fash and Stuart, this volume; Schele and Mathews, this volume).

After 810, the historical record at Quirigua ceases, and the fate of both Jade Sky and Yax Pac remains unknown. As at Copan, it appears that Quirigua's traditional dynastic order broke down shortly thereafter. Yet unlike Copan, monumental construction in the site core continued after the end of the historical era. The Acropolis was modified and expanded on a large scale after AD 810, with construction continuing until perhaps the mid-ninth century. The latest occupational debris at Quirigua includes new pottery types and forms that derive from the northern lowlands – indicative of new contacts or even new masters at the very end of the Classic era (Sharer 1985b). But the last-gasp efforts to maintain the old Motagua trade routes from Quirigua ultimately failed. The civic and ceremonial core of Copan was apparently abandoned by this time, and, although large populations remained at many sites, including Copan, for decades or even centuries, the economic and political order of much of the central lowlands was significantly transformed. In the process, Quirigua, like most of the traditional centers of Classic elite power, was eventually bypassed and ultimately abandoned.

## CONCLUSION

Our concepts about Classic Maya civilization in general, and the origins and nature of the ruling elite segment of ancient Maya society in particular, have been shaped by a rather uniformitarian theoretical perspective (Webster 1988). Recognition of the diversity within Classic Maya civilization – seen across both time and space – forces a reexamination of the utility of models based on outmoded uniformitarian assumptions and general analogies with European and other Old World civilizations. The simplistic "rise and fall" model of political history emphasizes the sequential collapse and disappearance of civilizations, and de-emphasizes their continuities. In the Maya case we have an evolutionary process of considerable cultural continuity marked by the episodic growth and decline of a system of independent polities, roughly synchronized by a network of complex relationships between these states. These cycles of growth and decline seem to reflect shifts in the basis of political power within the components of this system over time.

In the emergent Maya polities of the Late Preclassic, political authority may not have been centralized or focused in a single ruler, but diffused among several offices held by members of the theocratic elite. This is reflected in the archaeological record by huge expenditures on monumental public ritual architecture that was dedicated to the gods, rather than to individual rulers – the unsurpassed scale of El Mirador's Preclassic temples being the most dramatic example. At the same time there was little investment on behalf of individual members of the elite – a relative lack of emphasis on palace architecture or funerary embellishments. The Early Classic period in the Maya lowlands was an era of crucial transition, for by the Late Classic, of course, we see nearly the opposite pattern. The greatest architectural investments were made on behalf of individual rulers in the construction of great funerary temples (together with their tombs) and palaces. But, although many of the Preclassic polities dramatically declined, or were completely abandoned, at the onset of the Classic period, no one has been compelled to label this process a collapse of Maya civilization. Rather, it seems reasonable to view this as an evolutionary transformation – one centered on the kind of changes in the elite political order described above – within the overall trajectory of Maya lowland development.

Yet when we consider the contrasts in the archaeological record between the Classic and Postclassic eras, there has been a long-standing assumption that they reflect a much more profound event – that there was a catastrophic collapse of Classic Maya civilization. Except for the scale of the observable changes, reflecting a greater population at the end of the Classic in comparison to the close of the Preclassic (size of sites, number of sites occupied and subsequently abandoned, and so forth), the distinctions in the archaeological record seen at the end of the Classic are little different from those observed at the close of the Preclassic.

Lowland dynastic monuments provide the one qualitative distinction between these two episodes; in fact the timing and distribution of the "collapse" are measured by the disappearance of the Classic-period custom of erecting carved stones adorned with ruler portraits and historical texts. This cessation is followed by population decline and ultimate abandonment of most (but not all) central lowland centers within 100–200 years. Obviously, for polities like Tikal and the others that were eventually abandoned, the end result of this process was total collapse. But, just as obviously, this process does not mark the end of Maya civilization. Rather, it provides a convenient boundary for a block of time, the termination of the Classic period, defined by the custom of erecting dynastic monuments. But by emphasizing this transition as a catastrophic collapse, we often lose sight of the overwhelming cultural continuities that existed both in the greatly diminished central lowlands, and in those areas, such as Yucatan, where Maya civilization was vigorously expanded and renewed in the Terminal Classic and Early Postclassic (Sabloff and Andrews 1986).

Most importantly, however, by emphasizing the catastrophic nature of the lowland Classic collapse we have tended to ignore the true meaning of the process: the significance of the cessation of dynastic monument erection as a reflection of a specific breakdown in the political system. While Maya civilization did not disappear, the particular political institution that characterized the Classic era – that based on the abilities of individual rulers who derived their power from their ancestors and maintained their authority by military and ritual achievements (as proclaimed on their monuments and buildings) – did cease. Although the causes for this are still debated, it appears that Maya society was transformed around a new political system (which, in part, may have triggered the failure of the old system), and new centers of power emerged in the Puuc region, and at Chichen Itza (Sabloff and Andrews 1986; Wren and Schmidt, this volume).

Thus, the realities apparent in our data are, at times, obscured by the very models applied to interpret them. This problem can be minimized if, rather than imposing general analogies drawn from other areas of the world, more emphasis is given to particularistic studies of the diverse manifestations of Maya civilization in both time and space (Sharer 1985c). The resulting reconstructions of the past should then be more firmly based on inferences drawn first and foremost from Maya archaeological, historical, ethnohistorical, and ethnographic data. General analogies from non-Maya societies should not be excluded out of hand, but should be applied with rigorous care to insure their appropriateness, and then only after being tested against new evidence from the Maya area itself.

Over the past few decades of Maya research we have moved from viewing Maya civilization as a monolithic entity that rose and fell in an evolutionary lockstep (Fig. 8.1a), to being able to describe the individual developmental trajectory of independent polities (Fig. 8.1b). In the future, using conjunctive research, we should be able to trace the detailed career of each Classic Maya polity, correlating the historical events of rulers and dynasties, the impact of their alliances and wars, with evidence of architectural activity, settlement growth and decline, and other archaeological data (Fig. 8.1c). This kind of historical synthesis has already begun, as at Copan (Fash and Stuart, this volume), Quirigua (Sharer 1978; Ashmore and Sharer 1978; Ashmore 1984), and Tikal (Jones, this volume).

It is clear, therefore, that the continued advances in decipherment

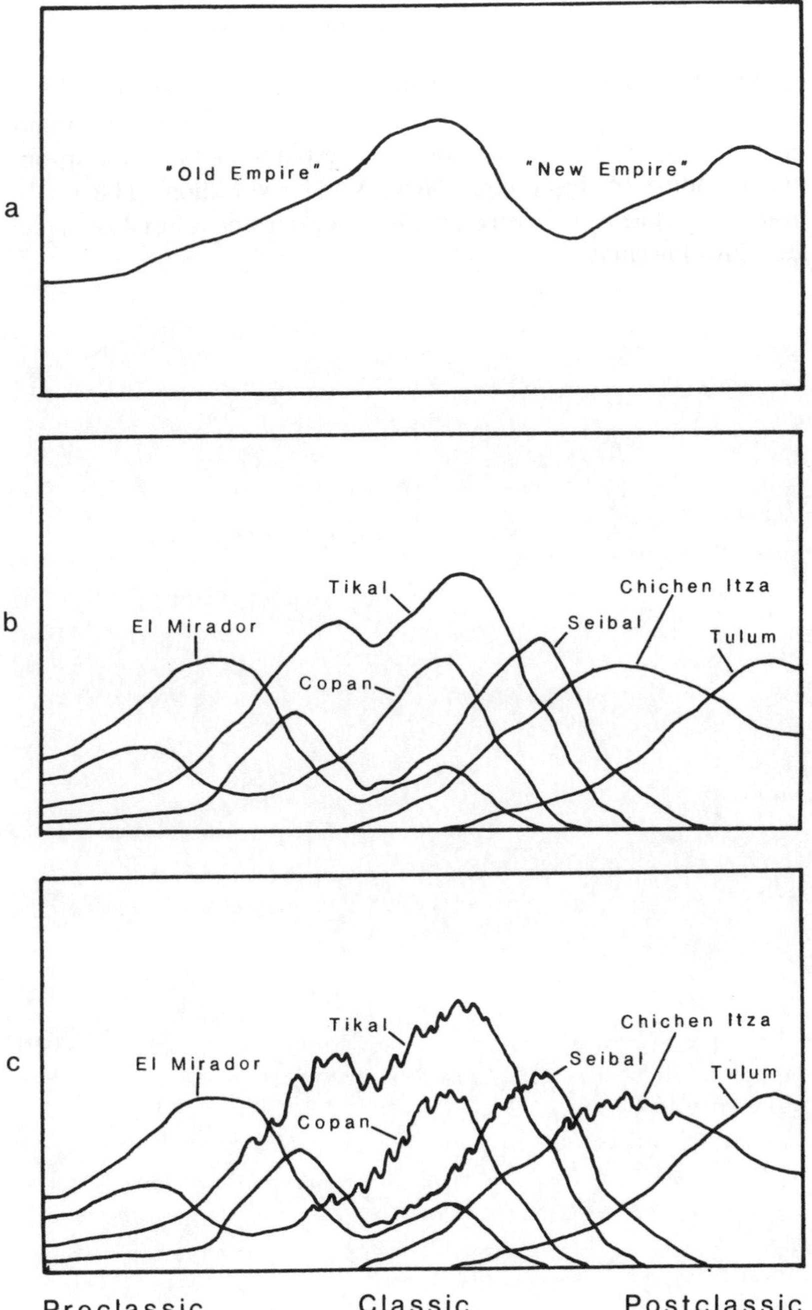


Fig. 8.1 Schematic models of the development of Maya civilization.

of Maya texts, and new interpretations of Maya representational art, when combined with further increases in Maya archaeological information, place us at the threshold of a revolutionary increase in our understanding of this unique New World civilization. The era of historical archaeology based on conjunctive research is just dawning in the Maya lowlands.

# 9
# Elite interaction during the Terminal Classic period: new evidence from Chichen Itza

LINNEA H. WREN and PETER SCHMIDT

Chichen Itza in Yucatan, Mexico has been studied almost continuously since 1842 when John Lloyd Stephens and Frederick Catherwood visited the site and, shortly afterwards, published a vivid account of the ruins (Stephens 1963). The site was impressive to them not only because of the presence of the Sacred Cenote but also because of the vast size of the ceremonial plazas, the immense scale of the architectural structures and the rich diversity of style, composition, and motif in the art and architecture that survives. Since the nineteenth century Chichen Itza has been recognized as having played a pivotal role in Maya lowland history during the Late Classic and Early Postclassic periods. Nonetheless, both the nature of the relationships that existed between the elite of Chichen Itza and of other polities in both Yucatan and in central Mexico and the internal character of the distinctive polity that was formed at Chichen Itza have been poorly understood and have been issues of considerable debate.

The traditional reconstruction of the history of Chichen Itza has postulated that the occupation of the site in the Late/Terminal Classic and Early Postclassic periods can be divided into two discrete, sequent chronological periods demarcated by the military conquest of the native population of Chichen Itza by intruders foreign to the northern

Maya lowlands (Tozzer 1957; Thompson 1970). These intruders have been identified as a people with strong Mexican cultural affinities and, more specifically, as the Toltecs from the site of Tula in central Mexico (Tozzer 1930, 1957) or, possibly, as the Putun Maya from southern Campeche and Tabasco, a people with strong cultural ties to central Mexico (Thompson 1970:3–47). On the basis of ethnohistorical evidence, their *entrada* has generally been dated at 10.8.0.0.0 Katun 4 Ahau (AD 968–87 in the Goodman-Martínez-Thompson correlation in which all dates in this paper will be given) (Roys 1933:204; Thompson 1937:190; Morley 1946:87). Arguments have also been made for earlier dates of 10.6.0.0.0 (AD 948) and 10.4.9.7.3 (AD 918) (Tozzer 1957:25–32; Thompson 1970:22–5).

The entrada has been thought to postdate the collapse of Maya civilization in the southern lowlands and, therefore, to have had little direct impact upon events in that region. In the northern lowlands, however, where Maya civilization was flourishing, the impact of the Mexican entrada has been seen as profound. According to the traditional view, Mexican and Maya peoples came into conflict as the foreign elite challenged native rulers for hegemony over the northern Yucatan Peninsula. The defeat of Maya armies at Chichen Itza and elsewhere by their Mexican opponents supposedly resulted in the eclipse of Maya polities, the abandonment of Maya cities and the enervation of Maya culture. According to this view, the only Maya site to survive was Chichen Itza. But even at Chichen Itza, which the Maya continued to occupy as the major population group, the native culture was subordinated to the foreign concepts and practices of a minority group of Mexican elite.

This process of subordination, affecting religious beliefs, ritual activities, and political and social patterns at Chichen Itza has been thought to be most clearly mirrored by changes in architectural and artistic styles. The traditional interpretation of monuments at Chichen Itza has been based upon the premise that the execution of all architectural and artistic works of art in a style native to the northern lowlands which had begun in the Late Classic period was suddenly halted by the Mexican entrada and was replaced, after a break in time, by a distinctive style that is Mexican in origin. The massive architectural complexes and their sculptural and mural decorations have been considered Postclassic in date and have been regarded as symptomatic of foreign cultural domination.

Chichen Itza has generally been regarded as a dramatic instance of a wider shift that occurred during the Terminal Classic period in the balance between two Mesoamerican cultures presumed to represent two radically different and incompatible world views. In this shift the pacific, refined culture of the Maya in the southern lowlands disintegrated over a period of at least a century while the aggressive, violent culture of central Mexican peoples associated with the Postclassic period rose to ascendancy (Morley 1946; Thompson 1966). Recent scholarship has re-examined the traditional interpretation of Maya culture as peaceful and harmonious and has formulated an interpretation that acknowledges the constant presence of military aggression between Maya polities and the violent sacrificial practices within Maya culture (Schele and Miller 1986). This paper will re-examine the interpretation of Chichen Itza as a site in which two supposedly hostile and culturally incompatible ethnic groups were united into a successful polity only by the forceful suppression of the native population. The authors accept the traditional view that a multi-ethnic polity emerged at Chichen Itza but we will argue that it did so at a date significantly earlier than previously thought, that it represented an instance of cultural convergence rather than opposition between the elite of two ethnic groups, and that it had a profound impact upon events in both the southern and northern Maya lowlands.

## PURE FLORESCENT AND MODIFIED FLORESCENT ART AND ARCHITECTURE AT CHICHEN ITZA

Many of the buildings at Chichen Itza share close stylistic features with Puuc architecture of northwestern Yucatan. Buildings constructed in the style variously known as Yucatec-Maya (Tozzer 1957), Chichen-Maya (Cohodas 1978) or – the term that will be employed in this paper – Pure Florescent (Andrews IV 1965), are generally low, multi-chambered structures resting on shallow plinths. Constructed of block masonry, they utilize stone lintels to span wall openings and corbeled arches to cover interior spaces. The exteriors are decorated with flying buttresses and with panels consisting of mosaic elements that are composed to create geometric patterns or combined to form frontal deity masks. The Pure Florescent style can be firmly assigned to the Late/Terminal Classic period by means of the dated hieroglyphic texts inscribed upon the lintels. The dates associated with Pure Florescent contexts span the brief period between 10.1.17.15.3 (AD 867) inscribed on the Watering Trough Lintel and 10.2.12.2.4 (AD 881) inscribed on Lintel 2 of the Temple of the Four Lintels.

Figural art is rarely associated with Pure Florescent architecture, although the human figure is depicted in relief on the lintel of the Akab Dzib (Maudslay 1889–1902, III:Plate 19) and on the east façade of the east wing of the Monjas (Bolles 1977:115). Because of their resemblances in composition and motif to portraiture found in Puuc sites of the northern lowlands (Kowalski 1987:149–81) as well as to portraiture of the southern lowlands (Proskouriakoff 1960, 1963, 1964; Schele 1974, 1976), these sculptures may be presumed to represent rulers at Chichen Itza.

Buildings constructed in the architectural style known as Toltec-Maya (Tozzer 1957), Chichen-Toltec (Cohodas 1978), or – the term employed in this paper – Modified Florescent (Andrews IV 1965), are frequently structures with one or two chambers set on steep pyramids. The interior spaces are often divided by rows of columns linked by wooden lintels supporting corbeled arches. The surfaces are decorated by motifs also found at Tula including columns carved as serpents and atlantean figures, low-relief carvings on columns and daises, images of skeletal figures, jaguars and eagles, and *chac mool* figures. Hieroglyphic texts have previously been known from only four Modified Florescent contexts (Ruppert 1935; Morley 1935; Thompson 1937; Proskouriakoff 1970). Only two Modified Florescent structures, the Caracol and the High Priest's Grave, have been datable on the basis of these inscriptions. The date on the Caracol stela has been read as either 10.2.17.0.0 (AD 886) (Thompson 1937:186) or as 10.3.17.0.0 (AD 907) (Kelley 1982:12); the date on the Caracol frieze has been read as either 10.7.0.5.1 3 Imix 9 Yax (AD 968) (Thompson 1937:186) or as 10.3.0.15.1 3 Imix 9 Zip (AD 890) (Kelley 1982:13); the second reading is preferable because of its contemporaneity with the date on the Caracol stela. The date on the High Priest's Grave, while badly eroded and open to many interpretations, has generally been accepted as 10.8.10.11.0 2 Ahau 18 Mol (AD 998) (Thompson 1937:186; Kelley 1982:12). Stratigraphic and ceramic evidence concerning the dating of Modified Florescent structures relative to Pure Florescent structures is inconclusive, but all Modified Florescent buildings have traditionally been considered to be Early Postclassic in date.

Figural art is associated with Modified Florescent structures in a quantity unprecedented at any other site in the Maya lowlands. Figural sculpture is carved in relief on both interior and exterior surfaces of buildings including walls, vaults, jambs, piers, columns, lintels, daises, and balustrades; figural murals further embellish the buildings. This decoration incorporates a wide range of visual motifs especially in the costumes and weapons associated with individual figures. Based on the recognition of frequently recurring clusters of costumery and weaponry traits that also occur in Maya art and in the Toltec sculpture at Tula, Alfred Tozzer (1930, 1957) classified the figures depicted in Modified Florescent contexts as members of either Maya or Mexican ethnic groups. Although they show few resemblances in either style or motif with the figures represented in Pure Florescent art at Chichen Itza, Maya figures in Modified Florescent art have been considered representative of the same population that occupied Chichen Itza during the Late Classic period, constructed its Pure Florescent structures, and, after their defeat by Mexican intruders, were incorporated into the new political order as a subjugated people. The Mexican figures have been considered members of a cohesive ethnic group that effected sudden change through military conquest (Tozzer 1957:25).

Tozzer's identification of Mexican figures in the art of Chichen Itza has been confirmed by excavations at Tula. The parallels in motifs between the sculpture at the two sites extend to the presence of identical pictographic signs that serve to name specific individuals (Ruz Lhullier 1964). Stylistic similarities in the sculpture at the same sites are also pronounced, although architectural similarities have apparently been emphasized by programs of restoration at Tula that have employed structures at Chichen Itza as models (Molina-Montes 1982:130–2). At the same time, the recognition that Chichen Itza was occupied by multi-ethnic groups has been expanded by the recognition of resemblances between the art and architecture of the site and of other regions including Oaxaca and Veracruz (Tozzer 1957:25; Kubler 1975:199–200).

## THE GREAT BALL COURT STONE AND A TERMINAL CLASSIC DATE FOR MODIFIED FLORESCENT ARCHITECTURE

Crucial to the understanding of the transformation of the Maya site of Chichen Itza into a multi-ethnic polity and of its impact upon other Maya cities is the data at which non-Maya peoples can be recognized as an important presence in the northern lowlands. The recent recovery of a sculptural monument, which we have termed the Great Ball Court Stone (Fig. 9.1), suggests that the ethnic diversification of Chichen Itza occurred significantly earlier than traditionally believed. The monument combines a Maya hieroglyphic inscription with figural relief in the Modified Florescent style.

The Great Ball Court Stone was located in the summer of 1983 in the *bodega* of the Museo Regional de Antropología in Merida. A reference in a museum catalog of the 1940s indicates that the hemispherical stone was recovered from the Great Ball Court of Chichen Itza during the excavation and restoration of the structure undertaken

Fig. 9.1 Great Ball Court Stone. Photograph by David Wren.

between 1923 and 1940. The provenience of the stone is confirmed by an undated memorandum written by Edward Thompson (n.d.) at the time of its discovery and by several short and essentially inaccurate accounts of the stone published by Cesar Lizardi Ramos (1936, 1937) and J. Eric S. Thompson (1937).

The Great Ball Court Stone is 52 cm in height, 99 cm in diameter and 311 cm at its outer circumference. Around its base is a rim which is 16 cm in height and 11 cm in width. Now broken into several pieces, the stone was originally monolithic. It can be clearly identified as a sacrificial stone used in heart excision rituals (Wren 1986). Although its surface is badly eroded, three panels of figurative relief can be seen on the curved surfaces of the Great Ball Court Stone. Two of these panels (Figs. 9.2, 9.3) depict opposing teams of ball players

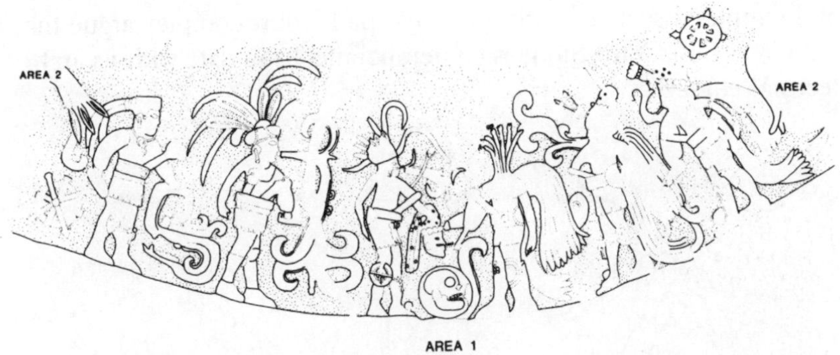


Fig. 9.2 Area I, Great Ball Court Stone. Drawn by Ruth Krochock after Peggy Diggs.

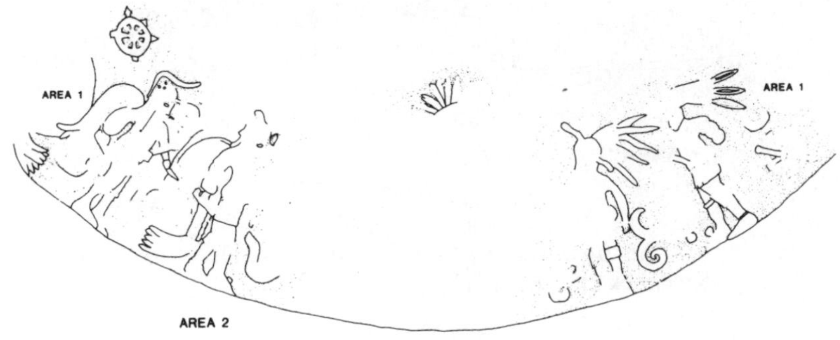


Fig. 9.3 Area II, Great Ball Court Stone. Drawn by Ruth Krochock after Peggy Diggs.

separated by balls inscribed with skulls. The central pairs of players consist of a victim who is decapitated with streams of blood stylized as serpents issuing from his neck and a sacrificer who wields a knife in one hand and holds the severed head of his opponent in the other. These panels are similar to the reliefs on the Great Ball Court benches. The third scene on the Great Ball Court Stone (Fig. 9.4) depicts three warriors, each outlined against a distinctive serpent form facing a fourth figure who holds a serpent staff. The processional format and the use of the serpent imagery are similar to the reliefs of the Lower Temple of the Jaguars in the Great Ball Court complex while the prominence of the serpent staff as an authority badge is underlined by the jamb figures of the South Temple in the same complex. The close similarities in style, subject, composition, and format between the scenes on the Great Ball Court Stone and the reliefs on the benches and temples associated with the Great Ball Court complex argue that the Great Ball Court Stone is contemporaneous in date with its architectural context.

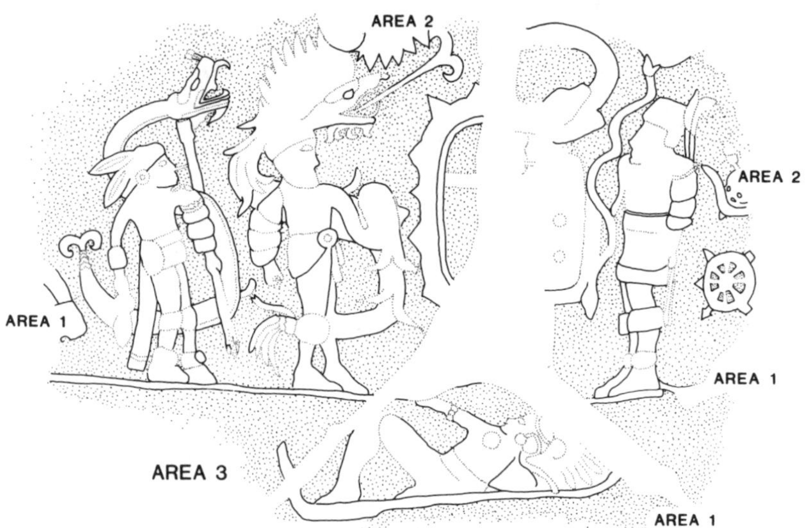


Fig. 9.4 Area III, Great Ball Court Stone. Drawn by Ruth Krochock after Peggy Diggs.

The inscription on the rim of the Great Ball Court Stone (Fig. 9.5) contains only one date, a Calendar Round date inscribed in glyphs

Fig. 9.5 Inscription, Great Ball Court Stone. Drawn by Ruth Krochock.

6–7, which records the date 11 Cimi 14 Pax. Although neither an Initial Series date nor a *Katun-Ahau* date is present, it is possible to posit a Long Count equivalent of 10.1.15.3.6 (AD 864) for the Calendar Round date recorded in the inscription. Evidence for this date is based on several parallels between the inscriptions on the Great Ball Court Stone and other inscriptions at Chichen Itza. First, a nominal phrase identical with that recorded on the column of Structure 6E1 is recorded at glyphs 21–2 on the Great Ball Court Stone. This phrase has been identified by David Kelley (1982:10) as an ideographic version of Kakupacal. Second, a phrase which frequently follows the name of Kakupacal in the inscriptions of Chichen Itza is also recorded following the nominal phrase on the Great Ball Court Stone at glyphs 23–4. The second of these glyphs can be read as *Ahpo Ahau*. Kelley initially proposed that this glyph represents the Emblem Glyph of Chichen Itza (1976:218) but more recently has read it as a title such as "ruler of lords" or "king of kings" (1982:8). James Fox (1984:13–18) has argued that Ahpo Ahau is the second glyph of a two-glyph compound that functions as the Chichen Itza Emblem Glyph. Third, an ideographic glyph referring to the ballgame event is recorded in glyph 5 of the Great Ball Court Stone. Ballgame events are also described in ideographic glyphs on Lintels 1 and 4 of the Temple of the Four Lintels and on Lintel 1 at Yula and seem to be closely associated with Kakupacal (Kelley 1982:5; Krochock, personal communication).

With the exception of the inscription recorded at the High Priest's Grave, all the dated inscriptions at Chichen Itza fall within the forty-year time period between 10.1.17.5.13 (AD 866) recorded on the Water Trough Lintel (Thompson 1937:186; for an alternative reading cf. Kelley 1982:13–14) and 10.3.8.14.4 (AD 906) recorded on the Caracol stela (Kelley 1982:Table 1; for an alternative reading cf. Thompson 1937:186). The earliest inscription containing the phonetic rendering of the name Kakupacal is the Casa Colorada band, dated 10.2.0.1.9 (AD 869; Kelley 1982:14; 1983:171; for an alternative reading, cf. Thompson 1937:186), and the latest inscription is Lintel 4 of the Temple of the Four Lintels, dated 10.2.12.2.4 (AD 881; Thompson 1937:186; Kelley 1982:Table 1). Although no date is recorded in the text containing the nominal phrase identified as the ideographic rendering of Kakupacal on Structure 6E1, Tatiana Proskouriakoff (1970:465) implicitly placed the text and its companion relief at approximately 10.1.0.0.0 (AD 849) on the basis of stylistic and iconographic evidence. Proskouriakoff's dating is strengthened by the probable date of 10.2.15.2.13 (AD 884) (Ruppert 1952:Fig. 151; Kelley 1982:12–13) associated with Structure 6E3 (The Temple of the Hieroglyphic Jambs) which is in the same complex as Structure 6E1.

It can therefore be argued that the Calendar Round date, 11 Cimi 14 Pax, recorded in the inscription on the Great Ball Court Stone should be placed at 10.1.15.3.6 (AD 864). This date is contemporaneous with the approximate date of Structure 6E1 in which the same historical individual is prominently described; it is only two years earlier than the Water Trough Lintel, the earliest of the dated inscriptions at Chichen Itza; and it is less than six years earlier than the Casa Colorada band, the earliest of the dated inscriptions in which Kakupacal is named. It can further be argued that the Great Ball Court, the largest and most prominently located ball court at Chichen Itza, was the setting for the ballgame events recorded in the inscriptions of Lintel 1 at Yula, dated 10.2.4.8.4 (AD 874) and Lintels 1 and 4 of the Temple of the Four Lintels, dated 10.2.12.1.8 (AD 881) (Thompson 1937; Kelley 1982).

If the Great Ball Court complex can be dated to the early Terminal Classic period, it raises the possibility that the expansion of the polity at Chichen Itza and the decline of the polities in the southern Maya lowlands may have been directly related. It further supports the model of partial overlap between the Pure Florescent sites of the northern lowlands and the Modified Florescent occupation of Chichen Itza. Finally, it not only strengthens the hypothesis that Pure Florescent and Modified Florescent construction at Chichen Itza were partially overlapping phenomena but also that the elite interaction between the ethnic groups at Chichen Itza was sharply different from that proposed by the traditional model.

## THE IMPACT OF CHICHEN ITZA UPON THE SOUTHERN MAYA LOWLANDS

The possible impact of the multi-ethnic polity at Chichen Itza upon the collapse of Maya civilization in the southern lowlands has been considered by a number of investigators. In his analysis of the murals of the Upper Temple of the Jaguars at Chichen Itza, Arthur Miller has argued that three scenes represent military campaigns undertaken by the chiefs of Chichen Itza in geographical regions outside the local area. According to Miller (1977:217–18, Figs. 8, 3, 9), the three murals at the south end of the inner chamber appear to illustrate the conquest and subjugation of a village in the southern tropical lowlands, probably in the Peten, by warriors from Chichen Itza, an interpretation with which Kelley is in basic accord (1984:12–13). The terrain depicted in battle scenes on the north end of the chamber (Miller 1977:Figs. 4, 5, 7) has been identified either as the slopes of southern Oaxaca (Miller 1977:212–13; Kelley 1984:12–13) or as the "red hills" of the Puuc region (Robles and Andrews 1986:84).

Miller's hypothesis that foreign invasions in the southern Maya lowlands during the Terminal Classic period may have originated from Chichen Itza is supported by data from numerous sites. At Becan, the appearance of northern ceramic types and forms suggests a northern intrusion at the beginning of the ninth century (Ball, 1974, 1977). At Altar de Sacrificios, a violent end to the late Boca ceramic phase and its replacement by an intrusive Fine Paste complex with Classic Maya and Mexican traits seem to be indicated (Adams 1973). Parallels between the architecture and the iconographic motifs in early Cycle 10 sculpture at Seibal and Chichen Itza also suggest an intrusion from the northern Maya lowlands (Adams 1973; Graham 1973; Sabloff 1973, 1975). Northern military activity may also be indicated by a pit containing twenty-eight human skulls and the presence of northern trade wares at Colha (Adams n.d.) and by ceramic evidence and stylistic features of Stela 4 at Rio Azul (Adams, personal communication).

Webb (1973) and Jones (1979) have proposed that Chichen Itza undertook far-reaching military incursions at the end of the Classic period in order to disrupt existing trade routes that linked central Mexico with the southern Maya lowlands and to establish a new long-distance trade network. The identification of Isla Cerritos, a site off the northern Yucatan coast, as a strategic trading post utilized by Chichen Itza in its long-distance trade supports this hypothesis (Andrews *et al.* 1986; Andrews and Gallareta Negrón 1986). The early Terminal Classic date proposed for the Great Ball Court Stone further argues for the connection between events in the northern and southern Maya lowlands.

## INTERACTION BETWEEN CHICHEN ITZA AND NORTHERN MAYA LOWLAND SITES

Recently, a number of investigators have become increasingly dissatisfied with the traditional chronology and interpretation of the northern lowlands that viewed the decline of Maya cities in northern Yucatan by AD 1000 as the result of foreign entrada and of the emergence of a multi-ethnic polity at Chichen Itza. Using ceramic and ethnohistorical evidence, Joseph Ball (1979a, b) has proposed an alternative reconstruction of Terminal Classic/Early Postclassic culture history that he terms the "non-linear, partial overlap" model. He has argued for a possible period of contemporaneity of as much as a century and a half or more between the formation of the new polity at

Chichen Itza and the demise of Maya centers such as Uxmal, Kabah, Sayil, and Labna in the northwestern zone of the Yucatan Peninsula. Ball's hypothesis is supported by the date proposed for the Great Ball Court Stone as well as by recent suggestions that Toltec Tula may date back to at least AD 900 (Andrews V 1979:9). It is further strengthened by the ceramic studies conducted by Rubén Maldanado (Lincoln 1986:175) and César Sáenz (1975) at Uxmal, as well as by the radiocarbon dates reported by E. Wyllys Andrews V (1979:8) for Modified Florescent architecture at Chichen Itza and for Mexican-style offerings in the Balankanche cave shrine. Direct contact between elites from Uxmal in its Pure Florescent phase and from the multi-ethnic polity at Chichen Itza seems to be confirmed by the possible inclusion of the name of the Uxmal ruler, Lord "Chac," in the hieroglyphic text inscribed on a column of Structure 6E1 at Chichen Itza (Kowalski 1987:74) and by the appearance of the name of the Chichen leader Kakupacal on an inscription from the Chan Chimez Group at Uxmal (Kelley 1982:10).

It also appears that the Maya polity of Coba in the northeastern zone survived long after the multi-ethnic polity was formed at Chichen Itza. Recent excavations indicate that Coba functioned as a powerful political and economic rival to Chichen Itza until as late as AD 1100 (Andrews and Robles 1985; Robles and Andrews 1986). David Freidel (n.d.) has further argued that Yaxuna, a small site in the north-central zone connected by a *sacbe* (causeway) to Coba, may have served as a frontier outpost against neighboring Chichen Itza.

## ELITE INTERACTION AND POLITY FORMATION AT CHICHEN ITZA

The argument that Modified Florescent architecture was constructed as early as early Cycle 10 not only supports the reconsideration of the elite interaction between Chichen Itza and other Maya sites in the northern and southern lowlands but also encourages the re-examination of polity formation within Chichen Itza. The construction of the Great Ball Court complex at a date contemporaneous with Pure Florescent structures such as the Temple of the Three Lintels, the Temple of the Four Lintels, and the Monjas suggests that Maya and Mexican elite interaction at Chichen Itza was not based upon conquest and subjugation but upon mutually beneficial alliances. As noted by Proskouriakoff (1970), Maya as well as Mexican elites are celebrated in the Modified Florescent sculpture. Arguing that it was unlikely that Mexican victors would honor their conquered foes in this manner, Proskouriakoff proposed that Mexican factions may have entered the northern lowlands, settled at Maya sites a considerable time prior to their emergence at Chichen Itza, and recruited groups of Maya as their allies. Thus some Maya elite, in Proskouriakoff's view, participated with Mexican intruders in campaigns of conquest and shared in important positions of power and prestige at Chichen Itza.

Proskouriakoff's hypothesis that military and political coalitions between Maya and Mexican factions crossed ethnic boundaries can be further substantiated by additional features of Modified Florescent sculpture. The reliefs at Chichen Itza not only celebrate Maya as well as Mexican warriors as conquerors but also parade both Mexican and Maya prisoners as humiliated captives (Morris *et al.* 1931:Plates. 93, 96, 97, 103; Tozzer 1957:179). In addition, Modified Florescent sculpture depicts many individuals whose costume and weaponry combine Maya and Mexican attributes (Tozzer 1957:151–5). Thus it can be argued that the Mexican peoples, like their Maya contemporaries, were politically fragmented and that some were drawn into alliances with Maya peoples that ended in defeat and disgrace. It can further be argued that the distance between the Maya and Mexican civilizations of the Terminal Classic period was far less than has been traditionally supposed and that, as common interests emerged, ethnic and cultural differences between the elite groups at Chichen Itza quickly blurred. As a result it appears that a multi-ethnic polity with distinctive political and social patterns of organization was formed.

Recent epigraphic studies suggest that the polity at Chichen Itza differed markedly from the pattern documented for polities in the southern Maya lowlands. In sites such as Piedras Negras, Yaxchilan (Proskouriakoff 1960, 1963, 1964) and Palenque (Schele 1974, 1976), inscriptions provide a chronological record of the events of an elite individual's life as a type of historical narrative. However, as Ruth Krochock (1988, n.d.) has noted, the pattern of recording information in the inscriptions of Chichen Itza is very different. She observes that "there are no birth dates, no accession dates, no death dates and no distance numbers stringing events together in an historical narrative" (Krochock n.d.). Instead, the same events, occurring on the same or on two closely related dates, are often inscribed on the multiple lintels of a single structure and are described as being performed by several different individuals (Kelley 1982; Krochock 1988, n.d.).

The most frequently recorded event in the inscriptions of Chichen Itza is the lintel dedication ceremony (Kelley 1982; Krochock 1988, n.d.). The most frequently named individual is Kakupacal (Kelley 1986). The name of Kakupacal is described in ethnohistorical sources as a military captain of the Itza who took part in the conquest of Motul, Itzamal and Chakanputun and in the establishment of an important state at Mayapan (Kelley 1968:259–66). The appearance of the name of Kakupacal in the inscriptions at Chichen Itza suggests that a historical figure bore the same name at an earlier date than the individual known from the ethnohistorical accounts. Further, the association of the name of Kakupacal with the Emblem Glyph of Chichen Itza suggests that this individual achieved a prominent role at the site. At the same time, the association of the same Emblem Glyph with the names of other individuals indicates that high status was enjoyed by elites besides Kakupacal. No epigraphic texts associate Kakupacal or any other figure at Chichen Itza with the events and ceremonies known in southern Maya lowland polities that celebrate the accession of an individual to the throne.

Not only is it impossible to identify a contemporary ruler at Chichen Itza, it is also impossible to reconstruct a dynastic sequence between individuals named in the texts. The effort made by Michel Davoust (1977, 1980) to identify such a sequence is marred by the contemporaneity of the events in which individuals are described as participants. The frequent appearance of the serpent-segment relationship glyph, recently read as "sibling," may indicate that the inscriptions at Chichen Itza record an alliance of ruling brothers (Krochock n.d.). Such an alliance may be similar to that described by Landa for the site (Tozzer 1941:19, 177). Krochock (n.d.) has inferred from the structure and content of Chichen Itza's hieroglyphic inscriptions that the political organization at the site has "moved away from the Classic period emphasis on one individual ruler and [has] moved toward the development of some sort of ruling class with the emphasis on the relationships of the co-rulers to each other and perhaps the status differences among them."

Modified Florescent art also indicates that the multi-ethnic polity at Chichen Itza emphasized a ruling class rather than a single individual. Moreover, it indicates that the elite class has been enlarged to include a far larger number of individuals than had ever occurred in any other Maya polity. This can be recognized by the simultaneous development of architectural and stylistic features that indicate increased inclusiveness in the privileges of elite status. These features can be seen in the Temple of the Warriors and in the Northwest Colonnade (Morris *et al.* 1931) as well as in other structures. In these structures an innovative engineering technique in architecture is combined with a multiplicity of sculptural images to produce permanent monuments that typify the distinctive features of the polity at Chichen Itza.

The architects of Chichen Itza were the first builders in Mesoamerica to exploit the characteristic tensile strength of wood in stone-vaulted architecture. In contrast to wood, stone is weak in tension, that is, in the ability to span distances unsupported by uprights. While wooden lintels were commonly used to span openings in both northern and southern Maya architecture, they functioned as substitutes for stone lintels and resulted in no major change in architectural form. The builders at Chichen Itza, however, evidently realized that, because of its tensile strength, wood could be used in ways that were dramatically different from stone. Wooden beams could do what stone beams could not: they could span wide spaces while still supporting heavy loads. Therefore, at Chichen Itza architects were able to substitute rows of piers spanned by wooden beams for the solid load-bearing walls that, in traditional Maya architecture, were necessary to support the heavy vaulted super-structure. They increased the distances spanned by wooden beams by two or even three times the distances traditionally spanned by stone lintels. As a result they were able to suspend parallel rows of corbeled vaults over widely spaced supports and to create interior vaulted spaces that dwarfed the interior spaces permitted by traditional architectural techniques.

The purpose for which these vastly expanded spaces were created is evidently engraved on the surfaces of the piers which support the vaults. The reliefs on these piers depict the long files of warriors and priests who were evidently permitted entrance into the citadels of administrative power and religious authority at Chichen Itza. These elite individuals, who are both Maya and Mexican in ethnic origin, created crowds too numerous to be contained in the small, enclosed spaces of Maya architecture and too diverse to be controlled except by direct inclusion in the process of governance.

## MONUMENTAL ART AS AN EXPRESSION OF ELITE INTERACTION

The formation of a multi-ethnic polity at Chichen Itza should be understood as the culmination of a long process of cultural convergence between several ethnic factions rather than as the abrupt confrontation of two diametrically opposed cultures. As in other sites in northern Yucatan, Maya culture at Chichen Itza does not appear to have been submerged by Mexican culture but rather seems to have responded to its impetus in dynamic ways. This process can be traced throughout the Classic period in northern lowland sites such as Xelha (Mayer 1983), Dzibilchaltun (Andrews IV and Andrews V 1980:74) and Acanceh (V. Miller 1985). At Chichen Itza this convergence resulted in a pattern of elite interaction that involved a process substantially different from either the subordination of Maya culture to Mexican concepts or the random combination of native traditions with foreign traits. Instead, interrelated and compatible sets of sociopolitical concepts and religious beliefs, of ceremonial activities and aesthetic practices, were drawn from native Maya and from central Mexican as well as from other non-Maya traditions and were shaped into a unique culture.

Monumental art appears to have been used at Chichen Itza as a means of elucidating the process of cultural synthesis. This can be illustrated by the reliefs carved on the interior surfaces of the North Temple, a single-chambered structure located at the north end of the Great Ball Court. The reliefs in this temple portray an extended cycle of ritual activity that parallels the accession ceremonies that are described in sixteenth-century texts for rulers of Tenochtitlan (Townsend n.d.) and that have been reconstructed from the art and epigraphy of Maya lowland sites, particularly Palenque (Schele 1974, 1976, 1978) and Bonampak (M. Miller 1986). Carved blocks recovered from the south vault by the junior co-author (Figs. 9.6, 9.7) depict skeletal and priestly figures in scenes that suggest the rituals surrounding the death of an elite individual, possibly a ruler. The central scene of the north wall (Fig. 9.8) depicts the vacant jaguar throne in the lowest register, the newly designated ruler in the central register where his importance is emphasized by his placement upon the skeletal jaw of a long-nosed deity, and an ancestral deity in a serpent circle in the highest register. The new ruler's distinctive garment and headdress resemble those

Fig. 9.6 South vault, North Temple. Drawn by Linnea Wren after Peter Schmidt.

described by Sahagún (1950–82, VIII:62) and by Durán (1967, II:301) that were donned by the ruler in his investiture ceremony. Similarly, Linda Schele (1974:46) has identified a particular costume assemblage associated with rites of accession of Palenque. In the North Temple relief, the ruler is flanked by three tiers of multi-ethnic warriors and elders. This group resembles the assembly of elites which gathered in Tenochtitlan to confirm the ruler's right to accession (Durán 1967, II:61; Motolinía 1971:338).

The reliefs on the north vault (Fig. 9.9) can be interpreted as representing the circuit of ceremonial visits to sacred shrines that was undertaken by the ruler after the investiture ceremony. Garbed in

Fig. 9.7 South vault, North Temple. Drawn by Linnea Wren after Peter Schmidt.

ceremonial attire, the ruler of Tenochtitlan entered the temples of the principal Mexican gods, offered incense to the image of the deity and performed acts of sacrifice or, very frequently, of auto-sacrifice (Sahagún 1950–1982, VIII:62, V:56, VIII:86; Durán 1967, II:301–2). The importance of bloodletting in Maya accession rites has also been well documented (Schele 1976; M. Miller 1986). The ruler on the north vault of the North Temple is depicted as he performs acts of penis and nasal perforation as well as sacrificial acts involving animals and birds. One ritual is performed at the edge of a cenote, presumably the Sacred Cenote of Chichen Itza.

In the scene extending across the west wall and the western edge of the north wall (Figs. 9.8, 9.10), the ruler is shown in the upper tier seated with a second figure as figures approach him. The register below depicts a warrior kneeling between two other warriors and an eagle, a symbol of one of the Mexican military orders. In the lowest register, celebrants costumed as birds dance to the accompaniment of the drum. This scene can be compared to the public festivities that were staged at Tenochtitlan to confirm the accession of a ruler (Durán 1967,

Fig. 9.8 North wall, North Temple. Drawn by Linnea Wren after Cohodas (1974:Fig. 28).

Fig. 9.9 North vault, North Temple. Drawn by Linnea Wren after Cohodas (1974:Fig. 31).

Fig. 9.10 West wall, North Temple. Drawn by Linnea Wren after Cohodas (1974:Fig. 29).

Fig. 9.11 East wall, North Temple. Drawn by Linnea Wren after Cohodas (1974:Fig. 30).

11:303). These festivities opened with a formal ceremony in which the elder Mexican statesman presented the ruler to the nobles of Tenochtitlan and its neighboring states. Guests approached the lord and offered him their homage. After delivering an oration to the assembly, the ruler joined the stately dance of magnificently garbed lords. Prisoners were also sacrificed to conclude the ceremonies. A similar sequence of events was enacted by the Maya in heir-designation ceremonies such as those depicted at Bonampak (M. Miller 1986:97).

The scene extending across the east wall and the eastern edge of the north wall of the North Temple (Figs. 9.8, 9.11) appears to represent the contest of physical prowess by which the ruler demonstrated his ability to rule. In the upper area of the scene a ball player, identifiable by his ballgame equipment, can be seen to kneel to the side of a large ball. Streams of blood, stylized as serpents, spurt from his severed neck. Around his neck is a rope held by the ruler who stands behind him. In the lowest register is a corpse around whom elite figures cluster. This scene suggests that one function of the ballgame at Chichen Itza was to serve as a substitute for the Flower Wars staged by Mexico to confirm the accession rites or for the war events that accompanied Maya heir-designation ceremonies (Schele 1984b: 12–14; M. Miller 1986:97).

The reliefs of the North Temple can be interpreted as illustrations of the accession ceremonies that were particular to the polity of Chichen Itza. At the same time, they appear to emphasize congruent elements between Maya and Mexican accession ceremonies in order to fuse the ethnically diverse elites of Chichen Itza into a single polity.

## DYNAMICS OF STYLE

Pure Florescent and Modified Florescent art and architecture have traditionally been defined as representing two markedly different art styles diagnostic of two successive chronological time periods at Chichen Itza. However, the contemporaneity of Pure Florescent and Modified Florescent monuments suggests that the art of Chichen Itza can be seen as a continuous spectrum of stylistic variation which was contemporaneously available to the inhabitants of the site. As it adapted to the increasingly distinctive needs of the multi-ethnic polity, the art became increasingly original and dynamic.

Chichen Itza has traditionally been interpreted as a remote center of Mexican culture established by Toltecs from Tula in the northern lowlands. Kubler (1961) has noted that the art of Chichen Itza surpasses that of Tula in its iconographic variety and stylistic quality. He has rejected the model of Chichen Itza as an outpost of Tula and has suggested that it is more characteristic of an artistic capital. More recently Charles Lincoln (1986) proposed that Modified Florescent art should be regarded as a regional variant of native Maya culture.

The appearance of many specific motifs such as chac mools, atlantean figures, feathered serpent columns, and skull racks at both Chichen Itza and Tula indicated that the two sites were in close contact during the Terminal Classic and Early Postclassic periods. It has been argued that many of these motifs have possible precedents in Maya art (Kubler 1961:64–7; Miller 1985). However, the disappearance of these motifs from the northern Maya lowlands after the collapse of Chichen Itza and their continued prominence in central Mexican art until the time of the Spanish conquest indicates that the motifs were Mexican in origin. Changes in the sociopolitical institutions evidently vitiated the significance of the motifs in the northern lowlands but left their importance to central Mexican peoples undiminished. Hence, the patterns of aesthetic continuity in central Mexico and of aesthetic disjunction in the northern Maya lowlands do not support the thesis that Chichen Itza was the source of artistic influence for the motifs shared between it and Tula and subsequently transmitted to later central-Mexican cultures.

We believe that a different model can be applied to Chichen Itza to explain why the Mexican motifs brought by Toltec intruders into the Yucatan Peninsula were elaborated into forms that far surpassed those achieved at the site of their origin. This model has been developed by Oleg Grabar (1978) to explain the development of Islamic art. As Grabar notes, the impetus for the development of Islamic art was as much, or more, a result of the spread of Islam as it was a result of the internal requirements of religious expression. The earliest forms of Islamic art are found outside central Arabia, the geographic region where the Islamic religion initially appeared. As Muslim armies moved across the Middle East and Spain, their commanders followed a pattern that was very rarely destructive. Earlier artistic traditions continued at almost every level of creation and patronage and were used by Muslims and non-Muslims alike. Indeed Grabar (1978:207) observes that "almost every decorative motif considered in isolation, every unit of planning, every detail of construction and every kind of object [in Islamic art] had a direct prototype in the earlier artistic traditions of the Near East and the Mediterranean." These very artistic traditions on which Islamic art was based proved to be both a source to be absorbed and a challenge to be countered. They were a rich source of artistic motifs and designs already imbued with religious, political, and social meaning that could be appropriated by the elite of the newly emerged polity. At the same time they expressed a world order and cemented allegiances to a cultural tradition that was undergoing a process of transformation. In order to serve the needs of a new polity and to maintain its unique identity, motifs derived from artistic vocabularies from all over the Islamic sphere of influence were drawn together. An Islamic style of art was created by sorting out the meanings associated with the forms according to directions necessitated by Islamic concepts of faith and politics. Only a limited number of new artistic elements were added, but original principals of composition and distribution of borrowed forms surfaced in the process of giving visual shape to the distinctive features of Islamic culture. The greatest achievement of the early centuries of Islamic art, according to Grabar (1978:211) was the successful creation of a monumental setting for a new culture, that is, a consistent body of forms which utilized the same external motifs as other contemporary cultures but arranged them in different patterns capable of expressing the distinctive internal dynamic of Islamic religion and thought.

The formation of Modified Florescent art can be interpreted in the same way. The culture of Chichen Itza was the creation of elite groups drawn from Maya polities throughout the northern lowlands and the central Mexican highlands. This culture represented neither a conscious rejection of the habits and practices of the northern Maya lowland cultures nor an uncompromising superimposition of Mexican concepts. Rather it was a reformulation of Maya society in accordance with the changing economic, social, and political pressures of the Terminal Classic period. The Mexican and Maya inhabitants of Chichen Itza developed an artistic style that responded to dual imperatives: the first, to speak to the native culture by absorbing its underlying structures and by utilizing the visual forms that gave them expression; the second, to utilize these forms in an original manner that conveyed the distinctiveness of the multi-ethnic polity. Because the task of the artists at Chichen Itza to address a multi-ethnic, multi-lingual, multicultural elite class was much more complex than the requirements faced by artists at Tula, the artistic vocabulary at Chichen Itza was enlarged and enriched until its themes were richly expressed in a multiplicity of images. The relief cycle of the North Temple of the Great Ball Court at Chichen Itza illustrates the resultant diversity in artistic expression and the fusion in cultural tradition that, for a brief time, supported one of the most successful polities in Mesoamerica.

# 10
# Royal visits and other intersite relationships among the Classic Maya

LINDA SCHELE AND PETER MATHEWS

Throughout the Maya lowlands, the Classic period was a time of great activity and magnificent achievement. The proximity of major centers to one another inevitably must have led to a great deal of interaction among them. Archaeologically this can be and has been detected through the presence of "foreign" objects – ones traded or brought in from another city or region – and through the spread of architectural features and styles, ceramic types, and the like. Hieroglyphic evidence can also be brought to bear on the question of site interaction and interrelationships, and many cases of specific intersite references can be documented (Fig. 10.1)

It is thirty years since site-specific hieroglyphs were detected by Heinrich Berlin (1958). These glyphs, of a fairly standard form, were called Emblem Glyphs by Berlin, because he felt they were emblematic of their site in some way: either they were the name of the city, or its patron deity, or of the royal family, or of the territory under its control.

In their standard form, Emblem Glyphs have a pair of affixes on the left of and above a "main sign." The top affix is one nicknamed *ben-ich* by Thompson (1950:160–2, 200–3): it is now quite clear that it is to be read *ahau*, "lord" (Lounsbury 1973; Mathews and Justeson 1984).

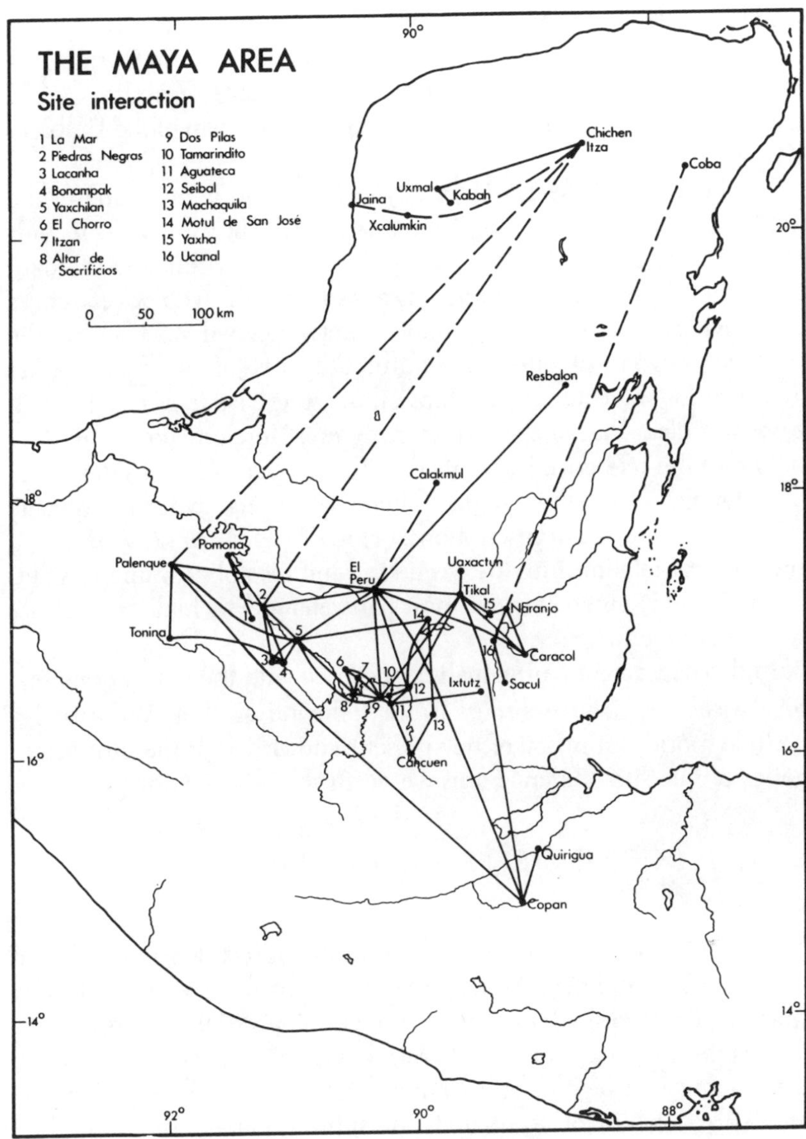


Fig. 10.1 Map of the Maya area, showing interaction between sites. The solid lines represent definite links between sites; the dashed lines refer to probable ties (shared dates at Naranjo–Coba and Calakmul–?El Peru; objects from Palenque, Piedras Negras and Xcalumkin found at Chichen Itza, and from Xcalumkin found at Jaina).

Emblem Glyphs invariably occur in the name phrases of royal individuals: as such, they appear to function as royal titles. A paraphrase of the Emblem Glyph would be "lord of *x*" (the actual reading order was "*x*"-lord), where "*x*" is the main sign of the Emblem Glyph.[1]

We believe that the Emblem Glyph main sign is the name of the polity controlled by the ruler (Mathews 1985, 1986). As such, records of the main signs of Emblem Glyphs – usually within the standard Emblem Glyph context, but not always so – are likely to be references to individual Classic Maya polities. References at one site to the Emblem Glyphs of other sites form the crux of the hieroglyphic evidence for intersite relationships among the Classic Maya. In such cases it is clear that one site is referring to a "foreign" polity, and the nature of the reference is specified in the passage which accompanies the "foreign" Emblem Glyph. There are several types of intersite reference in the Maya inscriptions: (1) royal marriage; (2) warfare; (3) hierarchical relationships (between king and his political inferiors); (4) royal visits; (5) others (for the most part references which are still not well understood).

In this paper we are principally concerned with the fourth of these – royal visits – which we discuss in the following section. We will also include a brief summary of our present knowledge of the other categories of intersite reference: this we do in the third section.

## ROYAL VISITS AMONG THE CLASSIC MAYA

The term "royal visit" may be defined as the peaceful visit of one lord to the city of another. Although instances of royal visits were only sporadically recorded, they were no doubt a common occurrence among the Classic Maya. Royal visits were most frequently recorded in the Usumacinta region, at Yaxchilan and Piedras Negras – sites that are both notable for the variety of subject matter found in their hieroglyphic inscriptions.

*Piedras Negras.* At Piedras Negras, royal visitors are portrayed on several lintels. Lintel 12 is the earliest dated monument at the site; it has four dates, three of which can be read securely: 9.3.19.12.12 9 Eb 11 Zec (the Initial Series Date, July 2, 514[2]), 9.4.0.0.0. (Oct. 18,

514), and 9.4.3.0.17 5 Caban 0 Zac (Oct. 19, 517). The eroded date is perhaps 9.4.3.10.1 7 Imix 19 Pop (Apr. 21, 518). Since the last event, "smoking k'in vase," also appears on Lintel 4, which has a similar scene, we may presume that the event portrayed occurred on 9.4.3.10.1.

The scene on Lintel 12 shows three people in lordly dress kneeling before an unidentified ruler who stands facing them. Behind the ruler crouches a prisoner, stripped of all symbols of rank and with his hands bound behind him. The three kneeling figures also appear to have their hands bound, but in front of their bodies, and by cloth rather than rope. They may in fact be captives, but they are deliberately contrasted in dress and bonds to the captive behind the king. Since the later monuments showing this type of scene (Lintels 2 and 4) do not show these kneeling attendants bound as captives, we suspect that the ones on Lintel 12 are shown as *symbolic* captives only, and that they are involved in some ritual that we do not yet understand, but which probably involves the ritual sacrifice of the captive behind the standing ruler.

Each of the kneeling nobles is named by a four-glyph phrase near his head. We have not been able to identify the two figures on the left, but the person closest to the king is clearly named Knot-eye Jaguar of Yaxchilan, a king whose reign can be dated to the late third and early fourth katuns of Baktun 9, thus matching the Piedras Negras Lintel 12 dates.

A similar scene is repeated on Lintel 2 (Fig. 10.2), which displays six kneeling figures, a ruler, and a smaller standing figure behind him. All the figures are dressed in a costume distinctive of the Tlaloc-war complex (Schele 1986d) and all carry spears and shields. Here the kneeling figures are clearly not captives. The text records two events: one occurring on 9.11.6.2.1 3 Imix 19 Ceh (Oct. 24, 658), and an earlier one of 9.3.16.0.5 8 Chicchan 3 Ceh (Nov. 13, 510). The events on both dates are written with an ahau-in-hand followed by a complement specifying the kind of object displayed in the ritual.[3] Ruler 2 is the protagonist of the later event, while a man called Ah-Chac-Ahau-K'in enacted the earlier ritual.

Interestingly, this earlier date is very close to the cluster of dates recorded on Lintel 12, and the later one is only thirteen days after a similar scene shown on Lintel 4. The later ahau-in-hand ritual is recorded in a couplet, first following an elaborate Long Count expres-

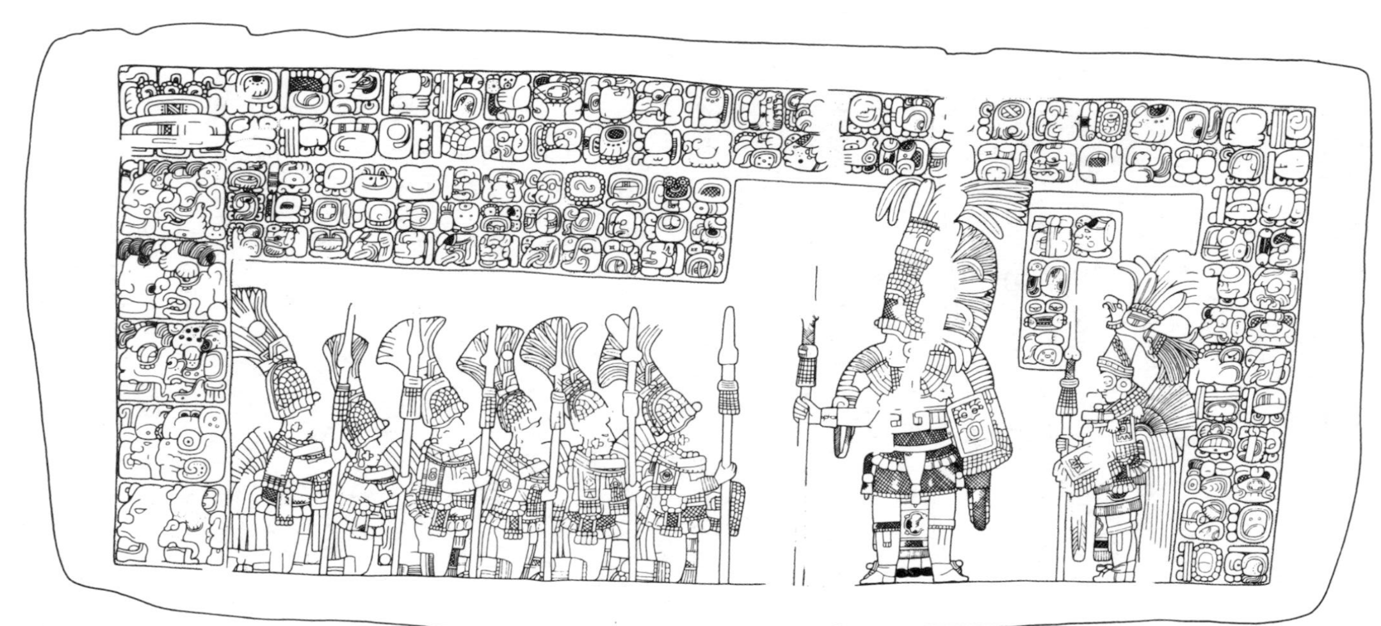

Fig. 10.2 Piedras Negras Lintel 2. Drawing by David S. Stuart.

sion of the date, and then linked by a Distance Number to the earlier event. This linkage and the deliberate use of the same verbal phrase to record both events are discourse devices used to emphasize the connection of the contemporary event to its Early Classic prototype.

In the scene on Lintel 2, the six kneeling figures and the small standing figure are all named. The date of the event is well after Ruler 2's accession on 9.10.6.5.9 (Apr. 15, 639), and is not associated with an anniversary of his accession. The beneficiary of the action seems to be the small figure standing behind the king; he appears to be an adolescent, perhaps the son of the king, being initiated into the role of warrior (Schele and Miller 1986:149). The kneeling figures in front of the king are each named by a double-column text above his head: the first, third, fourth and sixth figures are titled Lacanha ahau, while the second is a Yaxchilan ahau, and the fifth an ahau of Bonampak. If these visitors were standing, they would be the same height as the young Piedras Negras ahau, and considerably shorter than the standing ruler. We think it is likely that the six kneeling attendants are youths of ahau status sent by their respective kings to participate in this ritual. Their presence suggests an alliance between Ruler 2 of Piedras Negras and his contemporaries at Lacanha, Bonampak, and Yaxchilan.

Piedras Negras Lintel 3 (Fig. 10.3) depicts another royal visit, involving the later Ruler 4. The chronology and events recorded in the inscription are as follows:

| Date (Long Count) | Event | Protagonist |
|---|---|---|
| 9.15.18.3.13 (7/31/749) | 1-katun anniversary of accession | Ruler 4 |
| 9.15.18.3.15 (8/2/749) | came by canoe | Jaguar of Yaxchilan |
| 9.15.18.3.16 (8/3/749) | unknown | Ruler 4 |
| 9.16.6.11.17 (11/30/757) | death | Ruler 4 |
| 9.16.6.12.0 (12/3/757) | burial | Ruler 4 |
| 9.17.9.5.11 (3/28/780)[4] | unknown | Person in the land of Ruler 7 |

| Secondary text | | |
|---|---|---|
| 9.16.6.10.19 (11/12/757) | unknown | ?? |
| 9.16.6.9.16 (10/20/757) | T683 "bundle" | Bat-Jaguar of Yaxchilan |

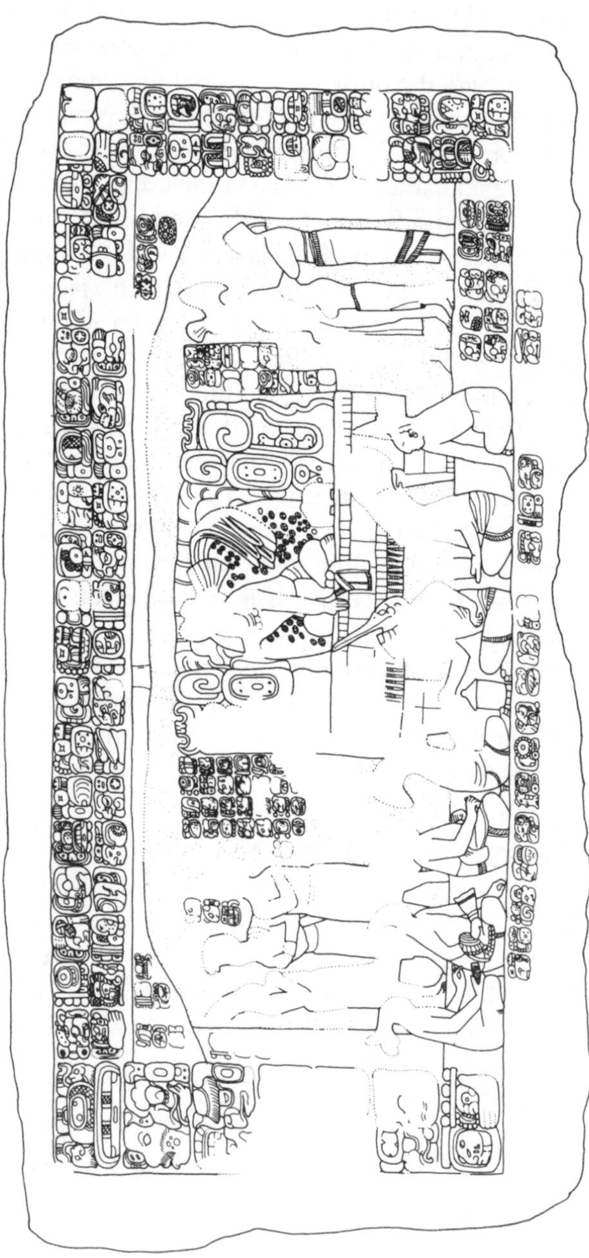

Fig. 10.3 Piedras Negras Lintel 3.

The scene depicts court activity, but we do not know which date is to be associated with it. The cluster of dates associated with the katun anniversary specifically mention a visit by canoe of a Yaxchilan lord, and the secondary texts to the left of the throne also include Yaxchilan names, contemporaries of Piedras Negras Ruler 4. Moreover, the bench on which the protagonist sits seems to depict Throne 1, associated by its dates and texts with Ruler 7: the last passage in the main text of Lintel 3 also names Ruler 7. Thus the inscription of Lintel 3 appears to record several royal visits, while the scene depicts one of them.

The figures in the scene are divided into four groups. The Piedras Negras king (Ruler 4, we suspect) sits on the throne, leaning forward and to his right. On the same level as the throne, three figures stand to the king's right and four to his left (viewer's right). Seven figures sit on a lower level: four on one side of a vessel and three on the other. These seven lower figures are named in incised captions below or near their bodies as *cahals*; we believe them to be members of the Piedras Negras elite – but they are of a lower rank than the standing figures.

The group of figures to the left of (behind) the king consists of three small figures and one adult (Proskouriakoff 1961a:21); they appear to be named in incised phrases on the curtain above and on the step below them. If we assume that the upper text names the adult, then the ten glyphs below (divided into groups of four, two, and four glyphs, respectively) should name the three youngsters. The first name includes a rabbit head and *chi* hand as personal names, followed by the "rodent-bone" title and concluding with the Piedras Negras Emblem Glyph. The middle pair of glyphs includes a macaw-God GI conflation (also used as the name of Ruler 2), and the "rodent-bone" title. The final name is "Ah Cacaw Chan God K": this name is identical to that of Ruler A of Tikal – but the chronology indicates that he is another person bearing the same name.

The three figures to the king's right (the viewer's left) appear to be visitors. The left figure has three name phrases positioned near him, but we do not know which is his. The center figure is named above his head with a turtleshell over a *te* sign, and with the Yaxchilan Emblem Glyph. He appears to be an attendant for the third figure of the group, who is probably the protagonist of the large text incised between him and the king. This text may record the event portrayed in the scene. It begins with an undated clause recording some event done by a Piedras Negras personage "in the land of" Bat-Jaguar of Yaxchilan, a name long recognized as a substitution for Bird-Jaguar (Proskouriakoff 1964:181). The second passage ties an unknown event on 9.16.6.10.19 (Nov. 12, 757) to a "bundle"[5] event which took place twenty-three days earlier. The actor was the same Bat-Jaguar, but this event was "in the land of" a man called "God N-turtleshell". Since a turtleshell glyph is found in Ruler 4's name, but not in Ruler 7's, we may interpret this phrase as recording "in the land of Ruler 4."

Proskouriakoff (1961a:21) has suggested that this scene represents the heir-designation of the next king of Piedras Negras, and we agree. The date in the incised text precedes Ruler 4's death by only forty-one days, and the figures to his left appear to be youngsters, perhaps his sons. Houston (1983) has argued that Rulers 5 and 6 were the same person, or at least that the names are the same. If he is right, then Ruler 5/6 is named on several occasions (Stela 16 and Throne 1) with the same rabbit glyph that appears in the first of the three names discussed above. Thus the event shown on Lintel 3 seems to correspond to the incised text and to the designation of this child as the next king. The "bundle" event, then, might record not the accession of Bird-Jaguar of Yaxchilan (his accession at Yaxchilan occurred on 9.16.10.0.0; Mar. 17, 761), but rather his participation in the designation of the Piedras Negras child as heir to the throne of Piedras Negras. If this interpretation is correct, then Ruler 4 insured the successful enthronement of his son by securing the participation of the largest neighboring polity with which he was allied. Furthermore, the "royal visit" reinforced a long-standing and successful way of forging and maintaining alliances, as we shall now see from inscriptions at Yaxchilan.

*Yaxchilan.* The earliest and longest record of royal visits now known was recorded at Yaxchilan, in a series of lintels (Fig. 10.4) probably carved around 9.5.10.0.0±10 tuns (AD 549±10 years) but re-used in a later building by the famous king Bird-Jaguar IV. These texts record the dynastic history of Yaxchilan and a series of visitors from other polities who participated in rites associated with accession. As first noted by Proskouriakoff (1964:182–3), the Yaxchilan royal names are accompanied by glyphs which set them in numerical order. Proskouriakoff suggested that these names "may be those of the 'first men' who became heads of different lineages after the founding of the town" (Proskouriakoff 1964:184). In analyzing the same texts,

Mathews (1975) identified the numbered glyphs as a sign for "succession" prefixed by an ordinal number and followed by T168:700, a glyph for accession known also at Palenque (Mathews and Schele 1974). Thus Mathews argued for a series of royal accessions, each marked by the "successor" glyph giving their numerical position in Yaxchilan's dynasty: the then-known lintels recorded the sixth through the tenth rulers. Mathews also noted that each of the Yaxchilan names was followed by a constant glyph and then by one or more different names. In some examples, these names designated foreigners who could be identified in contemporary inscriptions from other sites. The two Calendar Round dates that occur in the set of lintels were able to be placed in the Long Count by considering other, dated references.

The dynastic sequence was completed in 1983 when Roberto García Moll discovered the first lintel in the series (see *National Geographic Magazine,* October 1985, p. 541). Having drawn the new lintel *in situ* at Yaxchilan, David Stuart (personal communication 1984) recognized that the name phrase at C6–C7 on the new lintel also occurs on Hieroglyphic Stair 1 at 60–62 and that the Yaxchilan king named in both inscriptions is Bird-Jaguar (Fig. 10.5). Furthermore, he noted the glyph that stands between the names of the king and the foreigner on the lintel also precedes the foreigner's names on the stairs. More importantly, this glyph on the stairs is preceded by a Distance Number, a Posterior Date Indicator, and a Calendar Round date, thus demonstrating that it is a verb recording an event enacted by the foreigner some time after the accession of the Yaxchilan ruler. The pattern is as follows:

On the lintels, all of the temporal data (with the exception of two Calendar Round dates) were deleted, giving the alternative pattern of:

Ordinal succession number/"he acceded (T700)"/Yaxchilan ruler/
he did something/foreigner

Calendar Round date 1/"he was seated as king"/Yaxchilan ruler
Distance Number/"and then it came to pass"/date 2/
he did something/foreigner

The foreigners' names appear in two forms: a single name phrase and a compound consisting of two or more names separated by T126.168:518. Houston and Mathews (1985:Fig. 12) identified this variant of ahau as a glyph specifying the relationship between a noble

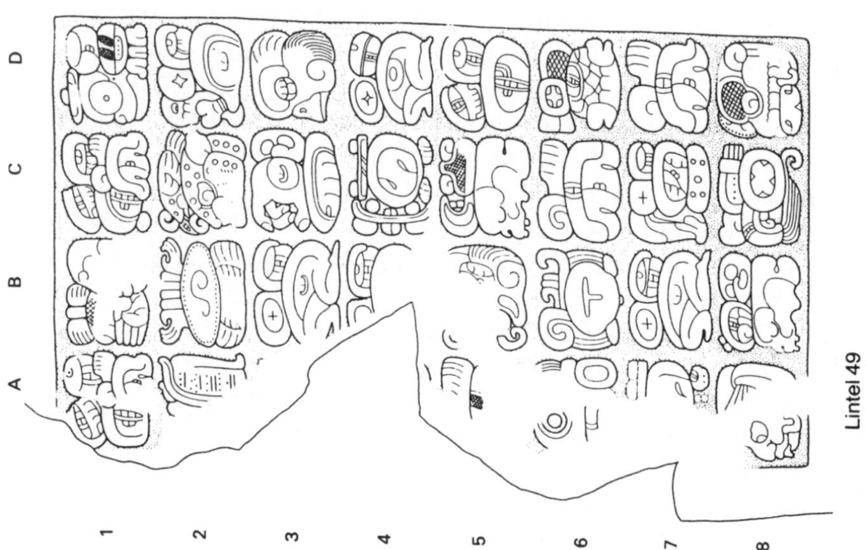


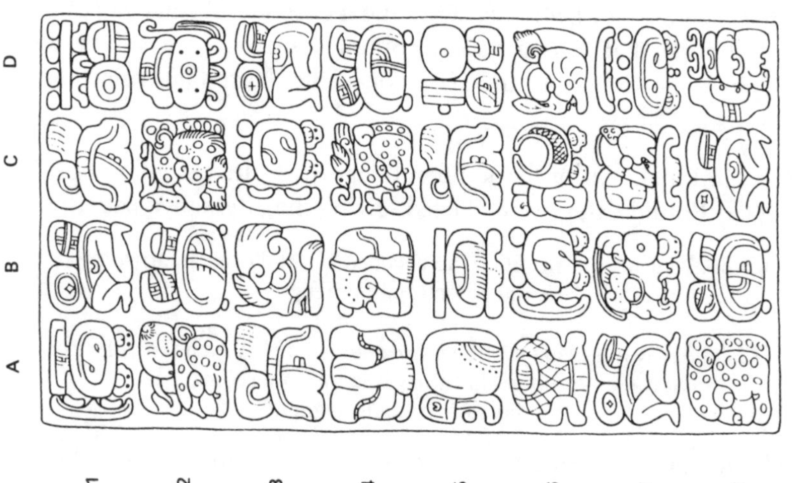


Fig. 10.4 Yaxchilan: Lintels 11, 49, 37, and 35.

Lintel 37

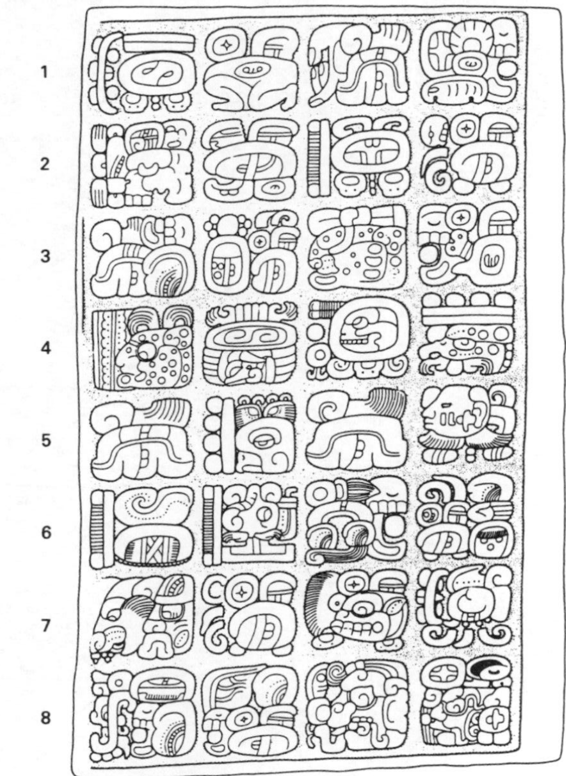


Lintel 35

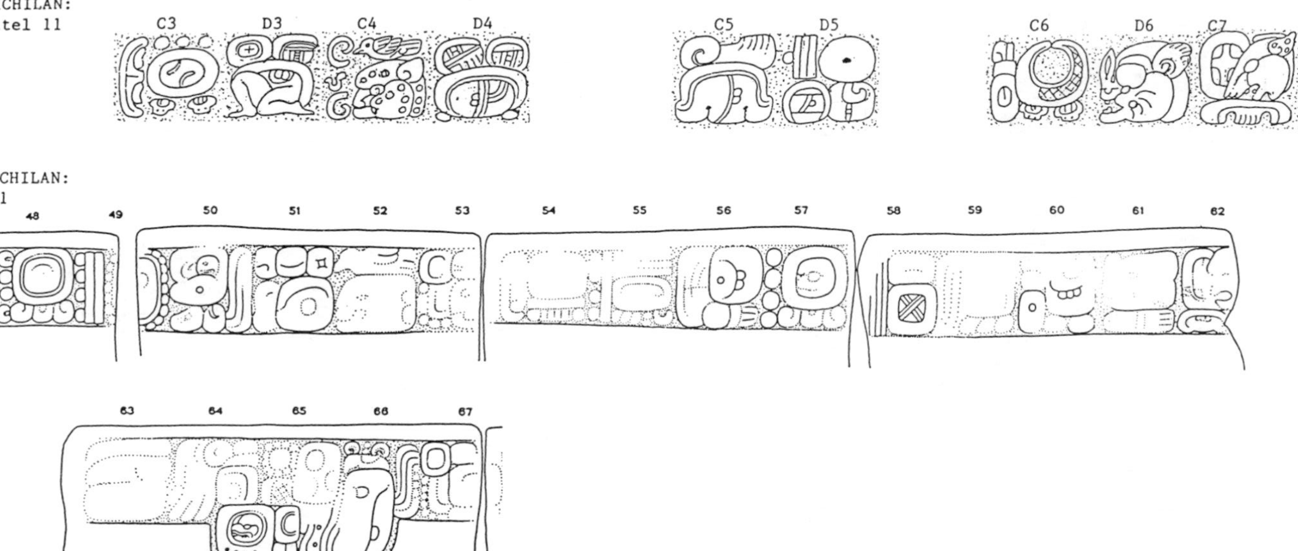


Fig. 10.5 References to Bird-Jaguar I of Yaxchilan and his royal visitor Zac-Hal-Zotz.

Table 10.1. *Royal visitors to Yaxchilan as recorded on Lintels 11, 49, 37, and 35*

| | | |
|---|---|---|
| 1st successor Penis-Jaguar | visited by | Ah-Cauac-Turtleshell |
| 2nd successor Shield-Jaguar | visited by | Muan-Yax-Be |
| 3rd successor Bird-Jaguar | visited by | Zac-Hal-Zotz on 8.17.2.11.5 (May 29, 379) |
| 4th successor Yax-Antler-Skull | visited by | Tree-Diving Bird |
| 5th successor missing | visited by | Ik |
| 6th successor Tah-Skull I | visited by | Bird-Jaguar of Bonampak |
| 7th successor Moon-Skull I | visited by | Turtleshell of Piedras Negras |
| | visited by | Uinal-Serpent |
| 8th successor Bird-Jaguar | visited by | Zac-Imix, the ahau of Turtleshell of Piedras Negras |
| 9th successor Knot-eye Jaguar | visited by | Yax-Uc, the ahau of Fish-Fin of Bonampak |
| | visited by | Kan-Te, the ahau of Fish-Fin of Bonampak |
| | visited by | Upended Frog, the ahau of Jaguar Paw-Skull of Tikal on 9.3.13.12.19 (Aug. 9, 508) |
| 10th successor Tah-Skull II | visited by | Ah Cauac, the ahau of Jaguar-Diving Bird |
| | visited by | 9-Bird, the ahau of Chaan-Ah Cauac-Te-Tun Ahau |
| | visited by | Ah Chuen, the ahau of Knot-eye Jaguar of Bonampak |
| | visited by | Arcing-Cauac, the ahau of Ix of Site Q (El Peru?) on 9.5.2.10.6 (Jan. 16, 537) |

and his overlord, while David Stuart (personal communication 1985) has suggested it should be read as *yahau*, literally "his ahau" or "the ahau of," with the possessor being the high king of a specific site. Thus, we have visitors who are kings and others who are lords of the rank ahau sent as representatives of their kings. The visitors are listed in Table 10.1.

These lintels with their early dynastic history were commissioned by the tenth Yaxchilan ruler, but they were re-used by Bird-Jaguar IV. The Structure 5 Hieroglyphic Stairway recorded the same events, but in greater detail. Both the 10th king and his eventual successor, Bird-Jaguar IV, considered these visits to have been political information important enough to be recorded in permanent and public form.

*Bonampak.* At Bonampak there are implicit references to royal visits (see Fig. 10.6 and Table 10.2 for these and all other instances in which the origins of visitors are known). Lintel 2 of Structure 1 records

Table 10.2. *Royal visits between known polities in the Classic Maya lowlands*

| | Ruler | Polity | | Visitor | Polity | Date |
|---|---|---|---|---|---|---|
| 1 | Tah-Skull II | Yaxchilan | | Bird-Jaguar | Bonampak | *c.* 9.0.0.0.0 |
| 2 | Moon-Skull I | Yaxchilan | | Turtleshell | Piedras Negras | *c.* 9.1.0.0.0 |
| 3 | Bird-Jaguar II | Yaxchilan | | Turtleshell | Piedras Negras | *c.* 9.2.0.0.0 |
| 4 | Knot-eye Jaguar | Yaxchilan | Yax-Uc, ahau of | Fish-Fin | Bonampak | *c.* 9.3.10.0.0 |
| 5 | Knot-eye Jaguar | Yaxchilan | Kan-Te, ahau of | Fish-Fin | Bonampak | *c.* 9.3.10.0.0 |
| 6 | Knot-eye Jaguar | Yaxchilan | Upended Frog, ahau of | Jaguar Paw-Skull | Tikal | 9.3.13.12.19 |
| 7 | Ah-Cauac-Ahaw-Kin? | Piedras Negras | | Knot-eye Jaguar | Yaxchilan | 9.4.3.10.1 |
| 8 | Tah-Skull II | Yaxchilan | 9 Bird, ahau of | Chaan-Ah-Cauac | (Te-Tun polity) | *c.* 9.5.0.0.0 |
| 9 | Tah-Skull II | Yaxchilan | Ah-Chuen, ahau of | Knot-eye Jaguar | Bonampak | *c.* 9.5.0.0.0 |
| 10 | Tah-Skull II | Yaxchilan | Ta-?-Nah, ahau of | Cu-hand-Ix | El Peru | 9.5.2.10.6 |
| 11 | Ruler 2 | Piedras Negras | | Ta-cu-be | Lacanha | 9.11.6.2.1 |
| 12 | Ruler 2 | Piedras Negras | | K-an-Ah-? | Yaxchilan | 9.11.6.2.1 |
| 13 | Ruler 2 | Piedras Negras | | Zac-la | Lacanha | 9.11.6.2.1 |
| 14 | Ruler 2 | Piedras Negras | | Mo'-ta-la-ah-ta | Lacanha | 9.11.6.2.1 |
| 15 | Ruler 2 | Piedras Negras | | God K-? | Bonampak | 9.11.6.2.1 |
| 16 | Ruler 2 | Piedras Negras | | God K-?-lu-nab | Lacanha | 9.11.6.2.1 |
| 17 | Ruler E | Tamarindito | | Ruler 2 | Dos Pilas | *c.* 9.14.0.0.0 |
| 18 | Ruler 4 | Piedras Negras | | Bird-Jaguar IV | Yaxchilan | 9.15.18.3.15 |
| 19 | La Pasadita cahal | Yaxchilan | | Bird-Jaguar IV | Yaxchilan | 9.16.15.0.0 |
| 20 | Chan-Muan | Bonampak | | Shield-Jaguar II | Yaxchilan | 9.18.0.3.4 |

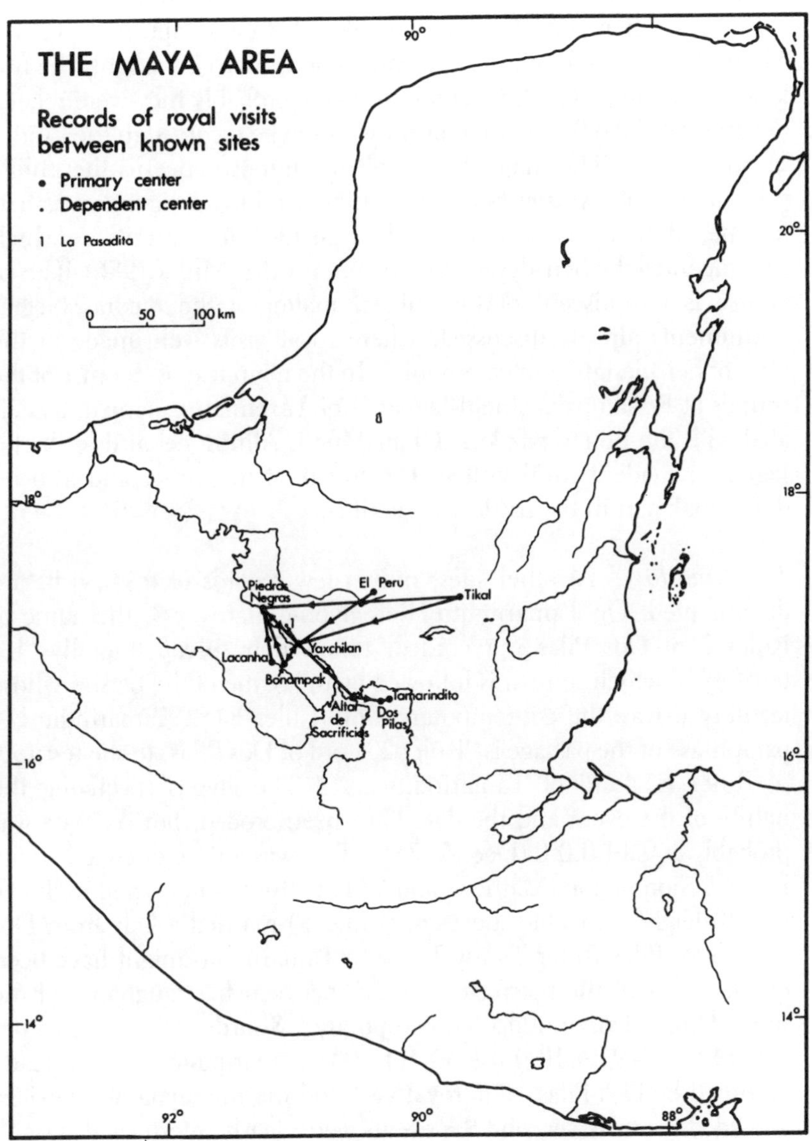


Fig. 10.6 Records of royal visits between known cities in the Classic Maya lowlands. (The arrows indicate the direction of the visit.)

a capture by Shield-Jaguar II of Yaxchilan. The date of the capture is 9.17.16.3.8 (Jan. 8, 787), just four days before a capture by Chan-Muan, the king of Bonampak (recorded on Lintel 1). Probably the two kings were campaigning together, and very probably they were related (Mathews 1980:67). A similar event seems to be recorded in the murals of Structure 1. The major theme of the murals concerns the public presentation of a young Bonampak prince and his designation as heir to the Bonampak throne, and a battle and sacrifice which accompanied the heir-designation ceremony (M. Miller 1986). This of course is reminiscent of the subject matter of the Piedras Negras monuments already discussed, where royal visits were made at the time of heir-designation ceremonies. In the main text of Room 1 of the murals at Bonampak, Shield-Jaguar II of Yaxchilan is named, associated with the Bonampak king Chan-Muan. Almost certainly, Shield-Jaguar II made a royal visit to Bonampak at this time, and also no doubt took part in the battle and sacrifice.

*Tamarindito.* At other sites, only a few records of royal visits are documented. On Tamarindito Hieroglyphic Stairway 3, the name of Ruler 2 of Dos Pilas is recorded, followed by *u-cab* (literally "his territory"), which in turn is followed by the name of the person whose territory it was: the contemporary king (Ruler E) of Tamarindito. A paraphrase of the passage is "Ruler 2, Lord of Dos Pilas, in the territory of Ruler E, Lord of Tamarindito . . ." The glyphs specifying the nature of the event and the date have been eroded, but the date was probably *c.* 9.14.0.0.0 (Dec. 5, 711). This was a time of great activity in the Pasion region (Mathews and Willey, this volume), and we know that Ruler E's probable successor (Ruler F) married a lady from Dos Pilas. Dos Pilas Ruler 2's royal visit to Tamarindito might have been connected with the marriage, perhaps between his daughter and the son of his Tamarindito contemporary. Shortly after this time, *c.* 9.14.0.0.0–9.14.10.0.0 (AD 711–21), Tamarindito was politically absorbed by Dos Pilas. The royal visit and the interdynastic marriage preceded the takeover, and the events were clearly interrelated. For all known royal visits between polities see Fig. 10.6 and Table 10.2.

*La Pasadita.* There are also records of royal visits within polities. The two lintels of La Pasadita, as well as a looted panel now in New York City (Simpson 1976) portray and name the local ruler of La

Pasadita, who is of cahal rank. The three monuments also portray and name the contemporary rulers of Yaxchilan: Lintels 1 and 2 name Bird-Jaguar IV (on 9.16.15.0.0 [Feb. 19, 766] and 9.16.8.3.18 [Jun. 14, 759], respectively), and the New York panel Shield-Jaguar II (undated, but presumably after 9.17.0.0.0 [Jan. 24, 771]). It is clear that the local cahal remained as governor of La Pasadita following the death of Bird-Jaguar. It is also obvious that these monuments portray royal visits, but it is not clear which person visited the other: these could be monuments ordered by the governor to commemorate his visit to the capital of the polity, and his participation in various events there. But is is also likely that the Yaxchilan kings visited La Pasadita, and that such important events were commemorated locally. Certainly royal visits within the polity, by the king to his deputies, are known from elsewhere, namely at Copan.

*Copan.* William Fash and David Stuart (this volume) have cogently argued that the ruler of Copan, Yax-Pac, made royal visits to outlying residential groups in the Copan Valley. These were acts of mutual support in a society where the traditional Maya sociopolitical organization was beginning to break down, and where the central authority was beginning to lose effective political control. In fact, Yax-Pac (Yax Sun-at-Horizon) is also named, apparently, as a royal visitor, at Quirigua (Structure 1). The date is 9.19.0.0.0 (Jun. 26, 810) and the action was a "scattering" rite for the katun-ending.

## OTHER TYPES OF INTERSITE RELATIONSHIP

### *Royal marriage*

At several sites, there are references to women whose name phrases include a "foreign" Emblem Glyph (Fig. 10.7 and Table 10.3 list all instances known to us). These have been presumed to indicate royal marriages between the dynasties of the two Maya sites. Of course, some of the examples could represent royal visits only, but in most cases (6, 8, and 9 of Table 10.3 are the only exceptions), the presumption of royal marrige is confirmed by parentage statements, stating that the "foreign" woman was the mother of a local ruler, and the wife of his father (Schele, Mathews and Lounsbury n.d.).

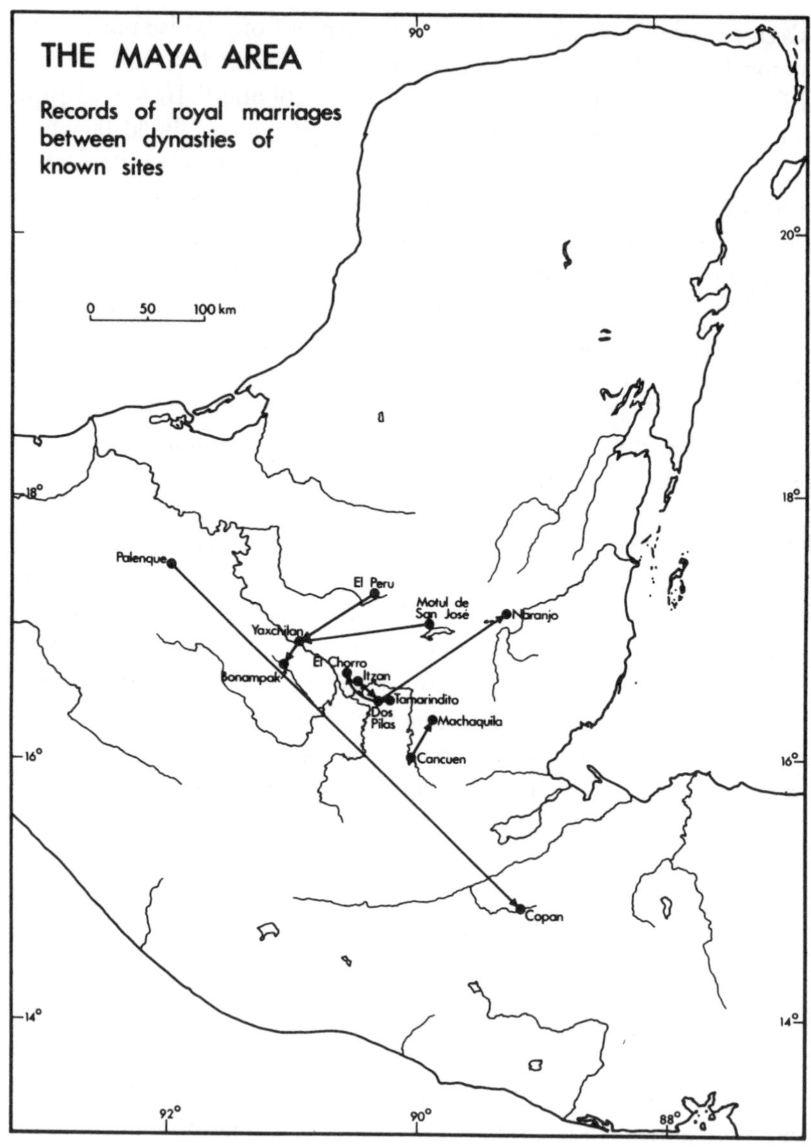


Fig. 10.7 Records of royal marriages between dynasties of known cities in the Classic Maya lowlands. (The arrows indicate the direction of travel of the bride.)

Table 10.3. *Royal marriages between known polities in the Classic Maya lowlands*

| Polity of husband | Polity of wife | Date |
|---|---|---|
| 1 Dos Pilas | Itzan | c. 9.11.10.0.0 |
| 2 El Chorro | Dos Pilas | c. 9.11.15.0.0 |
| 3 Naranjo | Dos Pilas | c. 9.13.0.0.0 |
| 4 Yaxchilan | El Peru | c. 9.13.0.0.0 |
| 5 Tamarindito | Dos Pilas | c. 9.13.10.0.0 |
| 6 Yaxchilan | Motul de San Jose | c. 9.15.0.0.0 |
| 7 Machaquila | Cancuen | c. 9.15.10.0.0 |
| 8 Copan | Palenque | c. 9.15.10.0.0 |
| 9 Bonampak | Yaxchilan | c. 9.17.10.0.0 |

Much has been made of these interdynastic marriages and their implications for sociopolitical organization among the Classic Maya (Marcus 1973:914, 1976 passim; Molloy and Rathje 1974:435–42). In fact there are relatively few cases of royal interdynastic marriage – fewer than the number of known cases of royal visits or of warfare between polities. It appears that there could have been various reasons behind interdynastic marriage alliances. Some (e.g. 9 in Table 10.3) were between old friends and allies; others (1) to gain local prestige; others (7, 8) contacts made at times of political stress; still others (5) might have been royal marriages imposed upon the weaker partner. All known instances of royal interdynastic marriages date to Late Classic times; some were between neighboring polities, while others involved polities hundreds of miles apart.

## *Warfare*

Warfare among the Classic Maya has long been recognized, and there has been steady progress in the decipherment of war-related hieroglyphic texts, so that now several verbs and many warrior titles have been identified (e.g. Proskouriakoff 1960:470, 1963:152; Riese 1984a). It now appears that most Maya warfare probably consisted of relatively small-scale raiding, the main aim of which was to obtain live victims for sacrifice. Although there is evidence of defensive fortifications at several Maya sites, most sites were very open and vulnerable – as though the inhabitants were not concerned about a major attack on their city by a large invading army. Rather, most attacks seem to have been small raids made just outside the raiders' own territory and in the

Table 10.4. *Occurrences of warfare between known polities in the Classic Maya lowlands*

| | Victor | Defeated | | Date (Long Count) | | |
|---|---|---|---|---|---|---|
| 1 | Yaxchilan | Lacanha | | 9.6.10.14.15 | 4 Men | 3 Mac |
| 2 | Caracol | Naranjo | | 9.9.18.16.3 | 7 Akbal | 16 Muan |
| 3 | Tikal | El Peru | | 9.13.3.7.18 | 11 Etz'nab | 11 Ch'en |
| 4 | Naranjo | Ucanal | | 9.13.6.10.4 | 6 Kan | 2 Zac |
| 5 | Tonina | Palenque | | 9.13.19.3.3 | 13 Akbal | 16 Yax |
| 6 | Yaxchilan | Lacanha | | 9.14.17.15.11 | 2 Chuen | 14 Mol |
| 7 | Dos Pilas | Seibal | | 9.15.4.6.4 | 8 Kan | 17 Muan |
| 8 | Quirigua | Copan | | 9.15.6.14.6 | 6 Cimi | 4 Zec |
| 9 | Aguateca | Cancuen | before | 9.15.9.17.17 | | |
| 10 | Machaquila | Motul de San Jose | before | 9.15.10.0.0 | | |
| 11 | Tikal | Yaxha | | 9.15.12.2.2 | 11 Ik | 15 Ch'en |
| 12 | Dos Pilas | Yaxchilan | | 9.15.10.0.0–9.16.10.0.0 | | |
| 13 | Aguateca | El Chorro | c. | 9.17.0.0.0 | | |
| 14 | La Mar | Pomona | | 9.17.3.5.19 | 1 Cauac | 2 Uayeb |
| 15 | ?? | Yaxchilan | | 9.17.11.6.10 | 8 Oc | 8 Zotz'? |
| 16 | Piedras Negras | Pomona | | 9.18.3.9.12 | 9 Eb | 10 Zotz'? |

boundaries between polities. Emphasis was always given in the Maya monuments to the "single-combat" nature of warfare – to the many one-on-one struggles within the larger context of the battle itself. In most cases, the identity of captives was given by one or two name glyphs, without an Emblem Glyph. Presumably the captured individual in such cases was important, but not always of the highest ahau rank. The individual conquests were prominently recorded among the winner's titles: the "captor of . . . (name)" (Proskouriakoff 1963) expressions, and the title stating how many captives were taken (Stuart 1985a). There are, however, just over a dozen cases where an Emblem Glyph is associated with the loser of a battle and thus where the polities of both combatants are known (Fig. 10.8 and Table 10.4).

It should be emphasized that these are but a small portion of the records of battle and capture in the Maya hieroglyphic corpus. However, they represent all the instances we know where the place of origin of both protagonists is known. The impression one gets is that it was not the place of origin of the captive that was important. Rather, it was the individual himself, and his rank, that mattered: the Emblem Glyph of the captive was recorded not to give his place of origin, but for the inclusion in the glyph of the title ahau, "lord."

Not all battles yielded the same political results, as can be seen in a few of the battles listed in Table 10.4.

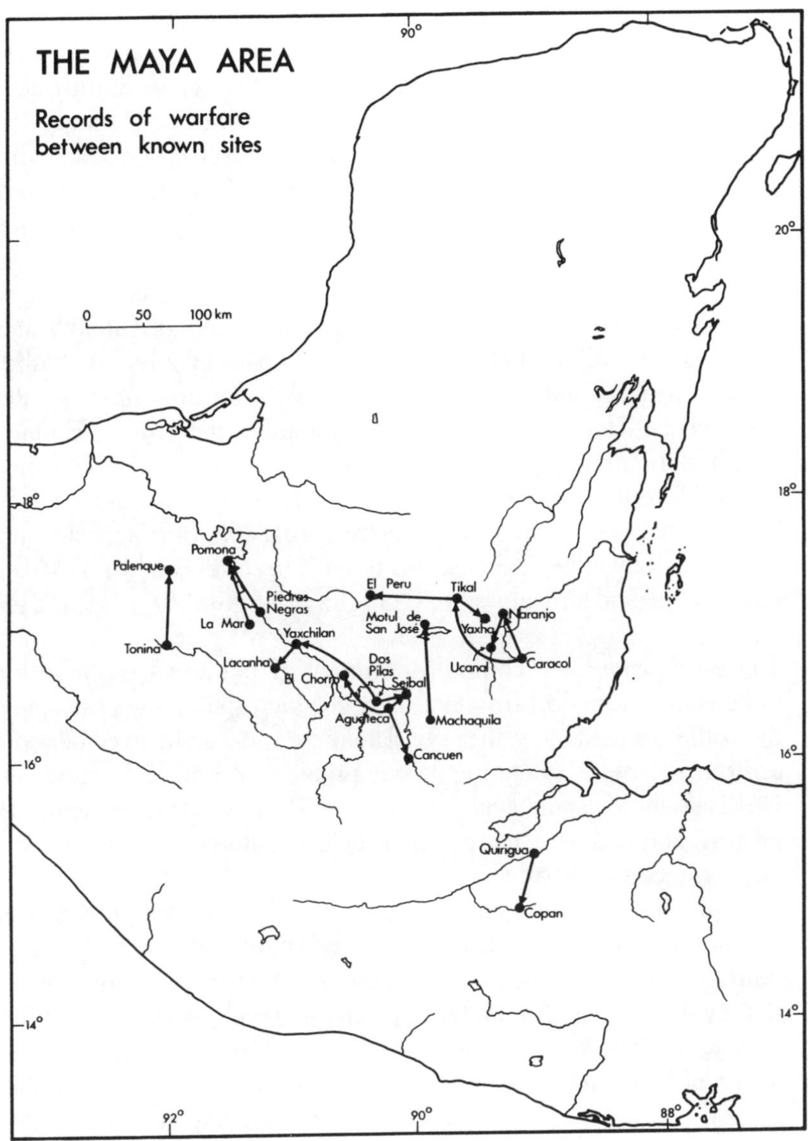


Fig. 10.8 Records of warfare between known cities in the Classic Maya lowlands. (The arrows indicate the direction of the attack.)

*Caracol–Naranjo.* Records of this battle were made at both sites. Significantly, the record at Naranjo was inscribed on a monument carved in Caracol style, and glorifying Caracol Ruler V. Shortly afterwards there began a thirty-year inscriptional hiatus at Naranjo. It is almost certain that Naranjo was politically controlled by Caracol during this period – the price paid for its defeat. In fact, Naranjo only reasserted its independence *c.* 9.13.0.0.0 (Mar. 18, 692), at which time Caracol itself was in decline.

*Quirigua–Copan.* This battle was also commemorated at both sites, but it was not followed at the losing site, Copan, by a hiatus. Rather, the following period at Copan was arguably the time of its greatest florescence. The later Copan rulers included the Copan Emblem Glyph in their name phrases, and referred to earlier (pre-battle) Copan rulers. Nevertheless, the date of the defeat was recorded at Copan on the Hieroglyphic Stairs of Structure 10L-26. Furthermore, any hostility felt by either polity seems to have been resolved by Yax-Pac's reign for he paid a royal visit to Quirigua at 9.19.0.0.0 (Jun. 26, 810).

*Tonina–Palenque.* Tonina Monument 22 portrays a captured lord of Palenque, Kan-Xul II, and a short glyphic caption gives the date of the battle. Immediately after this date there was a short-lived period of crisis at Palenque, centering on the problem of Kan-Xul's successor. However there is no evidence of any Tonina interference in this process, and both sites continued as before, autonomous, and making no reference to one another.

From these three cases it can be seen that there were various possible outcomes to battles in which a polity ahau was captured – from outright political control over the loser by the winner, to the imposition by the winner of some terms (such as a royal marriage) – but both sites remaining autonomous, to relatively little interruption of the affairs of both sites, and no effect on the losing site's royal dynasty.

### *Hierarchical relationships*

Joyce Marcus (1973, 1976) has pioneered the study of hierarchical relationships among Classic Maya sites. Her studies were based largely on statistical counts of foreign Emblem Glyph usage at Maya sites, which she felt to be implicit evidence for site hierarchies (Marcus

1976:16). In this paper we shall confine ourselves to explicit references to site hierarchies. Such references are of two types: (1) visits by the king to subsidiary rulers in charge of dependent centers within the king's own domain; and (2) references by the ruler of a dependent center to his overlord, the ruler of the polity.

The first category has already been dealt with in the second section, the second consists of just a few inscriptions, again from the Usumacinta and Pasion regions. For example, Lintel 1 of Lacanha portrays and names the local ruler, Ah-zac-te-le-s(e), the cahal of Lacanha. He is recorded as presiding over period-ending ceremonies on 9.15.15.0.0 (Jun. 4, 746), having acceded to the office of cahal a few years earlier, on 9.15.11.17.3 (Jun. 3, 743). The text also records the names of his father and mother, but before that (D3–D6) says that he is the cahal of Knot-eye Jaguar, the ahau of Bonampak. In other words, he is acknowledging his overlord.

A similar text is on Arroyo de Piedra Stela 2, in which the local ruler of Arroyo de Piedra says that he is the ahau of Ruler 2 of Dos Pilas. In this case, both individuals are of ahau rank, but the Arroyo de Piedra lord is of inferior political status, and acknowledges the fact. (See Houston and Mathews 1985, Figs. 11 and 12 for illustrations of these texts.)

This type of hierarchical relationship was first identified by Stephen D. Houston. In these records there is no indication of royal visits by the king (although that might well have happened); it is simply the hierarchical relationship that is being recorded.

## *Other intersite relationships*

Many other references to foreign sites are recorded in the Classic Maya inscriptions. In some cases, the glyphs specifying the nature of the reference have been eroded; in other cases we are not yet able to define the nature of the relationship. For example, the "Altar Vase" (Adams 1971, 1977b) apparently shows the visit by lords of Yaxchilan and Dos Pilas (or, far less likely, Tikal) to Altar de Sacrificios. Adams and others (e.g. Molloy and Rathje 1974:440–1) have speculated on the events surrounding these possibilities.

The bone texts of Tikal Burial 116 record many foreign lords, some of whom (e.g. Ruler 2 of Dos Pilas) are recognized from inscriptions at their own site. Do these bone texts represent a record of royal visits to

Tikal, or are they just a record of Tikal Ruler A's friends and relations?

A major problem concerning the nature of intersite relationships revolves around "Site Q," a site that is still not securely identified, but which might be El Peru. There are more foreign references to Site Q than there are to any other site in the Maya lowlands: Caracol, Copan, Dos Pilas, Palenque, Piedras Negras, Resbalon, Seibal, Tikal, and Yaxchilan all make reference to the site, and there are at least two dozen looted monuments that can be ascribed to Site Q. The Emblem Glyph of Site Q (with a serpent-head main sign) occurs quite frequently on monuments from El Peru, though as Stephen Houston (personal communication 1982) has pointed out, there is another Emblem Glyph commonly recorded at El Peru, so the identification of Site Q with El Peru (a very large site with over thirty stelae) is by no means firmly established. Some of the external references to Site Q are understood – a royal marriage with Yaxchilan, a capture by Tikal – but others are still unspecified. In this paper, we have assumed the identification of the "serpent-head" Emblem Glyph with El Peru.

## CONCLUSIONS

Royal visits, as we have defined them, are of three types: (1) the visit of the king of one polity to the king of another; (2) the visit of an ahau, who serves as the representative of the king, to the king of another polity; (3) the visit of the king of the polity to a subsidiary site within his political domain, and whose ruler could be either an ahau or a cahal.

Most of the surviving records of royal visits come from sites in the Usumacinta region, and we can speculate on the nature of alliances among the various polities involved (Piedras Negras, Yaxchilan, Bonampak, and Lacanha) especially when we consider records of conquest and interdynastic marriage as well as records of royal visits.

Yaxchilan monuments record visits by ahaus of the Piedras Negras and Bonampak polities (as well as those of Tikal and ?El Peru), between *c.* 9.1.0.0.0 (455) and 9.5.0.0.0 (534). Piedras Negras monuments record visits by ahaus of Yaxchilan (*c.* 9.4.0.0.0 [514]–9.16.0.0.0 [751]) and Lacanha (*c.* 9.10.0.0.0 [633]). Lacanha appears to have been the junior partner in these exchanges. Yaxchilan and Bonampak had a long record of alliance, beginning with the royal visits of *c.* 9.1.0.0.0 and extending through the interdynastic marriage and military alliances of *c.* 9.18.0.0.0 (790). Although its ahaus participated in royal visits to Piedras Negras *c.* 9.10.0.0.0, no such visits are recorded at Bonampak or Yaxchilan. Indeed, the captures of Lacanha lords are recorded at Yaxchilan (9.6.10.14.15 [Nov. 19, 564] and 9.14.17.15.11 [Jul. 14, 729]), and by 9.15.15.0.0 (Jun. 4, 746) Lacanha had become politically absorbed by Bonampak.

Our present view of the Classic Maya lowlands is one of many small political units, each ruled over by a king, of ahau status, who had under him various other ahaus and cahals, some of whom were in charge of subsidiary centers within the polity. There are many references in the inscriptions to one site by another.

Records of interdynastic marriage and royal visits indicate that many Classic Maya polities were joined in loose alliances. However, warfare records show that, in other cases, relations were not so friendly, and that perhaps alliances could even be broken. In short, the Classic Maya were human. The small polities which made up their world were constantly jostling for more widespread power and influence. They were proud of their conquests and careful to record their alliances. By Late Classic times they appear to have achieved a sort of delicate political equilibrium, which they were able to maintain, despite local fluctuations of fortune, until the advent of the Classic Maya collapse, some 300 years later.

## ACKNOWLEDGMENTS

We would like to thank Ian Graham, Stephen D. Houston, and David Stuart for access to their unpublished field notes and drawings; we have also greatly benefited from discussions with them on points raised in this paper.

## NOTES

1. At this point we should perhaps define our use of terms of noble titles. As we see it, ancient Maya nobility consisted of two main ranks: ahau and cahal. Ahau was the highest rank in Classic Maya society, and the head of the polity (in this paper we call him "king") was invariably an ahau (but by no means the only ahau, "lord," in the polity). Cahal was apparently the next rank below ahau, and in many cases the rulers of subsidiary centers in the polity were cahals ("governors"), although ahaus could also rule over dependent centers. The hierarchy can be summarized as follows:

| Rank | Title | English paraphrase |
|---|---|---|
| *ahau* | (the) *ahau* | king |
| *ahau* | *ahau* | lord |
| *cahal* | *cahal* | governor (if ruler of dependent site) |
| *cahal* | *cahal* | noble |

2. In this paper we use the original Thompson correlation (584285) between the Maya and Christian (Gregorian) calendars.
3. Schele (1979:28 and 1982:185) identified the T[533]760 glyph – "ahau-in-hand" – as a verb recording the display of various scepters and other objects which are specified by a second glyph adjoined to T670.
4. This Calendar Round, located at V8, is preceded by a Posterior Date Indicator and a Distance Number reading 1.?.?.?. The Calendar Round is damaged but some of the elements can be discerned. The *tzolkin* has a coefficient of 10 or above and the *haab* 15 or above. The month is clearly Zip and Ruler 7 is named at the end of the phrase. 10 Chuen 19 Zip appears on Throne 1 as an important event associated with Ruler 7; this event is perhaps also recorded here.
5. T684 was identified by Proskouriakoff (1960) as a verb recording "inauguration." Although this glyph functions as a standard verb for accession to office, here it must refer to some other kind of ritual event, for Bird-Jaguar had acceded five years earlier on 9.16.1.0.0 (AD 752) according to the Yaxchilan inscriptions. It may simply refer to the presentation or offering of a "bundle" with its contents.

# 11
# Inside the black box: defining Maya polity

NORMAN HAMMOND

The Classic period with which this volume is concerned is defined by the first appearance of formal documentary records, presently thought to be *c.* AD 200, and by their cessation, in any form that survives today, *c.* AD 910. Polity formation and maintenance occurred throughout this period, but the temporal limitation imposed by the presence of written records does not constrain the archaeological evidence for the emergence of a complex society with an undoubted political dimension among the lowland Maya, which occurred several centuries earlier in the Late Preclassic period (Hammond 1986a). Nor does it mark the end of Maya polities: the Postclassic period, especially in northern Yucatan, and on a different cultural trajectory in the southern highlands of Guatemala, is notable for the range of fractious statelets for which we have both ethnohistorical and archaeological evidence.

The limits of the Classic period are those within which Maya rulers in parts of the lowland zone chose to commemorate significant events, both historical and calendric, in their reigns by erecting monuments to themselves embodying dynastic and political information in the context of a complex and unified vision of the progress of time and the structure of the cosmos. Like the public monuments of Imperial

Rome, those of the Maya were capable of fudging strict historical accuracy for reasons of policy, and were intended to impress not just the generation living at their erection, but generations to come. Like the Roman inscriptions they repeated already-known facts, listing titles and conquests in formulaic fashion, fixing the reign of a temporary king within the quasi-infinity of cosmic history. The common acceptance by the Classic Maya polities of this system forms part of the elite culture which defines them as a collective entity (first recognized as such by John Lloyd Stephens a century and a half ago), of which the internal dynamics may usefully be investigated.

The external limits of the Maya ecumene can be drawn on the basis of both ethnographic and ethnohistoric distribution of language and prehispanic material culture ranging from ceramics to cities (this volume, chapter 1). Language in particular may have established the psychological frontier of a cognitive interaction sphere that marked the Maya off from their Mesoamerican neighbors to the west and the polities of lower Central America on the east. It may also have separated the lowlands, where Yucatecan and Choloid languages, mutually interpenetrating and both used in Classic-period inscriptions (Justeson *et al.* 1985), seem to have been the twin tongues of Maya civilization, from the highlands and Pacific slope where (apart from the Chol-related Tzeltalan) the Greater Quichean and Kanjobalan languages are estimated to have diverged from the lowland group by 1,000 BC (Fox 1983:Fig. 15.2). The coherence of Classic Maya material culture, especially in its elite manifestions of monumental architecture, iconography, and hieroglyphic writing, is a clear indication that, whether language did or did not perform such an encapsulating function, it coexisted with it.

Within this cultural membrane the Maya polities seem to have formed what Wesson (1978:vii, 11) calls a "state system," a term used to "designate a group of closely interacting and therefore competing independent sovereignties that collectively dominate their world . . . and for whom interrelations are comparable in importance to domestic affairs." Such state systems are a commonplace of Old World history, from Sumer in the third millennium BC through the Greek *poleis* and the Warring States of late Zhou China, to the familiar political mosaics of the Holy Roman Empire and Renaissance Italy. Wesson (1978:81, 11, 13) notes that it is "implicit in the definition of a state system that the units of political control are small in comparison with the sphere of interaction and awareness," that these units have "an indefinite number of histories" recorded in parallel, as against the single history of empire, and that "politics are of incessant concern . . . the climactic event is war and victory over fellow states." A state system is a pluralistic civilization, in which methods of government may vary, law is more community right than legal or divine ukase, bureaucracy is relatively unimportant but the hereditary principle the reverse: these features are sufficiently close to what we know of the Colonial Maya, and to what we can elucidate about their Classic ancestors (Farriss 1984), that we are quite justified in seeking illumination from outside the Maya sphere as well as from all possible sources within it.

Two recent formal models which may be thus useful are Price's (1977) "cluster-interaction" model, and the revamped version presented by Renfrew and Cherry (1986) as "peer-polity interaction," a descriptive rather than analytical schema applicable to any level of political development in which autonomous political units are closely enough juxtaposed to have substantial dealings with each other. Like Wesson's state systems, the Price/Renfrew–Cherry model (which I have conflated to "peer cluster interaction" and abbreviated "PCI") might have been designed to describe the patterns of Classic Maya polity distribution and interaction that have in recent years become common knowledge (cf. Hammond 1982; Morley *et al.* 1983), and extract meaning from the bare spatial relationships defined by Hammond (1972, 1974a) and the hierarchies proposed by Marcus (1973, 1976), as well as to formalize the pragmatic historical interpretation of Pasion Valley protohistory advanced by Mathews and Willey (this volume).

Renfrew (Renfrew and Cherry 1986:1) observes that the model

> designates the full range of interchanges taking place (including imitation and emulation, competition, warfare, and the exchange of material goods and of information), between autonomous (i.e. self-governing and in that sense politically independent) socio-political units which are situated beside or close to each other within a single geographical region, or in some cases more widely. The framework of analysis . . . avoids laying stress upon relations of dominance and subordination between societies, although such relations are indeed common enough . . . [it] does not simply consider the socio-political unit in isolation . . . most early states . . . do not exist in isolation. On the contrary, it is possible to identify in a given region several autonomous political centres which, initially at least, are not brought within a single unified jurisdiction. It is such autonomous territorial units, with their

administrative centres, which together constitute what is often termed a civilization . . . the underlying principle is conceived here primarily with reference to fairly complex societies (developed chiefdoms or early states).

Autonomy can subsist even under conditions of formal subordination, as the cases of late Shang China and the Holy Roman Empire show clearly: the transition from ceremonial to effective dominance, when it occurs, marks (in terms of the PCI model) the end of peer interaction. The polity itself, as Renfrew (Renfrew and Cherry 1986:5) notes, is not a permanent feature of the cultural landscape: it exists only while it is autonomous, and may be absorbed into a larger entity, or absorb others itself, or split between two or more successor polities. The creation of Czechoslovakia, the elastic frontiers of Poland, and the fates of Tannu-Tuva and Biafra are all recent examples of this mutability. In the past, leagues or confederacies of peer polities existed in China, India, and Greece (where three to five centuries passed before the emergence of a dominant polity); this seminar considered in some detail the question of "regional states" in which the fusion of two or more pre-existing polities by conquest changed the overall Maya system of states, and whether such processes were atypical of the Classic Maya world (Culbert, this volume, chapter 6).

How are we to define the Classic Maya polities that we wish to study in interaction, given the diachronic lack of stability of state systems and the relative paucity of synchronic data on economic and political structure? While the epigraphic and archaeological developments summarized in this book have suddenly and greatly increased the factual basis for our reconstructions, we must not ignore the sobering reality that they have brought the Maya from the margins of prehistory into merely liminal history. A dozen royal marriages, a score of battles or royal visits, and the genealogies of a handful of dynasties do not give us a broad historical foundation on which to build, in the absence of economic information or any documentation of Maya society below the uppermost elite.

We must, perforce, employ the good archaeological principle of working from the known to the unknown: those areas in which we have data from both "bottom-up" and "top-down" sources (see chapter 1) are the best in which to try and formulate polity definitions which look realistic beside such related Mesoamerican comparanda as the *cuchcabalob* of Postclassic Yucatan (Roys 1957), their colonial *partido* successors (Farriss 1984) or the small states of Postclassic central Mexico (Bray 1972), as well as more exotic parallels such as the Early Historic city-states of the Ganges basin (Erdösy 1987), the "galactic polities" of Southeast Asia (Tambiah 1977), and the emergence of the dynastic state in Capetian France (Lewis 1982).

On the basis of present knowledge, the northeast Peten and Pasion regions (Fig. 1.1) are those in which sites of known scale and distribution can best be matched with epigraphic data to define the spatial relationships of polities. Equally useful evidence comes from the inscriptions of the Usumacinta, but rather less archaeological information. The southeast region has a rapidly increasing data base in both stratigraphic and epigraphic fields (Sharer, this volume; Fash and Stuart, this volume), but contains only two interacting polities, while areas such as northern Belize have a substantial amount of archaeological evidence but few known inscriptions to bring them out of prehistory.

I shall try to utilize this information within the format of a "black box" model (Fig. 11.1) such as was defined by Leach (1973:Fig. 2) to

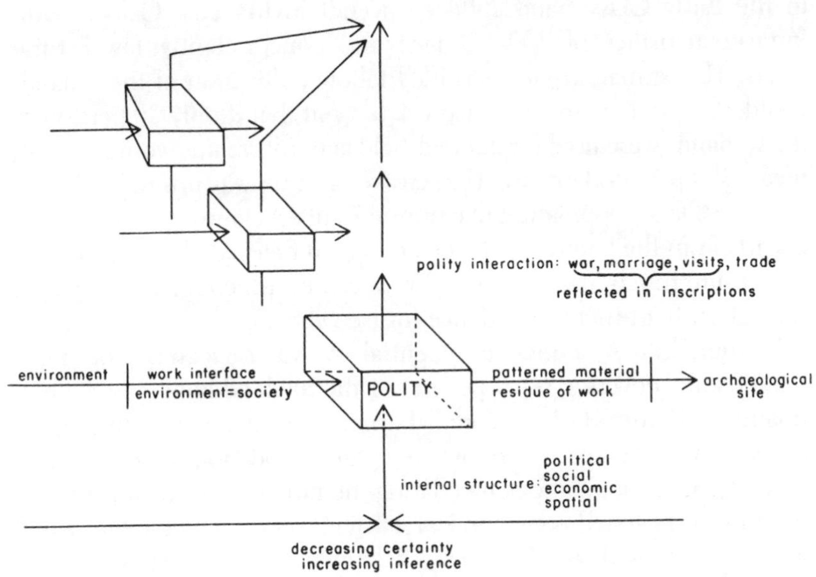


Fig. 11.1 Polities as "black boxes," with partly known input, output and relationships, but unknown internal structures and processes.

examine successively the traditional archaeological concerns of demography and economy, then the social structure derivable from them, and finally the spatial definition and internal organization of Maya polities which a combination of archaeology, epigraphy, and eclectic external parallels suggests.

## POPULATION SIZE

Whatever the precise scale and historical patterns of development of Maya polities, they were well populated, as is clear from the abundance of sites of all sizes. The low-density model of empty ceremonial centers and rural hamlets favored by earlier scholars has long been superseded (Ashmore 1981a), but the extraction of even approximate population totals and concentrations is a topic that still owes more to inspired extrapolation than to accurate knowledge. Culbert (1988a) has made a detailed assessment of potential agricultural production and its risks, and argues for movement of basic foodstuffs on a regional scale in the Late Classic. His estimates are of 20 persons/km$^2$ in the Middle Preclassic, 50 in the Late Preclassic, 100 in the Early Classic and 200/km$^2$ overall in the Late Classic, with intrasite densities of 300–500/km$^2$ and concomitantly lower rural levels. He estimates that intensified fallow cultivation of the uplands could support a mean 180 persons/km$^2$, and that if only 20 percent of the wetlands were used for drained-field agriculture this would rise to a mean 300 persons/km$^2$. Such intensive farming was not needed until the Late Classic population maximum, Culbert claims: his model here departs from the known existence of drained fields (and hillside terracing) from much earlier, but also specifies much greater wetland utilization than there is evidence for (see above).

Turner (n.d.) defines a "Central Maya Lowlands" of some 22,700 km$^2$, covering 6–10 percent of the lowland zone and approximating to Rathje's (1971) "core." Turner scales sites within this region on a rank-order basis, following Adams and Jones (1981), and estimates their populations by relating the rank relative to Tikal to the minimum suggested population of Tikal (40,000) as a baseline. Rural areas are assessed as 65 percent habitable land, and a population density assessed from a house-mound count (ignoring the possible impact of non-mound or "invisible" occupation), assuming a 100 percent Late through Terminal Classic usage of house sites. Turner extracts from these superimposed arguments and assumptions a central lowland population of 242,000 in 300 BC and 2.42 million in the Late Classic, with overall densities of 11/km$^2$ in the Preclassic, 45 in the Early Classic, 150 in the Late and 22 in the Terminal Classic, with the urban population being some 20 percent of the total. Turner does not care to extrapolate these figures (somewhat lower than Culbert's estimates for the Classic period) direct to the entire Maya lowlands, which would give a Late Classic population of 26–34 million, because he assumes the central region to be more capable of supporting high densities. For some areas, such as eastern Belize and Quintana Roo, and the wetlands of northwest Peten, he is surely correct, but nevertheless ancient Maya population would seem to have been higher than earlier intuitive estimates. Culbert's mean figure, applied to a "typical" polity of 2,000 km$^2$ (see below), would give a polity population of 400,000, 80,000 of them resident, in Turner's terms, in the urban or semi-urban nuclei. Such figures match well with external comparanda, such as Classical Athens with its 275,000 people in 2,600 km$^2$, or Sumerian Lagash with 80–100,000 people at 2400 BC, while lying below the estimates for Zhou China, where single cities had over 100,000 people.

## ECONOMIC ORGANIZATION

There are no written sources for the economic organization of Maya polities: like the structure of non-elite society, it can be studied only through the archaeological evidence. Economic activity can heuristically be divided into two categories, production and exchange (leaving aside the periodic economic boost provided by successful warfare with its influx of booty and captives); production can in turn be divided, into subsistence and craft activities, with the extended-family household probably forming the normative productive unit if settlement pattern is an accurate reflection of social organization (Ashmore 1981a; Wilk and Ashmore 1988).

For Classic Maya subsistence production we have a plethora of evidence and speculation, most recently summarized in Harrison and Turner (1978) and Flannery (1982). What seems clear is that agriculture was based on maize, beans, squashes, root crops, orchard crops such as cacao and fruit, and collected forest resources, with crisis reserves such as *ramón* nuts. Most cultivation took place close to settlements, as is the habit with village farmers everywhere (Chisholm 1968). While artificial econiches for intensive agriculture existed in places, including hillside terracing that indicates permanent demarcation of land and hence an investment requiring perennial utilization, and wetland drained fields with a potential productivity many times that of dryland *milpa* fields, their temporal persistence, spatial extent, and economic impact may be much less than some scholars have argued, and many others have come to accept implicitly (Hammond 1984:7; Pope and Dahlin 1989).

From the producer, subsistence goods traveled in two directions: laterally within the local community as short-term surplus disposed of by local exchange (Hammond 1973:Fig. 1), and vertically by appropriation to support the administrative hierarchy, as well as (in my opinion) in regional intrapolity exchange to acquire craft products such as pottery and stone tools. This level of interaction could well have taken place in a market at the polity center: facilities for this have been identified with specific structures at Tikal (Jones, this volume) and with convenient central open spaces at other sites, although proof is in all cases lacking.

Craft goods were the output of the middle ranks of Classic Maya society, the upper *macehualob* (commoners: see below), and came out of facilities organized at levels ranging from the household to the factory (the latter, as at Colha, in fact probably consisting of household units with a superordinate organization specifying what was to be produced and dealing with the interpolity export trade for which there is abundant evidence). Some goods spread through all levels of society – pottery vessels, stone tools, obsidian blades – while others such as jade jewelry, and costume and headdresses for ceremonial use, were restricted in the number of both producers and consumers, and may have been made on a commission or patronage basis.

Exchange, particularly at the "external" or interpolity level designated by Hammond (1973), was intimately linked with craft production. While some interpolity transfers of sumptuary products may have been at the level of prestation, others were undoubtedly commerical in nature in view of their bulk, widespread occurrence, and deep social penetration. As is discussed below, the extent to which this exchange was controlled by the ruling elite and used by them to acquire surplus by exaction is not known: pragmatically, the facts that Maya rulers did dispose of some surplus, both to finance public works and to stock their tombs, and that purely agricultural produce would be a bulky and inefficient way of funding these activities, both suggest that control of external exchange was important to maintenance of the elite. As Farriss (1984:178) concludes, the integration of communities into states depends on elite relations of trade as well as alliance and warfare, all made without reference to the mass of the population.

## SOCIAL ORGANIZATION

The spatial distribution of communities and the hierarchical organization of Classic Maya society were intimately linked; that this society was both stratified and hierarchical has always been accepted, even when the structure of the hierarchy was simplified to levels of priests and peasants in the idealized interpretations of Morley and Thompson (for which see Becker 1979). How complex the social pyramid was, and how it articulated with both the economic substructure and the intellectual superstructure of Maya civilization, is only now becoming apparent with the decipherment of the hieroglyphic inscriptions, and with the changed assessment of the Preclassic period that has resulted from archaeological discovery since 1970 (Hammond 1986a) (Fig. 11.2). Most of the reassessment involves the nature and roles of the elite – not surprisingly, given the character of the evidence – but something of the lower layers in the social pyramid, estimated by Adams (1974:294–5) to have formed 98 percent of the Classic Maya population, can be elucidated from archaeological and ethnohistoric evidence.

### *Commoners*

Because they are anonymous, we know nothing of the lives of individual macehualob: while the elite move out of the shadows into the penumbra of history, the commoners remain resolutely and permanently prehistoric. This is not to say that they must be treated *en masse*, simply that the approach must be from the direction of the archaeological evidence, bottom-upwards, rather than from epigraphy. While historical data have been used to illuminate the activities of those at the base of the social pyramid in medieval Europe (e.g. Laslett 1965; LeRoy Ladurie 1978) from sources as diverse as parish registers and Inquisition transcripts, they are limited in their range.

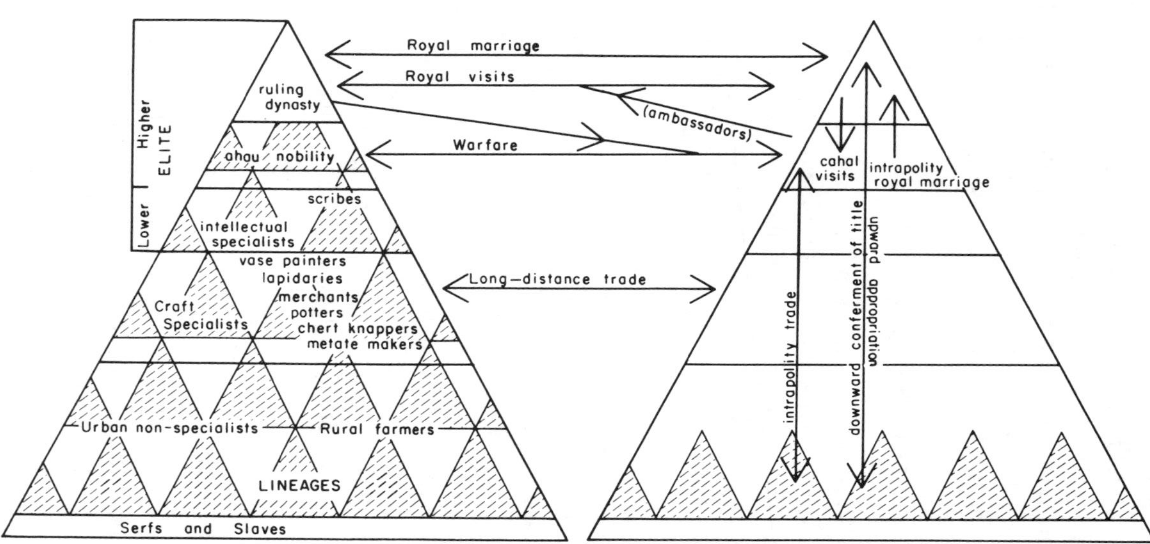


Fig. 11.2 The Maya social pyramid: internal polity structure and polity interaction.

This is pointed out by Ashmore and Wilk (1988:4–5), who note that the prehistoric archaeologist must perforce use material evidence, and especially the interpretation of spatial patterning, in studying households – the basic units of any society – as activity groups. They also emphasize the dangers of Mesoamerican archaeologists turning to fragmentary textual evidence as inscriptions are deciphered, and investing it with overmuch significance.

If we treat epigraphic evidence as confirmatory rather than revelatory so far as ancient Maya social structure is concerned, then the basis for archaeological reconstruction must come from two major classes of data: evidence for occupational specialization as a vertical, and of residential patterns as a locational, divider of society. The two are to some extent covariant, and together with documentary evidence on the relative statuses of occupations in the contact period may be used to suggest horizontal divisions for the Classic period.

Efforts to detect occupational specialization among the Classic Maya are not new: Adams (1970) argued for four classes based on the degree of knowledge and skill required, with unskilled labor forming the lowest, part-time semi-skilled workers such as masons and chert-knappers in the next, scribes, sculptors, costumiers, and armorers in the third, and administrators, architectural planners and religious and military leaders in the uppermost. Adams sees this fourth division, with the addition of trading (on the evidence of Thompson [1964]), as being elite occupations, and lists scribes and accountants, sculptors, makers of hierarchical costumes, servants, musicians and other entertainers, construction specialists, potters, armorers, and knappers as non-elite ones.

More specific studies included Becker's (1973) analysis of craft specialization at Tikal and Olga Puleston's (1969) analysis of a lithic workshop at the same site, Neivens and Libbey's (1976) suggestion of an obsidian workshop at El Pozito, Andrews IV and Rovner's (1973) identification of a mason's toolkit and jewelers' stocks-in-trade at Dzibilchaltun, and Wilk's (1973, 1975) identification of chert-tool workshops at Colha, the latter subsequently investigated by Shafer and Hester (1983) and shown to include massive production geared to inter-polity rather than local markets, and dating from the Late Preclassic through Early Postclassic period.

Potting has always been recognized as a specialized craft, with intra-polity movement of goods concomitant with market sale at the polity center (cf. Rands *et al.* 1975; Hammond, Harbottle and Gazard 1976), intracommunity production for local consumption (cf. Fry and Cox 1974; Culbert and Schwalbe 1987), and production for a market that included long distance export (cf. Sabloff *et al.* 1982) as well as local uptake.

The sheer bulk of pottery and stone tools produced makes it likely that commoners were the makers and major consumers of these goods; some had a clear elite-linked function, as with the "eccentric cherts" found in caches and most jade items, but this does not imply an elite artisan so much as an attached specialist serving elite needs. In only a few cases, where, not just the esoteric knowledge needed but documentary evidence can also be brought to bear, can an elite individual be firmly identified as the maker of a craft object: a recent case is Stuart's (1986a) identification of *u-dzib* as the vase-painter's signature, in which he shows that the painter was a member of the ruling family of Naranjo, a child of the ruler Lord Smoking-Batab.

That scribes were elite persons, rather than skilled but probably non-elite craftworkers, is also demonstrated by the façade sculptures of structure 9N-82 at Copan (Fash and Stuart, this volume), which depict figures holding inkpots made from shells; their social rank is also supported by the first-tier elite status of the *escribano* in colonial Yucatan (Farriss 1984:Fig. 8.1). That sculptors may also have had a higher status than Adams (1970) reckoned is hinted at by the naming (if Stuart's reading of the "*lu*-bat" glyph as "he carved" is correct) of the several individuals who created Stelae 12 and 14 at Piedras Negras.

Adams' classification thus suggests three probable levels of work specialization within the commoner class – unskilled, semi-skilled (and possibly part-time), and skilled (and possibly full-time) – while Farriss (1984:Fig. 8.1) perceives the likelihood of two strata of commoners based on the documented ranking of offices in colonial times. Among these are musicians, who are in the upper stratum: since musicians feature in the lowest or second-lowest of the four social strata identified in the Bonampak Room 1 murals (see below), we might tentatively suggest either four or five levels to Classic Maya society from the artisan upwards.

Hammond (1982:197) proposed that seven levels of economic action could be deduced in Classic Maya society from the archaeological evidence: the three uppermost formed the governing apparatus (see below), the lower four the commoners. The uppermost level of these macehualob may well, given the colonial parallels, have supplied the executive bureaucracy, putting into effect the decisions of the administration above them; they are also likely to have included skilled artisans such as potters, lapidaries, and stucco-workers, as well as any scribes or sculptors not belonging to the elite. Traders may also have been of this rank, even if control of commerce was vested in the elite, and goods such as obsidian may well have been both traded and worked by the same person. Chert-working apparently ranged from the factory-level production of Colha, where other communities in the region would receive the goods as trade items, to skilled or semi-skilled working of local raw material, and perhaps even domestic production.

Some of those employed on a major Classic-period public-works program, such as the construction of Ah Cacau's funerary pyramid (Temple I) at Tikal, would have been from the literate and iconographically educated elite, including those responsible for the conception, detailed design and execution of the project; but many more would have been skilled artisans, including stone- and wood-carvers, stucco-workers, and painters, and yet others would have been unskilled laborers, quarriers of fill and haulers of stone. These common laborers were presumably part of the basal stratum of urban Maya society, a layer which also supplied the cleaners, porters, and other people needed to keep any complex society operating. Outside the main population concentrations, where neither urban elite nor the skilled artisans servicing them were to be found, the lowest stratum would have been that of rural farmers, producing the food to support the entire edifice of Classic society.

Less socially visible are the poor, the servants or serfs equivalent to the *mayaques* of central Mexico, and slaves. Colonial sources tell us that slaves could be born to that state, sell themselves from freedom into slavery, or be captives who had escaped sacrifice. The term is evocative, and it may well be that Maya slavery was less exploitative, and more like the villeinage of medieval England, or the patron-client relationship with mutual obligations that Tambiah (1977:90) notes for medieval Southeast Asia.

Also invisible until recently, though not necessarily congruent with a serf class, were those ancient Maya who did not live in houses raised on platforms. While Tourtellot (1983:957), Bronson (n.d.), and others have noted the existence of "hidden house-mounds" with very low platforms buried by humus, the presence of a class of dwelling built directly on the land surface and marked archaeologically by nothing more than a plaster floor or trash spread had not been recognized until the work of Wilk and Wilhite (1980) at Cuello, based on Wilk's ethnographic observations among Kekchi swidden farmers in southern Belize. The work of Pyburn (1987, 1988) at Nohmul shows that such dwellings can be detected using a predictive model, and that the visible universe of mound-based residence present on Maya site maps may require substantial augmentation. The implications for intrasite population density and overall community size are at least as important as those for the presence of a stratum hitherto unseen and unconsidered in discussions of Classic Maya social organization.

Social interpretations have long been implicit in studies of prehistoric lowland Maya settlement patterns; they became explicit with the work of Bullard (1964), Haviland (1966, 1970, 1972) at Tikal, and Tourtellot (1983) at Seibal in the southern lowlands, and Kurjack (1974) in Yucatan, the latter perceiving a complexity of social organization closer to a preindustrial state than to a chiefdom. Organization of residential units into discrete clusters which might be equated with neighborhood *barrios* and perhaps with lineages and/or endogamous groups has been proposed (from the initial stimuli of Bullard [1960; 1964] and Vogt [1969]) by Fash (1983b) for Copan, with a median forty-three households, and also by Folan, Kintz and Fletcher (1983) for Coba, and Ashmore (1988) for Quirigua. Wilk (1988:142–4), reviewing the congruence of archaeological with ethnographic evidence for Maya community structure, suggests that most of the informal-cluster and patio-group patterns defined by Hammond (1975b) and Ashmore (1981b) housed multiple-family households, and that some single house-platforms housing nuclear families would also be related to the larger units, which have organizational advantages both as productive units and in the generational transmission of valuable resources, especially land. Evidence for occupational specialization within such barrios on the organized level demonstrated for the *calpulli* of Mexican Tenochtitlan by Calnek (1976) is presently lacking, however.

Detailed analyses of intrasite settlement patterns led Tourtellot (1983:943–58) to propose at least four social strata embodied in residential groups of varying size and volume:area ratio; the uppermost of these, including central administrators, peripheral temple (?) administrators and (presumably high-ranking) military personnel would fall within the elite range of occupations (see below), but craft specialists and "major temple servitors" could well belong to the upper level of the macehualob as easily as to the second-tier elite. Tourtellot (1983:952, 956) notes, however, that these "more or less identifiable occupational statuses still leave many [residential] units unaccounted for," and that "house architecture exhibits such variation, continuity and groupings that a complex social structure must have existed as well." The variation ranged from stone-walled buildings close to the site center, through four classes of perishable-superstructure dwellings on basal platforms of highly variable volume:area ratio (used as an index of wealth and negatively correlated with unit population size), to an "invisible" level of very low platforms acknowledged to exist, but thought to be sufficiently rare not to controvert the assumption that most commoners lived on the abundant house-mounds which formed the bulk of the structures recorded in mapping Maya sites.

A similar approach in the Copan Valley led Willey and Leventhal (1979) to classify residential units into four classes, of which the most complex (e.g. CV-68 of Class 4) would approximate to Bullard's (1960) "minor ceremonial center," and the next (CV-20 of Class 3) to a plazuela group. Fash (1983c) showed that locally distinct *sian otot* (approximating to Bullard's "cluster" and Vogt's (1969) *sna* waterhole group) included a mixture of these types, with Class 4 units occurring as far out from the center as the Ostuman pocket 5.5 km west of the ceremonial precinct. These units were, however, more frequent around the center, a centralization of inferred wealth and status seen also at Seibal, and more recently noted for the Late Preclassic at Komchen (Ringle and Andrews V 1988). That Class 3 units as well as those of Class 4 were elite residences is demonstrated by the discovery of hieroglyphic benches of the reign of Yax Sun-at-Horizon (Yax-Pac) in both CV-36 (in a building now redesignated Structure 9N-82) of Class 4 and CV-43 (9M-18) of Class 3. Such segmentation of a continuum of increasing residential complexity is, of course, a matter of classification, not necessarily a precise reflection of acknowledged social layering.

### *Maya elites*

That elites and forms of elite culture both preceded and persisted after the Classic period is not in question. What Coles and Harding

(1979:535) term "the rise of the privileged" is evident in the acquisition of exotic goods such as jade, from the middle of the first millennium BC onwards, and their deposition in select burials, including those of children. The Middle Preclassic beginnings of monumental architecture also suggest a society that was ranked, if not yet stratified.

How such elites came into being in general is still a matter of contention. The functionalist position, that elites engage in managerial activities that benefit the whole population, has been challenged by Gilman (1981:5) with the argument that they emerge coevally with productive subsistence technologies, less by organizing them than by taxing their developers, who cling to their capital investment even in the face of exaction. Subsistence technology absorbing enough investment for this to work does not appear in the Maya archaeological record before the middle of the Late Preclassic, after 100 BC, when drained-field complexes are first identified at sites such as Cerros, but Gilman also includes in this category field clearance for permanent agriculture, and polyculture including orchard trees that do not crop for years after planting. While there is no evidence for such investment in the Maya lowlands (and it would be archaeologically exiguous), the population nucleation, overall demographic increase, and growing complexity of Late Preclassic communities from 400 BC onwards indicates that a subsistence regime more intensive than milpa agriculture might have been needed in some areas.

While control of redistribution has often been suggested as a function of elites, it is doubtful that the Maya upper class were involved directly in it: the lineage-based settlement pattern documented by ethnography and indicated by archaeology suggests rather an upward appropriation of basic resources to support the successive levels of hierarchy, which did not result in a large ultimate surplus (cf. Tambiah 1977:85). Even chiefdoms (the level at which we might perceive Middle Preclassic Maya polities as existing) are not usually characterized by redistribution, contrary to popular belief; chiefly authority comes rather from alliance, leadership in warfare, sanctification and prestation (Spencer 1987:376).

Tambiah (1977:86) suggests that the resources to underwrite independent action on the part of a ruler came not from the pyramid of politico-economic relations within the polity, but from control of the supply of non-subsistence goods from outside the system. Rathje (1971) argued that such control was the pathway to power of Maya elites at the beginning of the Classic period, but the specifics of his model have been disproved, in that what he saw as essential imports have acceptable local substitutes, and the existence of elites has been perceived at a time when any long-distance exchange was so low in bulk that it was probably sporadic in occurrence. What remains is the impression that certain kinds of exotic goods were concentrated in the hands of the elite; but whether they got there by control of the means of supply, or simply by possession of the wherewithal to purchase them within an exchange network disengaged from political control, as Wesson (1978:13) would infer from his cross-cultural study of state systems, is not archaeologically detectable. Here the lack of economic records of the kind common in West Asian and Aegean civilizations renders discussion of Maya modes of acquisition moot, although their absence in itself argues for a strictly limited administrative role for the elite. We can still say with some confidence, however, that the Maya elite had at its disposal three kinds of economic resources: human labor for communal projects such as construction or warfare, extracted either by upward appropriation or by direct corvée; internally produced subsistence and craft goods; and exotic imports, including utilitarian goods of limited production area, such as salt and obsidian, together with craft products such as polychrome pottery, and ritually functional goods such as stingray spines.

The Maya elites of the Classic period differed from their precursors and successors in their creation of dynastic records preserved on public monuments, but whether this implies any structural difference in society is not clear: the retrodictive *hel* or *dzac* recording of rulers back to *c.* 8.6.0.0.0 (AD 150) at Tikal and Copan, and to 9.1.0.0.0 (AD 455) at Quirigua, shows that dynastic descent of rulership preceded the public proclamation of the fact, while the colossal public buildings of Late Preclassic sites such as El Mirador, Nakbe, Calakmul, Seibal, Tikal, Lamanai, Nohmul, and Cerros attest to centralized control of manpower and other economic resources several centuries earlier. The entire dynastic monument complex (aka "stela cult") may be epiphenomenal to the emergence of powerful elites in the lowlands, a spreading fashion diffusing along established economic pathways (cf. Hägerstrand 1953; Haggett 1965:58–9): nevertheless, it is the key to understanding both the structure of the ruling elite and its role in regulating Classic Maya society.

Hammond (1982:197) proposed three levels of elite activity in the

Classic period, of which the uppermost was the ruling individual or lineage, self-perpetuating and impossible to enter from below except by dynastic marriage. This level controlled central administration of government, of religion, and of interpolity contacts such as warfare. The ruler's enduring role as maintainer of order and link with the cosmos was punctuated by episodes of heroic activity as war leader to maintain status and control of population within fluidly drawn boundaries, to acquire loot and bring in additional manpower either for labor or sacrifice. Occasionally this would extend into territorial acquisition also, and then multi-center or complex polities emerged for anything from a few generations to several centuries, but enlargement beyond roughly doubling the original territory was very rare.

Associated with the ruling dynasty was an aristocracy, the *ahau* class, which might also include former dynastic lineages (cf. Haviland 1981), and which acted as ambassadors and probably as the administrative class of the bureaucracy. Local rulers of *cahal* rank, perhaps equivalent to the Postclassic and colonial *batab*, may also have been of ahau class: the presence of funerary pyramids and richly stocked burials in small sites suggests that nobles were present not only in the polity capital, but formed the top tier of provincial society also (as in Early Dynastic Egypt). Below the aristocracy were the gentry, the colonial *principales*, rulers of perhaps only a few square kilometers, local administrators, and denizens of the minor ceremonial centers outside the main population concentrations.

It seems clear that the elite as such had at least two strata within it, with the ruling family forming part of the upper level or a separate third stratum. In colonial times the *almehenob*, nobles who could trace their ancestry through both male and female lines, were divided into batab lineages and principales, "lords" and "gentry" (Farriss 1984:241). The batab lineages controlled the positions of *batab* (in Postclassic times a war leader, in colonial the town ruler, either autonomous or under a provincial *halach uinic*); of *maestro cantor*, head of the religious hierarchy and the direct successor to the Postclassic *ahcambecah* and probably also to the high priest, *ah kin* (Collins 1977); of *escribano* or town clerk, requiring literacy and conferring control over documents, including land-titles; and of patron of the *cofradía* (Farris 1984:Fig. 8.1; 1986:97–9). The office of batab was hereditary within the lineage (but see Thompson 1985 for a variant interpretation), that of maestro cantor with a succession controlled by the incumbent (Farris:1984:236); both men were addressed by the honorific *yum*, placing them at a level above the other high offices.

The batab was served by an executive bureaucracy of *ahkulelob*, apparently principales, and by a legislature (*cabildo*) of *ahcuchcabob* representing the wards (*parcialidades*) of the town. The ahcuchcabob were also principales, and the cabildo was self-perpetuating in its membership, so that colonial Maya society was an effective oligarchy. The second-tier elite also included other secular and religious offices, clearly distinguished from those open to macehualob commoners (Farriss 1984:Fig. 8.1).

The general structure of this two-tiered elite, with the highest ruling offices distinguished within the upper level, can be perceived in the Classic period. The class of ahau would seem to correspond with the batab lineages, in that *ahauob* were not just territorial rulers, but also nobles who could be sent on embassy by their own superiors, while the *cahalob*, who were clearly subordinate, may be equated with either subordinate membership of batab lineages or with the principales (since cahal may have been a conferred title of office, and ahau an inherited one of class: David Stuart's [1989] suggestion that the office of cahal was inheritable, on the basis of La Pasadita Lintel 2, is not incompatible with this, given that assigned titles often become frozen into heritability by the arrogation of economic power).

Mary Miller (1986) identifies a number of ahauob in the Room 1 murals at Bonampak: several of the captions name the persons portrayed as "ahau," including Chan-Muan, ruler of Bonampak, while others wear the same costume and stand on the same level and are by inference ahauob. Miller (1986:41) distinguishes between the white-robed ahauob and those bearing the title *ah nabe* (which Floyd Lounsbury suggested be read "young lord"), who are bare-chested. The difference in rank may be one of age, not birth, since all the rulers of Palenque take the ah nabe title at some point.

Four social levels can be distinguished in the Room 1 murals: the highest are the ahauob, wearing white robes and spondylus-shell pectoral ornaments, and apparently including royal visitors from other polities. Below them the *ah nabeob* wear jade jewelry, elaborate individualized headdresses and elaborate loincloths (*ex*) of rich fabric. The third level also have elaborate loin/hipcloths, but wear a standardized headdress and lack jade ornaments. The masquers (Human Figures [HF] 45–50) fall between the second and third groups in their attire, suggesting that they were of high rank (cf. the "ah'nabe" title in the accompanying Caption 33). The lowest level wear a simple loincloth, a standardized headdress and no jade: but given the importance of the heir-designation ceremony portrayed, it is likely that even these individuals are of at least lower elite status and not commoners. This suggests a more subtle layering within the Classic elite than in colonial times.

While Chan-Muan is described simply as "ahau" (and the person HF 62 in Caption 40 as a "vulture-ahau," with a possible Emblem Glyph), there is evidence that a ruling dynasty was separated from the rest of the upper elite: the notion of rulers in a hel/dzac succession from the dynastic founder onwards sets the dynasty apart as a vertical sequence in time, distinct from the lateral web of relationships of a coeval elite, as does the "blood-line" or "holy" meaning assigned to the T35-41 ("water group") prefix of the Emblem Glyph. This separation may have come as the ruler changed from being the community's representative to the gods, to the gods' agent in society, or to a dual role as a conduit of cosmic power as suggested by Schele and Miller (1986:301) – divinity hedged the Maya kings. This second vertical relationship can be seen in its most elaborate and aggrandizing form in the Twin Pyramid Groups of Tikal, where the living ruler is equated with the Sun God at the blazing zenith of his power, but also passes unscathed through Xibalba, realm of the Nine Lords of the Night (Coggins 1980). This symbolism may be of Preclassic origin (Hammond 1987), and certainly by the Early Classic the heavens are enlisted in commemorating the life-cycle of an elite individual, as Coggins (1986) shows for Rio Azul Tomb 12 at AD 450.

Once distinct, the dynasty was at pains to emphasize the fact and to record its validating ancestry, at Palenque invoking the gods as ancestors in a manner reminiscent of the Mikados of Japan. Several of the papers in this volume (Schele; Mathews and Willey; Jones; Sharer; Fash and Stuart) deal with the successions elucidated for polities in the Usumacinta basin, the Peten and the southeast, and it is not my intention to examine these in detail. In general the patrilineal succession suggested for Tikal by Haviland (1977) has been accepted, albeit with the need to explain exceptions such as the female rulers Lady Kanal-Ikal (9.7.10.3.8–9.8.11.6.12: AD 583–604) and Lady Zac-Kuk (9.8.19.7.18–9.9.2.4.8; AD 612–615) at Palenque (Schele, this volume). While the latter can be seen as a regent for her young son

Pacal II, who acceded at the age of twelve, the former is more difficult to fit into a patrilineal succession except by the argument that dynastic descent was by the seventh century AD so important that the direct bloodline, even in a female, overrode the claims of male collaterals.

A challenge to the patrilineal model has been offered by Fox and Justeson (1986), who argue for matrilineal succession to the sister's son allied with cross-cousin marriage (the latter known in colonial Yucatan) to keep the rulership within the lineage. The problem is that matrilineal institutions, if they existed, do not seem to have persisted even into the Postclassic. Edmonson's (1978) reconstruction of Yucatecan society at this period has the same patrilineal, patrilocal, and patriarchal framework as Haviland's (1972) model for Classic Tikal and Farriss' (1984) observations on colonial Yucatan. Wilk (1988:141–2) argues, in contrast, that "there does not seem to be any consistent patrilocal rule of residence . . . there is no evidence that the household was ever a formally organized patrilineal segment in the lowlands . . . the Maya seem to fit well into the overall southern Mesoamerican pattern of social organization in which corporate descent groups . . . are missing and in which the household is the most important social unit below the level of the community."

Whichever means of descent was employed, membership of the dynasty seems, so far as the inscriptions allow us to establish, to have been tightly controlled: there is no proliferation of titles such as "son of the ruler" used by nobility on funerary ceramics or provincial inscriptions (although the undeciphered glyphs which we know to be titles of some sort may hold surprises for us). The rank of ahau could in theory be applied to royal cadets, but there are few enough of these to suggest that it did not apply beyond the first descendant generation. The arrogation of patrimony and title to a single heir in each generation, the method of dynastic consolidation employed by the Capetians (Lewis 1982), is one which could on the evidence have well been used by the Classic Maya.

The dynasty ruled, and in polities where the Emblem Glyph was used proclaimed its right to a territory defined more by its center than its boundaries (see below). Whether it ruled by "devolution of graduated power on a scale of decreasing autonomies" (Tambiah 1977:33), with land tenure distributed from the top downwards in return for upward appropriation of basic resources, by direct control of satellite rulers (cahalob) or ahau members of the ruling lineage, or as a *primus inter pares* exerting executive control of the polity only for purposes such as warfare, is unknown, although the site hierarchies adduced from the archaeological record suggest that the first of these is most congruent with the evidence. There is nothing to refute a model similar to Tambiah's (1977) "galactic polity," in which there is congruence of elite structure, elite reward by prebendal assignment or appanage, with the duties of the prebend forming the mechanism of administration. As Tambiah (1977:89) shows, the tension between the royal cadets outside the direct line of succession, and the non-royal nobility among which they found themselves operating, could fruitfully be used to maintain the ruler's power, something documented also by Lewis (1982) for Capetian France. The variety of elites, and the struggle among them, may have been a significant factor in the stability and growth of the Classic Maya polities, although the frozen nature of the Late Classic elite proposed by Rathje (1970) or the accelerated upward movement to higher elite status of local gentry suggested by Fash and Stuart (this volume) would both fit Fourquin's (1978) model of social instability in medieval Europe, and be equally significant in their eventual dissolution.

What mechanisms linked these social levels, elite and commoners, together? Adams and Smith (1977, 1981) argue for a feudal system based on that of medieval Europe, with aspects of Tokugawa Japan in addition, while Sanders (1981) is equally in favor of a generalized feudal model, drawing his specific parallels from West Africa. Both are related to Tambiah's (1977:92) model of the "galactic polity," "whose building blocks are circles of leaders and followers that form and reform in highly unstable factions" in "a political-economic system premised on the control of manpower as its chief resource." These polities were driven by an agricultural economy with a particular relation of people to land and to mobilization of services, and the ruler's attempt to monopolize and tax foreign trade as a way of acquiring the surplus wealth necessary to sustain independent royal action.

The vision of both the pyramid of politico-economic relations within the society and the core:periphery/center:satellite relationships as reflections of a cosmic order (*mandala*), giving a sacred rationale for what may well have been pragmatic aspects of government, as seen by Tambiah in both thirteenth-century Thailand and fourteenth-century Java, is one that extends to interpolity relationships of enmity or alliance in a way closely paralleled by the Classic Maya situation in the Pasion region (Mathews and Willey, this volume).

As Willey (1981:414–15) remarks, the classic feudal models of both Adams and Smith and of Sanders underestimate the role of trade, while the mercantilist models of Webb (1973) and Rathje (1971) overemphasize it. Freidel's (1981) "pilgrimage-fair" construct imposes too constrained a linkage between religious and commercial activity, and lacks evidence for its existence at all in the Maya area. Whether trade was free or administered in Classic times is unknown: the degree of control covaries in the minds of scholars with the presumed social rank of the traders – the more elite, the greater the chances of a centralized monopoly.

The role of religion in vertically integrating Maya society is axiomatic, whether the cult was that of a pantheon of celestial and chthonic deities as outlined by Schele (Schele and Miller 1986) of a henotheistic creator in whom every aspect of the universe was manifested, as in Thompson's (1970) proposed Late Classic primacy of Itzamna, or of venerated ancestors at all levels from the local lineage to the ruling dynasty.

Finally, the function of elite marriage in cementing ties between the ruling dynasty and the nobility should be noted: Mathews estimates that 90 percent of elite marriages recorded on the monuments took place within the polity, and those deciphered are presumably only a proportion of those originally commemorated, which were in turn only a fraction of the total matrimonial interaction. Here the explicit is a guide to the implicit, but does not by any means encompass it.

## THE TERRITORIAL STRUCTURE OF CLASSIC MAYA POLITIES

The existence of Maya polities in the Classic period has been unquestioned since the 1840s; their autochthonous rather than secondary development, and their organization at the level of the state rather than the developed chiefdom, have conversely been a matter of energetic dispute to the present day. Hundreds of sites are known, ranging in size and complexity from hamlets up to pre-industrial cities in many aspects of form and almost all of function (Hammond 1975a:83–4), but their political organization remained an enigma until the historicity of the inscriptions was demonstrated and their contents elucidated. Even so, the dynastic emphasis of this content and the absence of territorial declarations beyond the actual existence of the polity designated by the Emblem Glyph made the delineation of boundaries difficult. The "bottom-up" approach of Hammond (1972, 1974a), defining the territory closer to a given center than to any other, and adjusting to a best fit with apparent natural borders, has some support in the ethnographic record (e.g. Riesenberg 1968), but depends on assumed parity between the polities and the location of the capital at the territorial center of each. (Numerous exceptions to this are suggested by specific topography in the Maya lowlands; weighted Thiessen polygons were explicitly eschewed beause of the then [in 1971] lack of accurate data on Maya site hierarchy.) The "top-down" approach of Marcus (1973, 1976), using Barthel's (1968b) model of four "regional capitals" derived from his reading of Copan Stela A and Seibal Stela 10, makes equally explicit assumptions about the existence of specific hierarchical relationships, and their integration into a central-place model derived from quantitative economic geography. This approach also has its weaknesses including the uncertainty of Barthel's initial exegesis of the inscriptions, the paucity of lower-order sites to flesh out the hinterland of the central-place hierarchy, and the lack of economic administrative data on production and demand to justify the use of such a model at all.

Polity definition still depends on assumptions, in the present case this volume's consensus that possession of an Emblem Glyph is *ipso facto* evidence of autonomy, and the concomitant acceptance that the appearance of new and disappearance of old Emblem Glyphs marked changes in the political landscape. This consensus is based on the detailed but plausible history of the Pasion region's changes offered by Mathews and Willey (this volume) and the equally striking evidence for political stability downstream on the Usumacinta presented by Schele (this volume), supported by that from Copan and Quirigua (Fash and Stuart, Sharer, this volume). There are some uncomfortable details, such as the use of dual Emblem Glyphs by the rulers of Yaxchilan, which suggest that things were not quite as simple as they seem, but the overall model appears robust.

The concentration of inscriptions within the assumed polity centers or capitals, their sporadic appearance in subordinate communities, and the lack of frontier markers (with possible exceptions at El Pabellon and Tres Islas on the Pasion, and on the hills around Copan) all suggest that boundary maintenance and territorial integrity were not of prime importance to the Maya rulers. The Southeastern Asian *muang* concept of "center-orientated" as opposed to "bounded" space, with the name of the capital also standing for that of the polity, is an appropriate parallel (Tambiah 1977:74). Moertono (1968:112) cites the Javanese metaphor of a torch, the radiant power of which determines the distance it can illuminate, to explain the "pulsating polities" of the Majapahit kingdom where "territorial jurisdiction could not be strictly defined by permanent boundaries, but was characterized by a fluidity or flexibility of boundary dependent on the diminishing or increasing power of the center."

What was important to center-orientated polities was control of manpower, a mobile resource, rather than static territory: the Maya propensity for recording capture of individuals, only rarely distinguished by a polity identifier, may be a specific instance of this, and these rare cases are one of the few ways in which we can gain an idea of where frontiers lay. Mathews (in Schele and Mathews, this volume) has tabulated the recorded instances of interpolity warfare and capture and shown that two identified rulers (Kan-Xul of Palenque and 18 Rabbit of Copan) were captured without their polities being taken over by the captor states, which were respectively 64 and 47 km distant (all distances are in airline); Jaguar Paw-Jaguar of Seibal was captured by Ruler 3 of Dos Pilas, 24 km away, and his capital subordinated to Dos Pilas. That there was sometimes a territorial dimension to warfare is suggested by the occasional substitution of the *caban*, "earth" glyph for a specific polity Emblem Glyph in the "shell-star" compound signifying war (Justeson, personal communication), and the role of boundary warfare in reinforcing central control by the elite has been discussed by Webster (1975). About a dozen men of ahau status are recorded as captured in major battles (such as that portrayed on the Bonampak Room 2 murals), and raiding for victims for sacrifice, and also to prove manhood and ability, just beyond the frontiers of the polity would explain why few of these ahauob are mentioned in inscriptions at the polity center. The mean distance between polity centers that record war is 49 km (n=17), giving a mean radius of 25 km; an assumption that the polity capital lies at the territorial center would give a realm of *c.* 2,000 km$^2$.

That this mean figure is plausible is suggested by Mathews' tabula-tion of royal marriages, which tend to take place not with the nearest neighbor – who is often the partner in warfare – but with a slightly more distant polity. As the *Arthasastra* (6.2.14–15) puts it: "Encircling [the king] on all sides with territory immediately next to his is the constituent called the enemy. In the same manner, one with territory separated by one [other territory] is the constituent called the ally." The mean distance for the seven interpolity royal marriages known (excluding that between Palenque and Copan) is 64 km (for the eight including Palenque–Copan it is 109 km).

External parallels such as Erdösy's (1987) study of Early Historic (100 BC–AD 300) cities on the Ganges, with polity centers spaced at 35–40 km, and Tambiah's (1977:75) citation of the thirteenth-century multi-center Thai polity of Sukothai as embracing muang two days' march away (i.e. *c.* 60–70 km), suggest that a polity radius of *c.* 25 km for Classic Maya territories is realistic. This is supported by Scarborough's (1985) assessment of Late Preclassic polities in northern Belize, where the intercenter distances average 39 km (n=6) to give a "territory" of *c.* 1,300 km$^2$; and, more distantly in time, space, and organizational relevance, the partido capitals of colonial Yucatan where the mean distance is 67 km (n=12), giving an hypothetical territory of *c.* 3,400 km$^2$ (Farriss 1986:Fig. 6.1).

The royal visits described by Schele and Mathews (this volume) are of less use in defining polity size because of their mixed nature and small number, although it should be noted that visits to subordinate cahalob are over smaller distances than the hypothesized polity radius of 25 km, while most of those to ahauob of equal status are over distances greater than 25 km. It is interesting that the patterns of visits and warfare are mutually exclusive, while those of visits and royal marriages are partly congruent, as between Yaxchilan and Bonampak, and Yaxchilan and El Peru; it may also be politically significant that the longest-distance visits, for example those to Bird-Jaguar, Knot-eye Jaguar, and Tah-Skull II of Yaxchilan between 9.2.0.0.0 (AD 475) and 9.5.2.10.6 (AD 537), were all made by ahauob acting as ambassadors for their rulers, and not by the rulers themselves, while rulers did make shorter excursions (for example the 45 km from Yaxchilan to Piedras Negras directly downriver, or the 22 km across country from Yaxchilan to Bonampak). Rulers may not have liked to travel too far from their power base.

What the pattern of royal visits does suggest is the existence of spheres of influence within which there was reciprocal elite interaction: an area of concentrated interaction ran down the Usumacinta basin from Petexbatun and the Rio Lacantun, as far downstream as Piedras Negras (and possibly Pomona), and this lay within a larger sphere that embraced the northeast Peten as far as Tikal.

At intervals in Classic Maya history there emerged what we designate multi-center polities or complex polities. These grew from "normal" single-center polities by accretion, either by marriage (e.g. Dos Pilas–Tamarindito at *c.* 9.14.0.0.0 [AD 711]) or conquest (Tikal–Uaxactun on 8.17.1.4.12 [AD 378], Dos Pilas–Seibal on 9.15.4.6.4 [AD 735]); Dos Pilas is estimated to have had a polity of *c.* 3,500 km$^2$ for some forty years, and one of 1,800 km$^2$ for at least a century, while the realms of Tikal and pehaps Caracol may have been more than 2,500 km$^2$ in area, and Culbert (this volume) makes the case for an even larger Tikal state. Apart from this last case of special pleading, however, even the multi-center polities are not that much larger than the rest: provided our basic equation of Emblem Glyph=autonomous polity is correct, the model of a mosaic of small units first adumbrated by Morley (1946) would still appear valid.

Morley's inspiration was the *polis* of Classical Greece, and the division of the *poleis* into the central *asty* and the rural *demes* parallels what we know of the internal structure of the Maya states: the asty, the political center, also stood synecdochically for the entire polity (as in "Athens" for Athens plus Attica); law and leadership were focused there in the hands of the noble families, and the shrines of rural cults in Peisistratid Athens reflected the binding of the demes, with their hereditary priesthoods forming a network of local government, to the central administration in the asty (Frost 1987).

Thus the Emblem Glyph of, for example, Dos Pilas, designated both the realm controlled by the rulers based at that polity center, and the center as a location and community. The identification by Stuart and Houston (1988) of toponyms that are not Emblem Glyphs and lack the specifically dynastic elements of T35–41 and T168, the "bloodline/holy" and "ahau" affixes, not only emphasizes the dual nature of the Emblem Glyph but allows places and even specific structures within Maya polities to be named.

Nevertheless, outside the polity centers, with their dynastic records, we know little of the spatial structure of Classic Maya realms except from archaeological evidence. Local governors of cahal rank are known in a few instances in the Usumacinta valley, as at La Pasadita in the realm of Yaxchilan, Lacanha under Bonampak, and of ahau rank at Arroyo de Piedra under Dos Pilas (Schele and Mathews; Schele, this volume). The archaeological settlement pattern, however, demonstrates the presence of numerous communities with a polity ranging in size and complexity from small "major ceremonial centers" with the architectural appurtenances of a polity capital but lacking dynastic monuments, through the "minor centers" that, from their frequency, formed the basis of local elite residence and rule, to clusters of residential groups with no buildings larger than lineage shrines, located where agricultural resources could be exploited (cf. Bullard 1960; Hammond 1975b; Ashmore 1981a,b). The spatial distribution of population (and therefore of archaeological sites) is at the less complex end of the site hierarchy clearly a function of the subsistence economy; some medium-sized sites may have gained their ascendancy from control of aspects of the craft-production economy, as with the chert workshops of Colha (Shafer and Hester 1983) or of distribution as "gateway communities" (Hirth 1978). Polity centers themselves may initially have emerged where they did primarily for economic reasons, as seems to have been the case with Lubaantun (Hammond 1972), although their survival combines tactical (intrapolity) with strategic (interpolity) control of resources, and with the coeval overall pattern of polity relationships (Hammond 1974a). Because of this economic basis for its existence the single-center polity is a remarkably durable entity: apart from the Maya examples, many of which survived over half a millennium, we have the poleis of Greece, the city-states of Sumer, and the nomes of Egypt, persisting through Pharaonic times as the units into which the realm broke in times of severe stress and loss of central control.

This single-center structure could also be interpreted in cosmic terms, however: the mandala model of South and East Asian polities combines the core (*manda*) with a periphery of satellites (*la*), the core being seen also as the *axis mundi* that links the terrestrial to the supernal plane (Tambiah 1977:69–70, Figs. 1–2). Such a conflation of vertical with horizontal distance enables rulers to use exotic goods to symbolize control of distant domains (Helms 1987), and may explain some of the power of Teotihuacanoid imports and images in the Maya lowlands. Barthel's (1968b) interpretation of Copan Stela A and Seibal Stela 10 as listing four "capitals" of a quadripartite Maya domain is a model of cosmic order which, while now known to be invalid in its basic argument, fits well into Tambiah's scheme, and the latter's demonstration of the congruence of the cosmological, territorial, economic, and administrative facets of mandala could usefully be applied to the Maya situation.

A broad description of the structure of a Classic Maya polity would place at the strategic center of its territory (whether or not this was the geographical center) the capital, which was also the largest community. This housed the ruling dynasty, noble and a substantial number of commoner lineages, some of them engaged in intellectual and craft-specialist occupations. In the case of a very small polity this community and its sustaining hinterland might be all that there was, but in the constructed type of the Maya polity of about 2,000 km$^2$ which we have defined there would be many other foci of population. Some of these would be not just self-supporting argricultural communities, but also seats of local administration ruled by a cahal or an ahau. That a social hierarchy was spread through the polity, rather than the nobility living only in and near the capital, is indicated both by the cahal inscriptions and by the recorded captures of ahauob lacking Emblem Glyphs, whose residence in the border regions of polities would accord with Mathews' view of warfare as essentially the raiding of marginal territory.

The administrative/elite residential compounds in these communities are represented archaeologically by long "palace" or "range" structures on plazas which echo in miniature the architectural format of the polity capital, and which are often juxtaposed with a more public plaza bordered by shrines. Such elite plazas are most easily isolated in areas such as the Motagua valley (Sharer, this volume), where a system of administration was imposed on the region, or adopted by acculturation of an existing rural elite: in either case these "quadrangles" stand out in the local site hierarchy, reflecting in their layout a simpler version of the core of Quirigua and in their frequency the "minor ceremonial centers" of northern Belize (which are more widely spaced than those in the northeastern Peten, reported by Bullard [1960]).

These centers usually have pyramidal shrines, formerly seen as local manifestations of a state religion, but now recognized as foci of ancestor veneration for the ruling lineage of the community (Sanders 1981:359). These satellite rulers not only flourished in concert with their polity, but when central control broke down many of them arrogated to their own communities symbols of power formerly controled by the ruling dynasty. Such balkanization in the Terminal Classic can be seen in the appearance of stelae and public architecture at previously insignificant sites such as Xunantunich, Baking Pot, and Cahal Pech in the Belize valley, and Jimbal and Ixlu near Tikal, the erection of inscribed lintels by nobles at Chichen Itza (Krochok 1988), and also in the ladling-out of previously restricted titles to nobles at Copan (Fash and Stuart, this volume).

In the smallest communities the ranking lineage may not have been of noble standing: these sites appear in the archaeological record as "clusters" (Ashmore 1981b:Figs. 3.3–3.6), but still exhibiting in their range of variation differential statuses expressed by investment in domestic architecture. Such clusters were originally defined by Bullard (1960) as the remains of lineages of related extended families, in parallel with the sna waterhole groups of the Tzotzil at Zinacantan (Vogt 1969). While the higher-order structure of Vogt's interpretation of Classic Maya society has not survived the influx of new data, his model still has much to offer in understanding the relationship between landscape, resources, and lineage organization, as we try to peer into the black box of the past.

The picture of a "typical" Classic Maya polity outlined above is in reality made much more complex by the variable developmental trajectories of polities through time (Sharer, this volume, Fig. 8.1); while the history of each polity is unique, some prevailing patterns can be perceived among them (Fig. 11.3). These can be tagged as the "Cerros" pattern of Late Preclassic rise and subsequent desuetude; the "Nohmul/Seibal" pattern in which a Cerros trajectory is followed by a

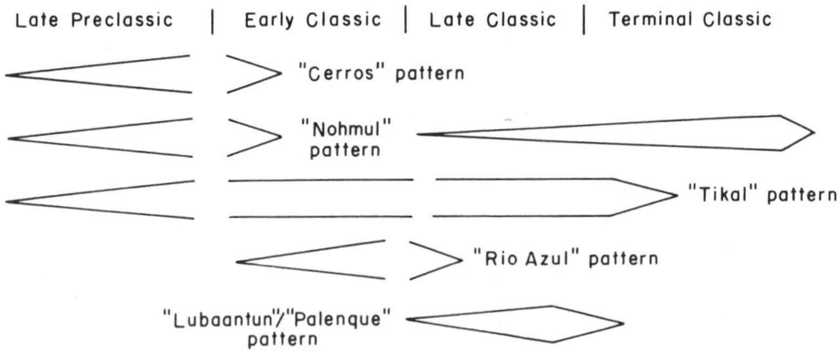


Fig. 11.3 Contrasting trajectories of polity-center florescence.

Late/Terminal Classic renaissance (in both exemplars, although not axiomatically, with an intrusive cultural tradition); a "Rio Azul" pattern of Early Classic florescence with insignificant prior and posterior status; a "Tikal" pattern of sustained prosperity, albeit with patches of political misfortune; and a "Lubaantun/Palenque" pattern of Late Classic rise from previous obscurity, with in Yucatan a parallel "Puuc" development. The emergence of Chichen Itza could be seen as either a late Puuc-pattern example, a substantial and temporarily successful polity commanding central northern Yucatan, or as Wren and Schmidt (this volume) argue, *sui generis* and the beginning of a new order.

## CONCLUSION

While the internal dynamics of Classic Maya polities must always be the subject of speculative reconstruction rather than observation, a combination of archaeological, ethnohistoric, and epigraphic evidence from the Maya lowlands, and a judicious admixture of external parallels from other preindustrial societies organized at levels between chiefdoms and feudal monarchies can enable us to make some defensible propositions about them. Recent demographic studies suggest an overall population density and level higher than previously envisaged, with polities such as Tikal controlling as many as 1.5 million subjects (Turner n.d.: Table 8), and a typical small polity of 2,000 $km^2$ having some 400,000 people. Polity capitals were preindustrial cities in their range of administrative and economic functions, and may have had populations exceeding 50,000. The social pyramid was multi-layered, with at least two classes of elite below the ruling dynasty, and two further classes of commoners below that, with a possible substratum of serfs and slaves. Occupational specialization was probably class-specific, with the intellectual activities requiring literacy confined to the elite, and skilled crafts to the upper levels of commoner society, and may also have been lineage-specific. Residence in clusters of compounds, long acknowledged to have a lineage basis, may also have defined occupational barrios similar to those of the Mesoamerican highland zone, although specific evidence is presently scanty. The conduct of war, government, and relations with the cosmos was reserved to the ruling elite, but atavistic cults formed both the heart of lineage worship and powerful vertical links between rulers and ruled: the royal palace compound was but the plazuela on a larger scale. Social control and resource appropriation probably utilized a pyramidal set of relationships in which the downward conferment of honor and affirmation in office was balanced by upward movement of goods to support the local and central hierarchies. At the time of the collapse in the ninth century AD the topmost levels of this pyramid were truncated, leaving the lower separate community organizations as the framework of Postclassic society. The removal of the Classic ruling dynasties, with their archaeologically striking material output of buildings, monuments, inscriptions, and patronage art, pushed the Maya from marginally historic to ahistoric status; the social dissolution that accompanied the process included major diminution in population, as the managerial apparatus for feeding and servicing large, dense communities ceased to exist. The elite culture which defined Classic Maya civilization for over half a millennium ceased to have meaning, and lost its currency among the epigonal population: the black box was sealed.

# 12
# Maya elite interaction: through a glass, sideways

NORMAN YOFFEE

## ELITES AND THE EVOLUTION OF ANCIENT CIVILIZATIONS

There's a new skyscraper going up in downtown Tucson. It's at least twenty storeys high. Now in downtown Tucson there are two main sorts of buildings, derelict stores and office buildings, especially government office buildings. Nonetheless, there are big plans for a downtown revival and the new skyscraper, which is another office building, replaces some of the derelict stores. The shell of this new office building is now complete and one can see that the building will have an entablature, an ornamented cornice, and a most unusual set of structures (or "pitched roofs") at its top, smaller ones in front on all sides and one large structure rising over them in the middle.[1]

This new office building is the only one of its kind in the Old Pueblo. All the other skyscrapers are built in accord with the Bauhaus rule that dictates roofs must be flat (Wolfe 1981). Pitched roofs and cornices, apparently, were considered by the Bauhaus, which completely dominated normative ideas of American architecture for decades, as elite symbols of Old World nobility, which both the European and American bourgeoisie had long insisted on emulating. Tucson architects, who constructed honest, functional governmental and office buildings free of applied decoration and with roofs making clean right-angles to the façades, were clearly demonstrating their distaste with that elite ideology.

As most signs of normal bourgeois life leave downtown Tucson, it strikes me as quite "Mayan" for Tucson to erect an elite symbol of the transformation of downtown into a governmental/ceremonial center (much as Maya central cities were regarded in the olden days of Mesoamerican scholarship, about twenty years ago). Presumably, Tucson's new office building is a symbol that reflects the Reaganomic ideology that elitism is a good thing, so the more crown-like a building's roof appears the better.[2]

Just what does it mean to call a cornice "elite"? Why are elites railed against or alternatively held as a vision of *laissez-faire* splendor? What does elite mean and how is the term used in social and political writings and what, if anything specific, is denoted by the term "elite interaction"? Finally, what does the existence of elites have to do with evolutionary theory, particularly the development and nature of ancient states and civilizations?

The word "elite" is a bare anglicism, of course, of the French *élite*, which is derived from Old French *eslite*, a feminine past participle of *eslire*, "to choose," which in turn derives from a (vulgar?) Latin infinitive *eligere*, "elect" (Morris 1976; I shall not dwell on the possible *PIE forms). Indeed, through the nineteenth century in France, *élite* mainly meant "choice," especially referring to commodities of choice, but also grew to refer to superior social groups. In English, used first in 1823, "elite" already had picked up this social connotation. By the late nineteenth and early twentieth century the term became increasingly used in sociological and political theory, especially in the writings of V. Pareto (Bottomore 1966).

"Elite," for Pareto, referred to the highest rank in any category and denoted inequality in ability or endowment. The "governing elite," as used by Lasswell *et al.* in the influential book *The Comparative Study of Elites* (1952), isolated specifically that minority occupying political command and who may or may not represent other types of elites. The classical sociological theory of elites, therefore (here much abridged from Bottomore [1966], see also G. Marcus [1983]), is concerned with identifying various forms of elites and examining the social and/or economic or other bases of their power.

Theories of elites are also usually associated with arguments directly intended to rebut Marxist social theory. That is, "elite" is an analytical concept that stands in contradistinction to that of "class," especially that of "ruling class." Now standard Marxist usage of the term ruling class must contain minimally the notion that it is explained "by possession of the major instruments of economic production although it maintains power through military force and the control of the production of ideas" (Bottomore 1966:24).

"Ruling class," therefore, seems a much more specific term than is useful in most investigations of the character of ancient governments, both for the Maya and elsewhere: "class" is a term that entails the idea that there is an economic cause for its existence and "ruling class" denominates a theory that an economic class rules politically (after C. Wright Mills after Bottomore).

Now in every complex society it is clear that a minority group wields political power. It is less clear, however, what is the source of that power. Indeed, I have argued (1985, 1986; similar Weberian ideas have been discussed recently by others, notably Runciman 1982, Mann 1986) that power needs to be divided into three and perhaps only into three components: economic, social, and political power. All of these sources of power need to be present for an evolutionary trajectory toward state formation to ensue in a society. It is from the "tensions" among the various societal organizations and thus their various different elites that the sort of central ruling apparatus emerges that is usually called the state. The specialized ruling elite, of course, must legitimize its new, integrative role, especially by inventing and/or controlling the most important symbols of cultural commonality, by regularizing social relations, especially in settling disputes, and by representing the entire society in defensive/expansionist policies. The ruling elite must also be able to reproduce itself, in part by providing access to its own inner structure.

Such a theory of elites, which I shall use in explicating certain Mesopotamian data and which I suppose can also be applied to explore the Maya case, avers that various types of elites exist within any state-level society. It further expresses the principle that across ancient states political power can be represented and legitimized through different kinds of elites. Thus, it is in the nature of elites in ancient states, as much as in any environmental circumstances, that we find the important distinctions in the "character" and in the socio-economic stability of those polities.[3]

The evolutionary significance of the study of elites, then, consists in the alternative weightings in the different forms of power, all of which appear, but not in the same proportions, among ancient states. This theory further challenges the notion that all social institutions in a complex society are "inextricably intertwined" (Henderson 1981:151). Rather, certain social organizations can be tied to specific forms of power which not only are (analytically) separable, but also inherently express conflicting aspirations and possess differing means for establishing political authority. In the following remarks on the papers in this volume I shall try to cull such observations on Maya elite interaction that address this theme of political struggle.[4]

I also intend to discuss several issues pertinent to the study of Mesopotamian elites that are occasioned by way of the examination of the Maya material. This "sideways" approach, as discussed by Norman Hammond in this volume, has an explicit justification. Everyone uses analogies in their analytical work, just because no one, not even Mesopotamian archaeologists and historians, have yet managed to achieve the blessed state of *tabula rasa*, even if some of them seem to aspire to it. Indeed, the process of expanding basic inferences from patterns of data to the construction of models of human behavior and social change requires making clear what analogies and assumptions are being employed in the analysis. Analogies are posited because they are assumed to yield data and patterns of data from a known example that resemble the data and patterns being investigated in the unknown one. Salmon calls these analogies "prior probabilities" (1982); they are derived from history, ethnography, ethno-archaeology, or "common sense." They are used because they give the investigator confidence that his or her models are "probable," that is, not wholly unique and so unlikely. Some of the authors in this volume, like Norman Hammond, have used analogies explicitly, and often. In his chapters in this volume he refers to political organizations in Capetian France, the Holy Roman Empire, Peru, Egypt, Sumer, the Indus Valley, Biafra, Poland, Renaissance Italy, and Greece. Such comparisons may or may not be considered valid, but that's as may be. What is required is that all investigators state clearly, as Hammond usually does, what are the premises of choosing this or that example for comparison as opposed to some other example. Many of the debates on archaeological explanations do not, of course, refer to arguments over data. Rather, disputes over rival claims of knowledge proceed endlessly and without resolution because the premises of analogies are left unstated or the analogies themselves remain subconscious and hence are "untestable."

The goals of comparison, furthermore, are not to homogenize the universe of cases, for example, by implying that all ancient states are similarly structured. Rather, the point of social evolutionary theory is to promote investigations that illuminate why certain social institutions exist or do not exist in one area of the world by showing under what conditions similar institutions may or may not be found in another area. Only by comparison, in other words, can an evolutionary theory be generated in which particular social forms can be assessed and explained or, as the adage has it, *testis unus testis nullus*, "one witness no witness." Too often evolutionary theory has been structured simply to separate states from those forms of society thought antecedent to states. Little attention has been given to the varieties of ancient states themselves and to the study of the conditions of such variability.

One prominent feature justifies the comparison of Maya and Mesopotamian civilization as well as providing the context for examining important areas of contrast. Neither Mesopotamia nor the Maya existed as a unified pan-regional state. That is, the focus of political struggle and elite tension in early Mesopotamia was in the various city-states. Only rarely did the southern Sumerian or Babylonian city-state form a regional state and these state-agglomerations were highly unstable and evanescent. Assyria to the north differed significantly from the south and was never incorporated with it to form a single, political Mesopotamian state.

The Maya have similarly been described in this volume as a "system of states" (Sharer) and "a fractured group of quarreling states" (Wren and Schmidt), and the clear common opinion is that these city-states (usually called "polities" in this volume) were engaged in a more-or-less endemic struggle for dominion and/or independence with other such city-states (see Culbert's summary chapter for a discussion of the various meanings of Maya warfare).

In both the Maya and Mesopotamian cases, then, we cannot speak of Maya or Mesopotamian overall states, in a political sense. What is just as clear, however, is that we can speak of Maya and Mesopotamian civilizations. That is, there are Maya/Mesopotamian cultural boundaries that overarch real political diversity. These boundaries are palpable and they separate Maya/Mesopotamia from their neighbors as effectively as political borders, if in a different way. These boundaries change over time as they alternately incorporate or resist foreign elements and as they were actively and consciously reproduced over generations. They mark Maya and Mesopotamia as different kinds of ancient civilizations from those of Egypt, China, Teotihuacan, or Peru, all of which maintained and defined such pan-regional political boundaries. Although there are major differences between Maya and Mesopotamia – differences as clear and important as in tropical as opposed to desert irrigation argricultural systems of production – the nature of the boundaries of the civilizations provides an appealing point of entry to the ensuing discussion. The following remarks are meant in no way as critical appraisals of this volume's papers; I am incompetent for the purpose. Rather, I hope I have learned enough from the papers to provide a few controls for the comparative method I seek to employ.

## MAYA ELITE INTERACTIONS

In days of yore, when Maya subsistence agriculture was characterized as slash-and-burn, it seemed the limits of ecological credibility were mightily strained. How could so many Maya be supported with such a non-intensive agricultural system? Today, having learned about root crops, ramon nuts, and especially about raised fields, the question seems to be why weren't there more Maya since there was so much food? Similarly, interpretations of sparsely populated ceremonial centers have given way to estimates of as much as 600–1,000 persons per km$^2$ in Late Classic urban megalopoloi (Culbert 1988a). Peaceful priests "contemplating the stately procession of time that was commemorated in the hieroglyphic inscriptions" (Culbert 1986; see also Hammond 1982) are now bloody-minded kings seeking to control the volatile forces of nature through elaborate ritual. In the new S & M (Schele and Miller 1986) version of Maya art, bloodletting (of the good guys) and torture-sacrifices (of the bad guys) are the mortar of this ritual life. Warfare was endemic since sacrificial victims needed procuring. Various manipulations of the kinship system were recorded in the process of celebrating alliances, victories, and royal gore. In the old days big-time ceremonial centers and elite activity were thought to be characteristic only of the Classic (especially Late Classic); now the super-novas of El Mirador and Calakmul require a reassessment of the nature of the Preclassic and perhaps of the entire sequence of development of Maya civilization (see also Hammond [1986a] on evolutionary developments throughout the Preclassic). The earliest Maya were once thought (about twenty years ago) to have appeared about 800 BC. Maya are now known to have hacked their way through the rainforest at least by 2000 BC and perhaps considerably before that (MacNeish *et al.* 1980). Until the 1986 seminar there was no Maya history. Our fearless leader has now informed me that the credo of this Advanced Seminar volume is "Let there be History".[5]

Things are moving rapidly in the world of Maya studies and Maya scholars are delightfully adaptive. Among the most significant changes that have occurred are the new perspectives on the nature of boundaries in Maya civilization and, perhaps beginning with this volume, the investigation of the nature of interactions within the various levels of those boundaries.

In several recent accounts (Freidel 1979; Henderson 1981) and in this volume represented by Sharer and Hammond most explicitly, Maya civilization has been described as an "interaction sphere." It is my understanding that this term, as used by Caldwell (1964) and latterly by Struever and Houart (1972) – although the concept was also employed in Peru by Willey (1948) and Kroeber (1944) as "horizon styles"; see Schortman and Urban (1987) – is meant to denote how a series of ("politically") independent "cultures" are linked through participation in a larger, specifically non-political inter-regional culture. Sharer thus speaks of the development of a mosaic of Maya states, "a system of states," within an environmentally circumscribed sphere that was "reinforced and perpetuated by social circumscription." Hammond and Culbert (following Hammond) speak of the mosaic of Maya states whose "ethnic identity" was (possibly, according to the "peer-polity" notion) generated through participation in an interaction sphere. For Sharer, ethnic identity is less clear; Cholan Maya and Yucatec Maya are distinct dialects and Mixe-Zoquean ethnics (based presumably on linguistic definition) also participated in the overarching Maya identity.

What all Mayanists seem presumably capable of identifying as "Maya" is a series of material-culture traits. These include various "exotics" (e.g., jade, shell), bark-beaters, corbeled arches, art, ceramics, ceremonial architecture, the dynastic monument (stela) complex (sometimes oddly called the "stela cult"). These material traits reflect Maya "culture," specifically a Maya belief system, that overarches local political, productive, and even cultural differences and which can be identified in the specific symbols required in that superordinate system.

This approach is clearly Hammond's "downward direction" in understanding Maya civilization. It implies that what is distinctively Maya is not derived from the forces of production or from productive relations but from an ideological edifice of symbols and beliefs. Sharer explicitly identifies these material traits as representing an apparent unity of the elite subculture, while a considerable diversity among the non-elite can be discerned beneath that social level. I shall return to the matter of "elite unity" below.

Breakthroughs into the nature of writing, the meaning of artistic representation, and the interrelations of sites have reshaped the understanding of this Maya cultural entity. The gist of these studies is to demonstrate how a common fund of linguistic and artistic expressions are drawn upon to reinforce local political power throughout Maya territory. Thus, for Schele and Miller "public art and architecture . . . define the nature of political power" (1986:103); for J. Marcus (1976:37) writing "legitimizes each ruler's right to accede to the throne"; for Justeson (1986:445), the original use of a writing system borrowed from the Olmec was to "reinforce elite power and prestige" by depicting "elite males in ritual contexts," presumably to demonstrate their fitness to rule – their appropriate place in the state of the cosmos.

All this reminds an Old World on-looker of ancient Egypt. There, writing was a royal accomplishment that had the ceremonial purpose to commemorate the achievements of the king and the status of courtiers and the king's relations (Ray 1986:311). Furthermore writing and pictorial representation were not distinct in Egypt. Indeed, the complex of pictorial representations included writing (Baines 1981:576). History was a presentation of the ordered world in which writing gave prestige to the elite presenters. Of course, the political nature of Egyptian and Maya civilizations could not be more different. Egypt was unified politically at a stroke at the very beginning of its history and remained so for more-or-less the next 3000 years.

Schele and Miller (1986:105) claim that writing and art function to "tie disparate groups into a cultural whole." These sociopolitical reasons for pictorial representation, that is, the political context of writing and art, are very common in ancient states. Irene Winter (1981) has noted that Neo-Assyrian reliefs function precisely to communicate an intended social cohesion and integration in an empire that was anything but coherent and integrated. The Assyrians nevertheless produced a fully developed narrative in their palace reliefs that told a story of political order. K. C. Chang (1983) presents the argument that art, myth, and ritual together form the critical elements through which political authority was ultimately effected in ancient China. Even though there are enormous differences in the aesthetic expressions among Maya, Mesopotamian, Egyptian, and Chinese art, the political function of the art depends on two identical criteria: the intention to legitimize a created and changing world as being in harmony with an unchanging and given cosmos (see Baines 1981) and an audience to whom that message is comprehensible.

For Schele and Miller (1986) that audience is not only the "entire elite class" which could read the texts and interpret the art but a general public who could at least read the dates and names of rulers and get the picture, as it were, of their rightful place in the Maya universe. The nature of the vast public plazas and the scale of the messages themselves certainly lends plausibility to the intention of communicating the message to a wide audience. In Mesopotamia the evidence that such messages of royal action and legitimacy were widely disseminated is minimal. Some, maybe most Mesopotamian texts, even the most famous poetic compositions and royal hymns, may have been known only within the precincts of higher scribal learning. In Egypt the various levels of communication seem rather more similar to the Maya case than they are in Mesopotamia.

If it can be taken that a common fund of symbols and written conventions united Maya people into a cultural identity, it is also clear that important regional differences existed in Maya territory. That is, if all Maya presumably shared certain conceptions of the Maya universe (such as Coggins [1986] has discussed: the levels of the underworld, the significance of directions, the iconic representations of the deities, and so on), various regional expressions of political ideology and changes in their structure can also be observed. Wren and Schmidt have convincingly shown, for example, how a new and fruitful amalgam of Maya and Mexican motifs represents an admixture of elite cultural behaviors that gave vitality to the city-states in the northern lowlands. If there is an overarching Maya civilizational boundary, then there are also significant sub-regional political structures that are characteristic of Maya civilization.

Several of this volume's papers (as summarized by Culbert) concentrate on these regional boundaries, their organizing principles and the histories of their development. Regionalism has been detected in many aspects of the "upward direction" in Maya studies: through rank-size distribution in courtyard counts (Adams 1981; Adams and Jones 1981) and ceramic distributions that imply local manufacture and distribution within a larger stylistic conformity (Hammond 1982).

Mathews and Willey here argue for a "political-territorial unit" on the Pasion, a "subdivision of the greater Maya lowlands," on the basis of various local hierarchical arrangements in site-sizes and in monumental inscriptions. The historical correlate of this sphere is most clearly realized in the establishment of the Dos Pilas dynasty which, even if it ultimately came from Tikal, was an independent authority on the Pasion. Culbert notes that the various relations between Tikal and Uaxactun (and perhaps Rio Azul) form part of a Tikal regional state in which elite affairs are significant features (see below). Jones delineates a history of Tikal and concludes that the regional state seemed so flexible and resilient that its collapse must have been caused by outside forces. Fash and Stuart document the "indigenous, highlands/Pacific coast interaction sphere" around Copan. Copan alternately sought ties with Kaminaljuyu, Tikal, and lower Central America in its historical and dynastic changes. Finally, regionalism is most clearly demonstrated, if on a macro-Maya scale, in the consideration of the Classic Maya collapse. As is well known, not all Maya centers did collapse and thus some regions (in the northern lowlands) clearly had effected enough differences from the Peten (this is all very clearly illustrated in Wren and Schmidt's paper) to survive the catastrophe. These regional sub-boundaries must be considered part of the theme of elite interaction because the struggle for independence and dominion is played out in the search for marital and other alliances that necessitated alternately elite visitations (as read by Mathews and Schele) and military action.

If Maya regional boundaries can now be taken as demonstrated, although the principles of regional boundary-formation and specific alliance-patterns are on-going subjects of research, we may pass to the more complex subject of internal differentiation among elites and the consequences of such differing elite orientations. In the Pasion expansionist state, Mathews and Willey pinpoint various oscillations in the locus of political power and in dynastic successions. While this history does not allow specification of the possible differences in the sources of power of such elites, the existence of elite political struggle is clearly indicated. Furthermore, their analysis of the origin of the Dos Pilas dynasty as a cadet lineage of the ruling house at Tikal suggests one endemic source of conflict among the central Peten elite.

Although Jones and Culbert see a certain continuity among Tikal elite, the picture seems, on the basis of their own data and analyses, less certain to me. For example, Culbert (this volume) and Adams (1986a) have described the tension that must have arisen at Uaxactun and Rio Azul when "local leaders were replaced by those from the capital" (Culbert 1986) at Tikal. Jones discusses the violent history of various Tikal dynasties in which deliberate erasing and breaking of carved monuments cannot be ascribed solely to conquest by outsiders. He also describes the replacement of a Twin Pyramid ceremonial precinct by a new ball court. In the first draft of his seminar paper, Jones argued that such a change was easy for the Tikaleños since both structures "focused on duality." While that interpretation may be plausible, this sort of architectural replacement at Tikal may also qualify as an example of the sort of ideological-political re-legitimation that may be associated with internal dynastic change.

Fash and Stuart argue that precisely this sort of intra-elite struggle was taking place throughout the history of Copan. Indeed, not only did Copan shift allegiances and alliances toward various other Maya regional states, perhaps because of the geographically peripheral location of Copan within the Maya interaction sphere, but elite interaction within the Copan state can be seen and assessed. Fash and Stuart discuss the evidence for conflict between the last ruler of Copan and various elite lineage heads and other members of the royal family. Monuments were raised to the glory of these nobles, who were attracting clients outside their direct kinship organization, and they even managed to claim the Emblem Glyph of Copan itself. For Fash and Stuart it was this political struggle among diverse strands of elites that contributed to or was symptomatic of the growing weakness of centralized leadership in the Copan city-state.

Finally, Wren and Schmidt discuss, on the basis of Mexican analogies that they justify as singularly appropriate at Chichen Itza, that assemblies of nobles existed in the northern lowlands, that noblemen shared power with the rulers, and that there was a rotation in the royal succession.

These themes provide exciting and important advances that go beyond the task of reconstructing the overarching cultural boundaries of Maya civilization. The study of ancient states and civilizations has seen too many declarations of state monopolies on production and exchange or totalitarian direction of political action. The nature of differentiation as an evolutionary phenomenon for many archaeologists appears to end in the rise of the state. Nowhere, however, where there exist historical documents is such a conclusion drawn, for all such documents are full of accounts of political struggle, not only between rulers and ruled, but between differing orientations of social groups and tensions within social groups. It is of critical significance that this sort of theoretical outlook is now being explored from the Maya data presented in this volume.

If elite interaction can be seen, on the one hand, within a Maya "civilizational" boundary and, on the other hand, within a subregional mosaic of Maya states, it is finally appropriate to consider in these few remarks the models of "feudal" Maya and of "peer-polity" interaction that have been proposed to explain the character of Maya social and political organization.

Adams and Smith's (1981) feudal analogy appeals initially because it tries to model the "diffusion of authority" and the "dispersal of elites" that is characteristic in the absence of a dominant Maya political authority in Maya territory. It furthermore is consonant with interpretations of the endemic condition of warfare among Maya states and the significance of a military aristocracy. As Adams and Smith have noted, however, the analogy breaks down in consideration of the importance of religious sanctions for Maya governmental institutions and for the formation of Maya elites and in exceptionally thoroughgoing kinship, rather than personal, relations (see Marcus 1983).

In addition to these problems, much of the nature of feudal conditional land-holdings cannot be shown to have occurred among the Maya and it seems doubtful that the low level of commercial activity that is required for a feudal model fits the Maya case (Jones 1979). Another flaw in the feudal model, however, is that the exteme diffusion of authority and the existence of large land-holdings intermixed with personal relationships of fiefdoms that characterize feudal societies are generally thought (e.g., by Coulborn 1956 and by Bottomore 1966) to have evolved in the specific conditions of the collapse of previously centralized governments. To my knowlege, such a condition of historical development has not been and perhaps cannot be suggested for the Maya.

Peer polity interaction (Renfrew 1986) posits a universalist historical scenario in which there are not only no "hearths of civilizations," but in which civilizations themselves are seen as members of larger interregional systems of "peers." When change occurs in one member of this system of polities, then the entire system changes at about the same time and in the same direction. Further, "ethnicity," and even languages, are seen as creations of the interactional process itself rather than as something that might be antecedent to the existence of the system.

As in other forms of systems theories, peer polity interaction does not seem to further the purpose of discerning detailed patterns of complexity that are formed by many overlapping and conflicting points of organizational behavior and which are the result of constantly changing strategies designed to meet long- and short-term risks and opportunities. Peer polity interaction passes over the internal development of political institutions and asymmetries among competing social and political organizations. It assumes not only that states, but even blocks of states, are really highly integrated or at least are so interrelated that they corporately become the constituent elements of social evolution. The abstractions of peer polity interaction theory thus impede our ability to break down complex data and prevent the examination of social institutions that are normally not well integrated. In the specific instance of collapse (from which consideration the above points were originally made [Yoffee and Cowgill 1988]), and especially that of the Maya collapse, it is clear that when ancient states and civilizations disintegrate not all social institutions fail as "peers" nor do they do so at the same pace.

To conclude this brief and certainly cursory review of the papers in this volume, I stress that one must investigate both the overarching "civilizational" boundaries and the various political sub-boundaries in order to grasp the nature of Maya elites and dynamic tensions that characterize Maya elite enmity as well as cooperation. The logic of social evolution is, in part, one of twin processes of differentiation and integration – processes that are resolved, not dissolved, in the formation of ruling elites. The civilizational boundaries are not "givens," either by environment or culture, but must be made and remade through time as the various sources of power themselves shift, especially as responses to the kinds of elite interaction that are discussed in the chapters of this volume.

## ASPECTS OF ELITE INTERACTION IN MESOPOTAMIA

To offer a kind of social chiaroscuro to the vivid tropical colors of Maya civilization, I now turn to the types of civilizational and political boundaries and explore the nature of elite interaction in the drab alluvial and relatively featureless Mesopotamian plain. I conclude with some observations on how the comparisons and contrasts that may be drawn between the two civilizations can be accommodated within an appropriate evolutionary theory.

As in the Maya case, the difference between Mesopotamian civilization and Mesopotamian states is real and easily apparent. In the political sense of the state, historians and archaeologists are well aware that the term "Mesopotamia" is by no means easy to define, since "Mesopotamia" consisted predominantly as a cellular pattern of city-states that rarely acted in political concert. Nevertheless, there can be demonstrated a very specific and shared *cultural* sense of Mesopotamia that is independent of a pan-Mesopotamian political system (Yoffee 1988a).

One particularly visible element of the overarching civilizational boundary that united city-states and regions in Mesopotamia consisted in those cultural institutions that were systematized in scribal academies throughout the land into what has been called "a stream of tradition" (Oppenheim 1964; Machinist 1986). Conspicuous in this "stream of tradition" are god-lists, rituals, and a standard corpus of *belles-lettres* that were preserved through millenniums, carefully transmitted in named catalogues, and occasionally revised into a kind of shifting "canon" of texts. Although one could also discuss various shared artistic conventions and a formal belief system that underwent a similar process of revision within an orthodox tradition, it is the standard corpus of texts themselves that stand as the clearest expression of Mesopotamian-ness. The preservation and transmission of these texts is especially impressive since various ethnic groups not only participated in Mesopotamian social interactions, but leaders of these ethnic groups became rulers of Mesopotamian cities and regions. If Gutians, Amorites, and Kassites, for example, ruled in the early stages of Mesopotamian history, they did so by appealing to normative Mesopotamian traditions to establish the legitimacy of their rule. No texts in Gutian, Amorite, or Kassite have been found. Indeed, it may be argued that these various ethnic groups were not so much assimilated into Mesopotamian society but actually became prime sponsors of Mesopotamian cultural institutions (Yoffee 1988b).

Within this civilizational boundary, the focal arenas for political struggle were the various city-states and beyond them several regional spheres of interaction. Although Mesopotamian political ideals, especially as are portrayed in the Sumerian King List, held that only one city-state should rule at any one time over all the other city-states in the third millennium BC, it can easily be shown that city-states listed sequentially were contemporaneous and that some powerful cities were omitted entirely from the Sumerian King List. Sargon's conquest of these city-states imposed an ephemeral unity in Mesopotamia, but this pan-Mesopotamian state faced rebellions throughout its existence and eventually disintegrated into the autonomous building blocks from which it had been composed. Similarly, the Ur III state, *c.* 2100–2000 BC, quickly collapsed into autonomous city-states.

In the third millennium and in the first part of the second, southern Mesopotamia can be considered to be composed of two regional entities, a northern and a southern one. The southern region was the location of the most venerable Sumerian city-states, that is, those city-states in which Sumerian was the language of official communication. In the north, especially around Kish, Akkadian seems to have been the common language and, in the dynasty of Sargon, official texts in this region were written in Akkadian. Of course, the admixture of Sumerian and Akkadian ethnolinguistic elements cannot simply be divided into north and south, since Akkadian scribes wrote in Sumerian (Biggs 1967; and Sumerian is written in far-away Ebla) and Akkadian and Sumerian identities were not as important as "citizenship" in individual city-states (Jacobsen 1939; see Kraus 1970). In any case, whatever the differences between central and southern Mesopotamia (Gelb 1981), it is clear that they were both part of a single Mesopotamian sphere of interaction. In the early second millennium BC, political coalitions formed in the aftermath of the breakdown of Ur III that replicated these regional differences. The southernmost region eventually came to be led by Rim-Sin of Larsa while the central Mesopotamian area was controlled by Sumula'el of Babylon. Finally, Hammurabi united both these regions into a pan-Mesopotamian state (save for the Assyrian north). The Babylonian state, however, did not outlast the reign of the successor of Hammurabi and the city-states were again able to re-establish their traditional autonomy.

If southern Mesopotamia could be divided into two sub-regions that were seldom united, the north of Mesopotamia, Assyria, was never subject to lasting southern political dominance. Although Sargonic and Ur III kings controlled Assyrian territories, the city-states of Assyria were but far-flung provinces of evanescent empires. The history of Assyria in the early second millennium is one of independence and political parity with the south. In the first millennium, however, the Assyrian state became transformed into an expansionist imperial organization led by warrior-kings. In this period, Assyria had what has been called its "Babylonian problem." That is, for the Assyrians, while Babylonia seems to have been the heartland of Mesopotamian Culture, it was also politically chaotic (lots of independent city-states there) and morally decadent (most vividly portrayed in Vidal 1981). Assyrian kings occasionally descended into Babylonia to set things right and eventually got caught up in a debilitating civil war that severely diverted manpower and material from Assyria's other foreign policy needs.

Details about this picture need not be supplied here (see Yoffee 1988a for a capsule account of the final collapse of Assyria and Babylonia). It is sufficient to note that Assyria and Babylonia were both part of a larger Mesopotamia in the civilizational sense which I have been discussing. Assyrians copied the same texts, used a Standard Babylonian literary language for some of their inscriptions, and one Assyrian king even ordered that collections of Mesopotamian texts be brought from the south to his library in the north. This overt display of Mesopotamian-ness by the Assyrian kings seems to have been an attempt to stress their traditional ties with a Mesopotamian past that they themselves were undermining through policies of forced incorporation of foreigners in Assyria and in the systematic replacement of the old-line Assyrian aristocracy by new generals and bureaucrats.

The shape of Mesopotamian civilization, I suggest therefore, looks remarkably like that of Maya civilization. One observes an overarching "civilizational" boundary and within it local and regional political boundaries that are the prime foci of political struggle. Of course, there are vast differences between the two civilizations. (It will suffice at this time only to recall the differences in writing – and in the kinds of things that were written – and in the nature of urbanism in the two areas.) At this point, however, I turn briefly to a discussion of elite political and economic struggle in Mesopotamia.

Many studies of the evolution of political power have embraced the notion that temples and priests provided initial leadership in stratified societies (Hocart 1936; Wittfogel 1957; Wheatley 1971; Netting 1972). Many of these opinions seem based on Mesopotamian data and interpretations of the "Tempelstaat" (temple-state) that were initially formulated in the 1920s and then forcefully in the 1950s (Falkenstein 1954). This theory held that all land in each city-state was owned by the temples and that the entire population was dependent on those temple estates. Kingship developed from the temple structure in times of war when extraordinary powers were temporarily granted to appropriate leaders but became permanent over time. This theory was thoroughly discredited in 1969 in two profoundly significant articles (Gelb 1969; Diakonoff 1969): temples did not own all land in city-states in the early third millennium. Royal estates and large "communal" estates also can be documented and councils of community leaders are significantly apparent. In a recent essay one commentator has even suggested not only that the "temple-state" was not the original locus of political leadership in Mesopotamian city-states, but that it arose in specific response to the trend toward areal centralization that culminated in the state created by Sargon (Nissen 1982). The standard interpretation of the so-called "Reforms of UruKAgina" supports this view in that just before the rise of Sargon, in the city-state of Lagash, the temples seem to be reacting to the growing power of the crown.

If elite tension between palace and temple organizations can be seen in the early third millennium BC, another kind of elite interaction can be observed at the start of the second. After the collapse of the Third Dynasty of Ur (*c.* 2000 BC), autonomous city-states battled with their neighbors, seeking autonomy and/or hegemony. The contest over political leadership in these city-states was usually resolved in the accession of ethnic Amorite leaders. The success of these individuals seems to have occurred by means of mobilizing ties of ethnic solidarity that extended beyond the borders of the particular city-states. That is, alliances among related Amorite "chieftains" were forged across city-state lines and these alliances gave a selective advantage in the intracity state struggle for political power (see especially the Uruk-Babylon alliance recorded in the correspondence of King Anam of Uruk). Beyond the level of city-states, however, these Amorite leaders fought among themselves for possession of key cities, especially the venerable cities of Nippur and Kish, which represented claims for traditional Mesopotamian leadership rather than actually being themselves powerful.

Mesopotamian elites were also formed through sources of economic power. The entrepreneurial long-distance trade known in the Old Assyian period (Larsen 1976) rested on the organizational knowledge of how to get goods from where they were plentiful and how to move them to where they were scarce. Vast profits were made through this mercantile system in which the state played almost no role. Indeed, the elite merchant families in Assyria formed powerful councils that shared power with the Assyrian king. The collapse of the Old Assyrian system seems to have occurred, in part, when newly centralized states emerged in Babylonia and Anatolia, two key points in the long-distance trading system, thus cutting off the easy access of goods to Old Assyrian merchants. Deprived of much of the economic foundation for the state's prosperity, the political system itself disintegrated and a subsequent Dark Age in Assyria lasted about 400 years.

In Babylonia to the south before the formation of the Old Babylonian southern and northern cores, under Rim-Sin and Hammurabi respectively, land was bought and sold as family estates grew in power. Rules of partible inheritance were skirted in amazing ways. In one of them, elite women were placed in religious organizations and forbidden to marry and so have legitimate heirs. However, these *nadītus*, although they could not alienate the immovable property that was part of their "dowries" (since this property would pass to their brothers or their brothers' children upon the death of a nadītu), possessed vast sums of "ring-money" which they used to buy enormous amounts of land and other real property. These excellent businesswomen then bequeathed their gains to other nadītus or to slave women who took care of them in their old age and performed the necessary funeral rites after which they were manumitted. The nature of all this enterprise, however, was changed especially when Hammurabi united (briefly) all of Babylonia and attempted to control the economic opportunities of Babylonians (especially in the conquered city-states).

To conclude this regrettably brief section on elite interaction in Mesopotamia, let me only emphasize that the administrative powers of the state, however coercive and encompassing they may have been at various times in Mesopotamian history, were by no means unlimited. Elites who were organized in different social and occupational associations – which exercised a certain autonomy in their own affairs – participated in a struggle for political and economic power. In the Old Assyrian trading colonies, the merchants were organized in councils and the home city of Assur was in part governed through councils of elites. In the Old Babylonian period all extant cases of divorce were settled in local courts, not in the judicial venues of the crown (Yoffee 1988b). The implication of such elite interaction is that ancient Mesopotamian states were not monolithically organized in order to dominate all forms of production, exchange, and political and legal action. An observer from the Mesopotamian social landscape indeed may wonder whether any ancient state can be described as a "functioning whole." Rather, it seems (at least to one of the discussants in the seminar on "The Collapse of Ancient States and Civilizations," Kaufman 1988), that ancient states (no less than modern ones) function with a good deal of bungling and generating conflict within themselves as well as with their neighbors. States were (and are) at best half-understood by the various peoples who made them, coped with them, and struggled against them.

## A REFRACTED IMAGE OF MAYA ELITES

For purposes of direct Maya/Mesopotamia comparison, only a few suggested topics will be considered concerning the separable nature of power that I have outlined (see also Yoffee 1986). Elite competition for political power in Mesopotamia is in large measure focused in the struggle among the elites of the great estates to lead city-states (and, latterly, regions) in the arenas of war, in securing the flow of long-distance goods, and in settling trouble-cases. While a ruling estate achieved dominance within city-states, it did not, nor could it legitimately eliminate all local organizations with their traditional political powers, especially the "community" organizations and the temple estates. For the Maya it seems either that the inter-connection between the palace and the temple estates is very close or that there is no real difference between the two (e.g., Willey 1985b:16). Nevertheless, the nature of Maya palaces themselves remains ambiguous, at least in the sense that such "range structures" seem to be administrative units and not just (royal) living quarters. George Cowgill has recently argued that the Street-of-the-Dead complex at Teotihuacan functioned as a ruler's residence (1983). His point is not that religion and the state at Teotihuacan are in fact totally independent but that there is an institutional (and geographic) integrity to the palace and its personnel and that state-ceremonial rites were not celebrated in temples or by temple elite. Although Mesopotamian leaders were much concerned with claiming a divine legitimacy and even, in some periods, portrayed themselves as divine, the closeness or identity between Maya religious and political authority does seem very different than is the case in Mesopotamia. As a further comparison makes clear, the government in ancient China was completely distinct from the priestly/religious structure (Keightley 1986) which itself was not a participant in political struggle. Thus there exist three different paths to elite political authority in these three cases.

In China, moreover, a key path to political authority lay in the restructuring of "societal" power (in the terms I have adapted from Runciman), in which control of the symbols of cultural commonality was affected through manipulation of the means of communication with the ancestors. Such strategic control enabled the creation of wealth and eventually the unification of the entire countryside. This kind of societal power was never so manipulable in either the Maya or Mesopotamian regions since symbols of pan-regional commonality seemed less effective in mobilizing support than did (traditional) kinship ties and other localized territorial allegiances within city-states/regional-states. In Mesopotamia, specifically, the path to political authority lay far more in the struggle for control over local economic resources and access to long-distance trade goods than in area-wide symbols of literature and art. The individual identities of local ethnic groups and of city-states could not be universalized into any pan-Mesopotamian system of values.

Further separating the Maya and Mesopotamians from the Chinese was the lack of any ideology in the former two cases in which some elites could become "autonomous," that is, owed their organizational existence and status to a transcendental vision rather than to a traditional social organization (Eisenstadt 1986). Such elites "strive to present a comprehensive view of the world, not merely of any particular group, and argue that the main task is to remake present reality, corrupt and imperfect as it is, in accordance with the dictates of a higher moral order." The existence of such elites does "not depend finally on the political establishment, nor on traditional kinship ties, but on individual qualifications, especially intellectual ability" (Machinist 1986:183). The Confucian literati in China were organized according to just such an ideology. These professional bureaucrats, armed with a vision of the Mandate of Heaven and essentially in control of the access to their elite status, maintained an ideal of the Chinese state that transcended the success or failure of any dynast or dynasty. The absence of any indication of this sort of elite among the Maya or in Mesopotamia is striking, while its existence goes far towards explaining the continued ability to remake Chinese civilization after the numerous collapses of specific Chinese states. If, then, it might be considered that the collapses (and kinds of collapses) of ancient states and civilizations are strongly related to the nature of elite interaction in them, it is appropriate that I close this section with a few comments on the enduring question of the Maya collapse.

It can reasonably be inferred from this volume's papers that, whatever other demographic reason, or however exhausted the Maya soil became, intra-elite as well as inter-elite conflict played an important role in the demise of Maya city-states. Such conflict as I have in mind is not allied to the models of warfare presented by Hamblin and Pitcher (1980) and Webster (1977). Rather, my concern is with the organizational difficulty of maintaining an administrative and economic stability in the face of constant drain on manpower and economic reserves that was exacerbated by conditions of endemic warfare. Mathews and Willey explicitly refer to the kind of administrative problem that seems involved in the extension of power by the Dos Pilas dynasty and the nature of resistance to that power. Arguments by Culbert and especially by Fash and Stuart point to the kind of administrative problems that might have been occurring.

For Culbert (this volume) and Adams (1984) provincial elites at Uaxactun and Rio Azul were increasingly caught up in the political situation at Tikal. These elites needed to receive support through participation in political-religious ceremonies at Tikal, to obtain access "to the full panoply of royal prerogatives, inscriptions, elite burials, mortuary temples" (Culbert 1986). At the same time, apparently, "local leaders were being replaced by those from the capital" presumably to administer the borderland area of the Tikal "regional state" more efficiently, at least in the short-term perspective of the capital. Although Jones is impressed with the vitality and resilience of the Tikal state, an outsider is suspicious about the ability of Tikal to insure legitimate support – and important manpower and resources with which to fund its external political affairs – if the scenario portrayed by Culbert is correct.

Fash and Stuart focus in their essay also on the evidence of internal conflict among the Copan elite. In the reign of the last ruler, lineage heads and royal pretenders are able to commemorate their own power at the expense of the ruler of Copan. These elites commission and dedicate sculpture and monuments, even to the extent of using the Emblem Glyph of Copan. Furthermore, these elites are engaged in attracting clients to their own organizations quite outside the normal ties that are imposed by kinship.

It seems that one important component in the Maya collapse might therefore lie in the increasing difficulty of maintaining the regional polities that were put together with so much blood and pain in the Late Classic. In the end, the ideology of leadership, necessitating on the one hand vast ceremonial displays in the urban centers that incorporated rural elites and, on the other hand, an urban managerial interference in provincial districts, undermined the very integrity of regional governance. Since all the regional polities seem to have been caught up in the process of expansion and thus conflict with their neighbors, which increasingly required rural support and rural agricultural intensification, the scale of the Maya collapse might at least in part be described as the fruits of the policy of regional state building itself.

In considering the collapse the most important questions still remain. Why did the collapse process not halt at some lower level of political integration than the city-state and why was there no recovery of a "Classic Maya" state following the collapse? I assume (following especially Culbert) that the growing capitals, which included an increasingly larger proportion of urban ceremonial specialists and attendants of state, were competing with their peers not only for captives but for diminished agricultural resources (imperiled through the slow regenerative qualities of tropical soils upon which unprecedented demands from the regional capitals were being made [Santley *et al.* 1986]). Such competition, then, seems to have restructured both countryside and capital in mutually deleterious ways.

In one way, as portrayed by Culbert and Adams in reference to Tikal's satellite communities of Uaxactun and Rio Azul, the fall of the capital (for whatever complex of reasons) also threatened the viability of the provincial outliers. That is, as governing elites were increasingly being supplied by the capital and tied to the ritually legitimizing ceremonies there, traditional authority in the hinterland was progressively eroded. In the absence of support from the capital, elites with few ties to the people they ruled were presumably "delegitimized" and the hinterland became reduced to its rural base in economy and social organization. In another way, as Fash and Stuart have described at Copan, local elites within the city-state took advantage of royal political weakness. In the ensuing loss of centralized authority that proceeded from intra-elite struggle at Copan, not only was there uncertainty in the succession to political leadership but also the cosmological underpinnings that required royal participation and justified the structure of Maya social and political life were jeopardized. If one is allowed to conflate these admittedly hypothetical cases, then whatever the ecological and demographic pressures that led to progressive abandonment of city-states over the last century or so at the end of the Late Classic, the result was also a loss of the ideological grounding for elite leadership both in the capitals and in the countryside. In the absence of an elite independent of the seats of collapsing royal power (the kind of elite which existed, for example, in the Han and thereafter in China) and who carried an idea of Maya government apart from their own connection to such political power, not only were aspirants unable to exercise power over subject populations, but the Maya "great tradition" – those identifying features that made the Maya Maya – was irrevocably lost.

Nevertheless, ways of Maya life did go on in the northern lowlands and Wren and Schmidt (this volume) may supply the reasons why they did. A new ideology, an amalgam of Mexican and Maya cultural forms, and a new elite had arisen at Chichen Itza. Not only did northern populations have access to different resources than did those in the south, but new ideologies underlay the existence of the rituals that justified a different kind of political leadership and permitted new sorts of alliances with food-producing regions. Rural elite structures may also have been tied into the northern centers in different ways than they were in the south, but with this speculation I must beat my retreat from the brave New World of Maya studies.

## A CASE OF COMPARISON

In *A Study in Scarlet*, when Watson first meets Sherlock Holmes and decides to share lodgings with him, he sets out to catalogue his new friend's interests and idiosyncracies. So, for example, Watson determined that Holmes had vast professional skills in geology. He could tell at a glance at a mud stain on a trouser-cuff where in London a crime had been committed. Similarly, Watson learned that Holmes was no mean botanist. He might not have comprehensive experience, but he was very knowledgeable about certain poisons, especially belladonna. In his entries of Holmes' abilities, however, Watson expressed extreme surprise that Holmes had almost no knowledge of astronomy and was even ignorant about the fact that the earth revolved around the sun! Being a good Victorian scientist himself, Watson thus set forth informing Holmes about the Copernican theory and disabusing him of the notion that the sun revolved around the earth, which had seemed quite natural to Holmes.

After absorbing the good doctor's lecture, however, Holmes retorted that it was all very well that the earth revolved around the sun instead of the reverse, but that this information was of no practical use to him. "You see, Watson," Holmes announced, "my business is detection. There are certain things a detective needs to know and there are other things that are quite irrelevant. Since the brain can only hold so much information, one can't clutter it up with irrelevancies or the real work of detecting won't get done."[6] Holmes then excused himself to get his slipper of cocaine and violin and to begin the process of forgetting the Copernican theory.

Having absorbed the subtle debates on the origin of the Dos Pilas dynasty, the six episodes of expansion at Tikal, the splendor and imagery attendant on Burial 10 (of Curl Nose) at Tikal among other of the important events in Maya history, I hope I may be excused at this point so as to get back to my real work of elucidating administrative and legal structures within Mesopotamian civilization. Perhaps my various musings on the nature of Maya elite interaction have been only so many irrelevant vapors from such a distant perspective as I have on Maya civilization.

If, however, by some happy fluke it is held that a comparative perspective such as I have screwed up my courage to offer does have some interest to experts on the Maya, then I may be permitted one last comment. When all the Maya documents are discovered and completely deciphered and all the complex codes of Maya art become clear and the History of the Maya is authoritatively written, with all the names of the persons and places neatly ordered and phonetically spelled, it is this outsider's prediction that all born-again Maya historians will suddenly remember they were once anthropologists.

Mesopotamianists have battled hard to learn to distrust their ancient texts and to find ways of evaluating the propaganda of the past so as to understand the nature of the civilization those historical materials often seek to disguise or more often simply ignore. By means of hard-fought battles, which are a long way from over, we have found that a comparative perspective can be crucial in guiding us to the questions we need to be asking of our sources. And it is from these questions that we are able to establish the unique qualities of Mesopotamian civilization and better appreciate the fund of data we have at our disposal. It is also from the comparative method that we can catch an occasional glimmer of understanding about what data do not exist in Mesopotamia, data that are critical for the reconstruction of an extinct social system whose extant fragmentary and hopelessly biased remains can never alone suffice for that reconstruction. In this task we are lucky to have the splendid vestiges of the Maya at hand, and especially the stalwart Mayanists who seek to understand them.

## *NOTES*

1. Only the shell of the building was completed in 1986 when the S.A.R. conference took place. Linnea Wren and Clemency Coggins informed me in Santa Fe that "pitched roofs" are not only not unusual, they are diagnostic features of post-modern architectural trends of the 1980s.
2. Clemency Coggins and Linnea Wren have instructed me that post-modernist architecture cannot be interpreted as an expression of Reaganomics. They are probably extrapolating to the Old Pueblo an East Coast view of architectural styles (which is perhaps analogous to the Tikalocentric view of Maya civilization that once dominated Maya studies).

3. My essay (Yoffee 1986) comparing ancient China with Mesopotamian civilization, each having very different sorts of elites and so differing evolutionary trajectories, represents an attempt to illustrate the utility of this theory.
4. My observations in this paper are obviously the result of having assiduously studied the essays that were submitted to the 1986 S.A.R. seminar (which essays and citations from them – but without specific page numbers – are occasionally referenced in this paper) and the discussions that subsequently took place in Santa Fe; they are not based on any original or substantial knowledge of Maya civilization. I am pleased not only to acknowledge my invitation to comment on the proceedings but also to thank all participants for putting up with my comments and for responding cheerfully and informatively to my questions. It was a relief to know that the real purpose of inviting a Mesopotamianist to a Maya conference was not to replicate some Maya ceremony without having to do away with a real Mayanist.
5. For "proto-historical" stirrings, i.e., those comments on Maya history made before this volume, see Norman Hammond's introductory chapter in this volume.
6. I have paraphrased Holmes' words. For the original see page 10 in *The Complete Sherlock Holmes* by A. Conan Doyle published by Doubleday and Company, Inc. (1956).

# 13
# Maya political history and elite interaction: a summary view

T. PATRICK CULBERT

This article draws together the results of our papers and our week of seminar discussions in Santa Fe. Substantively, this volume provides the first synthesis of the political history of the Classic period lowland Maya. The first section of this paper summarizes that history. The next section deals with elite interaction, a consideration of what the conjunction of epigraphic, iconographic, and archaeological data tells us about the mechanisms by which individuals, social groups, and polities interacted. Next, the more abstract models and comparisons that may be useful in understanding the structure of Classic Maya society are considered, before a final section that presents conclusions and the prospects for future development along the lines taken here.

## THE PRECLASSIC

The Late Preclassic (and Protoclassic for those who use the term) provides the base from which the dynastic structure evident in the Early Classic emerged. There can be no doubt that some sites, especially Mirador (Matheny 1986), were very large during the Late Preclassic. The Tikal evidence (Coe 1965a; Jones, this volume) shows that a complex that included large temples, elite burials covered by shrines, and murals that depict many of the royal trappings of Classic times had emerged by AD 1. There are also Preclassic monuments in the lowlands that include inscriptions that name individuals, even though such monuments have a stronger emphasis on ceremony than those of Classic times (Mathews 1985). The complexity and far-flung interconnections of the lowland Maya in the Preclassic are undeniable. Sharer (this volume) makes the important suggestion that this was a time during which interaction between polities both within and outside the lowlands contributed to the formulation of what was to be Classic civilization.

Was there a major change in political orientation between the Preclassic and the Classic? Freidel and Schele (1983) suggest that there was and that the cult of the king as an individual emerged from a more general theocratic elite at this time, an idea that Sharer (this volume) also espouses. The topic of the Preclassic–Classic transition was treated in papers and in seminar discussions and the strong consensus was that elements of continuity outweighed changes. Mathews and Willey (this volume) stress the continuity in architectural form and location at Pasion sites. Jones (this volume) raises the possibility that the Classic period dynastic list of Tikal kings may have started as early as AD 170, 13 katuns before Stormy Sky's inauguration. Schele reports that Copan inscriptions mention kings who predate the Classic dynastic list and stresses that the institution of kingship may well represent a cultural complex that spread throughout the lowlands in the Late Preclassic.

## THE EARLY CLASSIC: DATA

Dynastic inscriptions and the dynastic monument complex ("stela cult") began during the Early Classic. All Cycle 8 (before AD 435) monuments are at sites in the northeast Peten, although dynastic founders of this period are reported in later inscriptions of other regions. Early in Cycle 9 (AD 435–534), sites in other lowland regions began to erect monuments and by 9.5.0.0.0 (AD 534) hieroglyphic inscriptions had spread across the lowlands. For most sites, however, the Early Classic record is slim because of the scarcity of surviving monuments.

### *The western region* (Schele; Schele and Mathews, this volume)

Yaxchilan, Piedras Negras, and Bonampak carved inscriptions using Emblem Glyphs and naming rulers at various dates between 9.3.0.0.0 and 9.6.0.0.0 (AD 495 and 554). There is no indication that major sites were anything other than independent polities nor is there much evidence of interaction, except for Yaxchilan, whose inscriptions record royal visits from sites as distant as El Peru and Tikal.

There has been so little published archaeology for the western region that there is almost no information about the size of sites during the Early Classic. Even Palenque, which has frequently been cited as a place where the early rulers were no more than village headmen, provides hints of Early Classic burials and buildings in levels below those that have been investigated archaeologically. It does not seem likely to me, however, that any of the sites achieved the size of Early Classic sites in the Peten.

### *The Pasion region* (Mathews and Willey, this volume)

Altar de Sacrificios, Arroyo de Piedra/Tamarindito, and Tres Islas have written records that start between 9.1.0.0.0 and 9.2.0.0.0 (AD 455 and 475). The most complete record is from Altar de Sacrificios, where three rulers are named between 9.1.0.0.0 and 9.4.10.0.0 (AD 455 and 524) and another at the very end of the Early Classic. Arroyo de Piedra and Tamarindito shared the same Emblem Glyph and named the same rulers between 9.1.17.10.8 and 9.6.0.0.0 (AD 472 and 554), and were almost certainly parts of a single polity. None of the sites in the region is known to have been very large in the Early Classic, and the inscriptions suggest small-scale independent polities that give no record of interacting with each other.

### *Southeast region* (Fash and Stuart; Sharer, this volume)

Both Copan and Quirigua have Early Classic inscriptions beginning with a firm date of 9.0.0.0.0 (AD 435) at Copan and 9.2.3.8.0 (AD 478) at Quirigua. Although construction levels of this date are deeply buried and poorly explored at both sites, there is no evidence of large monumental architecture. Ceramically, Copan relates to the

Guatemalan highlands and Pacific coast rather than to the Maya lowlands, but Fash and Stuart favor the idea that the population was always Maya. They see the adoption of lowland elite art and writing as emulation of a prestigious model by a local Maya elite. For Quirigua, Sharer believes that elite culture was a result of an intrusion of low-landers, perhaps from Tikal, who ruled over a non-Maya indigenous population.

### *The northeast Peten* (Jones; Culbert, this volume)

The best combined record of archaeology and inscriptions for the Early Classic is from the northeast Peten. Eleven sites in the region have Early Classic inscriptions; six of them have their own Emblem Glyphs (Mathews 1985). Major research projects at Uaxactun, Tikal, and Rio Azul have produced extensive archaeological data, including critical information from elite burials.

The Tikal inscriptions provide a reasonably complete dynastic list between Moon Zero Bird, who acceded on 8.14.3.1.12 (AD 320), and Double Bird, who still occupied the throne at 9.6.13.17.0 (AD 567). Burials 10 and 48, identified with some security as those of the rulers Curl Nose and Stormy Sky (Coggins 1975), add detail to the dynastic record and show artifactual ties with Teotihuacan. Tikal is the only Early Classic site for which a domain can be estimated from the epigraphic evidence. Tikal's realm extended over a radius of some 25 km, including El Zapote to the south and Uaxactun to the north. The takeover of Uaxactun by Tikal on 8.17.1.4.12 (AD 378) is the only Early Classic case in which political (probably military) expansion of a site's territory is well attested. Given the concentration of monuments in the northeast Peten in the Early Classic, it is disappointing that more cannot be said about interaction, but further evidence may emerge when inscriptions from sites other than Tikal have been reported.

Archaeologically, Tikal, Uaxactun, and Rio Azul were all very large during the Early Classic. Their total mass of monumental construction far outweighs that known from other lowland regions. The contention that the northeast Peten was the core of Maya lowland civilization at least until the start of the hiatus (9.5.0.0.0; AD 534) seems to me to be supported by the archaeological, as well as the epigraphic, evidence.

## THE EARLY CLASSIC: DISCUSSION

The paucity of both epigraphic and archaeological data for the Early Classic makes reconstructions of events and institutions more tentative than for the Late Classic. Nevertheless, a set of conclusions and problems emerges that raise issues for future research.

### *Teotihuacan contact*

That Maya lowland sites were in contact with Teotihuacan is beyond dispute. The contact began early. Maya imitations of cylindrical tripods, the importation of green obsidian, and talud-and-tablero architecture go back at least to the beginning of the Early Classic at Altun Ha (Pendergast 1971), Becan (Ball 1979a), and Tikal (Laporte and Fialko n.d.).

The indications of Teotihuacan influence are strongest in the northeast Peten, and especially at Tikal, although this may be primarily a function of the greater amount of archaeological research done there. In seminar discussions, the participants were agreed that there were probably Teotihuacan colonies resident at some Maya sites. There was less agreement about the effect of Teotihuacan upon Maya culture, with opinions running the gamut noted in my paper (this volume) on the northeast Peten. I think it a mistake to downplay too much the role that Teotihuacan may have played in the lowlands. The evidence of quite direct Teotihuacan contact at Tikal has been strengthened by the research of the Proyecto Nacional Tikal (Laporte and Fialko n.d.) and it is likely that comparable evidence may be forthcoming when more research has been done on sites like Yaxha. I doubt that Teotihuacanos ever ruled at Maya lowland sites, but it is quite possible that they may have interfered in political affairs, and even dynastic succession, by throwing their strength behind local factions.

Current evidence suggests the strongest Teotihuacan contact occurred in the late fourth and early fifth centuries. It is not beyond the realm of possibility, however, that Teotihuacan may have been involved considerably earlier in the major realignments at the end of the Preclassic that saw the death of Mirador and the beginning of the northeast Peten surge (Coggins 1979). On the other hand, direct interaction with Mexicans probably ceased too early to have been responsible for whatever cultural disruption was associated with the monument hiatus at the end of the Early Classic.

### *Early Classic elite interaction*

The Early Classic lacks the abundant record of elite interaction that creates such a rich network of interconnections in the Late Classic. Nevertheless, most of the mechanisms that tied sites together were already in operation. The pattern of royal visits (Schele and Mathews, this volume) was already established at Yaxchilan in the Early Classic. The abundant depictions of prisoners show that warfare was already important and the Uaxactun-Tikal case demonstrates actual political takeover. Intersite marriages are the only mechanism not surely attested, although the problematic origin of Curl Nose of Tikal hints at intermarriage. The Early Classic Maya, then, seem to have interacted in the same ways as their Late Classic descendants. If there were differences in elite interaction between the two periods, they must have been ones of degree rather than of kind.

## THE HIATUS

There was considerable seminar discussion about the hiatus – the period at the end of the Early Classic (9.5.0.0.0 to 9.8.0.0.0; AD 534 to 593) when contemporary inscriptions are lacking at a number of sites. Willey, who had argued earlier (1974) that the hiatus was a period of cultural disruption, still considers the phenomenon a significant one for the central and western lowlands. Mathews and Schele question whether the hiatus is not a "Tikal-centric" concept based upon the gap in inscriptions at that site and not of general significance.

The data from the western (Schele, this volume) and Pasion (Mathews and Willey, this volume) regions are equivocal. Almost all sites have monument gaps of at least three katuns, and only Stela 4 at Tamarindito (9.6.0.0.0; AD 554), Altar 1 at Altar de Sacrificios (9.7.15.12.9; AD 589) and possibly Stela 29 at Piedras Negras fall into the traditional hiatus interval. But the data from these regions are fragmentary enough to argue that the apparent gaps may be filled by yet-to-be-discovered monuments.

At Tikal, there are two gaps in the monument record (Jones and Satterthwaite 1982; Jones, this volume). After Stelae 10 and 12 were erected at 9.4.13.0.0 (AD 527), there are no known monuments until Stela 17 was dedicated at some time between the middle and end of Katun 6. Jones believes, however, that monuments that dated to this gap were destroyed prehistorically. After Stela 17, there were no further monuments until Ruler A dedicated his first stela at 9.13.0.0.0 (AD 692).

The earlier monument gap may have been a time of political troubles at Tikal. The succession numbers of rulers indicate that seven rulers held the Tikal throne within a single katun before the inauguration of Double Bird at 9.5.3.9.15 (AD 537). Although Double Bird ruled at least twenty years, he was probably the victim of a defeat that Caracol inflicted upon Tikal at 9.6.8.4.2 (AD 562; Houston 1987) – a defeat that may have ended his career. After Double Bird, Tikal may have been under the control of a Caracol-imposed line of rulers and denied the prerogative of inscriptions until Ruler A reasserted that right eleven years after his inauguration (Schele and Freidel n.d.; Culbert, this volume). Elsewhere in the northeast Peten, the number of monuments between 9.5.0.0.0 and 9.8.0.0.0 (AD 534 and 593) is noticeably less than in both the preceding and following intervals, although both Uaxactun and El Peru celebrated the katun end at 9.6.0.0.0 (AD 554).

The eastern side of the lowlands was the area least affected by the hiatus. Caracol had a series of monuments during the interval and a strong dynasty that may have founded a multi-center polity (Chase and Chase 1987; Culbert, this volume). Copan also had an uninterrupted set of monuments, although the material they cover is unknown to me, and Fash and Stuart (this volume) speak of the Late Classic ruler Smoke-Imix-God K as the one who put Copan on the map, so to speak.

Although the breadth and meaning of the hiatus cannot be determined with certainty until more data have been recovered, it seems to me that a significant number of sites still show gaps in inscriptions toward the end of the Early Classic and the start of the Late Classic.

## THE LATE CLASSIC: DATA

The Late Classic was the peak period of Maya population and construction, as well as a time at which inscriptions were more abundant and more verbose. The dynastic records for many sites are nearly complete for this period, and most of the evidence for elite interaction comes from Late Classic inscriptions.

*The western region* (Schele; Schele and Mathews, this volume)

The rich inscriptional record of the western region provides a good picture of political structure and site interaction. Each major site had subsidiary sites within a 25 km radius whose inscriptions acknowledge allegiance to the central site. The major sites seem usually to have had friendly relationships and to have sought each other's support. Piedras Negras and Yaxchilan exchanged royal visits on the occasions of major political ceremonies. So did Yaxchilan and Bonampak where ties were also solidified by joint military campaigns and at least one royal intermarriage.

Both art and inscriptions from the western region make it clear that warfare was of considerable importance to royal prestige. Most of the engagements resulted in the capture of lords from small or unknown sites that may have been related to maintaining or extending local realms, or simply to the capture of prisoners for sacrifice. But there were also occasional conflicts between the major sites. Shield Jaguar of Yaxchilan captured a lord of Bonampak, and Tonina (in its peripheral location) seems to have been outside the sphere of friendly interaction and more generally bellicose. Tonina captured the ruler Kan-Xul of Palenque and possibly two other Palenque lords in what must have been a long-standing struggle. In addition, a lord of Bonampak acknowledges the overlordship of Ruler 3 of Tonina, suggesting at least a temporary extension of Tonina rule into an area close to the Usumacinta. This is the only case in the western region in which one major site seems to have been ruled by another.

Sites in the west occasionally attest interaction with sites in other regions. A representative of a Tikal ruler visited Piedras Negras and Bird-Jaguar of Yaxchilan seems to have attended the funeral ceremonies depicted on the famous vase from Altar de Sacrificios (Adams 1977b). Yaxchilan records intermarriages with women from El Peru and Motul de San Jose, while Palenque sent a woman to marry the ruler of distant Copan in the time of troubles after Copan was defeated by Quirigua. The only hostile interaction with other regions is the claim of Dos Pilas to have defeated a lord of Yaxchilan.

Overall, the western region gives the impression of major sites with relatively stable territories whose interrelations were more often friendly than belligerent.

*The Pasion region* (Mathews and Willey, this volume; Houston and Matthews 1985)

In the Pasion region, Dos Pilas established a multi-center polity that was both more expansionist and more strongly interconnected with the northeast Peten than any site in the other regions. The history of Dos Pilas begins with the accession of Ruler 1 (Flint Sky) in 9.10.12.11.2 (AD 645). Ruler 1 seems to have been an outsider, perhaps from Tikal, who established his position through both marriage and conquest. Marriages tied him to Itzan and El Chorro as well as to Naranjo in the northeast Peten. His records claim several military victories, although his captives cannot be identified with known sites. Ruler 2 extended the hegemony of Dos Pilas to include Arroyo de Piedra/Tamarindito where the local ruler expressed fealty in 9.15.0.0.0 (AD 731). This Tamarindito ruler was the son of a Dos Pilas woman, so marriage may have been the mechanism used to gain control of the site. Rulers 3 and 4 embarked upon adventuresome military campaigns that enlarged the polity substantially. On 9.15.4.6.5 (AD 735), Ruler 3 captured a lord of Seibal, an event that brought Seibal into the Dos Pilas realm for a period of sixty years. Ruler 4 captured lords of Cancuen and El Chorro and even claimed a successful military encounter against Yaxchilan.

At its maximum extent during the reign of Ruler 4 (9.15.9.17.17–9.16.9.15.3; AD 741–60), the Dos Pilas polity extended about 80 km north–south and 50 km east–west. Although the maximum realm may not have endured for more than about two katuns, at least half the territory was under Dos Pilas control for a century. Mathews believes that the scope and expansionist character of Dos Pilas was an anomaly, a view that I have challenged (Culbert, this volume). Whether or not anomalous, the Dos Pilas polity was not long lasting. By 9.17.0.0.0 (AD 771), a lord using the Dos Pilas Emblem Glyph was mentioned at several sites, but not at Dos Pilas (by this time centered at Aguateca). The polity seems to have split, either in an amicable joint rule or by political fragmentation. The latter may be more likely because by 9.18.0.0.0 (AD 790) inscriptions had ceased at

Dos Pilas and Aguateca and sites that had been part of the realm began to erect their own monuments.

Dos Pilas had strong ties with the northeast Peten. There was a close relationship with Jaguar Paw-Jaguar of El Peru or Calakmul, whose accession was recorded at Dos Pilas, a marital tie to Naranjo through Ruler 1's daughter, and the commemoration of Ruler 2's death on the carved bones in the tomb of Ruler A of Tikal (Jones 1986).

Elsewhere in the Pasion zone, Altar de Sacrificios has known rulers until 9.11.10.0.0 (AD 662) and then fades from the inscriptional record. El Chorro has six recorded rulers between 9.13.0.0.0 and 9.17.0.0.0 (AD 692 and 771) and Itzan has several rulers in the Late Classic, although there are also gaps in its monumental record. Mathews and Willey (this volume) believe that all these sites retained their independence through the Late Classic. This would make Dos Pilas an exception in the Pasion region, a single multi-center polity amidst small independent units.

### *The southeast region* (Fash and Stuart; Sharer, this volume)

Copan and Quirigua continued to dominate the southeast region in the Late Classic. Copan was the larger of the two sites and the one that had the greatest impact in pan-Maya elite interaction.

Copan's Late Classic eminence began with the reign of Smoke-Imix-God K (Smoke Jaguar). In addition to celebrating himself in numerous Copan monuments, he may have ruled Quirigua, for one of his monuments is located there. His successor 18 Jog (18 Rabbit) began his career with a flourish. It was 18 Jog who erected Stela A, the "four capitals" monument (Marcus 1973) that names Copan, Palenque, Tikal, and El Peru. His career was abruptly terminated, however, when he was captured and sacrificed by Cauac Sky of Quirigua in 9.15.6.14.6 (AD 738).

The defeat does not seem to have long affected Copan. Construction of Structure 10L–26 and its hieroglyphic stairway soon began as a testimony to the glories of past Copan rulers. Augmenting its prestige by intermarriage with a woman of Palenque, Copan prospered under Yax Sun-at-Horizon (Yax Pac), who was inaugrated in 9.16.12.5.17 (AD 763) and probably ruled until his successor, U Cit-Tok was inaugurated in 9.19.11.14.5 (AD 822; Grube and Schele 1987). Yax Sun-at-Horizon even resumed relations of some sort with Quirigua for he is noted as performing a scattering rite there on 9.19.0.0.0 (AD 811). Aside from Altar L, which records his accession but was never finished, there is no further notice of U Cit-Tok.

Quirigua must have gained its independence from Copan by the time of Cauac Sky's inauguration at 9.14.13.4.7 (AD 725) or soon thereafter. The capture of 18 Jog on 9.15.6.14.6 (AD 738) was certainly the most important event in Cauac Sky's life and perhaps in the history of Quirigua. The victory touched off a period of population expansion, major construction, and monument erection apparently intended to outshine the glories of Copan. The last Quirigua monument was erected by the ruler Jade Sky in 9.18.15.0.0 (AD 805), but even after that time construction continued in the Acropolis, although perhaps under the aegis of new leaders connected with Yucatan.

Perhaps because of the distances involved, there is not much indication that the southeastern sites interacted with other Maya centers. The long-distance marriage of a Copan ruler with a woman of Palenque and a possible mention of 18 Jog at Tikal in addition to the stela that mentions Tikal, Palenque, and El Peru are the only citations of other sites. In cultural affiliations below the elite level, the southeastern sites always looked away from the lowlands toward the southern highlands and lower Central America, and several participants at the seminar stressed the key location of the sites for trade to areas outside the Maya lowlands.

### *The northeast Peten* (Jones; Culbert, this volume; Schele 1986e)

The northeast Peten is a region with abundant Late Classic data, but substantial disagreements about interpretation. Just to the east of the region, Caracol had a vigorous dynasty at the end of the Early Classic and beginning of the Late Classic that embarked on military ventures into the Peten (Chase and Chase 1987). Caracol claims to have defeated Tikal on 9.6.8.4.2. (AD 562) and Naranjo on 9.9.18.6.3 and 9.10.3.2.12 (AD 631 and 636). After the last defeat, Naranjo was either abandoned or ruled by Caracol for nearly two katuns. The recent discovery by Schele and Freidel (n.d.) that Calakmul (or El Peru?) seems to have been involved in the conquest of Naranjo indicates political action of broader scope that may have involved the entire northeast Peten.

I have suggested (this volume, chapter 6) that Tepeu 1 (9.8.0.0.0 to 9.13.0.0.0; AD 593 to 692) was a period of relative weakness in the northeast Peten, a weakness probably related to the strength of Caracol. Rio Azul and Uaxactun both seem to have had diminished population and building activity. Naranjo was silent and Tikal had no monuments and may have been ruled by dynasts imposed by Caracol. Although Xultun and El Peru have Tepeu 1 monuments, they are too poorly reported to draw conclusions. It was not until halfway through Katun 12 (about AD 682) that northeast Peten sites began to show new vigor.

Naranjo began a campaign to regain its lost status on 9.12.10.5.12 (AD 682) with the arrival of Lady Six Sky, daughter of Ruler 1 of Dos Pilas, presumably to marry a surviving local lord. The birth of Smoking Squirrel five years later and his inauguration at the age of five led to a rapid series of military ventures that culminated in the capture of a lord of Ucanal. The movement was successful because Naranjo was thereafter a major site for most of the Late Classic.

El Peru, 80 km west of Tikal, was an important site although it is lamentably known almost entirely from looted materials. This creates a problem in identifying the site of Jaguar Paw-Jaguar, an important ruler of either El Peru or Calakmul, whichever is the home of the "Site Q" Emblem Glyph. Jaguar Paw-Jaguar's birth was recorded at both Calakmul and El Peru and his accession on 9.12.13.17.7 (AD 686) was noted at Dos Pilas as well as Site Q. He was closely linked with Ruler 1 of Dos Pilas and Schele and Freidel (n.d.) believe that he may have been little more than a puppet of the Dos Pilas king. His career seems to have been ended by his capture by Ruler A of Tikal on 9.13.3.7.18 (AD 695). Site Q, wherever it was, played an important role in regional contacts.

There are no stelae at Tikal from the Tepeu 1 horizon, but the burial of Animal Skull at 9.8.0.0.0 or 9.9.0.0.0 (AD 593 or 613) touched off major architectural development. Features of Animal Skull's burial and the fact that his father does not bear the Tikal Emblem Glyph suggest that he may have been an outsider (Coggins 1975; Jones, this volume) perhaps imposed by Caracol. The period until the inauguration of Ruler A (Ah Cacau) at 9.12.9.17.16 (AD 682) is not clear, but included Burials 23 and 24 and the life (and reign?) of Ruler A's father, Shield Skull.

The time of Ruler A (9.12.9.17.16–??; AD 682–??) and Ruler B

(9.15.3.6.8–at least 9.16.4.9.8; AD 734–55) was a period of glory for Tikal. Jones documents the passion of both rulers for monumental architecture and inscriptions. The iconography is replete with prisoners, although only Ruler A's capture of Jaguar Paw-Jaguar of El Peru in 9.13.3.7.18 (AD 695) and a defeat of Yaxha in Ruler B's reign (9.15.12.2.2; AD 743) refer to known sites. In addition to Jaguar Paw-Jaguar, Ruler A mentions 18 Rabbit (of Copan?), Ruler 2 of Dos Pilas, and a lord of Piedras Negras or El Peru in his inscriptions, demonstrating the breadth of his political connections.

The area under Tikal's political control during the reigns of Rulers A and B is a matter of debate. Everyone would agree on a minimal domain that extended from Lake Peten Itza northward through Uaxactun and was delimited by the territories of Naranjo and El Peru on the east and west. This would be about 2,500 $km^2$ and, given the dense populations indicated by surveys for the area, is estimated to have had a population in excess of 425,000 (Culbert *et al.* n.d.). I do not believe, however, that a full delineation of polity size and political structure will be possible until account has been taken of the interconnections between Tikal, Naranjo, Dos Pilas, and El Peru that may suggest coordinated political activity of a substantially larger scope (Culbert, this volume, chapter 6). We badly need more data on the inscriptions of Xultun and El Peru and the archaeology of these sites and that of Naranjo before we can make more solid interpretations of the history of the northeast Peten.

## LATE CLASSIC: DISCUSSION

Although the Late Classic was a time of huge population, massive construction projects and mighty rulers, it took several katuns for the most important sites to emerge in full flower. Between 9.8.0.0.0 and 9.10.0.0.0 (AD 593 and 633), only Caracol seems to have had a strong dynasty. In the next two katuns, Pacal at Palenque, Smoke-Imix-God K at Copan and Ruler 1 at Dos Pilas began to build the strength of their sites, at least the latter two partly by military means.

The period between 9.12.0.0.0 and 9.17.0.0.0 (AD 672 and 771) was a golden century for the Maya elite. Schele (1986e) has pointed out that the katun that opened this interval was distinguished by the overlapping of the most loudly acclaimed set of rulers in Maya history. Ruler 1 of Dos Pilas and Smoke-Imix-God K ruled throughout the katun and Pacal died at about its midpoint and was succeeded by Chan Bahlum. Shield Jaguar took the throne of Yaxchilan at 9.12.9.8.1 (AD 681), Ruler A was inaugurated at Tikal on 9.12.9.17.16 (AD 682), and Lady Six Sky arrived to rejuvenate Naranjo on 9.12.10.5.12 (AD 682). All of these sites raged out on multiple military campaigns to give katuns 13 and 14 (AD 692–731) a very warlike character (Schele 1986e). At least Dos Pilas and Tikal established multi-center polities during the century. Meanwhile, monument after monument and building after building proclaimed the marvels of the time. By 9.17.0.0.0 (AD 771), the luster had begun to fade and there were increasing signs of political fragmentation to be discussed in the next section. For the period before 9.17.0.0.0 (AD 771), I would call attention to several important research issues.

### *Understanding the Maya lowlands as a whole*

Inscriptions, art, and archaeology all provide data on individual sites. At thoroughly investigated sites, complicated series of events including royal careers, ceremonial activities, and pulses of construction emerge with increasing clarity. None of our evidence produces such clear information on interaction between sites. But the Maya lowlands were certainly an interactive whole in which events at one site influenced those at others and in which the elite actors were bound together by complicated networks of kinship, alliance, and ceremony. As a concrete example, there were complex interactions among Dos Pilas, El Peru, Naranjo, and Tikal in the Late Classic that involved a shared Emblem Glyph, movements of rulers, joint commemorations of events, intermarriages, and simultaneous military campaigns. We can hardly understand the history of any of these individual sites until we know more about how they interacted, a matter that is not an easy task – yet it is one that must absorb increasing effort in future research.

### *The role of the northeast Peten*

Several participants at the seminar suggested that many interpretations of Maya development have been "Tikal-centric"; i.e., strongly influenced by the weight of data from the site and by the number of archaeologists who have worked there and tend to see the Maya from a viewpoint that looks from Tikal outward. Mathews (1985:31) offers a contrasting view: "My impression is that from about 9.5.0.0.0 on, Tikal prefers to live with its memories of past political greatness, rather than to take a leading or even an active role in Late Classic regional politics."

The centrality of Tikal is clearly at issue, but by implication a broader question is involved – the role of the entire northeast Peten in Maya history. Undoubtedly the region was central in establishing the dynastic monument complex. After that time, however, we must ask whether it maintained some sort of centrality for the whole lowland area, or became simply another region, perhaps even conservative and isolated by the Late Classic.

### *The size of political units*

There was a strong consensus at the seminar in favor of the view that Maya political units were usually of small scale, probably in the order of single major sites and surrounding territories of 25 km radius. If Emblem Glyphs are used as the means to identify independent units, the number of units increased through time and the size of their territories decreased as Mathews' maps (1985) suggest. As indicated in my paper (this volume, chapter 6), I disagree with this interpretation and believe that the issue will be a matter for debate and research in coming years.

## END LATE CLASSIC AND TERMINAL CLASSIC

Towards the end of the Late Classic, a pattern emerged that I believe to be indicative of changing political conditions and the stresses that were soon to cause the Maya collapse. The pattern was first identified by Fash (1985; Fash and Stuart, this volume) at Copan. There, beginning at 9.17.10.0.0 (AD 780), carved inscriptions appeared in the residences of local nobles. The nobles are named and claim relationship to the ruler Yax Pac (Yax Sun–at–Horizon); one, a probable brother of Yax Pac (Schele and Grube 1987), was even seated in some office that conferred upon him the right to use the Copan Emblem Glyph. Fash attributes the practice to a move by Yax Pac to gain support from nobles at a time of increasing stress.

I believe that the phenomenon is represented on an even broader scale in other regions. In the northeast Peten, Uaxactun erected its first monument after a silence of 10 katuns in 9.16.0.0.0 (AD 751). At 9.17.0.0.0 or 9.17.10.0.0 (AD 771 or 780), Nakum, La Honradez, Ixcun, and Rio Azul erected either their initial monuments or the first after a long break. I believe this indicates that these sites were granted the prerogatives of stela erection and Emblem Glyphs by larger sites to which they were subservient, although it might also mean that lesser sites claimed their independence from their overlords. In the Pasion region, the appearance at 9.17.0.0.0 (AD 771) of a lord who uses the Dos Pilas Emblem Glyph but does not reign at Dos Pilas/Aguateca, could be another instance of the same process (Mathews and Willey, this volume). The mechanism of gaining support by honoring lesser nobles in inscriptions was not a new one because Bird-Jaguar had used it earlier to curry favor among the *cahals* of Yaxchilan (Schele, this volume). The proliferation of the process after 9.17.0.0.0 (AD 771) is almost surely, as Fash suggests, a sign of stress in much the same manner that a proliferation of royal titles in China signaled increasing instability at the end of each dynasty. Yoffee (1977) has noted a comparable phenomenon in Mesopotamia.

In Cycle 10 (after AD 830), there was a further burst of sites that began to erect monuments. Many of these sites were small and they tended to be located either very close to larger sites (e.g,. Jimbal and Ixlu near Tikal) or in peripheral areas like the Belize River Valley where inscriptions had previously not existed. Although there is no way of being certain, I suspect that by this late date minor nobles may simply have been taking advantage of a disintegrating political situation to claim independence and a brief moment of glory, a conclusion that Yoffee (this volume) also reaches.

The Cycle 10 inscriptions do not give much history. There are no inscriptions in the southeast region and only the remnant dynasty at Tonina in the west. Although there are more inscriptions in the northeast Peten and in Belize, the picture they give is confusing and fragmentary. Jimbal, Ixlu, and Tikal, for example, all use the Tikal Emblem Glyph and seem to name different rulers (Jones and Satterthwaite 1982). Most of the Cycle 10 monuments in the northeast Peten and Belize differ in some ways from the Classic tradition and many show elements that are thought to relate to Yucatan.

The most notable Cycle 10 flourish in the south was that at Seibal where a new dynasty had emerged by 10.0.0.0.0 (AD 830). Mathews and Willey (this volume) suggest that the new royal line may have been foreigners, and the possible Yucatecan elements in the late Seibal monuments have been noted frequently. The Seibal florescence resulted in major construction in Group A, but was short lived and disappeared after 10.3.0.0.0 (AD 889).

In Cycle 10, the northern lowlands began to assume the luster that had been lost in the south. The much-debated dating of Toltec Chichen Itza seems now thrust back into the early part of Cycle 10 with the Great Ball Court Stone having a likely date of 10.1.15.3.6 (AD 864; Wren 1986) and Kakupacal's inscriptions clustering between 10.2.0.1.9 and 10.2.12.2.4 (AD 869 and 881). Wren and Schmidt (this volume) suggest that the Chichen Toltec represented a new political order. Rather than a system created by an invading Toltec elite dominating a native Maya populace, the new order involved a variety of both Maya and Mexican factions whose elite merged elements from their two traditions in both a new art style and a new political style. The political change that allowed the Chichen-Toltec to adapt to changing conditions in a way that southern polities could not was the separation of political offices from the personalities of office-holders. Freed from an obsession with royal lineages and the charismatic leadership of rulers, the new focus allowed greater flexibility and social mobility. Most of the seminar participants were agreed that this change in institutional structure provided the Maya for the first time with the means to supercede the limiting boundaries of small scale polities and made possible a true regional state centered at Chichen Itza.

## ELITE INTERACTION

In addition to the substantive reconstruction of political history, the seminar was concerned with the ways in which the Maya elite interacted. The discussions of this topic involved an exciting exploration of new research territory that gradually unfolded as we shared ideas and information. The inscriptions provide only the *results* of elite interaction. The rules and regularities of Classic Maya social structure that underlie those results must be inferred by the kind of black-box procedure to which Hammond (this volume, chapter 10) refers. It is in the derivation of such structural regularities that the translation of Maya hieroglyphic writing seems to me to offer the most exciting possibilities and a precision of detail that would never be provided by other kinds of evidence.

*Emblem Glyphs* (Mathews 1985; this volume)

Although Emblem Glyphs can hardly be called a means of interaction, they are critical to interpretation of the inscriptions because they are the primary identifier of the sociohistoric context of individuals. An individual with a name but no Emblem Glyph is hopelessly adrift in the sea of inscriptions with neither point of origin nor social standing. A good case in point are the numerous named, but otherwise unidentified, prisoners in Maya art. We have no idea whether they were rival or rebellious nobles from the polities of their captors, chiefs of small sites, or military leaders from other sites who were not important enough to bear their homelands' emblems.

In chapter 2, Mathews reviews our knowledge of Emblem Glyphs. It now seems clear that the Main Signs of Emblem Glyphs are toponyms, identifying either a specific site or a polity (including both a site and its territory). The total assemblage that comprises an Emblem Glyph is a title, indicating the association of an individual with a particular place or polity. There are so many cases of individuals who were not rulers using Emblem Glyphs that it is obvious that this identifier was available to a *group* of upper-level elite, but the rules and restrictions governing its usage cannot yet be derived. In interpretation, the question of whether Emblem Glyph usage is or is not a sure indication of political autonomy is critical to a reconstruction of political history. Alternative viewpoints are discussed by Mathews (1985; this volume) and Culbert (this volume, chapter 6).

*Social status* (Schele; Fash and Stuart; Hammond, this volume; Schele and Miller 1986)

From the sheer complexity of Maya civilization, it has long been obvious that there must have been a number of social levels in Maya society. Archaeological evidence has shed some light on social variation by showing a gradation in the size and architectural sophistication of residential structures, as well as minor centers in rural areas surrounding major sites. The inscriptions now provide detailed information about named statuses, although these statuses are confined to the top levels of society and leave the remainder of the structure as the concern of archaeologists.

The uppermost status was the rank of *ahau* (Lord). Rulers were ahaus, but the group was considerably broader and included many individuals, both male and female, who did not rule. Ahaus were not all social equals because there are cases in which an ahau was called y'ahau ("his ahau") of another who obviously outranked him. A cahal status has now been identified in the inscriptions and is always at a level below the rank of ahau. Cahals served a variety of functions on behalf of their rulers. They are identified, especially in the western region, as battle companions of rulers and joint (although not necessarily equal) participants with them in ceremonies. Cahals were also governors of smaller sites where the inscriptions identify them as "cahal of Ruler X." Some cahals must have been influential because rulers were at pains to gain their support by associating themselves with cahals in their inscriptions. Cahal, like ahau, included both males and females. The rank seems to have been inherited because some cahals name their parents who were also cahals. There are instances in which a cahal woman marries an ahau; their children are of ahau status. Given the small sample of intermarriage, the fact that there are no cahal–ahau marriages in which the male is a cahal may be simply a matter of chance.

A fine example of a combined archaeological and epigraphic approach to the question of social status is the research at Copan that Fash and Stuart (this volume) describe. There, sites from each of the four levels of complexity originally identified by Willey and Leventhal (1979) have been excavated and the two uppermost levels (4 and 3) provide inscriptions that reveal the interaction of the ruler with members of the upper classes. In the Type 3 site, a hieroglyphic bench notes that the ruler Yax Pac honored the noble by performing a scattering rite, but the noble is not himself named. At the larger Type 4 site, where the façade sculpture indicates a long tradition of scribal occupation, the local noble is named, but seems to derive his status from an undetermined relationship with the ruler stated at the end of the inscription. A noble recently identified by Schele and Grube (1987) as a brother of Yax Pac, associated with the now-destroyed group at the site of the modern village, seems to have had an even higher status. He is named on the large Altars T and U at his site, named also on Altar

W in the Main Group and holds some office that allows him to use the Copan Emblem Glyph. The Copan example shows that when inscriptions can be located at the sites of lesser nobles, they can be very revealing about social structure.

*Dynasties and succession* (Hammond, this volume, chapter 11; Schele *et al.* n.d.)

The Maya had the concept of a line of rulership that led back to an original founder. Kings were numbered from the founder by *hel* (successor) numbers (Riese 1984b) so that, for example, Double Bird refers to himself as the 21 hel of Tikal and Animal Skull claims to be the 22 hel. Hel numbers would be a marvelous aid in reconstructuring dynasties if they had been used regularly. They were not, unfortunately, and even the best dynastic records include only a few rulers who give their numbers.

This line of rulers stretching back to an acknowledged founder is what Mayanists call a dynasty. We are bothered by the fact that our use of the term does not imply an unbroken line of descent and even decided at one point in seminar discussion that we *would* use the term with the stricter implication of descent line. We then promptly ignored our own stricture and returned to the looser definition I first described. Two factors make it nearly impossible to insist upon descent as a criterion for Maya dynasties. The first is that only a few rulers (Mathews estimates 20 percent) have surviving parentage statements. Consequently, although it is assumed – if there are no indications to the contrary – that a new ruler was a direct descendent of his predecessor, it is impossible in the great majority of cases to demonstrate that such was the case. Secondly, a few men known *not* to be direct descendents became rulers. These "outsiders" claimed the same founders as their unrelated predecessors and continued an unbroken line of hel numbers. Thus, for the Maya themselves a line of hels leading back to a founder was continuous even though direct descent lines were not invariably followed.

There is ample evidence, however, that the Maya were concerned with royal descent and that proper ancestry was a critical qualification for ruling. There are not enough parentage statements to resolve all debates about patterns of succession. Although Fox and Justeson (1986; also see Hammond, this volume, chapter 11) argue for matrilineal succession to the sister's son, the participants at the seminar believed that patrilineal succession was the standard practice. At Palenque, three sons of Pacal the Great reigned successively before the rule returned to the son of the eldest (Mathews and Schele 1974). This hints that age may have been important in guiding succession, but since the inscriptions almost never mention royal children who did not become rulers it would far exceed present information to speak of primogeniture. Sometimes the right to rule was gained through marriage. Curl Nose of Tikal, for instance, was certainly not a Tikal heir but may have married the daughter of his predecessor in the process of gaining the throne. In such cases, and in other rare instances where women themselves ruled, their sons claimed royal ancestry through their mothers' blood lines. There are indications that such situations were considered unusual and in need of justification and never did the rule pass through a female in a second successive generation.

Schele presented a penetrating analysis of two examples of "unusual" descent in seminar discussions. Pacal the Great traced royal descent through his mother, Lady Zac Kuk. Lady Zac Kuk was a direct descendant of Palenque kings through the male line. She briefly held the throne herself – perhaps as regent – until Pacal succeeded her at the age of 12. Schele believes that an enormous emphasis upon divine ancestors in Pacal's inscriptions was, in fact, an attempt to justify his inheritance through the female line by making his mother a counterpart of the mother of the gods.

A second fascinating example from Schele was Bird-Jaguar of Yaxchilan. Bird-Jaguar was undoubtedly the son of the preceding ruler, Shield Jaguar, but he did not succeed until eleven years after his father's death and after a period in which the rulership of Yaxchilan was – at least as far as inscriptions go – unclear. Bird-Jaguar's problem was that his mother was not of appropriate status. Shield Jaguar had several important wives whom he named in his inscriptions; Bird-Jaguar's mother was not among them. As Schele put it, "He was the son of a scullery maid." When Bird-Jaguar came to the throne many of his early inscriptions celebrate his mother's status, proclaiming that she had, indeed, done the same ceremonies as Shield Jaguar's more illustrious wives, and even done them on exactly the same days. In addition, Bird-Jaguar was very active in mustering political support in the early stages of his career. More than any other Yaxchilan ruler, he involved lower-ranking nobles of cahal rank in his art, and inscriptions cite them as battle companions and joint participants in ceremonies. These were undoubtedly gestures made to garner support which Bird-Jaguar probably needed to gain and hold the throne. Bird-Jaguar also visited Piedras Negras a few years before his inauguration, another probable effort to curry favor for his political ambitions. The evidence points strongly to a case of struggle over rulership at Yaxchilan in which the Maya equivalent of a bastard son wheeled and dealed his way onto the throne and then proclaimed – a bit too loudly – his right to be there.

There are also instances in which an individual who seems to have had no connection with previous royal lines became a ruler. Animal Skull of Tikal is one such case. Although his inscriptions name his parents, neither has the Tikal Emblem Glyph or any known relationship to earlier rulers (Jones, this volume). Outsiders without local royal connections could also start or rejuvenate dynasties. Ruler 1 of Dos Pilas came from Tikal to begin a dynasty at a site that seems to have had no previous inscriptions (Houston and Mathews 1985). Lady Six Sky, the daughter of Ruler 1, moved from Dos Pilas to Naranjo where she was certainly the force behind re-establishing the site's power in the Late Classic (Houston and Mathews 1985). Although it is usually assumed that she must have married a survivor from the old dynastic line at Naranjo, her inscriptions make no mention of the status of her husband; Smoking Squirrel, the next ruler and presumably her son, has no parentage statement despite a substantial corpus of inscriptions. Closs (1985) believes from this that Smoking Squirrel's father was without royal title at Naranjo or it would have been invoked to validate Smoking Squirrel's right to rule.

All of these examples suggest to me that there was far more turbulence in Maya succession than has generally been recognized. The fact that heir-designation ceremonies were used by Maya rulers suggests that troubles in succession were anticipated. More than half of Maya rulers did not say who their parents were; to assume, as is generally done, that they were sons of preceding rulers because they do not say otherwise may push negative evidence too far.

I am also struck by the number of important rulers whose accessions were in some way irregular. Curl Nose, Pacal, Bird-Jaguar, Animal Skull, Dos Pilas Ruler 1 and Lady Six Sky have all been noted among the examples of irregularities. This is an unusually influential group and one might posit that the ability to accede in the face of a less than clear claim to the throne may demand both a charisma and political sophistication that augurs well for a successful career.

### *Marriage* (Schele and Mathews, this volume)

The wives of rulers appear in several contexts in art and inscriptions. Their role is usually a ritual one, either associated with their husbands' ceremonial acts or conducting ritual on their own. They are also mentioned by their royal children in parentage statements. Some rulers record more than one wife, although there is no instance in which more than three wives were specifically mentioned.

Wives usually bear no Emblem Glyphs and are therefore assumed to be local women. It should be noted, however, that this is another bothersome instance of making an assumption on the basis of what is *not* said. Mathews estimates that less than 10 percent of marriages involve women with foreign Emblem Glyphs. He (Mathews 1986; see also Hammond, this volume, chapter 11, for calculation of mean distances of various kinds of interaction and inferences therefrom) points out that intermarriages between sites sometimes occur at substantial distances, in contrast to warfare which was usually between neighboring sites.

Several possible results of intermarriage can be inferred from the available cases. Sometimes sites in stressful circumstances seem to have bolstered their prestige by importing wives. The most notable example was Naranjo which, after having been twice defeated by Caracol and forced to erect an embarrassing hieroglyphic stairway telling of their defeat, resumed inscriptions after a lapse of forty years by bringing in Lady Six Sky from Dos Pilas (Schele 1986e). In a similar case, Copan, shortly after the loss of 18 Jog, imported a Palenque woman to marry his successor (Fash and Stuart, this volume). Marriages also seem to have been used to forge alliances useful in regional politics (Molloy and Rathje 1974). When Ruler 1 arrived at Dos Pilas, he married women from both Itzan and El Chorro, probably to help establish his position as a new dynast in the region (Mathews and Willey, this volume). Finally, marriage seems to have been used as a mechanism to gain influence at, or even control over, another site. The best example of this process is when Dos Pilas married a woman into the Tamarindito lineage whose son proclaimed himself subservient to the Dos Pilas ruler (Mathews and Willey, this volume). Speaking separately of the varying results of marriage probably distorts what was a single process with a variety of possible outcomes. One presumes that both sites involved in intermarriages must have hoped to benefit from the arrangement. Lesser sites might gain prestige, trade benefits, and the support of a more powerful ally. They ran the risk – which they probably recognized very well – of being exploited or even taken over as a result. The actual outcome in any individual case was probably a result of situational factors.

### *Trajectories of development* (Jones; Sharer, this volume)

That major construction projects were episodic rather than continuous became obvious from our papers and discussions. Jones' paper (this volume) demonstrates the surges and lulls in construction that occurred at Tikal, where meticulous attention to architectural stratigraphy made it possible to tie minute time-spans of construction and use across the entire central part of the site. The alternation between surges that concentrated upon remodeling the North Acropolis and others that stretched outward to plazas and non-acropolis structures is particularly fascinating. Many of the major building periods started soon after the placement of important burials, suggesting that new rulers felt constrained to refurbish the site and/or complete buildings honoring their predecessors. The association between specific rulers and structures has also, of course, been long recognized at Palenque and Yaxchilan and more recently at Quirigua and Copan. At Quirigua, it can be demonstrated that the major constructional expansion at the site followed hard on the heels of Cauac Sky's victory over Copan. We must now investigate whether spurts in construction activity at other sites correlated (either positively or negatively) with such political ventures as military campaigns. Did rulers embark on simultaneous building and political ventures, or did they alternate, marshalling available energy and manpower first for internal projects, then for external affairs? Perhaps data from sites such as Tikal or Copan are already precise enough to answer this question.

Sharer (this volume) recognizes the possibility of reaching a new level of interpretation when we have worked out fine-grained developmental trajectories for a number of sites. Some of the ups and downs will undoubtedly prove to be site-specific. Even in these cases, however, we will need to ask whether they are the result of purely internal factors such as weak rulers or outbreaks of factionalism or a reaction to what was happening at neighboring sites. In other instances, trajectories within a whole region may coincide. I already suspect, for example, that Tepeu 1 was a period of weakness for the entire northeast Peten. Here again the causes may prove either to be internal – factors that occur entirely within the region in question – or a reaction to external events in other regions. The Tepeu 1 dip in the northeast Peten may well be related to the fact that Belize sites, especially Caracol, were strong during the hiatus, a strength that might have retarded the beginning of Late Classic development in the neighboring Peten. Finally, of course, some characteristics of the site trajectories may be very widespread such as the growth spurt of Tepeu 2 and the collapse that followed, both of which affected the whole of the southern lowlands.

### *Warfare* (Schele and Mathews, this volume; Riese 1984a; Schele and Miller 1986; Schele and Freidel n.d.)

Maya art, in which prisoners are one of the most common themes, makes clear the importance of military achievements to royal prestige. Major captures were included as a part of royal titles and the recently noted captive count – "he of *x* captives" – shows cumulative martial prowess (Stuart 1985a). Warfare was strongly related to ritual. Captives were displayed in ceremonies and their sacrifice was an integral part of such rites as inauguation. That warfare served an important role in political legitimization is obvious, but there was a range of opinion about how often it was used as a means of territorial expansion. Some participants believed that warfare was almost gladiatorial in character with the capture of prisoners for ritual purposes its primary objective and political functions secondary. Others believed that the focus on the ritual aspects of war in art and epigraphy was a result of the character of the Maya system of communication and that political considerations, including territorial expansion, were of paramount importance – the "hidden agenda" beneath the ritualized cover of Maya writing.

Despite this divergence of opinion, some facts about the scope of warfare are clear from the inscriptions. Many of the captives depicted in Maya art are unnamed and most of those with name glyphs do not have Emblem Glyphs indicating their origins. Given the Maya rulers' penchant for proclaiming their achievements loudly, it seems safe to say that unnamed or unprovenienced captives can hardly have been the leaders of major sites. There are relatively few occasions of warfare between known sites and these usually involved two sites that were neighbors. Long-distance military campaigns were not the general policy among the Classic Maya, although when they did occur they were probably crucial in regional histories (Culbert, this volume, chapter 6).

The political results of war between known sites were variable. Sometimes (Dos Pilas's defeat of Seibal, Caracol's of Naranjo, and Tikal's of Uaxactun) the victors took over their opponents' site or at least changed elite life there for a number of generations. In other instances (the capture of Kan-Xul of Palenque by Tonina and of 18 Jog of Copan by Quirigua) the independence of the victim's site did not suffer. In the case of Quirigua, the site underwent a rapid expansion after the defeat of Copan, even though Copan remained independent (Sharer, this volume). One might speculate about the advantages of gaining trade routes, booty, or simply prestige even when there was no territorial expansion. The numerous unnamed or siteless captives tell us little about political process. They might have been either local or foreign captives taken solely for sacrifice, local rebels, or the leaders of small sites who were captured as part of expanding or maintaining the immediate territory of large sites.

### *Royal visits* (Schele and Mathews, this volume)

Schele and Mathews brilliantly document a pattern of royal visits in which rulers or their representatives visited foreign sites. Although the activities in which visitors participated have ritual aspects, they were primarily political events: accession ceremonies at Yaxchilan, heir designation rites at Piedras Negras and Bonampak, a possible puberty rite (but one also tied to heir designation?) at Piedras Negras. The function of such royal visits was obviously to gather political support from neighboring dynasts, although it is also easy to imagine trade agreements being arranged. The same pattern occurred within polities when subsidiary nobles visited paramounts (or vice versa). The visits between Yaxchilan rulers and La Pasadita cahals (Schele, this volume) are an example, as is probably the attendance of Yax Pac at ceremonies of his subsidiary nobles at Copan (Fash and Stuart, this volume).

Although most of the records of royal visits are from the western region, that is probably a result of the more expansive artistic format used there. The carved bones in the tomb of Ruler A at Tikal (Jones 1986) may be an alternative format for recording the same sort of interaction.

### *Trade*

Trade was certainly an important part of the network of interaction that tied Maya sites together. But it is a mechanism about which the inscriptions are mute, as they are about all economic matters. In the absence of an inscriptional record, we were forced to see whether patterns of trade recognizable from archaeology matched the patterns of political and ritual interconnections with which the inscriptions deal. Such a matter would be most likely for scarce, highly valued objects that circulated among the upper elite. Figure-painted polychrome vessels, for example, were produced at a limited number of centers as indicated by both chemical (Bishop *et al.* 1983) and stylistic (Coggins 1975; Reents and Bishop 1985) evidence. The products of these centers were widely distributed in a manner that may say something about political interconnections when more analyses have been completed. Possibilities other than trade may also be involved in stylistic similarities. Because some Lubaantun pieces that stylistically seemed certain to be trade pieces proved to be made from local clay, Hammond suggests that painters rather than pottery may have moved from site to site. Coggins' (1975) suggestion that the painted cylinders in the tomb of Ruler A at Tikal were painted at the site by visitors who had come to attend the burial ceremonies would reflect a similar situation. Another non-trade mechanism would have been operative if stone carvers were compelled to work at foreign sites after defeats in war as Schele and Miller (1986) suggest. Both trade and other mechanisms by which upper-elite products or their producers circulated have the potential to supplement information on interaction from the inscriptions, although much of the necessary analysis remains an objective for the future.

We also discussed the relationship between non-elite trade and political units. For ceramics, the degree of congruence is variable depending upon region and method of analysis. Mathews stressed that in the Palenque zone the data derived from petrographic analysis by

Rands and Bishop (1980) fits political reconstructions beautifully. Zones of distribution of kinds of pottery identified by inclusions are 20–25 km in radius, about the size of political units. In addition, areas that are political borders on the basis of Emblem Glyph distribution correspond with ceramic boundaries. The situation in the northeast Peten seems to me to be more complicated. There is ample evidence (Fry 1979; Fry and Cox 1974; Culbert and Schwalbe 1987) that Tikal was the site of several different centers for pottery manufacture. These centers had small spheres of distribution, so it is unlikely that they would have served Uaxactun. Nevertheless, I find the Late Classic ceramics from the two sites to be indistinguishable in typological characteristics and would be unable to sort out a mixed batch of ceramics according to site provenience. At Rio Azul, Late Classic ceramics mostly fall into types established for Tikal and Uaxactun, but would be easily separable on the basis of nuances of color and surface treatment. At Nohmul, which is closer to Rio Azul than Rio Azul is to Uaxactun, the ceramics do not fall within Peten types and a whole new typology would be necessary were I to do classification there. I believe these grades of variation to be meaningful, and to imply some sort of economic/stylistic border between Rio Azul and Nohmul that does not exist between Rio Azul and the Tikal/Uaxactun area. But it is not a border that relates directly to trade because everyday pottery, even including polychromes, was rarely moved the distances that would have been involved. Neither do I believe that the spheres denoted by stylistic similarity need necessarily correspond with political units. The degree of correspondence between economic and political spheres is a matter that must be determined by research rather than assumed. Because the glyphs contain no economic information, the question will be a difficult one to answer.

### *Ideology*

Maya art and writing focus more on cosmology and ritual than on any other topic. Consequently, they are a constant reminder of the ideological structure of Maya elite society. As Yoffee (this volume), Sharer (this volume), and Coggins (1986) emphasize, it was this ideological structure that defined Maya civilization by supplying the unifying theme that the fragmented political structure failed to provide. The charter for the Maya social order was made in heaven and was constantly validated and reaffirmed on earth through public rituals, especially the rituals of sacrifice (Schele and Miller 1986). The centrality of ideology in Maya culture is a theme in so many of the papers that it need hardly be discussed at length here.

Given this fact, I find it surprising that in our entire week of discussions the word "priest" was almost never mentioned, nor was the topic of religious specialists suggested for our agenda. What the Maya show us are not ceremonies conducted by priestly specialists. Instead, they show us individuals with political authority serving as the link with the cosmos and personally engaged in the rituals that maintained the cosmic order. What are we to make of this? Were the Maya a true theocracy with no religious practitioners who were not political figures? Surely not. The physical investment in religious infrastructure was too enormous for there not to have existed a corps of religious specialists. There are two alternative explanations for the absence of such specialists in art and writing. One is that the elite may have so controlled the ideological realm that the practioners were no more than lower-level minions carrying out the details of policies completely formulated and administered at the top by the political leaders. Such a structure would certainly not be impossible for a socieity in which ideology was so much at the core of the civilization itself. The second possibility is that there was a very real, and possibly powerful, structure of religious specialists that, like the structure of economic specialists who must also have existed, was simply outside the scope of art and writing.

## COMPARISON AND MODELS

After the considerations of Maya history and of the mechanisms of interaction among the Maya elite, we turned our attention to the question of where in other civilizations or in the models drawn from such civilizations we might find productive examples in comparison and contrast to the structure and operation of Classic Maya society. There was a range of opinion about how central comparison should be in understanding the nature of Maya society and to what degree a comparative approach can lead to oversimplification that obfuscates rather than clarifies analysis. Along a continuum of comparativeness, the balance of opinion seems to me to have inclined toward the position that we must first understand the Maya on their own terms and then use comparisons in a carefully controlled manner to avoid over-abstraction (see Sharer, this volume). We were certainly in agreement that no other specific civilization or model maps very well against Maya society as we reconstructed it. In our discussions, we considered a feudal model as suggested by Adams and Smith (1981), the cluster-interaction model of Price (1977), and a peer polity model after Renfrew and Cherry (1986), Freidel (1986a), and Sabloff (1986), and compared the Maya directly with other civilizations.

In consensus, we did not find a generalized feudal model applicable to Classic Maya society for reasons noted by Yoffee (this volume). The inability to determine land-holding patterns among the Maya, the greater importance of economic factors among the Maya than is characteristic of feudal societies and the fact that feudal societies are the products of disintegration of more centralized political structures (which was certainly not the case for the Maya) militate against classifying the Maya as feudal. Nevertheless, consideration of specific facets of individual feudal societies, on the lines of Hammond's suggestion of possible parallels between the Maya and the royal structure of Capetian France (this volume, chapter 11), may well hold promise for further investigation.

The peer polity model was discussed quite extensively and most participants agreed that it fits Maya political structure. We eschewed use of the term, however, because once it has been said that the Maya had peer polities it was not clear what analytical utility followed from the concept. Our analysis of mechanisms of interaction seemed to us to move to a depth of detail that might be obscured by speaking of peer polity interaction.

In comparison with other civilizations, Yoffee (this volume) suggests interesting parallels between the Maya and Mesopotamian civilizations. Both were politically fragmented societies united by an over-arching civilization – a tradition of shared elite culture mediated through art and writing. Like the Maya, early Mesopotamia had small-scale polities that retained their autonomy except for infrequent occasions when unusually ambitious and charismatic rulers created short-lived larger units. But there were also profound differences, Yoffee cautions. Of the three bases of power of which Runciman (1982) speaks, economic power, including control of both basic production and trade, loomed larger in Mesopotamia than we can see in the Maya case, while the control of ideological power seems more central for the

Maya. In addition, the function of writing differed, with extensive economic documents in Mesopotamia which, if they existed at all, are no longer evident for the Maya. As Hammond notes (this volume, chapter 1) and Yoffee (this volume) emphasizes, the strongest parallels in the use of writing are between the Maya and ancient Egypt. In both places, writing emphasized the place of a semi-divine ruler within the cosmos and focused upon public monuments. Egypt and the Maya, however, differed drastically in political structure with regional unification the characteristic form of the Egyptian state.

What, we must ask, should be the role of comparison in studying Maya civilization and what should we expect from comparison? Does the fact that no single model or single civilization matches the Maya very well indicate a failure in the comparative method? Or should we be heartened by the fact that Mesopotamian city-states and Egyptian writing are remindful of the Maya? The tension between uniqueness and cross-cultural similarities has long been recognized and is partly disciplinary in origin. The epigraphers and art historians at the seminar tended to dwell upon the unique configuration of Maya civilization while the anthropologists wished to find parallels. Whatever our disciplinary or individual inclinations, however, we can agree on the statement that comparisons that lead us to ask new and more detailed questions of the Maya data are useful.

## CONCLUSIONS AND PROSPECTS

What has happened to our understanding of Maya civilization now that a substantial number of Classic period inscriptions have been deciphered? The most obvious result is that we are inundated with a wealth of detail that has never before been available and that could have come from no source other than written records. These data tell us primarily of ritual, dynastic, and political history, and the mechanisms of elite interaction, and greatly increase the precision with which we can speak of the upper levels of Maya society. From archaeological evidence alone, it is difficult to infer the social structure of an ancient society. With historical information, we can see the Maya's own view of social structure and can even begin to comprehend social organization – the way in which the Maya situationally manipulated the principles of the elite order to fit individual circumstances and personalities.

How much have the new data changed our picture of Maya society? In most matters, I do not believe that profound disjunctions have been created between the way we conceptualized the Maya before and after impact of written records. Classic Maya polities may have been smaller than some of us believed previously, but nobody had ever believed that the entire lowlands was politically unified. We had thought of the Maya as a highly class-structured society dominated by a restricted elite class not much given to the creation of bureaucracies. This picture has been sharpened, but not substantially altered by the infusion of new data.

What lies in the future? Do new levels of understanding lie within reach if we continue to integrate a variety of data as we began to do at the School of American Research seminar? I believe that they do if we continue to communicate, cooperate, and appreciate the nature and limitations of each other's data. This does not mean that epigraphy, archaeology, and art history will meld into some monolithic entity in which all research is aimed at joint goals. We will continue to be different disciplines because our data, methods, and viewpoints only partially overlap. Each discipline is strong in considering some of the facets of Maya society and plays only a complementary role in the analysis of other facets.

Epigraphers deal with a wealth of detail on the careers and activities of individuals that is unmatched by anything that can be contributed by archaeological data. The inscriptions also provide information on cosmology and ritual that is beyond the reach of archaeologists, except for rare instances in which they can recover artifactual remains of individual rituals (like the recently discovered dedicatory blood-letting at Copan). The Maya calendar, by far the most precise chronological instrument available, is also tied more closely to epigraphic than to other kinds of data. Other kinds of information remain wholly within the realm of archaeology. Neither art nor inscriptions bear directly upon questions of demography, subsistence, or economics. In addition, the picture of social structure obtainable from inscriptions is limited to the very upper levels of a complex, multi-leveled society the remainder of which must be constructed from art and archaeology. The data with which art historians deal come mostly from the same elite levels covered by written records. Nevertheless, the social realm that appears in the Bonampak murals (M. Miller 1986) and perhaps in some painted pottery is broader than that of the inscriptions. In addition, the potential of stylistic studies and information on elite trade in art objects provides insight into economic matters about which the inscriptions are silent.

Interdisciplinary communication can take place at several different levels. At the most general level, results and conclusions can be juxtaposed to see whether those derived from one set of data are compatible with those derived from another. Interaction at this level during the seminar revealed both conjunctions and disjunctions. Nobody in Santa Fe questioned that the Classic Maya were a state-level society. We agreed that Maya civilization was the creation of shared elite ideas and institutions. The reconstruction of a society dominated by a restricted upper elite who created a network of interaction that overarched political boundaries was accepted by all. These important conclusions are strengthened by the fact that they arise from all the bodies of data with which we worked.

Perhaps more interesting as foci for future dialogue and research are issues about which reconstructions from different sets of data stretch the levels of credibility when juxtaposed. Many of these issues involve questions of scale and complexity. We must ask whether the polities with hundreds of thousands of inhabitants suggested by archaeological data could be run with the individualistic, non-bureaucratic style of rulership suggested by epigraphy. Or could polities under demographic stress and with such intensive agriculture as archaeologists posit have been so little concerned with warfare over territory as some epigraphers believe? We must re-examine our data and conclusions and undoubtedly engage in future problem-orientated research before all such disjunctions have been resolved.

There are many possibilities for collaborative research on specific problems for which several kinds of data are relevant. Although important work along these lines has already been accomplished, it was not until the range of information available from inscriptions became clear that it was possible to specify problems clearly and determine precisely what sorts of data would be useful. Epigraphers, for example, have now generated very detailed information about the careers of rulers. Most traditional archaeological information seems crude and imprecise by comparison because the problems with which archaeologists have dealt have not demanded a high level of precision. The focus on microprecision in architectural stratigraphy that characterized the work of the Pennsylvania Tikal Project (Coe 1965a, n.d.)

demonstrates what can be achieved. Jones' paper (this volume) indicates the potential richness of archaeological data when combined with the now-available historical record, as well as the manner in which archaeology helps fill the gaps for periods in which the inscriptional record is weak. Some of the research now underway at Copan is orientated toward the same level of precision. It is also clear that there is an urgent need for more elite burials, especially those that contain inscriptions or can be tied to monuments that have dates or name rulers. Archaeological hesitancy about a tombs-and-temples orientation must be overcome. Tombs and temples tell us about elite life which is now more than ever a critical component in understanding Maya society. Epigraphers could also tell us more about royal careers by paying greater attention to inscriptions in media other than stone. The fascinating glimpse into otherwise unknown elite interaction provided by the carved bones from the tomb of Ruler A of Tikal (Jones 1986) suggest that other media contain information that does not make its way into the formal statements on stelae or lintels. In part, this is a recovery problem and the excavation of more elite tombs will provide a greater corpus of non-monumental inscriptions. But one must also note that currently available inscriptions remain unread. One wonders, for example, what the inscription in the murals of Structure B. XIII at Uaxactun (although admittedly mostly calendrical) might tell us about the status of Uaxactun at a critical point in its history. Stylistic studies of elite art from non-monumental sources can also make contributions. Coggins' (1975) analysis of the interrelationship between Tepeu 1 Tikal and Caracol, for example, takes on added significance in the light of the new Caracol inscriptions (Houston 1987).

Below the level of rulers, collaborative research can throw substantial light upon the next levels of Maya social structure. The impressive example of work on structures of lesser elite at Copan (Fash and Stuart, this volume) shows how much can be accomplished when archaeological and epigraphic information can be located in such contexts. Discussions at the seminar on this point indicated a common impression that the Copan case is not anomalous but that similar data should be available at other sites. There has simply not been enough attention paid to investigation of precincts at intermediate social levels.

Finally, we need much more research on the interaction between sites. Even if Maya polities were small and autonomous, nobody would claim that they existed in vacuums. They were influenced by a structure of interaction that we can barely envision – a structure that is as critical to understanding individual polities as is internal information from the polities themselves. Some spectacular results on site interaction, such as the pattern of royal visits (Mathews and Schele, this volume), have already come from epigraphy. We need far more information and it is not clear to me how much more the inscriptions contain. Certainly all kinds of data must be marshalled in attacking the problem. Art-historical analysis of stylistic interaction between sites must be pursued. Archaeologists must contribute more precise information about periods of strength and weakness at individual sites in a variety of realms such as population, monumental construction, and participation in trade networks. Ways must be found to gather more information about economic spheres of interaction from archaeological data and to juxtapose it more closely with the sociopolitical interaction visible in art and inscriptions.

Eventually, although the difficulties of scale of research are enormous, we need a massive quantity of data to compare adjacent sites. At present, the closest we can come to such comparisons is in the southeast zone, where both Quirigua and Copan have been the focus of large projects. The southeast zone, however, may not be very typical because of the distance between the dominant sites, the relatively low populations in the area, and the presence of non-Maya inhabitants. Elsewhere, I am struck by how relevant the Uaxactun data, old though they are, seem in juxtaposition with Tikal. What might we not learn by a large project that investigated both Yaxchilan and La Pasadita, or, even more frightening in terms of scale, from a multi-year project at Naranjo to compare with Tikal?

We are at the beginning of a road that leads to completely new levels of understanding of Maya Classic civilization. The first steps that have been taken are already very exciting and the potential, when one imagines the research that might be done in the next generations, is breathtaking. If we are to realize this potential, we must augment interaction and collaboration and avoid the pitfalls of separatism that have plagued research in other areas where both historical and archaeological data are available.

*ACKNOWLEDGMENTS*

A summary article of this sort is, by its nature, a joint enterprise of the entire group of individuals who participated in the School of American Research Advanced Seminar. In preparing the summary, I have tried to be an accurate reporter of our papers and seminar discussions and to represent the consensus of the group as well as the opinions of those who differed from the consensus on one point or another. Citations of individuals that appear in the summary without bibliographic reference were derived from the tapes of seminar discussions. My colleagues sharpened my ideas and corrected my errors with their comments on an earlier draft of this article. I am deeply grateful to all of the participants at the seminar for their stimulation, kindness and encouragement. In addition, I would like to thank Jane Kepp, John S. Justeson, Michael B. Schiffer, and John W. Olsen for their suggestions on the preparation of this summary.

# References

Adams, Richard E. W. 1970. Suggested Classic Period occupational specialization in the southern Maya lowlands. In *Monographs and Papers in Maya Archaeology*, ed. William R. Bullard, Jr., pp. 489–502. Papers of the Peabody Museum of American Archaeology and Ethnology 61. Cambridge, Mass.: Harvard University

1971. *The Ceramics of Altar de Sacrificios*. Papers of the Peabody Museum of American Archaeology and Ethnology 63 (1). Cambridge, Mass.: Harvard University

1973. Maya collapse: transformation and termination in the ceramic sequence at Altar de Sacrificios. In *The Classic Maya Collapse*, ed. T. Patrick Culbert, pp. 133–63. School of American Research. Albuquerque: University of New Mexico Press

1974. A trial estimation of Classic Maya palace populations at Uaxactun. In *Mesoamerican Archaeology: New Approaches*, ed. N. Hammond, pp. 285–96. London: Duckworth

1977a, ed. *The Origins of Maya Civilization*. School of American Research. Albuquerque: University of New Mexico Press

1977b. Comments on the glyphic texts of the "Altar Vase." In *Social Process in Maya Prehistory: Essays in Honour of Sir Eric Thompson*, ed. Norman Hammond, pp. 409–20. London: Academic Press

1980. Swamps, canals, and the location of ancient Maya cities. *Antiquity* 80:206–14.

1981. Settlement patterns of the central Yucatan and southern Campeche regions. In *Lowland Maya Settlement Patterns*, ed. Wendy Ashmore, pp. 211–57. School of American Research. Albuquerque: University of New Mexico Press

1983. Ancient land use and culture history in the Pasion River region. In *Prehistoric Settlement Patterns: Essays in Honor of Gordon R. Willey*, ed. Evon Z. Vogt and Richard M. Leventhal, pp. 319–36. Albuquerque: University of New Mexico Press

1984, ed. *Rio Azul Project Reports 1: Final 1983 Report*. San Antonio: Center for Archaeological Research, University of Texas

1986a. *Rio Azul Reports 2: The 1984 Season*. San Antonio: Center for Archaeological Research, University of Texas

1986b. Rio Azul. *National Geographic* 169: 420–51

1987. The Rio Azul archaeological project, 1985 summary. In *Rio Azul Reports: The 1985 Season*, ed. Richard E. W. Adams, pp. 1–27. San Antonio: Center for Archaeological Research, University of Texas

n.d. A re-evaluation of Maya militarism in the southern lowlands. Unpublished manuscript

Adams, Richard E. W., Walter E. Brown, Jr., and T. Patrick Culbert. 1981. Radar mapping, archaeology and ancient Maya land use. *Science* 213:1457–63

Adams, Richard E. W., and Richard C. Jones. 1981. Spatial patterns and regional growth among Classic Maya cities. *American Antiquity* 46:301–22

Adams, Richard E. W., and Woodruff D. Smith. 1977. Apocalyptic visions: the Maya collapse and mediaeval Europe. *Archaeology* 30(5):292–301

1981. Feudal models for Classic Maya civilization. In *Lowland Maya Settlement Patterns*, ed. Wendy Ashmore, pp. 335–49. School of American Research. Albuquerque: University of New Mexico Press

Andrews, Anthony P., *et al.* 1986. Isla Cerritos Archaeological Project: a report of the 1985 field season. Report submitted to the Committee for Research and Exploration, National Geographic Society, Washington, DC

Andrews, Anthony P., and Fernando Robles C. 1985. Chichen Itza and Coba: an Itza-Maya standoff in Early Postclassic Yucatan. In *The Lowland Maya Postclassic*, eds. Arlen F. Chase and Prudence M. Rice, pp. 62–72. Austin: University of Texas Press

Andrews, Anthony P., and Tomás Gallareta Negrón. 1986. The Isla Cerritos Archaeological Project, Yucatan, Mexico. *Mexicon* 8:44–8

Andrews IV, E. Wyllys. 1965. Archaeology and prehistory in the northern Maya lowlands: an introduction. In *Handbook of Middle American Indians*, vol. 2, eds. Robert Wauchope and Gordon R. Willey, pp. 288–330. Austin: Univesity of Texas Press

Andrews IV, E. Wyllys, and E. Wyllys Andrews V. 1980. *Excavations at Dzibilchaltun, Yucatan, Mexico*. Middle American Research Institute, Publication 48. New Orleans: Tulane University

Andrews IV, E. Wyllys, and Irwin Rovner. 1973. Archaeological evidence on social stratification and commerce in the northern Maya lowlands: two masons' tool kits from Muna and Dzibilchaltun, Yucatan. In *Archaeological Investigations on the Yucatan Peninsula*, eds. Margaret A. Harrison and Robert Wauchope, pp. 81–102. Middle American Research Institute, Publication 31. New Orleans: Tulane University

Andrews V, E. Wyllys. 1977. The southeastern periphery of Mesoamerica: a view from eastern El Salvador. In *Social Process in Maya Prehistory: Essays in Honour of Sir Eric Thompson*, ed. Norman Hammond, pp. 113–34. New York: Academic Press

1979. Early central Mexican architectural traits in Dzibilchaltun, Yucatan, Mexico. *Actes de XLII Congrès International des Américanistes* 8:237–49, Paris

Ashmore, Wendy. 1980a. The Classic Maya settlement at Quirigua. *Expedition* 23(1):20–7

1980b. Discovering Early Classic Quirigua. *Expedition* 23(1):35–44.

1981a, ed. *Lowland Maya Settlement Patterns*. School of American Research. Albuquerque: University of New Mexico Press

1981b. Some issues of method and theory in lowland Maya settlement archaeology. In *Lowland Maya Settlement Patterns*, ed. Wendy Ashmore, pp. 37–70. School of American Research. Albuquerque: University of New Mexico Press

1983. Ideological structure in ancient Maya settlement patterns. Paper presented at the 82nd Annual Meeting of the American Anthropological Association, Chicago

1984. Quirigua archaeology and history revisited. *Journal of Field Archaeology* 11:365–86

1988. Household and community at Classic Quirigua. In *Household and Community in the Mesoamerican Past*, eds. Richard R. Wilk and Wendy Ashmore, pp. 153–69. Albuquerque: University of New Mexico Press

Ashmore, Wendy, and Robert J. Sharer. 1978. Excavations at Quirigua, Guatemala: the ascent of an elite Maya center. *Archaeology* 31(6):10–19

Ashmore, Wendy, and Richard R. Wilk. 1988. Household and community in the Mesoamerican past. In *Household and Community in the Mesoamerican Past*, eds. Richard R. Wilk and Wendy Ashmore, pp. 1–27. Albuquerque: University of New Mexico Press

Baines, John R. 1981. Literacy and ancient Egyptian society. *Man* 18:572–99

Ball, Joseph W. 1974. A coordinate approach to northern Maya prehistory: AD 700–1200. *American Antiquity* 39:85–93

1977. *The Archaeological Ceramics of Becan, Campeche, Mexico*. Middle American Research Institute, Publication 43. New Orleans: Tulane University

1979a. Southern Campeche and the Mexican plateau: Early Classic contact situation. *Actas del XLII Congreso Internacional de Americanistas* 8:271–80, Mexico

1979b. Ceramics, culture history, and the Puuc tradition: some alternative possibilities. In *The Puuc: New Perspectives*, ed. Lawrence Mills, pp. 18–35. Scholarly Studies in the Liberal Arts. Pella, Iowa: Central College

Barthel, Thomas S. 1968a. El complejo "emblema." *Estudios de Cultura Maya* 7:159–93

1968b. Historisches in dem Klassischen Mayainschriften. *Zeitschrift für Ethnologie* 93:119–56.

Baudez, Claude F., ed. 1983a. *Introducción a la arqueología de Copán*, 3 vols. Tegucigalpa, Honduras: Secretaria de Estado an el Despecho de Cultura y Turismo

1983b. La Estela 35. In *Introducción a la arqueología de Copán*, ed. Claude F. Baudez, vol. 1, pp. 186–90. Tegucigalpa, Honduras: Secretaria de Estado en el Despacho de Cultura y Turismo

1989. The House of the Bacabs: an iconographic analysis. In *The House of the Bacabs, Copan, Honduras*, ed. David L. Webster, pp. 73–81. Washington DC: Dumbarton Oaks

Beaudry, Marilyn P. 1987. Southeast Maya polychrome pottery: production, distribution, and style. In *Maya Ceramics: Papers from the 1985 Maya Ceramic Conference*, eds. Prudence M. Rice and Robert J. Sharer, pp. 503–23. BAR International Series 345. Oxford: BAR

Becker, Marshall J. 1971. The identification of a second plaza plan at Tikal, Guatemala, and its implications for ancient Maya social complexity. Ph.D. dissertation, University of Pennsylvania

1973. Archaeological evidence for occupational specialization among the Classic period Maya at Tikal. *American Antiquity* 38:396–406

1979. Priests, peasants, and ceremonial centers: the intellectual history of a model. In *Maya Archaeology and Ethnohistory*, eds. Norman Hammond and Gordon R. Willey, pp. 3–20. Austin: University of Texas Press

Becquelin, Pierre, and Claude Baudez. 1982. *Tonina, une cité Maya du Chiapas*. Etudes Mésoaméricaines 4. Paris: Mission archéologique et ethnologique française au Mexique. Editions recherche sur les civilisations

Berlin, Heinrich. 1958. El glifo "emblema" en las inscripciones Mayas. *Journal de la Société des Américanistes* (n.s.) 47:111–19

1959. Glifos nominales en el sarcófago de Palenque. *Humanidades* 2(10):1–8

Biggs, Robert D. 1967. Semitic names in the Fara period. *Orientalia* 36:55–66

Bishop, Ronald L., Garman Harbottle, Dorie J. Reents, Edward V. Sayre, and Lambertus van Zelst. 1983. Compositional attribution of non-provenienced Maya polychrome vessels. Paper presented at the 5th International Seminar, Applications of Science in Examination of Works of Art, Museum of Fine Arts, Boston

Bolles, John S. 1977. *Las Monjas: A Major Pre-Mexican Architectural Complex at Chichen Itza*. Norman: University of Oklahoma Press

Bottomore, Tom. 1966. *Elites and Society*. London: Penguin. First edn 1964.

Brasseur de Bourbourg, Charles Etienne. 1864. *Rélation des choses de Yucatan de Diego de Landa . . . accompagné de documents divers historiques et chronologiques*. Paris

Bray, Warwick M. 1972. Land-use, settlement pattern and politics in prehispanic Middle America: a review. In *Man, Settlement, and Urbanism*, eds. Peter J. Ucko, Ruth Tringham, and G. W. Dimbleby, pp. 909–26. London: Duckworth

Bronson, Bennet. n.d. Vacant terrain excavations at Tikal. Ms, dated 1966 on file, Tikal Project, University Museum, University of Pennsylvania

Bullard, William R., Jr. 1960. Maya settlement pattern in northeastern Peten, Guatemala. *American Antiquity* 25:355–72

1964. Settlement pattern and social structure in the southern Maya lowlands during the Classic period. *Actas y Memorias, XXXV Congreso Internacional de Americanistas* 1:279–87. Mexico

Caldwell, Joseph R. 1964. Interaction spheres in prehistory. In *Hopewellian Studies*, eds. Joseph R. Caldwell and Robert L. Hall, pp. 133–43. Illinois State Museum Scientific Papers 12. Springfield: Illinois State Museum

Calnek, Edward. 1976. The internal structure of Tenochtitlan. In *The Valley of Mexico: Studies in Pre-Hispanic Ecology and Society*, ed. Eric R. Wolf, pp. 287–302. School of American Research. Albuquerque: University of New Mexico Press

Campbell, Lyle R. 1976. The linguistic prehistory of the southern Mesoamerican periphery. *XIV Mesa Redonda, Sociedad Mexicana de Antropología* 1:157–83

1977. *Quichean Linguistic Prehistory*. University of California Publications in Linguistics 81. Berkeley and Los Angeles: University of California Press

Chang, K. C. 1983. *Art, Myth, and Ritual: The Path to Political Authority in Ancient China*. Cambridge, Mass.: Harvard University Press

Chase, Arlen F., and Diane Z. Chase. 1987. *Investigations at the Classic Maya City of Caracol, Belize: 1985–1987*. Pre-Columbian Art Research Institute, Monograph 3. San Francisco: Pre-Columbian Art Research Institute

Cheek, Charles D. 1983. Excavaciones en la Plaza Principal. In *Introducción a la arqueología de Copán*, ed. Claude F. Baudez, pp. 191–290. Tegucigalpa, Hondras: Secretaria de Estado en el Despacho de Cultura y Turismo

Chisholm, Michael. 1968. *Rural Settlement and Land-Use*. London: Hutchinson

Closs, Michael P. 1985. The dynastic history of Naranjo: the middle period. In *Fifth Palenque Round Table, 1983*, vol. ed. Virginia M. Fields; genl. ed. Merle Greene Robertson, pp. 65–77. Palenque Round Table Series 7. San Francisco: Pre-Columbian Art Research Institute

Coe, Michael D. 1973. *The Maya Scribe and his World*. New York: The Grolier Club

1974. A carved wooden box from the Classic Maya civilization. In *Primera Mesa Redonda de Palenque*, ed. Merle Green Robertson, Part 2:51–8. Pebble Beach: Robert Louis Stevenson School

1977. Supernatural patrons of Maya scribes and artists. In *Social Process in Maya Prehistory: Essays in Honour of Sir Eric Thompson*, ed. Norman Hammond, pp. 327–47. New York: Academic Press

Coe, Michael D., and Elizabeth P. Benson. 1966. *Three Maya Relief Panels at Dumbarton Oaks*. Studies in Pre-Columbian Art and Archaeology 2. Washington, DC: Dumbarton Oaks

Coe, William R. 1965a. Tikal, Guatemala, and emergent Maya civilization. *Science* 147:1401–19

1965b. Tikal: ten years of study of a Maya ruin in the lowlands of Guatemala. *Expedition* 8(1):5–56

1990. *Excavations in the Great Plaza, North Terrace and North Acropolis of Tikal*. Tikal Report 14. Philadelphia: The University Museum, University of Pennsylvania

Coe, William R., and John J. McGinn. 1963. Tikal: the North Acropolis and an early tomb. *Expedition* 5(2):24–32

Coggins, Clemency C. 1975. Painting and drawing styles at Tikal: an historical and iconographic reconstruction. Ph.D. dissertation, Harvard University

1976. Teotihuacan at Tikal in the Early Classic period. *Actes de XLII Congrès International des Américanistes* 8:251–69, Paris.

1979. A new order and the role of the calendar: some characteristics of the Middle Classic period at Tikal. In *Maya Archaeology and Ethnohistory*, eds. Norman Hammond and Gordon R. Willey, pp. 38–50. Austin: University of Texas Press

1980. The shape of time: some political implications of a four-part figure. *American Antiquity* 45:729–39

1986. There's no place like *hom*: variations in metaphors of death and birth in the excavated tombs of the Early Classic Maya. Paper prepared for Elite Interaction in Classic Maya Civilization. School of American Research Advanced Seminar, Santa Fe

1988. Classic Maya metaphors of life and death. *Res* 16:64–84

Cohodas, Marvin. 1978. *The Great Ball Court at Chichen Itza, Yucatan, Mexico*. New York: Garland Publishing, Inc.

Coles, John M., and A. F. Harding. 1979. *The Bronze Age in Europe*. London: Methuen

Collins, Anne C. 1977. The *Maestros Cantores* in Yucatan. In *Anthropology and History in Yucatan*, ed. Grant D. Jones, pp. 233–47. Austin: University of Texas Press

Coulborn, Rushton. 1956. Conclusion. In *The Idea of Feudalism*, ed. Rushton Coulborn, pp. 364–95. Princeton: Princeton University Press

Cowgill, George L. 1983. Rulership and the Ciudadela: political inferences from Teotihuacan architecture. In *Civilization in the Ancient Americas*, eds. Richard M. Leventhal and Alan L. Kolata, pp. 313–44. Albuquerque: University of New Mexico Press

Culbert, T. Patrick, ed. 1973. *The Classic Maya Collapse*. School of American Research. Albuquerque: University of New Mexico Press

1986. The Tikal regional state. Paper prepared for Elite Interaction in Classic Maya Civilization. School of American Research Advanced Seminar, Santa Fe

1988a. The collapse of Classic Maya civilization. In *The Collapse of Ancient States and Civilizations*, eds. Norman Yoffee and George L. Cowgill, pp. 69–101. Tucson: University of Arizona Press

1988b. Political history and the decipherment of Maya glyphs. *Antiquity* 62:135–52

Culbert, T. Patrick, Laura J. Kosakowsky, Robert E. Fry, and William A. Haviland, n.d. The population of Tikal, Guatemala. In *Precolumbian Population History in the Maya Lowlands*, eds. T. Patrick Culbert and Don S. Rice. Albuquerque: University of New Mexico Press

Culbert, T. Patrick, and Don S. Rice, eds. n.d. *Precolumbian Population History in the Maya Lowlands*. Albuquerque: University of New Mexico Press

Culbert, T. Patrick, and Larry A. Schwalbe. 1987. X-ray fluorescence survey of Tikal ceramics. *Journal of Archaeological Science* 14:635–57

Dahlin, Bruce H. 1984. A colossus in Guatemala: the Preclassic city of El Mirador. *Archaeology* 37(5):18–25

Davoust, Michel. 1977. *Etude epigraphique 2: les chefs Mayas de Chichen Itza et les glyphs de filiation*. Angers, France

1980. Les premiers chefs Mayas de Chichen Itza. *Mexicon* 2:25–9

del Rio, Antonio. 1822. *Description of the Ruins of an Ancient City Discovered near Palenque, in the Kingdom of Guatemala, in Spanish America*. London: Berthoud and Suttaby, Evance and Fox

Demarest, Arthur A. 1986. *The Archaeology of Santa Leticia and the Rise of Maya Civilization*. Middle American Research Institute, Publication 52. New Orleans: Tulane University

1988. Political evolution in the Maya borderlands. In *The Southeast Classic Maya Zone*, eds. Elizabeth H. Boone and Gordon R. Willey, pp.335–94. Washington, DC: Dumbarton Oaks

n.d. The Olmec and the rise of civilization in eastern Mesoamerica. In *The Olmec and the Development of Mesoamerican Civilization*, eds. Robert J. Sharer and David C. Grove. School of American Research. Cambridge, England: Cambridge University Press

Diakonoff, Igor M. 1969. The rise of the despotic state in ancient Mesopotamia. In *Ancient Mesopotamia*, ed. Igor M. Diakonoff, pp. 173–203. Moscow: Nauka

Dillon, Brian D. 1978. A Tenth Cycle sculpture from Alta Verapaz,

Guatemala. *Contributions of the University of California Archaeological Research Facility* 36:39–46

Doyle, Arthur Conan. 1956. *The Complete Sherlock Holmes*. New York: Doubleday and Company

Durán, Diego. 1967. *Historia de las Indias de Nueva Espana e islas de la tierra firma*, ed. Angel M. Garibay K., 2 vols. Mexico: Editorial Porrua

Edmonson, Munro S. 1978. Some Postclassic questions about the Classic Maya. *Third Palenque Round Table, 1978*, eds. Merle Greene Robertson and Donnan C. Jeffers, vol. 1: pp. 9–18. Palenque Round Table Series 4. Monterey: Pre-Columbian Art Research Center

Eisenstadt, Shmuel N. 1986. Introduction. In *The Origins and Diversity of Axial Age Civilizations*, ed. Shmuel N. Eisenstadt, pp. 1–25. Albany: SUNY Press

Erdösy, George. 1987. Early Historic cities of northern India. *South Asian Studies* 3:1–23

Falkenstein, Adam. 1954. La cité-temple sumérienne. *Cahiers d'histoire mondiale* 1:784–814

Farriss, Nancy M. 1984. *Maya Society under Colonial Rule: The Collective Enterprise of Survival*. Princeton: Princeton University Press

1986. Indians in Colonial northern Yucatan. In *Handbook of Middle American Indians, Supplement 4: Ethnohistory*, ed. Ronald Spores, pp. 88–102. Austin: University of Texas Press

Fash, William L. 1982. A Middle Formative cemetery from Copan, Honduras. Paper presented at the 81st Annual Meeting of the American Anthropological Association, Washington, DC

1983a. Reconocimiento y excavaciones en el valle. *Introducción a la arqueología de Copán*, ed. Claude F. Baudez, pp. 229–469. Tegucigalpa, Honduras: Secretaria de Estado en el Despacho de Cultura y Turismo

1983b. Maya state formation: a case study and its implications. Ph.D. dissertation, Harvard University

1983c. Deducing social organization from Classic Maya settlement patterns: a case study from the Copan Valley. In *Civilization in the Ancient Americas*, eds. Richard M. Leventhal and Alan L. Kolata, pp. 261–88. Albuquerque: University of New Mexico Press, and Cambridge, Mass.: Peabody Museum, Harvard University

1985. The evolution of the Copan polity. Paper presented at the 50th Annual Meeting of the Society for American Archaeology, Denver

1986a. History and characteristics of settlement in Copan, and some comparisons with Quirigua. In *The Southeastern Maya Periphery*, eds. Patricia A. Urban and Edward M. Schortman, pp. 72–93. Austin: University of Texas Press

1986b. La fachada esculpida de la Estructura 9N-82: contenido, forma, y significado. In *Excavaciones en el area urbana de Copan*, ed. William T. Sanders, pp. 319–82. Tegucigalpa, Honduras: Instituto Hondureño de Antropología e Historia

1986c. Lineage patrons and ancestor worship among the Classic Maya nobility: the case of Copan Structure 9N-82. Paper presented at the Sexta Mesa Redonda de Palenque, June, 1986, Palenque

1988. A new look at Maya statecraft from Copan, Honduras. *Antiquity* 62:157–9

1989. The sculptural façade of Structure 9N-82: content, form and significance. In *The House of the Bacabs, Copan, Honduras*, ed. David L. Webster, pp. 41–72. Washington, DC: Dumbarton Oaks

Fash, William L., and Kurt Z. Long. 1983. El mapa arqueológico del Valle de Copán. In *Introduccíon a la arqueología de Copán*, vol. 3, ed. Claude F. Baudez. Tegucigalpa, Honduras: Secretaria de Estado en el Despacho de Cultura y Turismo

Flannery, Kent V., ed. 1982. *Maya Subsistence: Studies in Memory of Dennis E. Puleston*. New York: Academic Press

Folan, William J., Ellen R. Kintz, and Loraine Fletcher. 1983. *Coba: a Maya Metropolis*. New York: Academic Press

Förstemann, Ernst W. 1880. *Die Maya-handschrift der Körniglichen Bibliothek Dresden*. Leipzig: Röder

1894. *Zur entzifferung der Mayahandschriften*, vol. 4. Dresden

Fourquin, Guy. 1978. *The Anatomy of Popular Rebellion in the Middle Ages*. Amsterdam: Elsevier

Fox, James A. 1983. Language and writing. In *The Ancient Maya*. Fourth edition, revised; eds. Sylvanus G. Morley and George W. Brainerd, revised by Robert J. Sharer, pp. 497–544. Stanford: Stanford University Press

1984. The hieroglyphic band in the Casa Colorado. Paper presented at the 83rd Annual Meeting of the American Anthropological Association, Denver

Fox, James A., and John S. Justeson. 1986. Classic Maya dynastic alliance and succession. In *Handbook of Middle American Indians, Supplement 4: Ethnohistory*, ed. Ronald Spores, pp. 7–34. Austin: University of Texas Press

n.d. Hieroglyphic evidence for the languages of the Classic Maya. Unpublished ms.

Freidel, David A. 1979. Culture areas and interaction spheres: contrasting approaches to the emergence of civilization in the Maya lowlands. *American Antiquity* 44:36–54

1981. The political economics of residential dispersion among the lowland Maya. In *Lowland Maya Settlement Patterns*, ed. Wendy Ashmore, pp. 371–82. School of American Research. Albuquerque: University of New Mexico Press

1983. Political systems in lowland Yucatan: dynamics and structure in Maya settlement. In *Prehistoric Settlement Patterns: Essays in Honor of Gordon R. Willey*, eds. Evon Z. Vogt and Richard M. Leventhal, pp. 375–86. Albuquerque: University of New Mexico Press

1986a. Maya warfare: an example of peer polity interaction. In *Peer Polity*

*Interaction and the Development of Socio-Political Change*, eds. Colin Renfrew and John F. Cherry, pp. 93–108. Cambridge, England: Cambridge University Press

1986b. Preface. In *Archaeology at Cerros, Belize, Central America. Vol. I. An Interim Report*, eds. Robin A. Robertson and David A. Freidel, pp. ix–x. Dallas: Southern Methodist University Press.

n.d. Yaxuna archaeological survey: a report of the 1986 field season. Report submitted to the Committee for Research and Exploration, National Geographic Society, Washington, DC

Freidel, David A., and Jeremy A. Sabloff. 1984. *Cozumel: Late Maya Settlement Patterns*. New York: Academic Press

Freidel, David A., and Linda Schele. 1983. Symbol and power: a history of the lowland Maya cosmogram. Paper presented at the Conference on the Origins of Classic Maya Iconography, Princeton University

Frost, Frank. 1987. Peisistratos and the unification of Attica. Paper presented at the 89th Annual Meeting of the Archaeological Institute of America, New York

Fry, Robert E. 1979. The economics of pottery at Tikal, Guatemala: models of exchange for serving vessels. *American Antiquity* 44:494–512

Fry, Robert E., and Scott C. Cox. 1974. The structure of ceramic exchange at Tikal, Guatemala. *World Archaeology* 6:209–25

Gelb, Ignace J. 1969. On the alleged temple and state economies in ancient Mesopotamia. In *Studi in onore di Edoardo Volterra*, vol. 6:137–54

1981. Ebla and the Kish civilization. In *La lingua di Ebla*, ed. L. Cagni, pp. 9–83. Naples: Instituto Universitario Orientale

Gerstle, Andrea. 1987. Maya and non-Maya ethnic interaction in Late Classic Copan, Honduras, Ph.D. dissertation, University of California, Santa Barbara

Gifford, James D. 1974. Recent thought concerning the interpretation of Maya prehistory. In *Mesoamerican Archaeology: New Approaches*, ed. Norman Hammond, pp. 77–98. London: Duckworth

Gilman, Antonio. 1981. The development of social stratification in Bronze Age Europe. *Current Anthropology* 22:1–23

Goodman, John T. 1905. Maya dates. *American Anthropologist* 7:642–7

Grabar, Oleg. 1978. *The Formation of Islamic Art*. New Haven: Yale University Press

Graham, Ian. 1967. *Archaeological Explorations in El Petén, Guatemala*. Middle American Research Institute, Publication 33. New Orleans: Tulane University

1982. *Corpus of Maya Hieroglyphic Inscriptions*, vol. 3, pt. 3: *Yaxchilan*. Cambridge, Mass.: Peabody Museum of American Archaeology and Ethnology, Harvard University

Graham, John A. 1972. *The Hieroglyphic Inscriptions and Monumental Art of Altar de Sacrificios*. Papers of the Peabody Museum of American Archaeology and Ethnology , 64(2). Cambridge, Mass.: Harvard University

1973. Aspects of non-Classic presences in the inscriptions and sculptural art of Seibal. In *The Classic Maya Collapse*, ed. T. Patrick Culbert, pp. 207–21. School of American Research. Albuquerque: University of New Mexico Press

1976. Maya, Olmecs, and Izapans at Abaj Takalik. *Actes de XLII Congrès International des Américanistes* 8:179–88, Paris

Grube, Nikolai. n.d. *Namenshieroglyphen mythologischer vorfahren in hieroglyphentexten der Maya*. Archiv für Völkerkunde, Vienna

Grube, Nikolai, and Linda Schele. 1987. *U Cit Tok, the Last King of Copan*. Copan Note 21. Copan Mosaic Project and Instituto Hondureño de Antropología e Historia

Hägerstrand, Torsten. 1953. *Innovationsforloppet ur korologisk synpunkt*. Lund: Royal University of Lund

Haggett, Peter. 1965. *Locational Analysis in Human Geography*. London: Edward Arnold

Hamblin, Robert L., and Brian L. Pitcher. 1980. The Classic Maya collapse: testing the class conflict hypothesis. *American Antiquity* 45:246–67

Hammond, Norman. 1972. Locational models and the site of Lubaantun: a Classic Maya centre. In *Models in Archaeology*, ed. David L. Clarke pp. 757–800. London: Methuen

1973. Models for Maya trade. In *The Explanation of Culture Change*, ed. Colin Renfrew, pp. 601–7. Pittsburgh: University of Pittsburgh Press

1974a. The distribution of Late Classic Maya major ceremonial centers in the Central Area. In *Mesoamerican Archaeology: New Approaches*, ed. Norman Hammond, pp. 313–34. Austin: University of Texas Press

1974b. On the "square" model of Maya territorial organization. *Science* 193:875–6

1975a. *Lubaantun: A Classic Maya Realm*. Monographs of the Peabody Museum of American Archaeology and Ethnology 1(2). Cambridge, Mass.: Harvard University

1975b. Maya settlement hierarchy in northern Belize. *Contributions of the University of California Archaeological Research Facility* 27:40–55

1977. The earliest Maya. *Scientific American* 236(3):116–33

1980. Early Maya ceremonial at Cuello, Belize. *Antiquity* 54:176–90

1982. *Ancient Maya Civilization*. New Brunswick: Rutgers University Press, and Cambridge, England: Cambridge University Press

1984. Holmul and Nohmul: a comparison and assessment of two lowland Maya Protoclassic sites. *Ceramica de Cultura Maya* 13:1–17

1986a. The emergence of Maya civilization. *Scientific American* 255(2):106–15

1986b. New light on the most ancient Maya. *Man* (n.s.) 21:399–413

1987. *The Sun Also Rises: Iconographic Syntax of the Pomona Flare*. Research Reports on Ancient Maya Writing 7. Washington, DC: Center for Maya Research

Hammond, Norman, and Wendy Ashmore. 1981. Lowland Maya settlement: geographical and chronological frameworks. In *Lowland Maya*

*Settlement Patterns*, ed. Wendy Ashmore, pp. 19–36. School of American Research. Albuquerque: University of New Mexico Press

Hammond, Norman, Catherine Clark, Mark Horton, Mark Hodges, Logan McNatt, Laura J. Kosakowsky, and Anne Pyburn. 1985. Excavation and survey at Nohmul, Belize, 1983. *Journal of Field Archaeology* 12:177–200

Hammond, Norman, Garman Harbottle, and Trevor Gazard. 1976. Neutron activation and statistical analysis of Maya ceramics and clays from Lubaantun, Belize. *Archaeometry* 18:147–68

Hansen, Richard D. 1987. *Informe preliminar de los estudios realizados en el sitio arqueológico Nakbé, Petén, Guatemala*. Guatemala: Instituto Nacional de Antropología e Historia

Harrison, Peter D. 1970. The Central Acropolis, Tikal, Guatemala: a preliminary study of the functions of its structural components during the Late Classic period. Ph.D. dissertation, University of Pennsylvania

1978. Bajos revisited: visual evidence for one system of agriculture. In *Pre-Hispanic Maya Agriculture*, eds. Peter D. Harrison and B. L. Turner II, pp. 247–53. Albuquerque: University of New Mexico Press

Harrison, Peter D., and B. L. Turner II, eds. 1978. *Pre-Hispanic Maya Agriculture*. Albuquerque: University of New Mexico Press

Hassig, Ross. 1988. *Aztec Warfare*. Norman: University of Oklahoma Press

Haviland, William A. 1966. Maya settlement patterns: a critical review. In *Archaeological Studies in Middle America*, eds. Margaret A. Harrison and Robert Wauchope, pp. 21–47. Middle American Research Institute, Publication 26. New Orleans: Tulane University

1967. Stature at Tikal, Guatemala: implications for Classic Maya demography and social organization. *American Antiquity* 32:316–25

1970. Tikal, Guatemala, and Mesoamerican urbanism. *World Archaeology* 2:186–99

1972. New look at Classic Maya social organization at Tikal. *Ceramica de Cultura Maya* 8:1–16

1977. Dynastic genealogies from Tikal, Guatemala: implications for descent and political organization. *American Antiquity* 42:61–7

1981. Dower houses and minor centers at Tikal, Guatemala: an investigation into the identification of valid units in settlement hierarchies. In *Lowland Maya Settlement Patterns*, ed. Wendy Ashmore, pp. 89–117. School of American Research. Albuquerque: University of New Mexico Press

1985. Population and social dynamics: the dynasties and social structure of Tikal. *Expedition* 27(3):34–41

Hellmuth, Nicholas M. 1976. Evidence of Teotihuacan contact in the Maya lowlands: a study of iconography. M.A. thesis, Yale University

Helms, Mary W. 1987. Thoughts on public symbols and distant domains relevant to the chiefdoms of lower Central America. Paper presented at Wealth and Hierarchy in the Intermediate Area. Seminar sponsored by Dumbarton Oaks, Washington, DC

Henderson, John B. 1981. *The World of the Ancient Maya*. Ithaca: Cornell University Press

Hirth, Kenneth G. 1978. Interregional trade and the formation of prehistoric gateway communities. *American Antiquity* 43:35–45

Hocart, Arthur M. 1936. *Kings and Councillors*, ed. Rodney Needham (1970). Chicago: University of Chicago Press

Houston, Stephen D. 1983. On "Ruler 6" at Piedras Negras, Guatemala. *Mexicon* 5:84–6

1987. Notes on Caracol epigraphy and its significance. Appendix II. In *Investigations at the Classic Maya City of Caracol, Belize: 1985–1987*, by Arlen F. Chase and Diane Z. Chase, pp. 85–100. Pre-Columbian Art Research Institute, Monograph 3. San Francisco: Pre-Columbian Art Research Institute

Houston, Stephen D., and Peter Mathews. 1985. *The Dynastic Sequence of Dos Pilas, Guatemala*. Pre-Columbian Art Research Institute, Monograph 1. San Francisco: Pre-Columbian Art Research Institute

Houston, Stephen D., and Karl A. Taube. 1987. "Name-tagging" in Classic Maya script: implications for native classifications of ceramics and jade. *Mexicon* 9:38–41

Jacobsen, Thorkild. 1939. The assumed conflict between the Sumerians and the Semites in early Mesopotamian history. *Journal of the American Oriental Society* 59:485–95

Joesink-Mandeville, L. R. V. 1987. The ethnological significance of the Copan Archaic. In *The Periphery of the Southeastern Classic Maya Realm*, ed. Gary W. Pahl, pp. 1–26. U.C.L.A. Latin American Studies Center, Publication 61. Los Angeles: University of California at Los Angeles

Johnston, Kevin. 1985. Maya dynastic territorial expansion: glyphic evidence for Classic centers of the Pasion River, Guatemala. *Fifth Palenque Round Table, 1983*. Vol. ed. Virginia M. Fields; genl. ed. Merle Greene Robertson, pp. 49–56. Palenque Round Table Series 7. San Francisco: Pre-Columbian Art Research Institute

n.d. A commentary on the hieroglyphic inscriptions of Piedras Negras, Guatemala. Unpublished ms. dated 1989

Jones, Christopher. 1969. The Twin-Pyramid Group pattern: a Classic Maya architectural assemblage at Tikal, Guatemala. Ph.D. dissertation, University of Pennsylvania

1977. Inauguration dates of three Late Classic rulers of Tikal, Guatemala. *American Antiquity* 53:28–60

1979. Tikal as a trading center. Paper presented at the 43rd International Congress of Americanists, Vancouver, BC

1983a. Monument 26, Quirigua, Guatemala. In *Quirigua Reports*, vol. 2, eds. Edward M. Schortman and Patricia A. Urban, pp. 118–23. University Museum Monograph 49. Philadelphia: The University Museum, University of Pennsylvania

1983b. New drawings of Monuments 23 and 24, Quirigua, Guatemala. In

*Quirigua Reports*, vol. 2, eds. Edward M. Schortman and Patricia A. Urban, pp. 137–40. University Museum Monograph 49. Philadelphia: The University Museum, University of Pennsylvania

1986. The life and times of Ah Cacau, Ruler of Tikal. Paper presented at the Primer Simposio Mundial de Epigrafía Maya, Guatemala

n.d. *Excavations in the East Plaza of Tikal*. Tikal Report 16. Philadelphia: The University Museum, University of Pennsylvania

Jones, Christopher, and Linton Satterthwaite. 1982. *The Monuments and Inscriptions of Tikal: The Carved Monuments*. Tikal Report 33A. Philadelphia: The University Museum, University of Pennsylvania

Jones, Christopher, and Robert J. Sharer. 1980. Archaeological investigations in the site-core of Quirigua. *Expedition* 23(1):11–19

Justeson, John S. 1986. The origin of writing systems: Preclassic Mesoamerica. *World Archaeology* 17:437–58

Justeson, John S., William M. Norman, Lyle Campbell, and Terrence S. Kaufman. 1985. *The Foreign Impact on Lowland Mayan Language and Script*. Middle American Research Institute, Publication 53. New Orleans: Tulane University

Kaufman, Herbert. 1988. The collapse of ancient states and civilizations as an organizational problem. In *The Collapse of Ancient States and Civilizations*, eds. Normal Yoffee and George L. Cowgill, pp. 219–35. Tucson: University of Arizona Press

Kaufman, Terrence S. 1976. Archaeological and linguistic correlations in Mayaland and associated areas of Mesoamerica. *World Archaeology* 8:101–18

Kautz, Robert, and Grant D. Jones. 1981. Introduction. In *The Transition to Statehood in the New World*, eds. Robert Kautz and Grant D. Jones, pp. 3–37. Cambridge, England: Cambridge University Press

Keightley, David. 1986. Early civilization in China: reflections on how it became Chinese. Paper prepared for Early China and Social Science Generalization. Conference at Airlie House, VA

Kelker, Nancy. 1981. Hieroglyphic inscription at Tortuguero. Paper prepared for the Seminar on Maya Hieroglyphic Writing, University of Texas at Austin

Kelley, David H. 1962a. Glyphic evidence for a dynastic sequence at Quirigua, Guatemala. *American Antiquity* 27:323–35

1962b. A history of the decipherment of Maya script. *Anthropological Linguistics* 4(8):1–48

1976. *Deciphering the Maya Script*. Austin: University of Texas Press

1982. Notes on Puuc inscriptions and history. Supplement to *The Puuc: New Perspectives*, ed. Lawrence Mills. Scholarly Studies in the Liberal Arts. Pella, Iowa: Central College

1983. The Maya calendar correlation problem. In *Civilization in the Ancient Americas: Essays in Honor of Gordon R. Willey*, ed. Richard M. Leventhal and Alan L. Kolata, pp. 157–208. Albuquerque: University of New Mexico Press

1984. The Toltec empire in Yucatan. *Quarterly Review of Archaeology* 5:12–13

Knorosov, Yurii V. 1952. Drevniaia Pis'mennost' Tsentral'noi Ameriki. *Sovetskaia Etnografia* 3:100–18

1958. The problem of the study of the Maya hieroglyphic writing. *American Antiquity* 23:284–91

Kowalski, Jeff K. 1987. *The House of the Governor: A Maya Palace at Uxmal, Yucatan, Mexico*. Norman: University of Oklahoma Press

Kraus, Fritz R. 1970. *Sumerer und Akkader*. Amsterdam: North Holland Publishing Company

Krochok, Ruth J. 1988. The hieroglyphic inscriptions and iconography of the Temple of the Four Lintels and related monuments, Chichen Itza, Yucatan, Mexico. M.A. thesis, University of Texas at Austin

n.d. Epigraphic evidence for political change at Chichen Itza. Unpublished manuscript

Kroeber, Alfred L. 1944. *Peruvian Archaeology in 1942*. Viking Fund Publications in Anthropology 4. New York: Viking Fund

Kubler, George. 1961. Chichen Itza y Tula. *Estudios de Cultura Maya* 1:47–80

1975. *The Art and Architecture of Ancient America*. London: Penguin Books

Kurjack, Edward B. 1974. *Prehistoric Lowland Maya Community and Social Organization: A Case Study at Dzibilchaltun, Yucatan, Mexico*. Middle American Research Institute, Publication 38. New Orleans: Tulane University

Lamb, Dana, and Ginger Lamb. 1951. *Quest for a Lost City*. New York: Harper and Brothers

Lamberg-Karlovsky, Carl C. 1986. The emergence of writing: Mesopotamia, Egypt and the Indus civilizations. In *Research and Reflections in Archaeology and History: Essays in Honor of Doris Stone*, ed. E. Wyllys Andrews V, pp. 149–58. Middle American Research Institute, Publication 57. New Orleans: Tulane University

Lange, Frederick W. 1971. Marine resources: a viable subsistence alternative for the prehistoric lowland Maya. *American Anthropologist* 73:619–39

Laporte Molina, Juan Pedro. 1988. Alternativas del Clásico Temprano en la relación Tikal-Teotihuacán: Grupo 6C-XVI, Tikal, Petén, Guatemala. Ph.D. dissertation, Universidad Nacional Autónoma de México

Laporte Molina, Juan Pedro, and Vilma Fialko C. n.d. Nuevas referencias para viejos problemas: enfoques dinásticos sobre el Clásico Temprano de Tikal. In *Vision and Revision in Maya Studies*, eds. Flora Clancy and Peter D. Harrison. Albuquerque: University of New Mexico Press

Laporte Molina, Juan Pedro, and Lillian Vega de Zea. 1986. Aspectos dinásticos para el Clásico Temprano en Mundo Perdido, Tikal. Paper presented at the Primer Simposio Mundial de Epigrafía Maya, Guatemala

Larsen, Mogens Trolle. 1976. *The Old Assyrian City-State and its Colonies*. Copenhagen: Akademisk Forlag

Laslett, Peter. 1965. *The World We Have Lost*. London: Methuen

Lasswell, Harold D., Daniel Lerner, and C. Easton Rothwell. 1952. *The Comparative Study of Elites*. Stanford: Hoover Institute Studies

Leach, Edmund R. 1973. Concluding address. In *The Explanation of Culture Change*, ed. Colin Renfrew, pp. 761–71. London: Duckworth

LeRoy Ladurie, Emmanuel. 1978. *Montaillon, Village Occitan de 1294 à 1324*. Paris: Gallimard

Leventhal, Richard M. 1979. Settlement patterns at Copan, Honduras. Ph.D. dissertation, Harvard University

Leventhal, Richard M., Arthur A. Demarest, and Gordon R. Willey. 1982. The cultural and social components of Copan. Paper presented at the 44th International Congress of Americanists, Manchester, England

Lewis, Andrew, 1982. *Royal Succession in Capetian France: Studies on Familial Order and the State*. Cambridge, Mass.: Harvard University Press

Liman, Florence F., and Marshall Durbin. 1975. Some new glyphs on an unusual Maya stela. *American Antiquity* 40:314–19

Lincoln, Charles E. 1985. Ceramics and ceramic chronology. In *A Consideration of the Early Classic Period in the Maya Lowlands*, eds. Gordon R. Willey and Peter Mathews, pp. 55–94. Institute for Mesoamerican Studies, Publication 10. Albany: State University of New York

1986. The chronology of Chichen Itza: a review of the literature. In *Late Lowland Maya Civilization: Classic to Postclassic*, eds. Jeremy A. Sabloff and E. Wyllys Andrews V, pp. 141–96. School of American Research. Albuquerque: University of New Mexico Press

Lizardi Ramos, Cesar. 1936. Los secretos de Chichén Itzá. *Excélsior*, December 21. Mexico

1937. New discoveries of Maya culture at Chichen Itza. *Illustrated London News*, July 3:12–15. London

Longyear, John M. 1952. *Copan Ceramics: A Study of Southeastern Maya Pottery*. Carnegie Institution of Washington, Publication 597. Washington, DC: Carnegie Institution

Lounsbury, Floyd G. 1973. On the derivation and reading of the "Ben-ich" prefix. In *Mesoamerican Writing Systems*, ed. Elizabeth P. Benson, pp. 99–143. Washington, DC: Dumbarton Oaks

1974. The inscription of the sarcophagus lid at Palenque. *Primera Mesa Redonda de Palenque*, ed. Merle Greene Robertson, Part 2: pp. 5–20. Pebble Beach: Robert Louis Stevenson School

1980. Some problems in the interpretation of the mythological portion of the hieroglyphic text of the Temple of the Cross at Palenque. In *Third Palenque Round Table, 1978*, ed. Merle Greene Robertson, vol. 2: pp. 99–115. Palenque Round Table Series 5. Austin: University of Texas Press

Lowe, Gareth W. 1977. The Mixe-Zoque as competing neighbors of the early lowland Maya. In *The Origins of Maya Civilization*, ed. Richard E. W. Adams, pp. 197–248. School of American Research. Albuquerque: University of New Mexico Press

Lowe, John W. G. 1985. *The Dynamics of Apocalypse: A Systems Simulation of the Classic Maya Collapse*. Albuquerque: University of New Mexico Press

Machinist, Peter B. 1986. On self-consciousness in Mesopotamia. In *The Origins and Diversity of Axial Age Civilizations*, ed. Shmuel N. Eisenstadt, 183–202. Albany: SUNY Press

MacNeish, Richard S., S. J. K. Wilkerson, and Antoinette Nelken-Terner. 1980. *First Annual Report of the Belize Archaeological Reconnaissance*. Andover, Mass.: Robert F. Peabody Foundation for Archaeology, Phillips Academy

Maler, Teobert. 1908. *Explorations of the Upper Usumasinta and Adjacent Region*. Memoirs of the Peabody Museum of American Archaeology and Ethnology 4(1). Cambridge, Mass.: Harvard University

Mann, Michael. 1986. *The Source of Social Power, Volume 1, A History of Power From the Beginning to AD 1760*. Cambridge, England: Cambridge University Press

Marcus, George E. 1983. "Elite" as a concept, theory, and research tradition. In *Elites: Ethnographic Issues*, ed. George E. Marcus, pp. 7–28. School of American Research. Albuquerque: University of New Mexico Press

Marcus, Joyce. 1973. Territorial organization of the lowland Classic Maya. *Science* 180:911–16

1976. *Emblem and State in the Classic Maya Lowlands*. Washington, DC: Dumbarton Oaks

1983. Lowland Maya archaeology at the crossroads. *American Antiquity* 48:454–88

Matheny, Ray T., ed. 1980. *El Mirador, Peten, Guatemala: An Interim Report*. Papers of the New World Archaeological Foundation 45. Provo, Utah: Brigham Young University

1986. Investigations at El Mirador, Peten, Guatemala. *National Geographic Research* 2:322–53

Matheny, Ray T., Deanne L. Gurr, Donald W. Forsyth, and F. Richard Hauck. 1983. *Investigations at Edzna, Campeche, Mexico: Volume 1, Part 1: The Hydraulic Systems*. Papers of the New World Archaeological Foundation 46. Provo, Utah: Brigham Young University

Mathews, Peter. 1975. The lintels of Structure 12, Yaxchilan, Chiapas. Paper presented at the Annual Conference of the Northeastern Anthropological Association, Wesleyan University

1980. Notes on the dynastic sequence of Bonampak, part I. *Third Palenque Round Table, 1978*, ed. Merle Greene Robertson, vol. 2: pp. 60–73. Palenque Round Table Series 5. Austin: University of Texas Press

1985. Early Classic monuments and inscriptions. In *A Consideration of the*

*Early Classic Period in the Maya Lowlands*, eds. Gordon R. Willey and Peter Mathews, pp. 5–55. Institute for Mesoamerican Studies, Publication 10. Albany: State University of New York

1986. Classic Maya site interaction and political geography. Paper presented at Maya Art and Civilization: The New Dynamics. Symposium sponsored by the Kimbell Art Museum, Fort Worth

1988. The sculptures of Yaxchilan. Ph.D. dissertation, Yale University

n.d.a. The ruins of Tortuguero, Tabasco, Mexico. A working notebook prepared in 1976

n.d.b. The dynastic sequence of Tonina, Chiapas, Mexico. Unpublished ms. dated approximately 1979

Mathews, Peter, and John S. Justeson. 1984. Patterns of sign substitution in Maya hieroglyphic writing: "the affix cluster." In *Phoneticism in Mayan Hieroglyphic Writing*, eds. John S. Justeson and Lyle Campbell, pp. 185–231. Institute for Mesoamerican Studies, Publication 9. Albany: State University of New York

Mathews, Peter, and David M. Pendergast. 1979. The Altun Ha jade plaque: deciphering the inscription. *Contributions of the University of California Archaeological Research Facility* 41:197–214

Mathews, Peter, and Linda Schele. 1974. Lords of Palenque – the glyphic evidence. *Primera Mesa Redonda de Palenque*, ed. Merle Greene Robertson, Part 1: pp. 63–75. Pebble Beach: Robert Louis Stevenson School

Maudslay, Alfred P. 1889–1902. *Biologia Centrali Americana: Archaeology*. 1 vol. text, four vols. plates. London: R. H. Porter and Dulau and Company

Mayer, Karl H. 1983. *Gewolgedecksteine mit Dekor der Maya-Kultur*. Archiv für Völkerkunde 37. Berlin: Museum für Völkerkunde

Miller, Arthur G. 1977. Captains of the Itza: unpublished mural evidence from Chichen Itza. In *Social Process in Maya Prehistory: Essays in Honour of Sir Eric Thompson*, ed. Norman Hammond, pp. 197–225. New York: Academic Press

1983. Stylistic implications of monument carving at Quirigua and Copan. In *Quirigua Reports II*, ed. Edward M. Schortman and Patricia A. Urban, pp. 129–40. University Museum Monograph 49. Philadelphia: The University Museum, University of Pennsylvania

1986. *Maya Rulers of Time*. Philadelphia: The University Museum, University of Pennsylvania

Miller, Mary Ellen. 1985. A re-examination of the Mesoamerican Chacmool. *Art Bulletin* 67:1–17

1986. *The Murals of Bonampak*. Princeton: Princeton University Press

Miller, Virginia. 1985. Eclecticism in the northern Maya lowlands. Paper presented at the 74th Annual Meeting of the College Art Association, Los Angeles

Moertono, Soemarsaid. 1968. *State and Statecraft in Old Java: A Study of the Later Mataram Period, 16th to 19th Century*. Ithaca: Cornell University Press

Molina-Montes, Augusto. 1982. Archaeological buildings: restoration or misrepresentation? In *Falsifications and Misreconstructions of Pre-Columbian Art*, ed. Elizabeth H. Boone, pp. 125–41. Washington, DC: Dumbarton Oaks

Molloy, John P. n.d. Tikal: an historical overview. Unpublished ms.

Molloy, John P., and William L. Rathje. 1974. Sexploitation among the Late Classic Maya. In *Mesoamerican Archaeology: New Approaches*, ed. Norman Hammond, pp. 431–44. London: Duckworth

Morley, Sylvanus G. 1920. *The Inscriptions at Copan*. Carnegie Institution of Washington, Publication 219. Washington, DC: Carnegie Institution

1935. Inscriptions at the Caracol. Appendix to *The Caracol at Chichen Itza, Yucatan, Mexico*, by Karl Ruppert, pp. 276–93. Carnegie Institution of Washington, Publication 454. Washington, DC: Carnegie Institution

1937–8. *The Inscriptions of the Peten*, 5 vols. Carnegie Institution of Washington, Publication 437. Washington DC: Carnegie Institution

1944. *Reconnaissance in Mexico and Guatemala*. Carnegie Institution of Washington, Yearbook 43. Washington, DC: Carnegie Institution

1946. *The Ancient Maya*. Stanford: Stanford University Press

Morley, Sylvanus G., and George W. Brainerd. 1956. *The Ancient Maya*. Third edition. Stanford: Stanford University Press

Morley, Sylvanus G., George W. Brainerd, and Robert J. Sharer. 1983. *The Ancient Maya*. Fourth edition, revised. Stanford: Stanford University Press

Morris, Earl H., Jean Charlot, and Ann A. Morris. 1931. *The Temple of the Warriors at Chichen Itza, Yucatan*. Carnegie Institution of Washington, Publication 406. Washington, DC: Carnegie Institution

Morris, William, ed. 1976. *The American Heritage History of the English Language*. Boston: Houghton Mifflin Company

Motolinía, Fray Toribio de Benevente. 1971. *Memoriales o libro de las cosas de la Nueva Espana y las naturales de ella*. Mexico: Universidad Nacional Autónoma de México

Nakamura, Seiichi. 1985. Informe del proyecto arqueológico La Entrada. Ms. on file at the Centro Regional de Investigaciones Arqueológicas, Copán, Honduras

Neivens, Mary D. and David Libbey. 1976. An obsidian workshop at El Pozito, Northern Belize. In *Maya Lithic Studies: Papers from the 1976 Belize Field Symposium*, eds. Thomas R. Hester and Norman Hammond, pp. 137–50. Center for Archaeological Research, University of Texas at San Antonio, Special Publication 4. San Antonio: Center for Archaeological Research

Netherly, Patricia J. 1984. The management of late Andean irrigation systems on the North Coast of Peru. *American Antiquity* 49:227–54

Netting, Robert McC. 1972. Sacred power and centralization: aspects of political adaptation in Africa. In *Population Growth; Anthropological Implications*. ed. Brian Spooner, pp. 219–44. Cambridge, Mass.: MIT Press

Nissen, Hans J. 1982. Die "Tempelstadt": Regierungsform der fruh-dynastischen Zeit in Babylonien? In *Gesellschaft und Kultur im alten Mesopotamien*, ed. H. Klengel, pp. 195–200. Berlin: Akademie Verlag

Oppenheim, A. Leo. 1964. *Ancient Mesopotamia*. Chicago: University of Chicago Press

Pahl, Gary W. 1977. The inscriptions of Rio Amarillo and Los Higos, secondary centers of the southeastern Maya frontier. *Journal of Latin American Lore* 3:133–54

Pendergast, David M. 1971. Evidence of early Teotihuacan-lowland Maya contact at Altun Ha. *American Antiquity* 36:455–60

1981. Lamanai, Belize: summary of excavation results 1974–1980. *Journal of Field Archaeology* 8:29–53

Pope, Kevin A., and Bruce H. Dahlin, 1989. Ancient Maya wetland agriculture: new insights from ecological and remote sensing research. *Journal of Field Archaeology* 16:87–106

Price, Barbara J. 1977. Shifts in production and organization: a cluster-interaction model. *Current Anthropology* 18:209–33

Pring, Duncan C. 1977. Influence or intrusion? The "Protoclassic" in the Maya lowlands. In *Social Process in Maya Prehistory: Essays in Honour of Sir Eric Thompson*, ed. Norman Hammond, pp. 135–65. New York: Academic Press

Proskouriakoff, Tatiana. 1960. Historical implications of a pattern of dates at Piedras Negras, Guatemala. *American Antiquity* 25:454–75

1961a. The lords of the Maya realm. *Expedition* 4(1):14–21

1961b. Portraits of women in Maya art. In *Essays in pre-Columbian Art and Archaeology*,eds. Samuel K. Lothrop and others, pp. 81–99. Cambridge, Mass: Harvard University Press

1963. Historical data in the inscriptions of Yaxchilan, part I. *Estudios de Cultura Maya* 3:149–67

1964. Historical data in the inscriptions of Yaxchilan, part II. *Estudios de Cultura Maya* 4:177–201

1970. On two inscriptions at Chichen Itza. In *Monographs and Papers in Maya Archaeology*, ed. William R. Bullard. Jr., pp. 457–68. Papers of the Peabody Museum of American Archaeology and Ethnology 61. Cambridge, Mass.: Harvard University

1973. The hand-grasping-fish and associated glyphs on Classic Maya monuments. In *Mesoamerican Writing Systems*, ed. Elizabeth P. Benson, pp. 165–73. Washington, DC: Dumbarton Oaks

Puleston, Dennis E. 1971. An experimental approach to the function of Classic Maya chultuns. *American Antiquity* 36:322–35

Puleston, Olga S. 1969. Functional analysis of a workshop tool kit from Tikal. M.A. thesis, University of Pennsylvania

Pyburn, Anne. 1987. Settlement patterns at Nohmul, a prehistoric Maya city in northern Belize, C.A. *Mexicon* 9:110–14

1988. The settlement of Nohmul: development of a prehistoric Maya community in northern Belize. Ph.D. dissertation, University of Arizona

Rafinesque, Constantine. 1827. Letter to the *Saturday Evening Post*. January 1st, 1827

Rands, Robert L. 1974. A chronological framework for Palenque. *Primera Mesa Redonda de Palenque*, ed. Merle Greene Robertson, Part 1:35–39. Pebble Beach: Robert Louis Stevenson School

1977. The rise of Classic Maya civilization in the northwestern zone: isolation and integration. In *The Origins of Maya Civilization*, ed. Richard E. W. Adams, pp. 159–80. School of American Research. Albuquerque: University of New Mexico Press

Rands, Robert L., P. H. Benson, Ronald L. Bishop, P.-Y. Chen, Garman Harbottle, Barbara C. Rands, and Edward V. Sayre. 1975. Western Maya fine paste pottery: chemical and petrographic correlations. *Actas del XLI Congreso Internacional de Americanistas* 7:534–41. Mexico

Rands, Robert L., and Ronald L. Bishop. 1980. Resource procurement zones and patterns of ceramic exchange in the Palenque region. In *Models and Methods in Regional Exchange*, ed. Robert E. Fry, pp. 19–46. Papers of the Society for American Archaeology 1. Washington, DC: Society for American Archaeology

Rands, Robert L., Ronald L. Bishop, and Jeremy A. Sabloff. 1982. Maya fine paste ceramics: an archaeological perspective. In *Excavations at Seibal: Analyses of Fine Paste Ceramics*, ed. Jeremy A. Sabloff, pp. 315–38. Memoirs of the Peabody Museum of American Archaeology and Ethnology 15(2). Cambridge, Mass.: Harvard University Press

Rathje, William L. 1970. Socio-political implications of lowland Maya burials. *World Archaeology* 1:359–74

1971. The origin and development of Classic Maya civilization. *American Antiquity* 36:275–85

Ray, John. 1986. The emergence of writing in Egypt. *World Archaeology* 17:307–16

Reents, Dorrie J., and Ronald L. Bishop. 1985. The Late Classic Maya "Codex Style" pottery. Paper presented at El Primer Coloquio Internacional de Mayistas. Centro de Estudios Mayas, Universidad Nacional Autónoma de México

Renfrew, Colin. 1972. *The Emergence of Civilization: The Cyclades and the Aegean in the Third Millennium* B.C. London: Methuen

1975. Trade as action at a distance: questions of integration and communication. In *Ancient Civilization and Trade*, eds. Jeremy A. Sabloff and Carl C. Lamberg-Karlovsky, pp. 3–59. School of American Research. Albuquerque: University of New Mexico Press

1986. Introduction: peer polity interaction and socio-political change. In *Peer Polity Interaction and Socio-Political Change*, eds. Colin Renfrew and John F. Cherry, pp. 1–18. Cambridge, England: Cambridge University Press

Renfrew, Colin, and John F. Cherry, eds. 1986. *Peer Polity Interaction and Socio-Political Change*. Cambridge, England: Cambridge University Press

Renfrew, Colin, and Eric V. Level. 1979. Exploring dominance: predicting polities from centres. In *Transformations: Mathematical Approaches to Culture Change*, eds. Colin Renfrew and Kenneth L. Cooke, pp. 145–68. New York: Academic Press

Ricketson, Oliver G., Jr., and Edith B. Ricketson. 1937. *Uaxactun, Guatemala, Group E, 1926–1937*. Carnegie Institution of Washington, Publication 477. Washington, DC: Carnegie Institution

Riese, Berthold. 1978. La inscripción del Monumento 6 de Tortuguero. *Estudios de Cultura Maya* 11:187–98

1983. Las esculturas de las Estructuras 10L-2 y -4. In *Introducción a la arqueología de Copán*, vol. 2, ed. Claude F. Baudez, pp. 143–84. Tegucigalpa, Honduras: Secretaria de Estado en el Despacho de Cultura y Turismo

1984a. Kriegsberichte der Klassischen Maya. *Baessler-Archiv* (n.f.) 30:255–321

1984b. Hel hieroglyphs. In *Phoneticism in Mayan Hierglyphic Writing*, eds. John S. Justeson and Lyle Campbell, pp. 263–86. Institute for Mesoamerican Studies, Publication 9. Albany: State University of New York

1986. Late Classic relationship between Copan and Quirigua: some epigraphic evidence. In *The Southeast Maya Periphery*, eds. Patricia A. Urban and Edward M. Schortman, pp. 94–101. Austin: University of Texas Press

Riesenberg, Saul. 1968. *The Native Polity of Ponape*. Washington, DC: Smithsonian Institution

Ringle, William M., and E. Wyllys Andrews V. 1988. Formative residences at Komchen, Yucatan, Mexico. In *Household and Community in the Mesoamerican Past*, eds. Richard R. Wilk and Wendy Ashmore, pp. 171–97. Albuquerque: University of New Mexico Press

Robicsek, Francis, and Donald M. Hales. 1981. *The Maya Book of the Dead: The Cermic Codex*. Charlottesville: University of Virginia Art Museum

Robles, Fernando C. and Anthony P. Andrews. 1986. A review and synthesis of recent Postclassic archaeology in northern Yucatan. In *Late Lowland Maya Civilization: Classic to Postclassic*, eds. Jeremy A. Sabloff and E. Wyllys Andrews V, pp. 53–98. School of American Research. Albuquerque: University of New Mexico Press

Rosny, Leon de. 1876. Essai sur le déchiffrement de l'écriture hiératique de l'Amérique Centrale. *Société Américain de France, Archives (n.s.)* 2:5–108

Roys, Ralph L. 1933. *The Book of Chilam Balam of Chumayel*. Carnegie

Institution of Washington, Publication 438. Washington, DC: Carnegie Institution

1957. *The Political Geography of the Yucatan Maya*. Carnegie Institution of Washington, Publication 548. Washington, DC: Carnegie Institution

Runciman, William G. 1982. Origins of states: the case of Archaic Greece. *Comparative Studies in Society and History* 24:351–77

Ruppert, Karl. 1935. *The Caracol at Chichen Itza, Yucatan, Mexico*. Carnegie Institution of Washington, Publication 454. Washington, DC: Carnegie Institution

1952. *Chichen Itza, Architectural Notes and Plans*. Carnegie Institution of Washington, Publication 595. Washington, DC: Carnegie Institution

Ruz Lhullier, Alberto. 1964. Influencias Mexicanas sobre los Mayas. In *Desarollo cultural de los Mayas*, eds. Evon Z. Vogt and Alberto Ruz L., pp. 202–41. Mexico: Seminario de Cultura Maya

Sabloff, Jeremy A. 1973. Continuity and disruption during Terminal Late Classic times at Seibal: ceramic and other evidence. In *The Classic Maya Collapse*, ed. T. Patrick Culbert, pp. 107–32. School of American Research. Albuquerque: University of New Mexico Press

1975. *Excavations at Seibal, Department of the Peten, Guatemala: The Ceramics*. Memoirs of the Peabody Museum of Archaeology and Ethnology 13(2). Cambridge, Mass.: Harvard University

1985. Ancient Maya civilization: an overview. In *Maya: Treasures of an Ancient Civilization*, eds. Charles Gallenkamp and Regina E. Johnson, pp. 34–46. New York: Harry N. Abrams and Albuquerque: The Albuquerque Museum

1986. Interaction among Classic Maya polities: a preliminary examination. In *Peer Polity Interaction and Socio-Political Change*, eds. Colin Renfrew and John F. Cherry, pp. 109–16. Cambridge, England: Cambridge University Press

Sabloff, Jeremy A., and E. Wyllys Andrews V, eds. 1986. *Late Lowland Maya Civilization: Classic to Postclassic*. School of American Research. Albuquerque: University of New Mexico Press

Sabloff, Jeremy A., Ronald L. Bishop, Garman Harbottle, Robert L. Rands, and Edward V. Sayre. 1982. Analyses of fine paste ceramics. In *Excavations at Seibal, Department of Peten, Guatemala: Ceramics*. Memoirs of the Peabody Museum of American Archaeology and Ethnology 15(2). Cambridge, Mass.: Harvard University

Sabloff, Jeremy A., and Gordon R. Willey. 1967. The collapse of Maya civilization in the southern lowlands: a consideration of history and process. *Southwestern Journal of Anthropology* 23:311–16

Saenz, César A. 1975. Cerámica de Uxmal, Yucatán. *Anales del Instituto Nacional de Antropología e Historia* 7:171–86

Sahagún, Fray Bernadino de. 1950–82. *Florentine Codex: General History of the Things of New Spain*. Charles E. Dibble and Arthur J. O. Anderson, translators. Santa Fe: Monographs of the School of American Research

Salmon, Merilee H. 1982. *Philosophy and Archaeology*. New York: Academic Press

Sanders, William T. 1981. Classic Maya settlement patterns and ethnographic analogy. In *Lowland Maya Settlement Patterns*, ed. Wendy Ashmore, pp. 354–69. School of American Research. Albuquerque: University of New Mexico Press

1989. Household, lineage, and state at eighth-century Copan, Honduras. In *The House of the Bacabs, Copan, Honduras*, ed. David Webster, pp. 89–105. Washington, DC: Dumbarton Oaks

Sanders, William T., and Carson N. Murdy. 1982. Cultural evolution and ecological succession in the Valley of Guatemala: 1500 B.C.–A.D. 1524. In *Maya Subsistence: Studies in Memory of Dennis E. Puleston*, ed. Kent V. Flannery, pp. 19–63. New York: Academic Press

Sanders, William T., and David L. Webster. 1988. The Mesoamerican urban tradition. *American Anthropologist* 80:521–46

Santley, Robert S., Thomas Killion, and Mark Lycett. 1986. On the Maya collapse. *Journal of Anthropological Research* 42:123–59

Satterthwaite, Linton S. 1979. Quirigua Altar L. (Monument 12). *Quirigua Reports vol. 1*, ed. Wendy Ashmore, pp. 39–43. University Museum Monograph 37. Philadelphia: The University Museum, University of Pennsylvania

Scarborough, Vernon L. 1985. Late Preclassic Northern Belize: context and interpretation. In *Status, Structure and Stratification: Current Archaeological Reconstructions*, eds. M. Thompson, M. T. Garcia, and F. J. Kense, pps. 331–44. Calgary: University of Calgary Archaeological Association

Schele, Linda. 1974. Observations on the cross motif at Palenque. In *Primera Mesa Redonda de Palenque*, ed. Merle Greene Robertson, Part 1: pp. 41–62. Pebble Beach: Robert Louis Stevenson School

1976. Accession iconography of Chan-Bahlum in the Group of the Cross at Palenque. In *The Art, Iconography, and Dynastic History of Palenque, Part* 3, ed. Merle Greene Robertson, pp. 9–34. Proceedings of the Segunda Mesa Redonda de Palenque. Pebble Beach: Robert Louis Stevenson School

1978. Genealogical documentation on the tri-figure panels at Palenque. *Third Palenque Round Table*, 1978, eds. Merle Greene Robertson and Donnan C. Jeffers, pp. 41–70. Palenque Round Table Series 4. Monterrey: Pre-Columbian Art Research Center

1978–89. Notebooks for the Maya hieroglyphic writing workshop at Texas. Austin: Institute of Latin American Studies, University of Texas

1982. *Maya Glyphs: The Verbs*. Austin: University of Texas Press

1984a. Some suggested readings of the events and office of heir-designate at Palenque. *Phoneticism in Mayan Hieroglyphic Writing*, eds. Johns S. Justeson and Lyle Campbell, pp. 287–307. Institute of Mesoamerican Studies, Publication 9. Albany: State University of New York

1984b. Human sacrifice among the Classic Maya. In *Ritual Human Sacri-*

*fice in Mesoamerica*, ed. Elizabeth Boone, pp. 7–48. Washington, DC: Dumbarton Oaks

1986a. *The Founders of Lineages at Copan and Other Maya Sites*. Copan Note 8. Copan Mosaic Project and Instituto Hondureño de Antropología e Historia

1986b. Architectural development and political history at Palenque. In *City-States of the Maya: Art and Architecture*, ed. Elizabeth P. Benson, pp. 110–37. Denver: Rocky Mountain Institute for Pre-Columbian Studies

1986c. The demotion of Chac-Zutz': lineage compounds and subsidiary lords at Palenque. Paper presented at the Sexta Mesa Redonda de Palenque, Palenque

1986d. The Tlaloc heresy: cultural interaction and social history. Paper presented at Maya Art and Civilization: The New Dynamics. Symposium sponsored by the Kimbell Art Museum, Fort Worth

1986e. A comparative study of the history of Katun 13 as recorded in the Maya inscriptions. Paper prepared for Elite Interaction in Classic Maya Civilization. School of American Research Advanced Seminar, Santa Fe

1988. *Revisions to the Dynastic Chronology of Copan*. Copan Note 45. Copan Mosaic Project and Instituto Hondureño de Antropología e Historia

Schele, Linda, and David A. Freidel. n.d. *A Forest of Kings: Royal Histories of the Ancient Maya*. New York: William Morrow

Schele, Linda, and Nikolai Grube. 1987. *The Brother of Yax-Pac*. Copan Note 20. Copan Mosaic Project and Instituto Hondureño de Antropología e Historia

Schele, Linda, Peter Mathews, and Floyd G. Lounsbury. n.d. Parentage expressions in Classic Maya inscriptions. Unpublished ms. dated 1977

Schele, Linda, and Mary Ellen Miller. 1986. *The Blood of Kings: Dynasty and Ritual in Maya Art*. Fort Worth: Kimbell Art Museum and New York: George Braziller and Co

Schortman, Edward M. 1980. Archaeological investigations in the lower Motagua Valley, Guatemala. *Expedition* 23(1):28–34

1986. Interaction between the Maya and non-Maya along the Late Classic southeast Maya periphery: the view from the lower Motagua Valley, Guatemala. In *The Southeast Maya Periphery*, eds. Patricia A. Urban and Edward M. Schortman, pp. 114–37. Austin: University of Texas Press

Schortman, Edward M., and Patricia A. Urban. 1987. Modeling interregional interaction in prehistory. *Advances in Archaeological Method and Theory* 11:37–95

Shafer, Harry J., and Thomas R. Hester. 1983. Ancient Maya chert workshops in northern Belize, Central America. *American Antiquity* 48:519–43

Sharer, Robert J. 1978. Archaeology and history of Quirigua, Guatemala. *Journal of Field Archaeology* 5:51–70

1985a. New perspectives on the origins of Maya civilization. Paper presented at the III Seminario Arqueológica Hondureña, Tela, Honduras

1985b. Terminal events in the southeastern lowlands: a view from Quirigua. In *The Lowland Maya Post-Classic*, eds. Arlen F. Chase and Prudence M. Rice, pp. 245–53. Austin: University of Texas Press

1985c. Archaeology and epigraphy revisited. *Expedition* 27(3):16–19

1988. Quirigua as a Classic Maya center. In *The Southeast Classic Maya Zone*, eds. Elizabeth H. Boone and Gordon R. Willey, pp. 31–65. Washington: Dumbarton Oaks

Sharer, Robert J., and David C. Grove, eds. n.d. *The Olmec and the Development of Mesoamerican Civilization*. School of American Research. Cambridge, England: Cambridge University Press

Sharer, Robert J., and David W. Sedat. 1987. *Archaeological Investigations in the Northern Maya Highlands, Guatemala: Interaction and the Development of Maya Civilization*. University Museum Monograph 59. Philadelphia: The University Museum, University of Pennsylvania

Sheets, Payson D. 1971. An ancient natural disaster. *Expedition* 14(1):25–31

1983, ed. *Archaeology and Vulcanism in Central America*. Austin: University of Texas Press

Siemens, Alfred H. and Dennis E. Puleston. 1972. Ridged fields and associated features in southern Campeche: new perspectives on the lowland Maya. *American Antiquity* 37:228–39

Simpson. Jon Erik. 1976. The New York Relief Panel and some associations with reliefs at Palenque and elsewhere, part I. In *The Art, Iconography and Dynastic History of Palenque, Part 3*, ed. Merle Greene Robertson, pp. 95–105. Proceedings of the Segunda Mesa Redonda de Palenque. Pebble Beach: Robert Louis Stevenson School

Smith, A. Ledyard. 1937. *Structure A-XVIII, Uaxactun*. Contributions to American Anthropology and History 4(20). Carnegie Institute of Washinton, Publication 483. Washington, DC: Carnegie Institution

1950. *Uaxactun, Guatemala: Excavations of 1931–1937*. Carnegie Institution of Washington, Publication 588. Washington, DC: Carnegie Institution

1972. *Excavations at Altar de Sacrificios: Architecture, Stelae, Burials and Caches*. Papers of the Peabody Museum of American Archaeology and Ethnology 62(2). Cambridge. Mass.: Harvard University

1982. *Excavations at Seibal, Department of Peten, Guatemala: Major Architecture and Caches*. Memoirs of the Peabody Museum of American Archaeology and Ethnology 15. Cambridge, Mass.: Harvard University

Smith, Robert E. 1937. *A Study of Structure A–I Complex at Uaxactun*. Contributions to American Anthropology and History 3(19). Carnegie Institution of Washington, Publication 456. Washington, DC: Carnegie Institution

1955. *Ceramic Sequence at Uaxactun, Guatemala*. Middle American

Research Institute, Publication 20. New Orleans: Tulane University

Spencer, Charles S. 1987. Rethinking the Chiefdom. In *Chiefdoms in the Americas*, eds. Robert D. Drennan and Carlos A. Uribe, pp. 369–89. Lanham: University Press of America

Spinden, Herbert J. 1913. *A Study of Maya Art: Its Subject Matter and Historical Development*. Memoirs of the Peabody Museum of American Archaeology and Ethnology 6. Cambridge, Mass.: Harvard University

Stephens, John L. 1841. *Incidents of Travel in Central America, Chiapas and Yucatan*, 2 vols. New York: Harper Brothers

1963. *Incidents of Travel in Yucatan*, 2 vols. New York: Dover

Storey, Rebecca. 1983. Paledemografía en Copán. Paper presented at the Segundo Seminario Arqueológica Hondureño, Tegucigalpa

Stromsvik, Gustav. 1952. The ball courts at Copan, with notes on courts at La Union, Quirigua, San Pedro Pinula and Ascencion Mita. Contributions to American Archaeology and History 11(55). Carnegie Institution of Washington, Publication 596. Washington, DC: Carnegie Institution

Struever, Stuart and Gail L. Houart. 1972. An analysis of the Hopewell interaction sphere. In *Social Exchange and Interaction*, ed. Edwin Wilmsen, pp. 47–79. University of Michigan Museum of Anthropology Papers 46. Ann Arbor: University of Michigan Museum of Anthropology

Stuart, David S. 1984. Royal auto-sacrifice among the Maya. *Res* 7/8:7–20

1985a. The 'count-of-captives' epithet in Classic Maya writing. In *Fifth Palenque Round Table, 1983*, vol. ed. Virginia M. Fields; genl. ed. Merle Greene Robertson, pp. 97–101. Palenque Round Table Series 7. San Francisco: Pre-Columbian Art Research Institute

1985b. The inscription on four shell plaques from Piedras Negras, Guatemala. In *Fourth Palenque Round Table, 1980*, vol. ed. Elizabeth P. Benson; genl. ed. Merle Greene Robertson, pp. 175–83. Palenque Round Table Series 6. San Francisco: Pre-Columbian Art Research Institute

1986a. The 'Lu-bat' glyph and its bearing on the primary standard sequence. Paper presented at the Primer Simposio Mundial de Epigrafía Maya, Guatemala

1986b. Subsidiaries and scribes: epigraphic evidence of Classic Maya social organization. Paper presented at Maya Art and Civilization: The New Dynamics. Symposium sponsored by the Kimbell Art Museum, Fort Worth

1987. Nuevas interpretaciones de la historia dinástica de Copán. Paper presented at the IV Seminario de Arqueología Hondureña, La Ceiba

1988. The Rio Azul cacao pot; epigraphic observations on the function of a Maya ceramic vessel. *Antiquity* 62:153–7

1989. Kinship terms in Mayan inscriptions. Paper presented at The Language of Maya Hieroglyphs. Conference held at the University of California at Santa Barbara, February, 1989

n.d. Epigraphic evidence of political organization in the Usumacinta Drainage. Unpublished ms. dated 1984

Stuart, David S., and Stephen D. Houston. n.d. *Classic Maya Place Names*. Research Reports on Ancient Maya Writing. Washington, DC: Center for Maya Research

Stuart, David S., and Linda Schele. 1986a. *Yax-K'uk-Mo', the founder of the lineage of Copan*. Copan Note 6. Copan Mosaic Project and Instituto Hondureño de Antropología e Historia

1986b. *Interim Report on the Hieroglyphic Stairs of Structure 26*. Copan Note 17. Copan Mosaic Project and Instituto Hondureño de Antropología e Historia

Tambiah, Stanley J. 1977. The galactic polity: the structure of traditional kingdoms in southeast Asia. In *Anthropology and the Climate of Opinion*, ed. Stanley A. Freed, pp. 69–97. Annals of the New York Academy of Science 293

Tate, Carolyn. 1986. The language of symbols in the ritual environment at Yaxchilan, Chiapas. Ph.D. dissertation, University of Texas at Austin

Thomas, Cyrus. 1882. A study of the manuscript Troano. *Contributions to North American Ethnology* 5:1–237. Washington, DC: U.S. Department of Interior

Thompson, Edward H. n.d. Newly discovered inscribed tablets of Chichen Itza. Memorandum in the Edward H Thompson Archives, Peabody Museum of American Archaeology and Ethnology, Harvard University

Thompson, J. Eric S. 1937. *A New Method of Deciphering Yucatecan Dates with Special Reference to Chichen Itza*. Contributions to American Archaeology and History 4(22). Carnegie Institution of Washington, Publication 483. Washington, DC: Carnegie Institution

1950. *Maya Hieroglypic Writing: An Introduction*. Carnegie Institution of Washington, Publication 589. Washington, DC: Carnegie Institution

1953. *Review of* La antigua escritura de los pueblos de America Central, by Yurii V. Knorosov. *Yan* 2:174–8

1954. *The Rise and Fall of Maya Civilization*. Norman: University of Oklahoma Press

1960. *Maya Hieroglyphic Writing: An Introduction*. Second edition. Norman: University of Oklahoma Press

1962. *A Catalog of Maya Hieroglyphs*. Norman: University of Oklahoma Press

1964. Trade relations between Maya highlands and lowlands. *Estudios de Cultura Maya* 4:13–49 (reprinted with revisions in Thompson 1970:124–58

1966. *The Rise and Fall of Maya Civilization*. Second edition. Norman: University of Oklahoma Press

1970. *Maya History and Religion*. Norman: University of Oklahoma Press

1971. *Maya Hieroglyphic Writing: An Introduction*. Third edition. Norman: University of Oklahoma Press

Thompson, Philip C. 1985. The structure of the civil hierarchy in Tekanto, Yucatan. *Estudios de Cultura Maya* 16:183–205

Tourtellot, Gair. 1983. Ancient Maya settlements at Seibal, Peten,

Guatemala: peripheral survey and excavation. Ph.D. dissertation, Harvard University

1988. *Excavations at Seibal: Peripheral Survey and Excavations: Settlement and Community Patterns*. Memoirs of the Peabody Museum of American Archaeology and Ethnology 16. Cambridge, Mass.: Harvard University

Tourtellot, Gair, Norman Hammond, and Richard M. Rose. 1978. *A Brief Reconnaissance of Itzan*. Memoirs of the Peabody Museum of American Archaeology and Ethnology 13(3). Cambridge, Mass.: Harvard University

Tourtellot, Gair, Jeremy A. Sabloff, and Robert Sharick. 1978. *A Reconnaissance of Cancuen*. Memoirs of the Peabody Museum of American Archaeology and Ethnology 14(2). Cambridge, Mass.: Harvard University

Townsend, Richard. n.d. Coronation at Tenochtitlan. Unpublished manuscript

Tozzer, Alfred M. 1913. *A Preliminary Study of the Prehistoric Ruins of Nakum, Guatemala*. Memoirs of the Peabody Museum of Archaeology and Ethnology 5(5). Cambridge, Mass.: Harvard University

1930, Maya and Toltec figures at Chichen Itza. *Proceedings of the 23rd International Congress of Americanists, New York*, pp. 155–64

1941. *Landa's Relación de las cosas de Yucatan: A Translation*. Papers of the Peabody Museum of American Archaeology and Ethnology 28. Cambridge, Mass.: Harvard University

1957. *Chichen Itza and Its Cenote of Sacrifice*. Memoirs of the Peabody Museum of American Archaeology and Ethnology 11–12. Cambridge, Mass.: Harvard University

Turner, B. L., II. 1978. Ancient agricultural land use in the central Maya lowlands. In *Pre-Hispanic Maya Agriculture*, eds. Peter D. Harrison and B. L. Turner II, pp. 163–83. Albuquerque: University of New Mexico Press

n.d. Population reconstruction of the central Maya lowlands: 1000 B.C. to A.D. 1500. In *Precolumbian Population History in the Maya Lowlands*, eds. T. Patrick Culbert and Don S. Rice, Albuquerque: University of New Mexico Press

Urban, Patricia A., and Edward M. Schortman, eds. 1986. *The Southeast Maya Periphery*. Austin: University of Texas Press

Vidal, Gore. 1981. *Creation*. London: Granada

Viel, René. 1983. La evolución de la ceramica en Copán: resultados preliminares. In *Introducción a la arqueología de Copán* I. ed. Claude F. Baudez, pp. 513–60. Tegucigalpa, Honduras: Secretaria de Estado en el Despacho de Cultura y Turismo

Vogt, Evon Z. 1964. The genetic model and Maya cultural development. In *Desarrollo cultural de los Mayas*, eds. Evon Z. Vogt and Alberto Ruz L., pp. 9–48. Mexico: Universidad Nacional Autónoma de México

1969. *Zinacantan*. Cambridge, Mass.: Harvard University Press

von Thünen, J. H. 1875. Der isolierte Staat in Beziehung auf Landwirtschaft und Nationalökonomie. Hamburg

Webb, Malcolm C. 1973. The Peten Maya decline viewed in the perspective of state formation. In *The Classic Maya Collapse*, ed. T. Patrick Culbert, pp. 367–404. School of American Research. Albuquerque: University of New Mexico Press

Webster, David L. 1975. Warfare and the evolution of the state: a reconsideration. *American Antiquity* 40:464–70

1977. Warfare and the evolution of Maya civilization. In *The Origins of Maya Civilization*, ed. Richard E. W. Adams, pp. 335–72. School of American Research. Albuquerque: University of New Mexico Press

1988. Copan as a Classic Maya center. In *The Southeast Classic Maya Zone*, eds. Elizabeth H. Boone and Gordon R. Willey, pp. 5–30. Washington, DC: Dumbarton Oaks

1989, ed. *The House of the Bacabs. Copan, Honduras*. Washington, DC: Dumbarton Oaks

Webster, David L., and Elliot M. Abrams. 1983. An elite compound at Copan, Honduras. *Journal of Field Archaeology* 10:285–96

Webster, David L., William L. Fash, and Elliot M. Abrams. 1986. Excavaciones en el Patio A, Grupo 9N—8. In *Excavaciones en el area urbana de Copán*, ed. William T. Sanders, pp. 155–318. Tegucigalpa, Honduras: Instituto Hondureño de Antropología e Historia

Webster, David L., and AnnCorrine Freter. n.d. The demography of Late Classic Copan. In *Precolumbian Population History in the Maya Lowlands*, eds. T. Patrick Culbert and Don S. Rice, Albuquerque: University of New Mexico Press

Wesson, Robert G. 1978. *State Systems*. New York: Free Press

Wheatley, Paul. 1971. *Pivot of the Four Quarters*. Edinburgh: University of Edinburgh Press

Wilk, Richard R. 1973. Operation 4C: Structure 100, Colha. In *British Museum–Cambridge University Corozal Project 1973 Interim Report*, ed. Norman Hammond, pp. 57–9. Cambridge, England: Centre for Latin American Studies, Cambridge University

1975. Superficial examination of Structure 100, Colha. In *Archaeology in Northern Belize: British Museum–Cambridge University Corozal Project 1974–1975 Interim Report*, ed. Norman Hammond, pp. 152–73. Cambridge, England: Centre for Latin American Studies, Cambridge University

1988. Maya household organization: evidence and analogies. In *Household and Community in the Mesoamerican Past*, eds. Richard R. Wilk and Wendy Ashmore, pp. 135—51. Albuquerque: University of New Mexico Press

Wilk, Richard R., and Wendy Ashmore, eds. 1988. *Household and Community in the Mesoamerican Past*. Albuquerque: University of New Mexico Press

Wilk, Richard R., and H. Wilhite. 1980. Patterns of household and settlement change at Cuello. Paper presented at the 45th Annual Meeting of the Society for American Archaeology, Philadelphia

Willey, Gordon R. 1948. A functional analysis of "horizon styles" in Peruvian archaeology. In A *Reappraisal of Peruvian Archaeology*, ed. Wendell C. Bennett, pp. 8–15. Memoirs of the Society of American Archaeology 4

1956. The structure of ancient Maya society. *American Anthropologist* 58:777–82

1973. *The Altar de Sacrificios Excavations: General Summary and Conclusions*. Papers of the Peabody Museum of American Archaeology and Ethnology 64(3). Cambridge, Mass.: Harvard University

1974. The Classic Maya hiatus: a "rehearsal" for the collapse? In *Mesoamerican Archaeology: New Approaches*, ed. Norman Hammond, pp. 417–30. Austin: University of Texas Press

1978. *Excavations at Seibal: Artifacts*. Memoirs of the Peabody Museum of American Archaeology and Ethnology 14(1). Cambridge, Mass.: Harvard University

1980. Towards an holistic view of ancient Maya civilization. *Man* (n.s.) 15:249–66

1981. Maya lowland settlement patterns: a summary review. In *Lowland Maya Settlement Patterns*, ed. Wendy Ashmore, pp. 385–415. School of American Research. Albuquerque: University of New Mexico Press

1982. Maya archaeology. *Science* 215:260–7

1985a. The Early Classic in the Maya lowlands: an overview. In A *consideration of the Early Classic Period in the Maya Lowlands*, eds. Gordon R. Willey and Peter Mathews, pp. 175–84. Institute for Mesoamerican Studies, Publication 10. Albany: State University of New York

1985b. Ancient Chinese – New World and Near Eastern ideological traditions: some observations. *Symbols*, Spring, 1985:14–17, 22–3

Willey, Gordon R., William R. Bullard, John B. Glass, and James C. Gifford. 1965. *Prehistoric Settlement Patterns in the Belize Valley*. Papers of the Peabody Museum of American Archaeology and Ethnology 54. Cambridge, Mass.: Harvard University

Willey, Gordon R., and Richard M. Leventhal. 1979. Prehistoric settlement at Copan. In *Maya Archaeology and Ethnohistory*, eds. Norman Hammond and Gordon R. Willey, pp. 76–102. Austin: University of Texas Press

Willey, Gordon R., Richard M. Leventhal, and William L. Fash. 1978. Maya settlement in the Copan Valley. *Archaeology* 31(4):32–43

Willey, Gordon R., and A. Ledyard Smith. 1969. *The Ruins of Altar de Sacrificios, Department of Peten, Guatemala: An Introduction*. Papers of the Peabody Museum of American Archaeology and Ethnology 62(1). Cambridge, Mass.: Harvard University

Willey, Gordon R., A. Ledyard Smith, Gair Tourtellot, and Ian Graham. 1975. *Excavations at Seibal, Department of Peten, Guatemala:*

*Introduction: The Site and Its Setting*. Memoirs of the Peabody Museum of American Archaeology and Ethnology 13(1). Cambridge, Mass.: Harvard University

Winter, Irene J. 1981. Royal rhetoric and the development of historical narrative in Neo-Assyrian reliefs. *Visual Communication* 7:2–38

Wittfogel, Karl A. 1957. *Oriental Despotism: A Study in Total Power*. New Haven: Yale University Press

Wolf, Eric. 1969. *Peasant Wars of the 20th Century*. New York: Harper and Rowe

Wolfe, Tom. 1981. *From Bauhaus to Our House*. New York: Farrar Straus Giroux

Wren, Linnea H. 1986. The Great Ball Court Stone. Paper presented at the Sexta Mesa Redonda de Palenque, Palenque

Yoffee, Norman. 1977. *The Economic Role of the Crown in the Old Babylonian Period*. Malibu: Undena

1985. Perspectives on "Trends toward complex society in prehistoric Australia and Papua New Guinea." *Archaeology in Oceania* 20:41–9

1986. Ancient China and Mesopotamia: comparisons, contrasts, and the evolution of ancient civilizations. Paper presented to conference Ancient China and Social Science Generalizations, Airlie House, Virginia

1988a. The collapse of ancient Mesopotamian states and civilization. In *The Collapse of Ancient States and Civilizations*, eds. Norman Yoffee and George L. Cowgill, pp. 44–68. Tucson: University of Arizona Press

1988b. Context and authority in early Mesopotamian law. In *State Formation and Political Legitimacy*, eds. Ronald Cohen and Judith D. Toland, pp. 95–114. Political Anthropology 6. New Brunswick: Transaction Press

Yoffee, Norman and George L. Cowgill, eds. 1988. *The Collapse of Ancient States and Civilizations*. Tucson: University of Arizona Press

# Index

Page numbers in *italics* refer to figures and tables

# Index

# Index

# Index

# Index

# Index

# Index

# *Index*